THE

HISTO

OF THE

REBELLION AND CIVIL WARS

IN ENGLAND,

TO WHICH IS ADDED

An Historical View of the Affairs of Ireland.

By EDWARD EARL OF CLARENDON.

A NEW EDITION,

EXHIBITING A FAITHFUL COLLATION OF THE ORIGINAL MS.,
WITH ALL THE SUPPRESSED PASSAGES;

ALSO THE

UNPUBLISHED NOTES OF BISHOP WARBURTON.

VOLUME III.

Oxford:
AT THE CLARENDON PRESS.

REPRINTED BY WELLS AND LILLY, BOSTON.
1827.

Printing Statement:

Due to the very old age and scarcity of this book,
many of the pages may be hard to read due to the
blurring of the original text, possible missing pages,
missing text and other issues beyond our control.

Because this is such an important and rare work, we
believe it is best to reproduce this book regardless of
its original condition.

Thank you for your understanding.

THE HISTORY

OF THE REBELLION, &c.

BOOK VI.

THE king's condition at Nottingham—Portsmouth besieged by the
parliament's forces—The marquis of Hertford's actions in Somersetshire, &c.—He retires to Sherborne—The earl of Bedford comes
against him—The king consults at Nottingham of sending a message for peace—The king sends to the two houses a message for
peace by the earl of Southampton, &c.—How it was received by
them—Their answer—The king sends another message to the two
houses—Their answer—The two houses' declaration to the kingdom—Another message from the king to the two houses in reply to
their answer—The king removes to Derby—The king's speech and
protestation at the head of his forces, after the reading his orders of
war—The king comes to Shrewsbury—Colonel Goring surrenders
Portsmouth—The marquis of Hertford's proceedings in the west—
Thence transporteth himself into Glamorganshire—Ezek. xxii. 25.—
The earl of Essex moves with his army from Northampton—A rencounter between the forces near Worcester, where prince Rupert
gets the better—The two houses' instructions to their general—The
petition of both houses to the king, sent to the general to be presented, but never delivered—Votes of both houses for raising and
procuring money—The two universities contributed their money
and plate to the king—The king comes to Shrewsbury—The substance of the king's speeches to the gentry and commonalty of the
several counties through which he passed—The strength of the
king's army at Shrewsbury—The king having formed an army,
marches from Shrewsbury towards London—Faction begun in the
king's army—The earl of Essex marches after the king—The battle
of Keinton or Edgehill—A character of the earl of Lindsey, the
king's general—Banbury castle surrendered to the king—The condition of the earl of Essex's army after the fight—Apprentices invited by the parliament to take arms—The two houses' declaration to

67*

the subjects of Scotland—The condition and inclinations of the kingdom of Scotland at that time—The king at Oxford recruits his army—The garrison of the parliament at Reading quitting it, the king marches thither—The king advances to Colebrook—A petition presented to the king from both houses—The king's answer—The king marches towards Brentford—The earl of Essex's army, and the city trained bands, opposed against them—The king's army drawn off to Kingston—Thence to Reading—The king sends a message to the houses—An ordinance for raising money upon the public faith—A declaration of both houses concerning their general's acceptable service—The houses' petition to the king, Nov. 24—The substance of the king's answer—The king having garrisoned Reading and Wallingford, and some other places, marches to Oxford—Marlborough garrisoned by the parliament—Marlborough taken by the king's forces under lieutenant-general Wilmot—The substance of the king's message to the privy-council of Scotland, upon occasion of the ·two houses' declaration to that kingdom—What means the king then used to raise money—The king makes new sheriffs—The substance of the declaration of the lords and commons to the states general of the United Provinces—The inclinations of foreign kings and states in this cause between the king and parliament—New ways of raising money by the two houses—His majesty's declaration upon occasion of the former ordinance—A petition of the city to the king—The king's answer—Commissioners sent to the king with propositions of peace about the end of January—Chichester possessed by the king's forces :—But surrendered to sir W. Waller—Cirencester won by the king's forces under prince Rupert —Sir Ralph Hopton and sir Bevil Greenvil's progress in Cornwall together with other gentlemen there—Sir Ralph Hopton beats the parliament's forces at Bradock-Down under Ruthen—·Saltash taken by the king's forces—Mr. Sidney Godolphin slain—The king's Cornish forces come to Tavistock—Captain Carteret supplies them with ammunition—A treaty between the two parties in Devon and Cornwall :—This protestation being first taken by both—A truce and cessation thereupon—An account of the northern parts disposition at that time—Articles of neutrality agreed in Yorkshire between both parties:—but disowned by the parliament: upon which they entered into acts of hostility there—The lord Fairfax made general of Yorkshire for the parliament—The earl of Newcastle comes from Newcastle into York—The queen arrives at Burlington from Holland—The earl of Newcastle fixed a garrison at Newark—Sir Hugh Cholmondley delivered up Scarborough castle to the queen—The condition at that time of Lancashire, Cheshire, and Shropshire—The condition at that time of the counties between Oxford and York

—The lord Brook shot in besieging the cathedral of Lichfield, which was soon after taken by sir John Gell—Stafford garrisoned by some gentlemen for the king—The earl of Northampton slain on Hopton-Heath near Stafford, having first vanquished the enemy's horse that opposed him—His character—The state of the principality of Wales at that time—The lord Herbert, son of the earl of Worcester, made general of South Wales—The lord Herbert raises a little army—Is surprised by sir William Waller, and routed—Sir Will. Waller takes Hereford and Tewkesbury: both which he presently left—The state of Ireland at that time with reference to the difference between the king and the two houses here—The king puts the two houses in mind of his proposition for a cessation of arms—Both houses agree there should be a treaty; and they send for a safe conduct—The king grants it to all they name but the lord Say—The two houses send their terms for a cessation—The houses pass an ordinance for a weekly assessment on the whole kingdom—The city of London fortified—The king's proposals of alterations in the two houses' articles of cessation—The petition of the general assembly of the kirk of Scotland presented to the king by Mr. Henderson, signed Jan. 4, 1642-3—His majesty's answer to the petition March 20, 1642—The transactions of the earl of Lowden and other Scottish commissioners at Oxford: that they might be mediators, and for a parliament in Scotland—The king's answer to them in both particulars—The parliament's commissioners to treat came to Oxford—The treaty begins upon the proposals of cessation; but that takes no effect—The advice and desires of the two houses concerning gaol-delivery—His majesty's answer—The two houses make an ordinance to forbid the next assizes, and gaol-delivery—An account and character of the privy-counsellors then attending the king, and those who staid with the two houses—Mr. Hyde made chancellor of the exchequer—Of the lord Littleton—Of the duke of Richmond—Of the marquis of Hertford—Of the earl of Southampton—Of the earl of Leicester—Of the earl of Bristol—Of the earl of Newcastle—Of the earl of Berkshire, and others—Of those of the privy-counsellors who staid with the parliament—Of the earl of Northumberland—Of the earl of Pembroke—Of the earl of Essex—Of the earl of Salisbury—Of the earl of Warwick—Of the earl of Holland—Of the earl of Manchester—Of the lord Say—Of sir Henry Vane the elder.

WHEN the king set up his standard at Nottingham, which was on the 25th of August, as is before remembered, he found the place much emptier than he thought the fame of his standard would have suffered it to be ; and received intelligence the next day, that the rebels' army, for such now he had declared them, was horse, foot, and cannon, at Northampton ; besides that great party which, in the end of the fourth book, we left at Coventry : whereas his few cannon and ammunition were still at York, being neither yet in an equipage to march, though sir John Heydon, his majesty's faithful lieutenant general of the ordnance, used all possible diligence to form and prepare it ; neither were there foot enough levied to guard it : and at Nottingham, besides some few of the trained bands, which sir John Digby, the active sheriff of that county, drew into the old ruinous castle there, there were not of foot levied for the service yet three hundred men. So that they who were not overmuch given to fear, finding very many places in that great river, which was looked upon as the only strength and security of the town, to be easily fordable, and nothing towards an army for defence but the standard set up, began sadly to apprehend the danger of the king's own person. Insomuch that sir Jacob Ashley, his serjeant-major-general of his intended army, told him, "that he could not give any assurance against his majesty's being taken out of his bed, if the rebels should make a brisk attempt to that purpose." And it was evident, all the strength he had to depend upon was his horse, which were under the command of prince Rupert at Leicester, and were not at that time in number above eight hundred, few better armed than with swords ; whilst the enemy had, within less than twenty miles of that place, double the number of horse excellently armed and appointed, and a body of five thousand foot well trained and disciplined ; so that, no doubt, if they had advanced, they might at least have dispersed those few troops of the king's, and driven his majesty to a greater distance, and exposed him to notable hazards and inconveniences.

When men were almost confounded with this prospect, his majesty received intelligence, that Portsmouth was so straitly besieged by sea and land, that it would be reduced in very few days, except it were relieved. For the truth is, colonel Goring, though he had sufficient warning, and sufficient supplies of money to put that place into a posture, had relied too much upon probable and casual assistance, and neglected to do that himself, a vigilant officer would have done: and albeit his chief dependence was both for money and provisions from the Isle of Wight, yet he was careless to secure those small castles and block-houses, which guarded the river; which revolting to the parliament as soon as he declared for the king, cut off all those unreasonable dependences; so that he had neither men enough to do ordinary duty, nor provisions enough for those few, for any considerable time.   And at the same time with this of Portsmouth, arrived certain advertisements, that the marquis of Hertford, and all his forces in the west, from whom only the king hoped that Portsmouth should be relieved, was driven out of Somersetshire, where his power and interest was believed unquestionable, into Dorsetshire ; and there besieged in Sherborne castle.

The marquis, after he left the king at Beverley, by ordinary journeys, and without making any long stay by the way, came to Bath, upon the very edge of Somersetshire, at the time when the general assizes were there held; where meeting all the considerable gentlemen of that great county, and finding them well affected to the king's service, except very few who were sufficiently known, he entered into consultation with them from whom he was to expect assistance, in what place he should most conveniently fix himself for the better disposing the affections of the people, and to raise a strength for the resistance of any attempt which the parliament might make, either against them, or to disturb the peace of the country by their ordinance of the militia, which was the first power they were like to hear of.   Some were of opinion, "that Bristol would be the fittest place, being a great, rich, and populous city ; of which being once possessed, they should be easily able to give the law to Somerset and Gloucestershire ; and could not receive any affront by a sudden or tumultuary insurrection of the people."   And if this advice had been followed, it would probably have proved very prosperous.   But, on the contrary, it was objected, "that it was not evident, that his lordship's reception into

the city would be such as was expected ; Mr. Hollis being
lieutenant thereof, and having exercised the militia there ;
and there being visibly many disaffected people in it, and
some of eminent quality; and if he should attempt to go
thither, and be disappointed, it would break the whole design : then that it was out of the county of Somerset, and
therefore that they could not draw that people thither ; besides, that it would look like fear and suspicion of their own
power, to put themselves into a walled town, as if they feared the power of the other party would be able to oppress
them.   Whereas, besides Popham and Horner, all the gentlemen of eminent quality and fortune of Somerset were
either present with the marquis, or presumed not to be inclined to the parliament."   And therefore they proposed
"that Wells, being a pleasant city, in the heart and near the
centre of that county, might be chosen for his lordship's residence."   Which was accordingly agreed on, and thither the
marquis and his train went, sending for the nearest trained
bands to appear before him ; and presuming that in little
time, by the industry of the gentlemen present, and his lordship's reputation, which was very great, the affections of the
people would be so much wrought upon, and their understandings so well informed, that it would not be in the power of the parliament to pervert them, or to make ill impressions in them towards his majesty's service.

Whilst his lordship in this gentle way endeavoured to
compose the fears and apprehensions of the people, and by
doing all things in a peaceable way, and according to the
rules of the known laws, to convince all men of the justice
and integrity of his majesty's proceedings and royal intentions; the other party, according to their usual confidence
and activity, wrought underhand to persuade the people that
the marquis was come down to put the commission of array
in execution, by which commission a great part of the estate
of every farmer or substantial yeoman should be taken from
them ; alleging, that some lords had said, "that twenty pounds
by the year was enough for any peasant to live by ; and so,
taking advantage of the commission's being in Latin, trans-
lated it into what English they pleased ; persuading the sub-

stantial yeomen and freeholders, that at least two parts of
their estates would, by that commission, be taken from them;
and the meaner and poorer sort of people, that they were to
pay a tax for one day's labour in the week to the king; and
that all should be, upon the matter, no better than slaves to
the lords, and that there was no way to free and preserve
themselves from this insupportable tyranny, than by adhering
to the parliament, and submitting to the ordinance for the
militia; which was purposely prepared to enable them to resist these horrid invasions of their liberties.

It is not easily believed, how these gross infusions generally prevailed.   For though the gentlemen of ancient families
and estates in that county were, for the most part, well affected to the king, and easily discerned by what faction the parliament was governed; yet there were a people of an inferior degree, who, by good husbandry, clothing, and other
thriving arts, had gotten very great fortunes; and, by degrees, getting themselves into the gentlemen's estates, were
angry that they found not themselves in the same esteem
and reputation with those whose estates they had;[1] and
therefore, with more industry than the other, studied all
ways to make themselves considerable.   These, from the
beginning, were fast friends to the parliament; and many of
them were now intrusted by them as deputy lieutenants in
their new ordinance of the militia, and having found when
the people were ripe, gathered them together, with a purpose on a sudden, before there should be any suspicion, to
surround and surprise the marquis at Wells.   For they had
always this advantage of the king's party and his counsels,
that their resolutions were no sooner published, than they
were ready to be executed, there being an absolute implicit
obedience in the inferior sort to those who were to command
them; and their private agents, with admirable industry and
secrecy, preparing all persons and things ready against a call.
Whereas all the king's counsels were with great formality

---

[1] What a miserable reason is here given for the jealousy of the king
and his actions, and the disaffection which it produced, when the true
cause lay so open, the king's preceding arbitrary measures.—W.

deliberated, before concluded : and then, with equal formality, and precise caution of the law, executed ; there being
no other way to weigh down the prejudice that was contracted against the court,[1] but by the most barefaced publishing
all conclusions, and fitting them to that apparent justice and
reason, that might prevail over the most ordinary understandings.

When the marquis was thus in the midst of an enemy that
almost covered the whole kingdom,[2] his whole strength was
a troop of horse, raised by Mr. John Digby, son to the earl
of Bristol, and another by sir Francis Hawley, (both which
were levied in those parts to attend the king in the north,)
and a troop of horse, and a small troop of dragoons, raised
and armed by sir Ralph Hopton at his own charge ; and
about one hundred foot gathered up by lieutenant-colonel
Henry Lunsford towards a regiment, which were likewise
to have marched to the king.   These, with the lord Pawlet, and the gentlemen of the country, which were about
eight and twenty of the prime quality there, with their servants and retinue, made up the marquis's force.   Then their
proceedings were with that rare caution, that upon advertisement that the active ministers of that party had appointed a general meeting at a town within few miles of Wells,
sir Ralph Hopton being advised with his small troop and some
volunteer gentlemen to repair thither, and to disappoint that
convention, and to take care that it might produce the least
prejudice to the king's service ; before he reached the place,
those gentlemen who stayed behind (and by whose advice
the marquis thought it necessary absolutely to govern himself, that they might see all possible wariness was used in
the entrance into a war, which being once entered into, he
well knew must be carried on another way) sent him word,
"that he should forbear any hostile act, otherwise they would
disclaim whatsoever he should do."   Otherwise the courage

---

[1] A strong proof of the arbitrary administration in the first fourteen
years of Charles's reign.—W.

[2] The disaffection, by this confession, was general, and therefore
must have as general a cause.—W.

and resolution of those few were such, and the cowardice of the undisciplined seditious rabble and their leaders was so eminent, that it was very probable, if those few troops had been as actively employed as their commanders desired, they might have been able to have driven the bigots out of the country, before they had fully possessed the rest with their own rancour : which may be reasonably presumed by what followed shortly after, when Mr. Digby, sir John Stawel and his sons, with some volunteer gentlemen, being in the whole not above fourscore horse, and fourteen dragoons, charged a greater body of horse, and above six hundred foot of the rebels, led by a member of the house of commons ; and without the loss of one man, killed seven in the place, hurt very many, took their chief officers, and as many more prisoners as they would ; and so routed the whole body, that six men kept not together, they having all thrown down their arms.

But this good fortune abated only the courage of those who had run away, the other making use of this overthrow as an argument of the marquis's bloody purposes ; and there-fore, in few days, sir John Horner and Alexander Popham, being the principal men of quality of that party in that coun-ty, with the assistance of their friends of Dorset, and De-von, and the city of Bristol, drew together a body of above twelve thousand men, horse and foot, with some pieces of cannon, with which they appeared on the top of the hill over Wells ; where the marquis, in contempt of them, stayed two days, having only barricadoed the town ; but then, find-ing that the few trained bands, which attended him there, were run away, either to their own houses, or to their fel-lows, on the top of the hill; and hearing that more forces, or at least better officers, were coming from the parliament against him, he retired in the noon day, and in the face of that rebellious herd, from Wells to Somerton, and so to Sherborne, without any loss or trouble. Thither, within two days, came to his lordship sir John Berkley, colonel Ashburnham, and other good officers, enough to have formed a considerable army, if there had been no other want. But they had not been long there, (and it was not easy to re-

solve whither else to go, they having no reason to believe
they should be any where more welcome than in Somersetshire, from whence they had been now driven,) when the
earl of Bedford, general of the horse to the parliament, with
Mr. Hollis, sir Walter Earl, and other ephori, and a complete body of seven thousand foot at least, ordered by Charles
Essex, their sergeant-major-general, a soldier of good experience and reputation in the Low Countries, and eight full
troops of horse, under the command of captain Pretty, with
four pieces of cannon, in a very splendid equipage, came to
Wells, and from thence to Sherborne. The marquis, by
this time having increased his foot to four hundred, with
which that great army was kept from entering that great
town, and persuaded to encamp in the field about three quarters of a mile north from the castle ; where, for the present,
we must leave the marquis and his great-spirited little army.

·When this news of Portsmouth and Sherborne came to
the king at Nottingham, the next day after the setting up his
standard, it will easily be believed that the spirits there were
not a little dejected : and indeed they who had least fear,
could not but reasonably think the king's condition very
desperate ; so that some of those of nearest trust and confidence about him, proposed to him, as the only expedient, to
send a gracious message to the two houses, to offer a treaty
for peace. His majesty received this advice very unwillingly, concluding that he should thereby improve the pride
and insolence of his enemies, who would impute it to the
despair of raising any force to resist them, and would demean themselves accordingly, and would to the same degree
dishearten and discountenance those who had appeared, and
upon the setting up his standard were now ready to appear
in any act of loyalty on his behalf, who would be all sacrificed to the revenge and fury of the others. On the other
side it was objected, that his majesty was not able to make
resistance ; that the forces before Sherborne, Portsmouth,
and at Northampton, were three several armies, the least of
which would drive his majesty out of his dominions; that it
was only in his power to choose, whether, by making a fair
offer himself, he would seem to make peace, which could

not but render him very gracious to the people, or suffer himself to be taken prisoner, (which he would not long be able to avoid,) which would give his enemies power, reputation, and authority to proceed against his majesty, and, it might be, his posterity, according to their own engaged malice.[1]

Yet this motive made no impression in him. "For, he said, no misfortune, or ill success that might attend his endeavour of defending himself, could expose him to more inconveniences than a treaty at this time desired by him, where he must be understood to be willing to yield to whatsoever they would require of him : and how modest they were like to be, might be judged by their nineteen propositions, which were tendered, when their power could not be reasonably understood to be like so much to exceed his majesty's, as at this time it was evident it did; and that, having now nothing to lose but his honour, he could be only excusable to the world, by using his industry to the last to oppose that torrent, which if it prevailed would overwhelm him." This composed courage and magnanimity of his majesty seemed too philosophical, and abstracted from the policy of self-preservation, to which men were passionately addicted : and that which was the king's greatest disadvantage, how many soever were of his mind, (as some few, and but few, there were,) no man durst publicly avow that he was so; a treaty for peace being so popular a thing, that whosoever opposed it would be sure to be, by general consent, a declared enemy to his country.

That which prevailed with his majesty very reasonably then (and indeed it proved equally advantageous to him afterwards) was, "that it was most probable" (and his whole fortune was to be submitted at best to probabilities) "that, out of their pride, and contempt of the king's weakness and want of power, the parliament would refuse to treat; which would be so unpopular a thing, that as his majesty would highly oblige his people by making the offer, so they would lose the hearts of them by rejecting it; which alone would

[1] The continuation of this account of the king's sending a message for peace, according to MS. B. will be found in the Appendix, A.

raise an army for his majesty.   That if they should embrace
it, the king could not but be a gainer; for by the propositions which they should make to him, he would be able to
state the quarrel so clearly, that it should be more demonstrable to the kingdom, than yet it was, that the war was,
on his majesty's part, purely defensive; since he never had,
and now would not deny any thing, which they could in
reason or justice ask: that this very overture would necessarily produce some pause, and delay in their preparations,
or motions of their armies; for some debate it must needs
have; and during that time, men's minds would be in sus-
pense; whereas his majesty should be so far from slackening
his preparations, that he might be more vigorous in them, by
hastening those levies, for which his commissions were out."
For these reasons, and almost the concurrent desire and importunity of his council, the king was prevailed with to send
the earls of Southampton and Dorset, sir John Colepepper,
chancellor of his exchequer, and sir William Udall, (whom
his majesty gave leave under that pretence to intend the
business of his own fortune,) to the two houses with this
message, which was sent the third day after his standard
was set up.

   " We have,[1] with unspeakable grief of heart, long beheld
the distractions of this our kingdom.   Our very soul is full
of anguish, until we may find some remedy to prevent the
miseries which are ready to overwhelm this whole nation by
a civil war.   And though all our endeavours, tending to the
composing of those unhappy differences betwixt us and our
two houses of parliament, (though pursued by us with all
zeal and sincerity,) have been hitherto without that success
we hoped for; yet such is our constant and earnest care to
preserve the public peace, that we shall not be discouraged
from using any expedient, which, by the blessing of the God
of mercy, may lay a firm foundation of peace and happiness
to all our good subjects.   To this end, observing that many
mistakes have arisen by the messages, petitions, and answers, betwixt us and our two houses of parliament, which

---

[1] *This message is in the handwriting of lord Clarendon's secretary.*

happily may be prevented by some other way of treaty, wherein the matters in difference may be more clearly understood, and more freely transacted ; we have thought fit to propound to you, that some fit persons may be by you enabled to treat with the like number to be authorized by us, in such a manner, and with such freedom of debate, as may best tend to that happy conclusion which all good men desire, the peace of the kingdom. Wherein, as we promise, in the word of a king, all safety and encouragement to such as shall be sent unto us, if you shall choose the place where we are, for the treaty, which we wholly leave to you, presuming the like care of the safety of those we shall employ, if you shall name another place ; so 'we assure you, and all our good subjects, that, to the best of our understanding, nothing shall be therein wanting on our part, which may advance the true protestant religion, oppose popery and superstition, secure the law of the land, (upon which is built as well our just prerogative, as the propriety and liberty of the subject,) confirm all just power and privileges of parliament, and render us and our people truly happy by a good understanding betwixt us and our two houses of parliament. Bring with you as firm resolutions to do your duty ; and let all our good people join with us in our prayers to Almighty God, for his blessing upon this work. If this proposition shall be rejected by you, we have done our duty so amply, that God will absolve us from the guilt of any of that blood which must be spilt ; and what opinion soever other men may have of our power, we assure you nothing but our Christian and pious care to prevent the effusion of blood hath begot this motion ; our provision of men, arms, and money, being such as may secure us from farther violence, till it please God to open the eyes of our people."

This message had the same reception his majesty believed it would have ; and was indeed received with unheard of insolence and contempt. For the earl of Southampton, and sir John Colepepper, desiring to appear themselves before any notice should arrive of their coming, made such haste, that they were at Westminster in the morning shortly after the houses met. The earl of Southampton went into the house of peers, where he was scarce sat down in his place, when, with great passion, he was called upon to withdraw; albeit he told them he had a message to them from the king, and there could be no exception to his lordship's sitting in the house upon their own grounds; he having had leave from the house to attend his majesty. However he was compelled to withdraw; and then they sent the gentleman usher of the house to him, to require his message; which, his lordship said, he was by the king's command to deliver himself, and refused therefore to send it, except the lords made an order, that he should not; which they did; and thereupon he sent it to them; which they no sooner received, than they sent him word, " that he should, at his peril, immediately depart the town, and that they would take care that their answer to the message should be sent to him." And so the earl of Southampton departed the town, reposing himself in better company, at the house of a noble person seven or eight miles off. Whilst the earl had this skirmish with the lords, sir John Colepepper attended the commons, forbearing to go into the house without leave, because there had been an order, (which is mentioned before,) that all the members, who were not present at such a day, should not presume to sit there, till they had paid a hundred pounds, and given the house satisfaction in the cause of their absence. But he sent word to the speaker, " that he had a message from the king to them, and that he desired to deliver it in his place in the house." After some debate, (for there remained yet some, who thought it as unreasonable as irregular to deny a member of the house, against whom there had not been the least public objection, and a privy-counsellor who had been in all times used there with great reverence, leave to deliver a message from the king in his own place as a member,) it was absolutely resolved, " that he should not sit in the house, but that he should deliver his message at the bar, and immediately withdraw;" which he did accordingly.

And then the two houses met at a conference, and read the king's message with great superciliousness; and within two days, with less difficulty and opposition than can be believed, agreed upon their answer. The king's messengers, in the mean time, being of that quality, not receiving ordinary civility from any members of either house ; they who were very willing to have paid it, not daring for their own safety to come near them ; and the other looking upon them as servants to a master whom they had, and meant farther to oppress. Private conferences they had with some of the principal governors ; from whom they received no other advice, but that, if the king had any care of himself or his posterity, he should immediately come to London, throw himself into the arms of his parliament, and comply in whatsoever they proposed. The answer which they returned to the king was this.

The answer[1] of the lords and commons to his majesty's message of the 25th of August, 1642.

" May it please your majesty :

" The lords and commons, in parliament assembled, having received your majesty's message of the 25th of August, do with much grief resent the dangerous and distracted state of this kingdom; which we have by all means endeavoured to prevent, both by our several advices and petitions to your majesty ; which have been not only without success, but there hath followed that which no ill counsel in former times hath produced, or any age hath seen, namely, those several proclamations and declarations against both the houses of parliament, whereby their actions are declared treasonable, and their persons traitors. And thereupon your majesty hath set up your standard against them, whereby you have put the two houses of parliament, and, in them, this whole kingdom, out of your protection ; so that until your majesty shall recall those proclamations and declarations, whereby the earl of Essex, and both houses of parliament, and their adherents, and assistants, and such as have obeyed and executed their commands and directions, according to their duties, are declared traitors or otherwise delinquents : and until the standard, set

[1] *This answer is in the handwriting of lord Clarendon's secretary.*

up in pursuance of the said proclamation, be taken down, your majesty hath put us into such a condition, that, whilst we so remain, we cannot, by the fundamental privileges of parliament, the public trust reposed in us, or with the general good and safety of this kingdom, give your majesty any other answer to this message."

When the king's messengers returned with this answer to Nottingham, all men saw to what they must trust; and the king believed, he should be no farther moved to make addresses to them. And yet all hopes of an army, or any ability to resist that violence, seemed so desperate, that he was privately advised by those, whom he trusted as much as any, and those whose affections were as entire to him as any men's, to give all other thoughts over, and instantly to make all imaginable haste to London, and to appear in the parliament-house before they had any expectation of him. And they conceived there would be more likelihood for him to prevail that way, than by any army he was like to raise. And it must be solely imputed to his majesty's own magnanimity, that he took not that course. However he was contented to make so much farther use of their pride and passion, as to give them occasion, by another message, to publish more of it to the people; and therefore, within three days after the return of his messengers, he sent the lord Falkland, his principal secretary of state, with a reply to their answer in these words.

" We will[1] not repeat, what means we have used to prevent the dangerous and distracted estate of the kingdom, nor how those means have been interpreted; because, being desirous to avoid the effusion of blood, we are willing to decline all memory of former bitterness, that might render our offer of a treaty less readily accepted. We never did declare, nor ever intended to declare, both our houses of parliament traitors, or set up our standard against them; and much less to put them and this kingdom out of our protection. We utterly profess against it before God, and the world; and, farther to remove all possible scruples, which may hinder the treaty so much desired by us, we hereby promise, so that a day be

---

[1] *This reply is also in the handwriting of lord Clarendon's secretary.*

appointed by you for the revoking of your declarations against all persons as traitors, or otherwise, for assisting us; we shall, with all cheerfulness, upon the same day recall our proclamations and declarations, and take down our standard.   In which treaty, we shall be ready to grant any thing, that shall be really for the good of our subjects: conjuring you to consider the bleeding condition of Ireland, and the dangerous condition of England, in as high a degree, as by these our offers we have declared ourself to do ; and assuring you, that our chief desire, in this world, is to beget a good understanding and mutual confidence betwixt us and our two houses of parliament."

This message had no better effect or reception than the former; their principal officers being sent down since the last message to Northampton to put the army into a readiness to march.   And now they required the earl of Essex himself to make haste thither, that no more time might be lost, sending by the lord Falkland, within two days, this answer to the king.

To the king's[1] most excellent majesty ;

The humble answer and petition of the lords and commons assembled in parliament, unto the king's last message.

"May it please your majesty :

"If we, the lords and commons in parliament assembled, should repeat all the ways we have taken, the endeavours we have used, and the expressions we have made unto your majesty, to prevent those distractions, and dangers, your majesty speaks of, we should too much enlarge this reply.   Therefore, as we humbly, so shall we only let your majesty know, that we cannot recede from our former answer, for the reasons therein expressed.   For that your majesty hath not taken down your standard, recalled your proclamations and declarations, whereby you have declared the actions of both houses of parliament to be treasonable, and their persons traitors; and you have published the same since your message of the

---

[1] *This answer is in the handwriting of lord Clarendon's secretary.*

25th of August, by your late instructions sent to your commissioners of array; which standard being taken down, and
the declarations, proclamations, and instructions recalled, if
your majesty shall then, upon this our humble petition, leaving your forces, return unto your parliament, and receive
their faithful advice, your majesty will find such expressions
of our fidelities, and duties, as shall assure you, that your
safety, honour, and greatness, can only be found in the affections of your people, and the sincere counsels of your parliament; whose constant and undiscouraged endeavours and
consultations have passed through difficulties unheard of, only
to secure your kingdoms from the violent mischiefs and dangers now ready to fall upon them, and every part of them;
who deserve better of your majesty, and can never allow
themselves (representing likewise the whole kingdom) to be
balanced with those persons, whose desperate dispositions
and counsels prevail still to interrupt all our endeavours for
the relieving of bleeding Ireland; as we may fear our labours
and vast expenses will be fruitless to that distressed kingdom.
As your presence is thus humbly desired by us, so it is in our
hopes your majesty will in your reason believe, there is no
other way than this, to make your majesty's self happy, and
your kingdom safe."

And lest this overture of a treaty might be a means to allay and compose the distempers of the people, and that the
hope and expectation of peace might not dishearten their party, in their preparations and contributions to the war, the
same day they sent their last answer to the king, they published this declaration to the kingdom.

"Whereas[1] his majesty, in a message received the fifth of
September, requires that the parliament would revoke their
declarations against such persons as have assisted his majesty
in this unnatural war against his kingdom; it is this day ordered, and declared by the lords and commons, that the arms,
which they have been forced to take up, and shall be forced
to take up, for the preservation of the parliament, religion, the
laws and liberties of the kingdom, shall not be laid down, un-

---

[1] *This declaration is copied into the MS. by an amanuensis.*

til his majesty shall withdraw his protection from such persons as have been voted by both houses to be delinquents,
or that shall by both houses be voted to be delinquents, and
shall leave them to the justice of the parliament to be proceeded with according to their demerits;[1] to the end that
both this and succeeding generations may take warning, with
what danger they incur the like heinous crimes : and also
to the end that those great charges and damages, wherewith
all the commonwealth hath been burdened in the premises,
since his majesty's departure from the parliament, may be
borne by the delinquents, and other malignant and disaffected persons: and that all his majesty's good and well affected
subjects, who by loan of monies, or otherwise at their charge,
have assisted the commonwealth, or shall in like manner hereafter assist the commonwealth in time of extreme danger, may
be repaid all sums of money lent by them for those purposes, and
be satisfied their charges so sustained, out of the estates of the
said delinquents, and of the malignant and disaffected party
in this kingdom."

This declaration did the king no harm; for besides that it
was evident to all men, that the king had done whatsoever
was in his power, or could be expected from him, for the prevention of a civil war, all persons of honour and quality plainly discerned, that they had no safety but in the preservation
of the regal power, since their estates were already disposed
of by them who could declare whom they would delinquents,
and who would infallibly declare all such who had not concurred with them.   And the advantage the king received by
those overtures, and the pride, frowardness, and perverseness
of the rebels, is not imaginable ; his levies of men, and all
other preparations for the war, being incredibly advanced from
the time of his first message.   Prince Rupert lay still with
the horse at Leicester ; and though he, and some of the prin-

---

[1] There cannot possibly be a stronger proof given that the parliament
was now become a faction, and a faction of the most destructive nature.
This declaration being the infallible means, and obvious to foresee, of
attaching the far greater part of the nobility and gentry to the king's
interest more firmly than ever. As they could not but foresee this, it
is plain their quarrel was now with the monarchy itself.—W.

cipal officers with him, were discontented to that degree, upon the king's first message and desire of a treaty, as like not
only to destroy all hopes of raising an army, but to sacrifice
those who were raised, that they were not without some
thoughts, at least discourses, of offering violence to the principal advisers of it, he now found his numbers increased, and
better resolved by it; and from Yorkshire, Lincolnshire, and
Staffordshire, came very good recruits of foot ; so that his
cannon and munition being likewise come up from York, within twenty days his numbers began to look towards an army;
and there was another air in all men's faces : yet Nottingham
seemed not a good post for his majesty to stay longer at; and
therefore, about the middle of September, the earl of Essex
being then with his whole army at Northampton, his majesty
marched from Nottingham to Derby : being not then resolved whither to bend his course, to Shrewsbury or Chester, not
well knowing the temper of those towns, in both which the
parliament party had been very active ; but resolving to sit
down near the borders of Wales, where the power of the parliament had been least prevalent, and where some regiments
of foot were levying for his service.   Before his leaving Nottingham, as a farewell to his hopes of a treaty, and to make
the deeper sense and impression, in the hearts of the people,
of those who had so pertinaciously rejected it, his majesty
sent this message to the houses.

" Who have taken[1] most ways, used most endeavours,
and made most real expressions to prevent the present distractions and dangers, let all the world judge, as well by
former passages, as by our two last messages, which have
been so fruitless, that, though we have descended to desire
and press it, not so much as a treaty can be obtained; unless
we would denude ourself of all force to defend us from a
visible strength marching against us ; and admit those persons as traitors to us, who, according to their duty, their
oaths of allegiance, and the law, have appeared in defence of
us, their king and liege lord, (whom we are bound in conscience and honour to preserve,) though we disclaimed all
our proclamations, and declarations, and the erecting of our

[1] *This message is in the same hand as the last declaration.*

standard, as against our parliament.   All we have now left
in our power, is to express the deep sense we have of the
public misery of this kingdom, in which is involved that of
our distressed protestants of Ireland ; and to apply ourself
to our necessary defence, wherein we wholly rely upon the
providence of God, the justice of our cause, and the affection
of our good people ; so far we are from putting them out of
our protection.   When you shall desire a treaty of us, we
shall piously remember, whose blood is to be spilt in this
quarrel, and cheerfully embrace it.   And as no other reason induced us to leave our city of London, but that, with
honour and safety we could not stay there ; nor raise any
force, but for the necessary defence of our person and the
law, against levies in opposition to both ; so we shall suddenly and most willingly return to the one, and disband the
other, as soon as those causes shall be removed.   The God
of heaven direct you, and in mercy divert those judgments,
which hang over this nation ; and so deal with us, and our
posterity, as we desire the preservation and advancement of
the true protestant religion; the law, and the liberty of the
subject ; the just rights of parliament, and the peace of the
kingdom."
    When the king came to Derby, he received clear infor-
mation from the well affected party in Shrewsbury, that the
town was at his devotion ; and that the very rumour of his
majesty's purpose of coming thither had driven away all
those who were most inclined to sedition.   And therefore,
as well in regard of the strong and pleasant situation of it,
(one side being defended by the Severn, the other having a
secure passage into Wales, the confines of Montgomeryshire
extending very near the town,) as for the correspondence
with Worcester, of which city he hoped well, and that, by
his being at Shrewsbury, he should be as well able to secure Chester, as by carrying his whole train so far north ;
besides that the other might give some apprehension of his
going into Ireland, which had been formerly mentioned, his
majesty resolved for that town ; and, after one day's stay at
Derby, by easy marches he went thither, drawing his whole
small forces to a rendezvous by Wellington, a day's march
short of Shrewsbury ; and that being the first time that they

were together, his majesty then caused his military orders
for the discipline and government of the army to be read at
the head of each regiment; and then, which is not fit ever
to be forgotten, putting himself in the middle, where he
might be best heard, not much unlike the emperor Trajan,[1]
who, when he made Sura great marshal of the empire, gave
him a sword, saying, "Receive this sword of me; and if I
command as I ought, employ it in my defence; if I do
otherwise, draw it against me, and take my life from me,"
his majesty made this speech to his soldiers.[2]

"Gentlemen,[3] you have heard those orders read: it is
your part, in your several places, to observe them exactly.
The time cannot be long before we come to action, therefore
you have the more reason to be careful: and I must tell you,
I shall be very severe in the punishing of those, of what
condition soever, who transgress these instructions. I cannot suspect your courage and resolution; your conscience
and your loyalty hath brought you hither, to fight for your
religion, your king, and the laws of the land. You shall
meet with no enemies but traitors, most of them Brownists,
anabaptists, and atheists; such who desire to destroy both
church and state, and who have already condemned you to
ruin for being loyal to us. That you may see what use I
mean to make of your valour, if it please God to bless it
with success, I have thought fit to publish my resolution to
you in a protestation; which when you have heard me make,
you will believe you cannot fight in a better quarrel; in
which I promise to live and die with you."

The protestation his majesty was then pleased to make
was in these words.

"I do promise in the presence of Almighty God, and as I
hope for his blessing and protection, that I will, to the utmost of my power, defend and maintain the true reformed

[1] The unlikeness was in this, the king's declaration was not till *after*
he had governed ill, the emperor's was *before.*—W.

[2] This speech is admirable, and has the advantage of most we meet
with in historians, that it was really delivered, and not a fiction of the
writer's.—W.

[3] *This speech and protestation is copied by the amanuensis.*

protestant religion, established in the church of England; and, by the grace of God, in the same will live and die.

"I desire to govern by the known laws of the land, and that the liberty and property of the subject may be by them preserved with the same care, as my own just rights. And if it please God, by his blessing upon this army, raised for my necessary defence, to preserve me from this rebellion, I do solemnly and faithfully promise, in the sight of God, to maintain the just privileges and freedom of parliament, and to govern by the known laws of the land to my utmost power ; and particularly, to observe inviolably the laws con-sented to by me this parliament. In the mean while, if this time of war, and the great necessity and straits I am now driven to, beget any violation of those, I hope it shall be im-puted by God and men to the authors of this war, and not to me ; who have so earnestly laboured for the preservation of the peace of this kingdom.

"When I willingly fail in these particulars, I will expect no aid or relief from any man, or protection from heaven. But in this resolution, I hope for the cheerful assistance of all good men, and am confident of God's blessing."

This protestation, and the manner and solemnity of making it, gave not more life and encouragement to the little army, than it did comfort and satisfaction to the gentry and inhabi-tants of those parts ; into whom the parliament had infused, that, if his majesty prevailed by force, he would, with the same power, abolish all those good laws, which had been made this parliament; so that they looked upon this protes-tation, as a more ample security for their enjoying the benefit of those acts, than the royal assent he had before given. And a more general and passionate expression of affections cannot be imagined, than he received by the people of those counties of Derby, Stafford, and Shropshire, as he passed ; or a better reception, than he found at Shrewsbury ; into which town he entered on Tuesday the 20th of September.

It will be, and was then, wondered at, that since the par-liament had a full and well formed army, before the king had one full regiment, and the earl of Essex was himself come to Northampton, some days before his majesty went from Not-tingham, his lordship neither disquieted the king whilst he staid there, nor gave him any disturbance in his march to Shrewsbury; which if he had done, he might either have taken him prisoner, or so dispersed his small power, that it would never have been possible for him to have gotten an army together. But as the earl had not yet received his instructions, so they, upon whom he depended, avoided that expedition out of mere pride, and contempt of the king's forces; and upon a presumption, that it would not be possible for him to raise such a power, as would be able to look their army in the face; but that, when he had in vain tried all other ways, and those, who not only followed him upon their own charges, but supported those who were not able to bear their own, (for his army was maintained and paid by the nobility and gentry, who served likewise in their own persons,) were grown weary and unable longer to bear that burden, his majesty would be forced to put himself into their arms for protection and subsistence; and such a victory without blood had crowned all their designs. And if their army, which they pretended to raise only for their defence, and for the safety of the king's person, had been able to prevent the king's raising any; or if the king, in that melancholic conjuncture at Nottingham, had returned to Whitehall, he had justified all their proceedings, and could never after have refused to yield to whatsoever they proposed.

And it is most certain, that the common soldiers of the army were generally persuaded, that they should never be brought to fight; but that the king was in truth little better than imprisoned by evil counsellors, malignants, delinquents, and cavaliers, (the terms applied to his whole party,) and would gladly come to his parliament, if he could break from that company; which he would undoubtedly do, if their army came once to such a distance, that his majesty might make an escape to them. And in this kind of discourse they were so sottish, that they were persuaded, that those persons, of whose piety, honour, and integrity, they had received heretofore the greatest testimony, were now turned papists; and that the small army, and forces the king had, consisted of no other than papists. Insomuch as truly those of the king's party, who promised themselves any support, but from the comfort of their own consciences, or relied upon any other means than from God Almighty, could hardly have made their expectations appear reasonable; for they were in truth possessed of the whole kingdom.

Portsmouth, the strongest and best fortified town then in the kingdom, was surrendered to them; colonel Goring, about the beginning of September, though he had seemed to be so long resolved, and prepared to expect a siege, and had been supplied with monies according to his own proposal, was brought so low, that he gave it up, only for liberty to transport himself beyond seas, and for his officers to repair to the king. And it were to be wished that there might be no more occasion to mention him hereafter, after this repeated treachery; and that his incomparable dexterity and sagacity had not prevailed so far over those, who had been so often deceived by him, as to make it absolutely necessary to speak at large of him, more than once, before this discourse comes to an end.

The marquis of Hertford, though he had so much discredited the earl of Bedford's soldiery, and disheartened his great army, that the earl of Bedford (after lying in the fields four or five nights within less than cannon shot of the castle and town, and after having refused to fight a duel with the marquis, to which he provoked him by a challenge) sent sir John Norcot, under pretence of a treaty and the godly care to avoid the effusion of Christian blood, in plain English to desire " that he might fairly and peaceably draw off his forces, and march away;" the which, how reasonable a request soever it was, the marquis refused; sending them word, "that as they came thither upon their own counsels, so they should get off as they could;" and at last they did draw off, and march above a dozen miles for repose; leaving the marquis, for some weeks, undisturbed at Sherborne: yet when he heard of the loss of Portsmouth, the relief whereof was his principal business, and so that those forces would probably be added to the earl of Bedford, and by their success give much courage to his bashful army, and that a good regiment of horse, which he expected, (for sir John Byron had sent him word from Oxford, that he would march towards him,) was retired to the king; and that the committees were now so busy in the several counties, that the people in all places declared for the parliament; and more particularly some strong and populous towns in Somersetshire ; as Taunton, Wellington, and Dunstar-Castle ; by reason whereof it would not be possible for him to increase his strength ; he resolved to leave Sherborne, where his stay could no way advance the king's service, and to try all ways to get to his majesty.   But when he came to Minhead, a port-town, from whence he made no doubt he should be able to transport himself and his company into Wales, he found the people both of the town and county so disaffected, that all the boats, of which there used always to be great store, by reason of the trade for cattle and corn with Wales, were industriously sent away, save only two ; so that the earl of Bedford having taken new heart, and being within four miles with his army, his lordship, with his small cannon and few foot, with the lord Pawlet, lord Seymour, and some gentlemen of Somersetshire, transported himself into Glamorganshire; leaving sir Ralph Hopton, sir John Berkley, Mr. Digby, and some other officers with their horse, (consisting of about one hundred and twenty,) to march into Cornwall, in hope to find that county better prepared for their reception.

On the other hand, the earl of Bedford, thinking those few fugitives not worth his farther care, and that they would be easily apprehended by the committee of the militia, which was very powerful in Devon and Cornwall, contented himself with having driven away the marquis, and so expelled all hope of raising an army for the king in the west; and retired with his forces to the earl of Essex, as sir William Waller had done from Portsmouth ; so that as it was not expected, that the forces about his majesty could be able to defend him against so puissant an army, so it was not imaginable that he could receive any addition of strength from any other parts.   For wherever they found any person of quality inclined to the king, or but disinclined to them, they immediately seized upon his person, and sent him in great triumph to the parliament ; who committed him to prison, with all circumstances of cruelty and inhumanity.

Thus they took prisoner the lord Mountague of Boughton, at his house in Northamptonshire, a person of great re-

verence, being above fourscore years of age, and of unblemished reputation, for declaring himself unsatisfied with
their disobedient and undutiful proceedings against the king,
and more expressly against their ordinance for the militia ;
and notwithstanding that he had a brother of the house of
peers, the lord privy seal, and a nephew, the lord Kimbolton, who had as full a power in that council as any man,
and a son in the house of commons very unlike his father ;
his lordship was committed to the Tower a close prisoner ;
and, though he was afterwards remitted to more air, he con‧
tinued a prisoner to his death.

Thus they took prisoner in Oxfordshire the earl of Berkshire, and three or four principal gentlemen of that county ;
and committed them to the Tower, for no other reason but
wishing well to the king ; for they never appeared in the
least action in his service.   And thus they took prisoner the
earl of Bath in Devonshire, who neither had, or ever meant
to do the king the least service ; but only out of the morosity of his own nature, had before, in the house, expressed
himself not of their mind ; and carried him, with many other
gentlemen of Devon and Somerset, with a strong guard of
horse, to London ; where, after they had been exposed to
the rudeness and reproach of the common people, who called
them traitors and rebels to the parliament, and pursued them
with such usage as they use to the most infamous malefac-
tors, they were, without ever being examined, or charged
with any particular crime, committed to several prisons ; so
that not only all the prisons about London were quickly
filled with persons of honour, and great reputation for sobriety and integrity to their counties, but new prisons were
made for their reception ; and, which was a new and barbarous invention, very many persons of very good quality,
both of the clergy and laity, were committed to prison on
board the ships in the river of Thames ; where they were
kept under decks, and no friend suffered to come to them,
by which many lost their lives.   And that the loss of their
liberty might not be all their punishment, it was the usual
course, and very few escaped it, after any man was committed as a notorious malignant, (which was the brand,) that

his estate and goods were seized or plundered by an order from the house of commons, or some committee, or the soldiers, who in their march took the goods of all catholics and eminent malignants, as lawful prize; or by the fury and licence of the common people, who were in all places grown to that barbarity and rage against the nobility and gentry, (under the style of cavaliers,) that it was not safe for any to live at their houses, who were taken notice of as no votaries to the parliament.

So the common people (no doubt by the advice of their superiors) in Essex on a sudden beset the house of sir John Lucas, one of the best gentlemen of that county, and of the most eminent affection to the king, being a gentleman of the privy chamber to the prince of Wales; and, upon pretence that he was going to the king, possessed themselves of all his horses and arms, seized upon his person, and used him with all possible indignities, not without some threats to murder him : and when the mayor of Colchester, whither he was brought, with more humanity than the rest, offered to keep him prisoner in his own house, till the pleasure of the parliament should be farther known, they compelled him, or he was willing to be compelled, to send him to the common gaol; where he remained, glad of that security, till the house of commons removed him to another prison, (without ever charging him with any crime,) having sent all his horses to the earl of Essex, to be used in the service of that army.

At the same time the same rabble entered the house of the countess of Rivers, near Colchester; for no other ground, than that she was a papist; and in few hours disfurnished it of all the goods, which had been many years with great curiosity providing, and were not of less value than forty thousand pounds sterling; the countess herself hardly escaping, after great insolence had been used to her person : and she could never receive any reparation from the parliament; so that these and many other instances of the same kind in London and the parts adjacent, gave sufficient evidence to all men how little else they were to keep, who meant to preserve their allegiance and integrity in the full vigour.

I must not forget, though it cannot be remembered without much horror, that this strange wild-fire among the people was not so much and so furiously kindled by the breath of the parliament, as of the clergy, who both administered fuel, and blowed the coals in the houses too. These men having creeped into, and at last driven all learned and orthodox men from, the pulpits, had, as is before remembered, from the beginning of this parliament, under the notion of reformation and extirpating of popery, infused seditious inclinations into the hearts of men against the present government of the church, with many libellous invectives against the state too. But since the raising an army, and rejecting the king's last overture of a treaty, they contained themselves within no bounds ; and as freely and without control inveighed against the person of the king, as they had before against the worst malignant ; profanely and blasphemously applying whatsoever had been spoken and declared by God himself, or the prophets, against the most wicked and impious kings, to incense and stir up the people against their most gracious sovereign.

There are monuments enough in the seditious sermons at that time printed, and in the memories of men, of others not printed, of such wresting and perverting of scripture to the odious purposes of the preacher, that pious men will not look over without trembling. One takes his text out of Moses's words in the 32d chapter of Exodus, and the 29th verse ; *Consecrate yourselves to-day to the Lord, even every man upon his son, and upon his brother, that he may bestow upon you a blessing this day :* and from thence incites his auditory to the utmost prosecution of those, under what relation soever of blood, neighbourhood, dependence, who concurred not in the reformation proposed by the parliament. Another makes as bold with David's words, in the 1st Chron. chap. xxii. verse 16. *Arise therefore, and be doing :* and from thence assures them, it was not enough to wish well to the parliament ; if they brought not their purse, as well as their prayers, and their hands, as well as their hearts, to the assistance of it, the duty in the text was not performed. There was more than Mr. Marshall, who from the 23d verse of the 5th chapter of Judges, *Curse ye Meroz, said the angel of the Lord; curse ye bitterly the inhabitants thereof, because they came not to the help of the Lord, to the help of the Lord against the mighty;* presumed to inveigh against, and in plain terms to pronounce God's own curse against all those, who came not, with their utmost power and strength, to destroy and root out all the malignants, who in any degree opposed the parliament.

There was one, who from the 48th chapter of the prophet Jeremiah, and the 10th verse, *Cursed be he that keepeth back his sword from blood,* reproved those who gave any quarter to the king's soldiers. And another out of the 5th verse of the 25th chapter of Proverbs, *Take away the wicked from before the king, and his throne shall be established in righteousness,* made it no less a case of conscience by force to remove the evil counsellors from the king, (with bold intimation what might be done to the king himself, if he would not suffer them to be removed,) than to perform any Christian duty that is enjoined. It would fill a volume to insert all the impious madness of this kind, so that the complaint of the prophet Ezekiel might most truly and seasonably have been applied; *There is a conspiracy of her prophets in the midst thereof, like a roaring lion ravening the prey; they have devoured souls; they have taken the treasure and precious things; they have made her many widows in the midst thereof.*

It was the complaint of Erasmus of the clergy in his time, that when princes were inclinable to wars, *alius e sacro suggesto promittit omnium admissorum condonationem, alius promittit certam victoriam, prophetarum voces ad rem impiam detorquens. Tam bellaces conciones audivimus,* says he. And indeed no good Christian can, without horror, think of those ministers of the church, who, by their function being messengers of peace, were the only trumpets of war, and incendiaries towards rebellion. How much more Christian was that Athenian nun in Plutarch, and how shall she rise up in judgment against those men, who, when Alcibiades was condemned by the public justice of the state, and a decree made that all the religious priests and women should

ban and curse him, stoutly refused to perform that office ;
answering, "that she was professed religious, to *pray* and to
bless, not to *curse* and to *ban*." And if the person and the
place can improve and aggravate the offence, (as without
doubt it doth, both before God and man,) methinks the
preaching treason and rebellion out of the pulpits should be
worse than the advancing it in the market, as much as poi-
soning a man at the communion would be worse than mur-
dering him at a tavern. And it may be, in that catalogue
of sins, which the zeal of some men hath thought to be the
sin against the Holy Ghost, there may not any one be more
reasonably thought to be such, than a minister of Christ's
turning rebel against his prince, (which is a most notorious
apostasy against his order,) and his preaching rebellion to
the people, as the doctrine of Christ ; which, adding blasphemy and pertinacy to his apostasy, hath all the marks
by which good men are taught to avoid that sin against the
Holy Ghost.

Within three or four days after the king's remove from
Nottingham, the earl of Essex, with his whole army, removed
from Northampton, and marched towards Worcester; of
which his majesty had no sooner intelligence, than he sent
prince Rupert, with the greatest part of the horse, on the
other side of the Severn, towards that city; as well to observe the motion of the enemy, as to give all assistance to
that place, which had declared good affections to him ; at
least to countenance and secure the retreat of those gentlemen, who were there raising forces for the king; but especially to join with sir John Byron, whom his majesty had
sent, in the end of August, to Oxford, to convey some money,
which had been secretly brought from London thither to his
majesty. And he, after some small disasters in his march,
by the insurrection of the country people, who were encouraged by the agents for the parliament, and seconded by
the officers of the militia, came safe with his charge to Worcester; where he had been very few hours, when a strong
party of horse and dragoons, being sent by the earl of Essex,
under the command of Nathaniel Fiennes, son to the lord
Say, came to surprise the town; which was open enough to

have been entered in many places, though in some it had an old decayed wall ; and, at the most usual and frequented entrances into the city, weak and rotten gates to be shut, but without either lock or bolt.

Yet this doughty commander, coming early in the morning, when the small guard which had watched, conceiving all to be secure, were gone to rest, and being within musket shot of the gate before he was discovered, finding that weak door shut, or rather closed against him, and not that quick appearance of a party within the town, as he promised himself, without doing any harm, retired in great disorder, and with so much haste, that the wearied horse, sent out presently to attend him, could not overtake any of his train; so that when prince Rupert came thither, they did not conceive any considerable party of the enemy to be near. However his highness resolved to retire from thence, as soon as he should receive perfect intelligence of the motion of the enemy, or where certainly he was, when on the sudden being reposing himself on the ground with prince Maurice his brother, the lord Digby, and the principal officers, in the field before the town, some of his wearied troops (for they had had a long march) being by, but the rest and most of the officers being in the town, he espied a fair body of horse, consisting of near five hundred, marching in very good order up a lane within musket shot of him. In this confusion, they had scarce time to get upon their horses, and none to consult of what was to be done, or to put themselves into their several places of command. And, it may be, it was well they had not; for if all those officers had been in the heads of their several troops, it is not impossible it might have been worse. But the prince instantly declaring, " that he would charge;" his brother, the lord Digby, commissary general Wilmot, sir John Byron, sir Lewis Dives, and all those officers and gentlemen, whose troops were not present or ready, put themselves next the prince ; the other wearied troops coming in order after them.

And in this manner the prince charged them, as soon as they came out of the lane ; and being seconded by this handful of good men, though the rebels being gallantly led by colonel Sandys, (a gentleman of Kent, and the son of a worthy father,) and completely armed both for offence and defence, stood well ; yet in a short time, many of their best men being killed, and colonel Sandys himself falling with his hurts, the whole body was routed, fled, and was pursued by the conquerors for the space of above a mile. The number of the slain were not many, not above forty or fifty, and those most officers ; for their arms were so good, that in the charge they were not to be easily killed, and in the chase the goodness of their horse made it impossible. Colonel Sandys, who died shortly after of his wounds, captain Wingate, who was the more known, by being a member of the house of commons, though taken notice of for having in that charge behaved himself stoutly, and two or three Scotch officers, were taken prisoners. Of the king's party none of name was lost : commissary general Wilmot hurt with a sword in the side, and sir Lewis Dives in the shoulder, and two or three other officers of inferior note ; none miscarrying of their wounds, which was the more strange for that, by reason they expected not an encounter, there was not, on the prince's side, a piece of armour worn that day, and but few pistols ; so that most of the hurt that was done was by the sword. Six or seven cornets were taken, and many good horses, and some arms ; for they who run away made themselves as light as they could.

This rencounter proved of unspeakable advantage and benefit to the king. For it being the first action his horse had been brought to, and that party of the enemy being the most picked and choice men, it gave his troops great courage, and rendered the name of prince Rupert very terrible, and exceedingly appalled the adversary ; insomuch as they had not, in a long time after, any confidence in their horse, and their very numbers were much lessened by it. For that whole party being routed, and the chief officers of name and reputation either killed or taken, though the number lost upon the place was not considerable, there were very many more who never returned to the service ; and, which was worse, for their own excuse, in all places, talked aloud of the incredible and unresistible courage of prince Rupert, and the king's horse. So that, from this time, the parliament begun to be apprehensive, that the business would not be as easily ended, as it was begun ; and that the king would not be brought back to his parliament with their bare votes. Yet how faintly soever the private pulses beat, (for no question many, who had made greatest noise, wished they were again to choose their side,) there was so far from any visible abatement of their mettle, that to weigh down any possible supposition that they might be inclined, or drawn to treat with the king, or that they had any apprehension that the people would be less firm, and constant to them, they proceeded to bolder acts to evince both, than they had yet done.

For to the first, to shew how secure they were against resentment from his allies, as well as against his majesty's own power, they caused the Capuchin friars, who, by the articles of marriage, were to have a safe reception and entertainment in the queen's family, and had, by her majesty's care, and at her charge, a small, but a convenient habitation, by her own chapel, in her own house, in the Strand, and had continued there, without disturbance, from the time of the marriage, after many insolencies and indignities offered to them by the rude multitude, even within those gates of her own house, to be taken from thence, and to be sent over into France, with protestation, " that if they were found again in England, they should be proceeded against as traitors :" and this in the face of the French ambassador, who notwithstanding withdrew not from them his courtship and application.

Then, that the king might know how little they dreaded his forces, they sent down their instructions to the earl of Essex their general, who had long expected them; whereby, among other things of form for the better discipline of the army, " they required him to march, with such forces as he thought fit, towards the army raised, in his majesty's name, against the parliament and the kingdom ; and with them, or any part of them, to fight at such time and place as he should judge most to conduce to the peace and safety of the kingdom : and that he should use his utmost endeavour by battle, or otherwise, to rescue his majesty's person, and the persons of the prince, and duke of York, out of the hands of those desperate persons, who were then about them.   They directed him to take an opportunity, in some safe and honourable way, to cause the petition of both houses of parliament, then sent to him, to be presented to his majesty; and if his majesty should thereupon please to withdraw himself from the forces then about him, and to resort to the parliament, his lordship should cause his majesty's forces to disband, and should serve and defend his majesty with a sufficient strength in his return.   They required his lordship to publish and declare, that if any who had been so seduced, by the false aspersions cast upon the proceedings of the parliament, as to assist the king in acting of those dangerous counsels, should willingly, within ten days after such publication in the army, return to their duty, not doing any hostile act within the time limited, and join themselves with the parliament in defence of religion, his majesty's person, the liberties, and law of the kingdom, and privileges of parliament, with their persons, and estates, as the members of both houses, and the rest of the kingdom, have done, that the lords and commons would be ready, upon their submission, to receive such persons in such manner, as they should have cause to acknowledge they had been used with clemency and favour; provided that that favour should not extend to admit any man into either house of parliament, who stood suspended, without giving satisfaction to the house whereof he should be a member; and except all persons who stood impeached, or particularly voted in either house of parliament for any delinquency whatsoever; excepting likewise such adherents of those who stood impeached in parliament of treason, as had been eminent persons, and chief actors in those treasons."   And lest those clauses of exception (which no doubt comprehended all the king's party, and if not, they were still to be judges of their own clemency and favour, which was all was promised to the humblest penitent) might invite those, whom they had no mind to receive on any terms, they vouchsafed a " particular exception of the earl of Bristol, the earl of Cumberland, the earl of Newcastle, the earl of Rivers, the duke of Richmond, the earl of Carnarvon, the

lord Newark, and the lord viscount Falkland, principal secretary of state to his majesty, Mr. Secretary Nicholas, Mr. En-
dymion Porter, and Mr. Edward Hyde ;" against not one of
whom was there a charge depending of any crime, and against
very few of them so much as a vote, which was no great
matter of delinquency.

It will be here necessary to insert the petition, directed to
be presented in some safe and honourable way to his majesty ; the rather for that the same was, upon the reasons hereafter mentioned, never presented; which was afterwards objected to his majesty as a rejection of peace on his part, when
they desired it.   The petition was in these words.

" We[1] your majesty's loyal subjects, the lords and commons
in parliament, cannot, without great grief, and tenderness of
compassion, behold the pressing miseries, the imminent dangers, and the devouring calamities, which extremely threaten,
and have partly seized upon, both your kingdoms of England
and Ireland, by the practices of a party prevailing with your
majesty; who, by many wicked plots and conspiracies, have
attempted the alteration of the true religion, and the ancient
government of this kingdom, and the introducing of popish
idolatry and superstition in the church, and tyranny and confusion in the state ; and, for the compassing thereof, have
long corrupted your majesty's counsels, abused your power,
and, by sudden and untimely dissolving of former parliaments,
have often hindered the reformation and prevention of those
mischiefs ; and being now disabled to avoid the endeavours
of this parliament, by any such means, have traitorously attempted to overawe the same by force ; and, in prosecution
of their wicked designs, have excited, encouraged, and fos-
tered an unnatural rebellion in Ireland ;[1] by which, in a most
cruel and outrageous manner, many thousands of your majes-

---

[1] *This petition is in the handwriting of lord Clarendon's secretary.*

[1] To hide their factious views, which would not suffer them to acquiesce in the satisfaction the king had given them by his consent to several salutary laws, which were a secure barrier against the return of
his arbitrary measures, they were forced to have recourse to popery
and Irelandish massacres ; neither of which could he be justly charged with.—W.

ty's subjects there have been destroyed ; and, by false slanders upon your parliament, and malicious and unjust accusations, have endeavoured to begin the like massacre here ; and being, through God's blessing, therein disappointed, have, as the most mischievous and bloody design of all, drawn your majesty to make war against your parliament, and good subjects of this kingdom, leading in your person an army against them, as if you intended, by conquest, to establish an absolute and unlimited power over them ;[1] and by your power, and the countenance of your presence, you have ransacked, spoiled, imprisoned, and murdered divers of your people ; and, for their better assistance in their wicked designs, do seek to bring over the rebels of Ireland, and other forces, beyond the seas, to join with them.

" And we, finding ourselves utterly deprived of your majesty's protection, and the authors, counsellors, and abettors of these mischiefs in greatest power and favour with your majesty, and defended by you against the justice and authority of your high court of parliament; whereby they are grown to that height and insolence, as to manifest their rage and malice against those of the nobility, and others, who are any whit inclinable to peace, not without great appearance of danger to your own royal person, if you shall not in all things concur with their wicked and traitorous courses ;[2] have, for the just and necessary defence of the protestant religion, of your majesty's person, crown, and dignity, of the laws and liberties of the kingdom, and the privileges and power of parliament, taken up arms, and appointed and authorized Robert earl of Essex to be captain general of all the forces by us raised, and to lead and conduct the same against these rebels and

---

[1] Raising an army against the two houses was certainly with no other intent than to preserve himself. But had they performed that service, it is not unlikely but he would have required much more of them. —W.

[2] The truth was indeed just the reverse ; for these *abettors of mischief* were so jealous of their master, and so apprehensive of his restoration by force of arms, that they constantly traversed the efforts of the military when they thought there was any danger of ending the war by conquest. By which policy they ruined their master.—W.

traitors, and them to subdue, and bring to condign punishment ; and do most humbly beseech your majesty to withdraw your royal presence and countenance from those wicked persons ; and, if they shall stand out in defence of their
rebellious and unlawful attempts, that your majesty will leave
them to be suppressed by that power, which we have sent
against them ; and that your majesty will not mix your own
dangers with theirs, but in peace and safety, without your forces, forthwith return to your parliament ; and, by their faithful counsel and advice, compose the present distempers and
confusions abounding in both your kingdoms ; and provide
for the security and honour of yourself and your royal posterity, and the prosperous estate of all your subjects ; wherein
if your majesty please to yield to our most humble and earnest desires, we do, in the presence of Almighty God, profess, that we will receive your majesty with all honour, yield
you all due obedience and subjection, and faithfully endeavour to secure your person and estate from all dangers ; and,
to the uttermost of our power, to procure and establish to
yourself, and to your people, all the blessings of a glorious
and happy reign."

Then, that it might appear they were nothing jealous or
apprehensive of the people's defection and revolt from them,
whereas before they had made the general desire of the kingdom the ground and argument for whatsoever they had done,
and had only invited men to contribute freely what they
thought fit to the charge in hand, without compelling any who
were unwilling ; they now took notice not only of those who
opposed their proceedings, or privately dissuaded other men
from concurring with them, but of those, who either out of
fear, or covetousness, or both, had neglected really to contribute ; and therefore they boldly published their votes,
(which were laws to the people, or of much more authority,)
" That all such persons, as should not contribute to the charge
of the commonwealth, in that time of eminent necessity,
should be disarmed and secured ;" and that this vote might
be the more terrible, they ordered, the same day, the mayor
and sheriffs of London, " to search the houses,' and seize the

---

¹ Things were now brought to that pass, that the *cause of liberty* was

arms belonging to some aldermen, and other principal substantial citizens of London," whom they named in their order; " for that it appeared by the report from their committee, that they had not contributed, as they ought, to the charge of the commonwealth."

And by this means the poorest and lowest of the people became informers against the richest and most substantial ; and the result of searching the houses and seizing the arms was, the taking away plate, and things of the greatest value, and very frequently plundering whatsoever was worth the keeping. They farther appointed, " that the fines, rents, and profits of archbishops, bishops, deans, deans and chapters, and of all delinquents, who had taken up arms against the parliament, or had been active in the commission of array, should be sequestered for the use and benefit of the commonwealth." And that the king might not fare better than his adherents, they directed " all his revenue, arising out of rents, fines in courts of justice, composition for wards, and the like, and all other his revenue, should be brought into the several courts, and other places, where they ought to be paid in, and not issued forth, or paid forth, until farther order should be taken by both houses of parliament ;" without so much as assigning him any part of his own, towards the support of his own person.

This stout invasion of the people's property, and compelling them to part with what was most precious to them, any part of their estates, was thought by many an unpolitic act, in the morning of their sovereignty, and that it would wonderfully have irreconciled their new subjects to them. But the conductors well understood, that their empire already depended more on the fear, than love of the people ; and that as they could carry on the war only by having money enough to pay the soldiers, so, that whilst they had that, probably they should not want men to recruit their armies upon any misadventure.

defended by injustice, and the *cause of prerogative* by law. In other words, they had changed hands, the parliament was become arbitrary and despotic, and the king was forced to struggle for liberty.—W.

It cannot be imagined, how great advantage the king received by the parliament's rejecting the king's messages for peace, and their manner in doing it. All men's mouths were opened against them, the messages and answers being read in all churches. When Mr. Hyde came from London towards York, to attend the king, he made Oxford his way ; and there conferring with his friend Dr. Sheldon, then warden of All Souls, of the ill condition the king was in, by his extreme want of money, with which there could be no way to supply him, the parliament being possessed of all his revenues, the doctor told him, and wished him to inform the king of it, that all the colleges in Oxford, and he did believe the like of Cambridge, were very plentifully supplied with plate, which would amount to a good value, and lay useless in their treasury ; there being enough besides for their use ; and he had given the king information of this, as soon as he came to York ; and when he was at Nottingham, in that melancholic season, he put him in mind again of it, and then two gentlemen were despatched away to Oxford, and to Cambridge, (two to each,) with letters to the several vice-chancellors, that he should move the heads and principals of the several colleges and halls, that they would send their plate to the king; private advertisements being first sent to some confidant persons to prepare and dispose those, without whose consent the service could not be performed.

This whole affair was transacted with so great secrecy and discretion, that the messengers returned from the two universities, in as short a time as such a journey could well be made ; and brought with them all, or very near all, their plate, and a considerable sum of money, which was sent as a present to his majesty from several of the heads of colleges, out of their own particular stores ; some scholars coming with it, and helping to procure horses and carts for the service ; all which came safe to Nottingham, at the time when there appeared no more expectation of a treaty, and contributed much to raising the dejected spirits of the place. The plate was presently weighed out, and delivered to the several officers, who were intrusted to make levies of horse and foot, and who received it as money ; the rest was carefully preserved to be carried with the king, when he should remove from thence ; secret orders being sent to the officers of the mint, to be ready to come to his majesty as soon as he should require them; which he meant to do, as soon as he should find himself in a place convenient.   There was now no more complaining or murmuring.   Some gentlemen undertook to make levies upon their own credit and interest, and others sent money to the king upon their own inclinations.

There was a pleasant story, then much spoken of in the court, which administered some mirth.   There were two great men who lived near Nottingham, Pierrepoint earl of Kingston, and Leake lord Dencourt, both men of great fortunes and of great parsimony, and known to have much money lying by them.   To the former the lord Capel was sent ; to the latter, John Ashburnham of the bedchamber, and of entire confidence with his master ; each of them with a letter, all written with the king's hand, to borrow of each ten or five thousand pounds.   Capel was very civilly received by the earl, and entertained as well as the ill accommodations in his house, and his manner of living, would admit.   He expressed, with wonderful civil expressions of duty, "the great trouble he sustained, in not being able to comply with his majesty's commands :" he said, "all men knew that he neither had, nor could have money, because he had every year, of ten or a dozen which were past, purchased a thousand pounds land a year; and therefore he could not be imagined to have any money lying by him, which he never loved to have.   But, he said, he had a neighbour, who lived within few miles of him, the lord Dencourt, who was good for nothing, and lived like a hog, not allowing himself necessaries, and who could not have so little as twenty thousand pounds in the scurvy house in which he lived ;" and advised, " that he might be sent to, who could not deny the having of money ;" and concluded with great duty to the king, and detestation of the parliament, and as if he meant to consider farther of the king, and to endeavour to get some money for him; which though he did not remember to send, his affections were good, and he was afterwards killed in the king's service.

Ashburnham got no more money, nor half so many good words. The lord Dencourt had so little correspondence with the court, that he had never heard his name; and when he had read the king's letter, he asked from whom it was; and when he told him, "that he saw it was from the king," he replied, "that he was not such a fool as to believe it. That he had received letters both from this king and his father;" and hastily ran out of the room, and returned with half a dozen letters in his hand; saying, "that those were all the king's letters, and that they always begun with *Right trusty and well-beloved*, and the king's name was ever at the top; but this letter began with Dencourt, and ended with *your loving friend C. R.* which, he said, he was sure could not be the king's hand." His other treatment was according to this, and, after an ill supper, he was shewed an indifferent bed; the lord telling him, "that he would confer more of the matter in the morning;" he having sent a servant with a letter to the lord Falkland, who was his wife's nephew, and who had scarce ever seen his uncle. The man came to Nottingham about midnight, and found my lord Falkland in his bed. The letter was to tell him, "that one Ashburnham was with him, who brought him a letter, which he said was from the king; but he knew that could not be; and therefore he desired to know, who this man was, whom he kept in his house till the messenger should return." In spite of the laughter, which could not be forborne, the lord Falkland made haste to inform him of the condition and quality of the person, and that the letter was writ with the king's own hand, which he seldom vouchsafed to do. And the messenger returning early the next morning, his lordship treated Mr. Ashburnham with so different a respect, that he, who knew nothing of the cause, believed that he should return with all the money that was desired. But it was not long before he was undeceived. The lord, with as cheerful a countenance as his could be, for he had a very unusual and unpleasant face, told him, "that though he had no money himself, but was in extreme want of it, he would tell him where he might have money enough; that he had a neighbour, who lived within four or five miles, the earl of Kingston, that never did good

to any body, and loved nobody but himself, who had a world
of money, and could furnish the king with as much as he had
need of; and if he should deny that he had money when the
king sent to him, he knew where he had one trunk full, and
would discover it; and that he was so ill beloved, and had
so few friends, that nobody would care how the king used
him." And this good counsel was all Mr. Ashburnham
could make of him : and yet this wretched man was so far
from wishing well to the parliament, that when they had
prevailed, and were possessed of the whole kingdom, as well
as of Nottinghamshire, he would not give them one penny;
nor compound for his delinquency, as they made the having
lived in the king's quarters to be; but suffered his whole estate to be sequestered, and lived in a very miserable fashion,
only by what he could ravish from his tenants; who, though
they paid their rents to the parliament, were forced by his
rage and threats to part with so much as kept him, till he
died, in that condition he chose to live in : his conscience
being powerful enough to deny himself, though it could not
dispose him to grant to the king. And thus the two messengers returned to the king, so near the same time, that he
who came first had not given his account to the king, before
the other entered into his presence.

And the same day, Mr. Sacheverel, who was a gentleman,
and known to be very rich, being pressed to lend the king
five hundred pounds, sent him a present of one hundred
pieces in gold ; " which," he said, " he had procured with
great difficulty ;" and protested, with many execrable im-
precations, " that he had never in his life seen five hundred
pounds of his own together ;" when, within one month after
the king's departure, the parliament troops, which borrowed
in another style, took five thousand pounds from him, which
was lodged with him, in the chamber in which he lay.
Which is therefore mentioned in this place, that upon this
occasion it may be seen, that the unthrifty retention of their
money, which possessed the spirits of those, who did really
wish the king all the success he wished for himself, was the
unhappy promotion of all his misfortunes : and if they had,
in the beginning, but lent the king the fifth part of what,

after infinite losses, they found necessary to sacrifice to his
enemies, in the conclusion, to preserve themselves from total
ruin, his majesty had been able, with God's blessing, to have
preserved them, and to have destroyed all his enemies.
The king was weary of Nottingham, where he had received
so many mortifications; and was very glad in so short a time
to find himself in a posture fit to remove from thence. The
general, earl of Lindsay, had brought to him a good regiment of foot out of Lincolnshire, of near one thousand men,
very well officered; and the lord Willoughby, his son, who
had been a captain in Holland, and to whom his majesty had
given the command of his guards, had brought up likewise
from Lincolnshire another excellent regiment, near the same
number, under officers of good experience. John Bellasis,
a younger son of the lord Falconbridge, and sir William Pen-
niman, were come up from Yorkshire to the standard, with
each of them a good regiment of foot, of about six hundred
men, and each of them a troop of horse. Though his train
of artillery was but mean, and his provision of ammunition
much meaner, yet it was all he could depend [upon,] and
therefore it was to be well spent, and as soon as might be,
all the impatience being now to fight. The lord Paget, who
left the parliament shortly after the king came to York, to
expiate former transgressions, had undertaken to raise a
good regiment of foot in Staffordshire, where his best interest was; and some other persons of condition had made
the same engagements for Wales. The lord Strange (for his
father the earl of Derby was then living) was thought to
have much more power in Cheshire and Lancashire than in
truth he had; and some of the best men of those counties
had commissions to raise both horse and foot in those counties; so that though the king was not resolved where to make
a stand, yet it appeared necessary to make his march towards
those parts. For all the reasons mentioned, Shrewsbury
was by all men thought to be the best post, because of the
communication it had with all the other counties; but they
could not be sure of admittance there. Some principal gentlemen of that county, and members of the house of commons, were then there to persuade the country to submit to

the ordinance of parliament; yet Mr. Hyde had kept an intelligence with the mayor of the town by a churchman who was a canon of a collegiate church there, and a dexterous and discreet person, who had been at Nottingham with him, and given him a full account of the humour and disposition of that people; and he had by his majesty's order sent him again thither, with such instructions and letters as were necessary for the negotiation. The first day's march was from Nottingham to Derby, in the middle way to which the army was drawn up, horse and foot, and was the first time his majesty had a view of them; and that day the lord Paget's regiment of foot increased the number; and the whole made so good an appearance, that all men were even wishing for the earl of Essex, and all fears were vanished. From Derby the king marched to Stafford, and gave order that no prejudice should be done to the earl of Essex his house or park at Chartley, which was in view of the way, and would otherwise have been pulled down and destroyed. Here Mr. Hyde received a letter from the canon of Shrewsbury, that the committee of parliament had left the town, and he believed there would not be the least pause in receiving the king. However the king would not declare which way he would march, till he had more assurance, and so sent Mr. Hyde to Shrewsbury, to give him speedy notice before he declined the way to Chester; and receiving from him the next day an account, that the town was well resolved and that the mayor, though an old humorous fellow, had prepared all things for his reception, the king came with the whole army to Shrewsbury before the end of September; prince Rupert, within few days after, marched on the Welsh side of Severn to Worcester, to countenance some levies of foot which were there preparing.

The news of the important victory before Worcester found the king at Chester, whither his majesty thought necessary to make a journey himself, as soon as he came to Shrewsbury, both to assure that city to his service, which was the key to Ireland, and to countenance the lord Strange (who, by the death of his father, became within few days earl of Derby) against some opposition he met with, on the behalf of the

parliament. Here Crane, sent by prince Rupert, gave his
majesty an account of that action ; and presented him with
the ensigns, which had been taken : and informed him of the
earl of Essex's being in Worcester; which made the king to
return sooner to Shrewsbury than he intended, and before
the earl of Derby was possessed of that power, which a little
longer stay would have given him.

Prince Rupert the same night, after his victory, finding
the gross of the rebels' army to be within five or six miles,
against which that city was in no degree tenable, though all
the king's foot had been there, retired from Worcester on the
Welsh side of the river, without any disturbance, and with
all his prisoners, (colonel Sandys only excepted, whom he
charitably left to die of his wounds there,) into his quarters
near Shrewsbury ; the earl of Essex being so much startled with his late defeat, that he advanced not in two days after ; and then being surely informed, that he should find no
resistance, he entered with his army into Worcester ; using
great severity to those citizens, who had been eminently inclined to the king's service, and sending the principal of them
prisoners to London.

Upon the king's coming to Shrewsbury, there was a very
great conflux of the gentry of that and the neighbours, which
were generally well affected, and made great professions of
duty to his majesty : some of them undertook to make levies
of horse and foot, and performed it at their own charge. The
town was very commodious in all respects, strong in its situation; and in respect of its neighbourhood to North Wales,
and the use of the Severn, yielded excellent provisions of all
kinds; so that both court and army were very well accom-
modated, only the incurable disease of want of money could
not be assuaged in either. Yet whilst they sat still, it was
not very sensible, much less importunate. The soldiers behaved themselves orderly, and the people were not inclined
or provoked to complain of their new guests ; and the remainder of the plate, which was brought from the universities, together with the small presents in money, which were made to
the king by many particular persons, supplied the present necessary expenses very conveniently. But it was easily discerned, that, when the army should move, which the king re-

solved it should do with all possible expedition, the necessity of money would be very great, and the train of artillery, which is commonly a spunge that can never be filled or satisfied, was destitute of all things which were necessary for motion. Nor was there any hope that it could march, till a good sum of money were assigned to it ; some carriage-horses, and waggons, which were prepared for the service of Ireland, and lay ready at Chester, to be transported with the earl of Leicester, lieutenant of that kingdom, were brought to Shrewsbury, by his majesty's order, for his own train : and the earl's passionate labouring to prevent or remedy that application, with some other reasons, hindered the earl himself from pursuing that journey ; and, in the end, deprived him of that province. But this seasonable addition to the train increased the necessity of money, there being more use of it thereby.

Two expedients were found to make such a competent provision for all wants, that they were at last broken through. Some person of that inclination had insinuated to the king, that, " if the catholics, which that and the adjacent counties were well inhabited by, were secretly treated with, a considerable sum of money might be raised among them ; but it must be carried with great privacy, that no notice might be taken of it, the parliament having declared so great animosity against them ;" nor did it in that conjuncture concern the king less that it should be very secret, to avoid the scandal of a close conjunction with the papists, which was every day imputed to him. Upon many consultations how, and in what method, to carry on this design, the king was informed, " that if he would depute Mr. Hyde, to that service, the Roman catholics would trust him, and assign one or two of their body to confer with him, and by this means the work might be carried on." Hereupon the king sent one morning for Mr. Hyde, and told him this whole matter, as it is here set down, and required him to consult with such a person, whom he would send to him the next morning. He was surprised with the information, that that classis of men had made choice of him for their trust, for which he could imagine no reason, but that he had been often of counsel with some persons of quality of that profession, who yet knew very well, that he was in no degree inclined to their persuasion ; he submitted to the king's pleasure, and the next morning a person of quality, and very much trusted by all that party, came to him to confer upon that subject ; and shewed a list of the names of all the gentlemen of quality and fortune of that religion, and who were all convict recusants, who lived within those counties of Shropshire and Stafford. Who appeared to be a good number of very valuable men, on whose behalf he had only authority to conclude, though he believed that the method, they agreed on there, would be submitted to, and confirmed by that people in all other places. He said, " they would by no means hearken to any motion for the loan of money, for which they had paid so dear, upon their serving the king in that manner, in his first expedition against the Scots." It was in the end agreed upon, that the king should write to every one of them to pay him an advance of two or three years of such rent, as they were every year obliged to pay to him, upon the composition they had made with him for their estates ; which would amount to a considerable sum of money. Which letters were accordingly writ, and within ten or twelve days between four and five thousand pounds were returned to his majesty ; which was a seasonable supply for his affairs.[1]

At his return to Shrewsbury, the king found as much done towards his march, as he expected. And then the other expedient (which was hinted before) for money offered itself. There was a gentleman of a very good extraction, and of the best estate of any gentleman of that country, one sir Richard Newport, who lived within four or five miles of Shrewsbury, who was looked upon as a very prudent man, and had a very powerful influence upon that people, and was of undoubted affections and loyalty to the king, and to the government both in church and state : his eldest son Francis

---

[1] *In MS. B. from which this part of the History is taken, here follows an account of the rencounter before Worcester, (a description of which is given in page 1091 from MS. C.) which will be found in the Appendix, B.*

Newport was a young gentleman of great expectation, and
of excellent parts, a member of the house of commons, had
behaved himself very well there, and was then newly married to the daughter of the late earl of Bedford.   This young
gentleman was well acquainted with Mr. Hyde, and formerly spoke to him as if he wished his father might be made a
baron ; for which, he did believe, he might be prevailed with
to present his majesty with a good sum of money. Mr. Hyde
had spoken to the king of it, but had no mind to embrace
the proposition, his majesty taking occasion often to speak
against " making merchandise of honour ; how much the
crown suffered at present by the licence of that kind, which
had been used during the favour of the duke of Buckingham ; and that he had not taken a firmer resolution against
many things, than against this particular expedient for the
raising money."   However, after he returned from Chester,
and found by the increase of his levies, and the good disposition all things were in, that he might in a short time be
able to march, and in so good a condition, that he should
rather seek the rebels, than decline meeting with them, if
the indispensable want of money did not make his motion
impossible ; the merit and ability of the person, and the fair
expectation from his posterity, he having two sons, both very hopeful, prevailed with his majesty to resume the same
overture ; and in few days it was perfected, and sir Ri.
Newport was made baron Newport of Ercall, and all preparations for the army were prosecuted with effect.[1]

   As soon as the king came to Shrewsbury, he had despatched his letters and agents into Wales, Cheshire, and Lancashire, to quicken the levies of men which were making
there.   And finding that the parliament had been very solicitous and active in those counties of Cheshire and Lancashire,
and that many of the gentry of those populous shires were
deeply engaged in their service, and the loyal party so much
depressed, that the house of commons had sent up an impeachment of high treason against the lord Strange, who be-

   [1] *The continuation of the History, according to MS. B. will be found
in the Appendix, C.*

ing son and heir apparent of the earl of Derby, and possessed of all his father's fortune in present, was then looked upon as of absolute power over that people, and accused him, that he had, with an intent and purpose to subvert the fundamental laws and government of the kingdom of England, and the rights and liberties, and the very being of parliaments, and to set sedition between the king and his people at Manchester of Lancaster, and at several other places, actually, maliciously, rebelliously, and traitorously summoned and called together great numbers of his majesty's subjects; and invited, persuaded, and encouraged them to take up arms, and levy war against the king, parliament, and kingdom. That he had, in a hostile manner, invaded the kingdom, and killed, hurt, and wounded divers of his majesty's subjects; had set sedition betwixt the king and the people, and then was in open and actual rebellion against the king, parliament, and kingdom. And upon this impeachment a formal order passed both houses, (which was industriously published, and read in many churches of those counties,) declaring his treason, and requiring all persons to apprehend him; whereby not only the common people, who had obeyed his warrants, but his lordship himself, (who had only executed the commission of array, and the seditious party at the same time executing the ordinance of militia, some blows had passed, whereof one or two had died,) were more than ordinarily dismayed. His majesty himself leaving his household and army at Shrewsbury, went in person with his troop of guards only to Chester, presuming that his presence would have the same influence there, it had had in all other places, to compose the fears and apprehensions of all honest men, and to drive away the rest; which fell out accordingly: for being received and entertained with all demonstrations of duty by the city of Chester, those who had been most notably instrumental to the parliament, withdrew themselves, and the nobility and gentry, and indeed the common people, flocked to him; the former in very good equipage, and the latter with great expressions of devotion: yet in Cheshire Nantwich, and Manchester in Lancashire, made some shows by fortifying, and seditious discourses of resistance and disaffection, and into those two places the seditious persons had retired themselves. · To the first, the lord Grandison was sent with a regiment of horse and some .few dragooners, with the which, and his dexterous taking advantage of the people's first apprehensions, before they could take advice what to do, he so awed that town, that after one unskilful volley, they threw down their arms, and he entered the town, took the submission and oaths of the inhabitants for their future obedience; and having caused the small works to be slighted, and all the arms and ammunition to be sent to Shrewsbury, he returned to his majesty. For Manchester, the lord Strange, who had by his majesty's favour and encouragement recovered his spirits, undertook, without troubling his majesty farther northward, in a very short time to reduce that place, (which was not so fortunately performed, because not so resolutely pursued,) and to send a good body of foot to the king to Shrewsbury. So that his majesty, within a week, leaving all parts behind him full of good inclinations or professions, returned through the northern parts of Wales, (where he found the people cordial to him, and arming themselves for him) to Shrewsbury. The king's custom was in all counties, through which he passed, to cause the high sheriff to draw all the gentlemen and the most substantial inhabitants of those parts together, to whom, (besides his caressing the principal gentlemen severally, familiarly, and very obligingly) he always spake something publicly, (which was afterwards printed,) telling them,

"That it was a benefit to him from the insolencies and misfortunes, which had driven him about, that they had brought him to so good a part of his kingdom, and to so faithful a part of his people. He hoped, neither they nor he should repent their coming together. He would do his part, that they might not; and of them he was confident before he came." He told them, "the residence of an army was not usually pleasant to any place; and his might carry more fear with it, since it might be thought, (being robbed, and spoiled of all his own, and such terror used to fright and keep all men from supplying him,) he must only live upon the aid and relief of his people." But he bid them "not be afraid;" and said,

" he wished to God, his poor subjects suffered no more by the insolence and violence of that army raised against him, though they had made themselves wanton with plenty, than they should do by his ; and yet he feared he should not be able to prevent all disorders ; he would do his best ; and promised them, no man should be a loser by him, if he could help it." He said, " he had sent for a mint, and would melt down all his own plate, and expose all his land to sale, or mortgage, that if it were possible he might bring the least pressure upon them." However, he invited them " to do that for him, and themselves, for the maintenance of their religion, and the law of the land, (by which they enjoyed all that they had,) which other men did against them ;" he desired them, " not to suffer so good a cause to be lost, for want of supplying him with that, which would be taken from them, by those who pursued his majesty with that violence. And whilst those ill men sacrificed their money, plate, and utmost industry, to destroy the commonwealth, they would be no less liberal to preserve it. He bad them assure themselves, if it pleased God to bless him with success, he would remember the assistance every particular man gave him to his advantage. However it would hereafter (how furiously soever the minds of men were now possessed) be honour and comfort to them, that, with some charge and trouble to themselves, they had done their part to support their king, and preserve the kingdom."

His majesty always took notice of any particular reports, which, either with reference to the public, or their private concerns, might make impression upon that people, and gave clear answers to them. So that with this gracious and princely demeanour, it is hardly credible how much he wan upon the people ; so that not only his army daily increased by volunteers, (for there was not a man pressed,) but such proportions of plate and money were voluntarily brought in, that the army was fully and constantly paid : the king having erected a mint at Shrewsbury, more for reputation than use, (for, for want of workmen and instruments, they could not coin a thousand pounds a week,) and causing all his own plate, for the service of his household, to be delivered there,

made other men think, theirs was the less worth the preserving.

Shortly after the earl of Essex came to Worcester, he sent
a gentleman (one Fleetwood, the same who had afterwards
so great power in the army, though then a trooper in his
guards) to Shrewsbury, without a trumpet, or any other ceremony than a letter to the earl of Dorset; in which he said,
" he was appointed by the parliament, to cause a petition,
then in his hands, to be presented to his majesty; and therefore desired his lordship to know his majesty's pleasure, when
he would be pleased to receive it from such persons, as he
should send over with it." The earl of Dorset, (by his majesty's command, after it had been debated in council what
answer to return) sent him word in writing, " that the king
had always been, and would be still, ready to receive any petition from his two houses of parliament; and if his lordship
had any such to be presented, if he sent it by any persons,
who stood not personally accused by him of high treason, and
excepted specially in all offers of pardon made by him, the
person who brought it should be welcome; and the king
would return such an answer to it, as should be agreeable to
honour and justice." Whether this limitation as to messengers displeased them, (as it was afterwards said, that the
messengers appointed to have delivered it were the lord Mandeville and Mr. Hambden, who, they thought, would have
skill to make infusions into many persons then about his majesty; and their access being barred by that limitation and
exception, they would not send any other,) or what other reason soever there was, the king heard no more of this petition,
or any address of that nature, till he found, by some new
printed votes and declarations, " that he was guilty of another breach of the privilege of parliament, for having refused to
receive their petition, except it were presented in such
manner as he prescribed : whereas they alone were judges
in what manner, and by what persons, their own petitions
should be delivered, and he ought so to receive them." And
so that petition, which is before set down in the very terms
it passed both houses, was never delivered to his majesty.

There cannot be too often mention of the wonderful providence of God, that from that low despised condition the king was in at Nottingham, after the setting up his standard, he should be able to get men, money, or arms, and yet, within twenty days after his coming to Shrewsbury, he resolved to march, in despite of the enemy, even towards London ; his foot, by this time, consisting of about six thousand ; and his horse of two thousand ; his train in very good order, commanded by sir John Heydon.   And though this strength was much inferior to the enemy, yet as it was greater than any man thought possible to be raised, so all thought it sufficient to encounter the rebels.   Besides that it was confidently believed, (and not without some grounds, of correspondence with some officers in the other army,) that, as soon as the armies came within any reasonable distance of each other, that very many soldiers would leave their colours, and come to the king ; which expectation was confirmed by some soldiers, who every day dropped in from those forces ; and, to make themselves welcome, told many stories of their fellows' resolutions, whom they had left behind.

And this must be confessed, that either by the care and diligence of the officers, or by the good inclinations and temper of the soldiers themselves, the army was in so good order and discipline, that, during the king's stay at Shrewsbury, there was not a disorder of name ; the country being very kind to the soldiers, and the soldiers just, and regardful to the country.   And by the free loans and contributions of the gentlemen and substantial inhabitants, but especially by the assistance of the nobility, who attended, the army was so well paid, that there was not the least mutiny or discontent for want of pay ; nor was there any cause ; for they seldom failed every week, never went above a fortnight unpaid,

The greatest difficulty was to provide arms ; of which indeed there was a wonderful scarcity, the king being exceedingly disappointed in his expectation of arms from Holland ; a vessel or two having been taken by his own ships, under the command of the earl of Warwick; so that, except eight hundred muskets, five hundred pair of pistols, and two hundred swords, which came with the powder, which was landed in Yorkshire, as is before mentioned, the king had none in

his magazine; so that he was compelled to begin at Nottingham, and so in all places as he passed, to borrow the arms
from the trained bands; which was done with so much wariness and caution, (albeit it was known that those arms would,
being left in those hands, be employed against him, or at least
be of no use to him,) that it was done rather with their consent, than by any constraint, and always with the full approbation of their commanders.   And therefore in Yorkshire
and Shropshire, where the gentlemen very unskilfully, though
with good meaning, desired that the arms might still be left
in the country men's hands, there was none of that kind of
borrowing.   But, in all places, the noblemen, and gentlemen
of quality, sent the king such supplies of arms, out of their
own armories, (which were very mean,) so that by all these
means together, the foot, all but three or four hundred, who
marched without any weapon but a cudgel, were armed with
muskets, and bags for their powder, and pikes; but, in the
whole body, there was not one pikeman had a corslet, and
very few musketeers who had swords.   Among the horse,
the officers had their full desire, if they were able to procure
old backs, and breasts, and pots with pistols, or carabines,
for their two or three first ranks, and swords for the rest;
themselves (and some soldiers by their examples) having gotten, besides their pistols and swords, a short pole-axe.

The foot were divided into three brigades; the first commanded by sir Nicholas Byron, the second by colonel Harry
Wentworth, and the third by colonel Richard Fielding, sir
Jacob Ashley being major general, and commanding the foot
immediately under the general.   For, though general Ruthen,
who came to the king some few days before he left Shrewsbury, was made field marshal, yet he kept wholly with the
horse to assist prince Rupert: and sir Arthur Aston, of whose
soldiery there was then a very great esteem, was made colonel general of the dragoons; which at that time, though consisting of two or three regiments, were not above eight hundred, or a thousand at the most.   Most of the persons of
honour and quality, except those whose attendance was near
the king's own person, put themselves into the king's troop
of guards, commanded by the lord Bernard Stewart; and

made indeed so gallant a body, that, upon a very modest computation, the estate and revenue of that single troop, might justly be valued at least equal to all theirs, who then voted in both houses, under the name of the lords and commons of parliament, and so made and maintained that war. Their servants, under the command of sir William Killigrew, made another full troop, and always marched with their lords and masters.

In this equipage the king marched from Shrewsbury, on the twelfth of October, to Bridgenorth, never less baggage attending a royal army, there being not one tent, and very few waggons belonging to the whole train; having in his whole army not one officer of the field who was a papist, except sir Arthur Aston, if he were one; and very few common soldiers of that religion. However the parliament, in all their declarations, and their clergy much more in their sermons, assured the people, " that the king's army consisted only of papists," whilst themselves entertained all of that religion, that they could get; and very many, both officers and soldiers, of that religion engaged with them; whether it was that they really believed, that that army did desire liberty of conscience for all religions, as some of the chief of them pretended, or that they desired to divide themselves for communication of intelligence, and interest. And here it is not fit to forget one particular, that, when the committee of parliament appointed to advance the service upon the proposition for plate, and horses, in the county of Suffolk, sent word to the house of commons, " that some papists offered to lend money upon those propositions, and desired advice whether they should accept of it," it was answered, " that if they offered any considerable sum, whereby it might be conceived to proceed from a real affection to the parliament, and not out of policy to bring themselves within their protection, and so to excuse their delinquency, it should be accepted of."

When the king was ready for his march, there was some difference of opinion which way he should take; many were of opinion that he should march towards Worcester, where the earl of Essex still remained; those countries were thought well-affected to the king; where his army would be supplied with provisions, and increased in numbers; and that no time should be lost in coming to a battle ; because the longer it was deferred, the stronger the earl would grow, by the supplies which were every day sent to him from London ; and he had store of arms with him to supply all defects of that kind.   However it was thought more counsellable to march directly towards London, it being morally sure, that the earl of Essex would put himself in their way.   The king had much confidence in his horse, (his nephew prince Rupert being in the head of them,) which were fleshed by their success at Worcester ; and if he had made his march that way, he would have been entangled in the inclosures, where his horse would have been less useful ; whereas there were many great campanias near the other way, much fitter for an engagement. And so, about the middle of October, the king marched from Shrewsbury, and quartered that night at Bridgenorth, ten miles from the other place, where there was a rendezvous of the whole army, which appeared very cheerful ; and so to Wolverhampton, Bromicham, and Killingworth, a house of the king's, and a very noble seat, where the king rested one day ; where the lord chief justice Heath, who was made chief justice for that purpose, (Bramston, a man of great learning and integrity, being, without any purpose of disfavour, removed from that office, because he stood bound by recognizance to attend the parliament, upon an accusation depending there against him,) began to sit upon a commission of oyer and terminer, to attaint the earl of Essex, and many other persons who were in rebellion, of high treason.

Some days had passed without any notice of that army ; some reporting that it remained still at Worcester ; others, that they were marched the direct way from thence towards London.   But intelligence came from London, " that very many officers of name, and command in the parliament army, undergone that service with a full resolution to come to the king as soon as they were within any distance ; and it was wished, that the king would send a proclamation into the army itself, and to offer pardon to all who would return to their obedience."   And a proclamation was prepared accordingly, and all circumstances resolved upon, that a herald should be sent to proclaim it in the head of the earl's army, when it should be drawn up in battle. But that, and many other particulars, prepared and resolved upon, were forgotten, or omitted at the time appointed, which would not admit any of those formalities.

When the whole army marched together, there was quickly discovered an unhappy jealousy, and division between the principal officers, which grew quickly into a perfect faction between the foot and the horse. The earl of Lindsey was general of the whole army by his commission, and thought very equal to it. But when prince Rupert came to the king, which was after the standard was set up, and received a commission to be general of the horse, which, all men knew, was designed to him, there was a clause inserted into it, which exempted him from receiving orders from any body but from the king himself;[1] which, upon the matter, separated all the horse from any dependence upon the general, and had other ill consequences in it: for when the king at midnight, being in his bed, and receiving intelligence of the enemy's motion, commanded the lord Falkland, his principal secretary of state, to direct prince Rupert, what he should do, he took it very ill, and expostulated with the lord Falkland, for giving him orders. But he could not have directed his passion against any man, who would feel or regard it less. And he told him, "that it was his office to signify what the king bad him ; which he should always do ; and that he, in neglecting it, neglected the king ;" who did neither the prince nor his own service any good, by complying in the beginning with his

[1] The king gave here just such a specimen of his conduct in war, as he had long given in peace. His exempting this young boy from the command of the general, an old experienced soldier, encouraged that undisciplined vigour in the prince's military exploits, which ruined all the advantages of his uncle's arms. The first and early effects were the misfortunes attending the action of Edge-hill. Had the general not been disgusted by this exemption from his authority, he had acted in his post as general, and consequently not have left the king's foot naked, to be cut to pieces by the enemy's horse. But that disgust made him retire to the post of a private colonel, and charge at the head of his own regiment of foot, where he fell.—W.

rough nature, which rendered him very ungracious to all men. But the king was so indulgent to him, that he took his advice in all things relating to the army, and so upon consideration of their march, and the figure of the battle they resolved to fight in with the enemy, he concurred entirely with prince Rupert's advice, and rejected the opinion of the general, who preferred the order he had learned under prince Maurice, and prince Harry, with whom he had served at the same time, when the earl of Essex and he, had both regiments. The uneasiness of the prince's nature, and the little education he had in courts, made him unapt to make acquaintance with any of the lords, who were likewise thereby discouraged from applying themselves to him; whilst some officers of the horse were well pleased to observe that strangeness, and fomented it; believing their credit would be the greater with the prince, and desired that no other person should have any credit with the king.   So the war was scarce begun, when there appeared such faction and designs in the army, which wise men looked upon as a very evil presage; and the inconveniences, which flowed from thence, gave the king great trouble in a short time after.[1]

Within two days after the king marched from Shrewsbury, the earl of Essex moved from Worcester to attend him, with an army far superior in number to the king's; the horse and foot being completely armed, and the men very well exercised, and the whole equipage (being supplied out of the king's magazines) suitable to an army set forth at the charge of a kingdom.   The earl of Bedford had the name of general of the horse, though that command principally depended upon sir William Balfour.   Of the nobility he had with him the lords Kimbolton, Saint-John's, Wharton, Roberts, Rochford, and Fielding, (whose fathers, the earls of Dover, and Denbigh, charged as volunteers in the king's guards of horse,) and many gentlemen of quality; but his train was so very great, that he could move but in slow marches.   So that the two armies, though they were but

---

[1] The account of the battle of Edge-hill, as given in MS. B. will be found in the Appendix, D.

twenty miles asunder, when they first set forth, and both marched the same way, they gave not the least disquiet in ten days' march to each other ; and in truth, as it appeared afterwards, neither army knew where the other was.

The king by quick marches, having seldom rested a day in any place, came, on Saturday the twenty-second of October, to Edgcot, a village in Northamptonshire, within four miles of Banbury, in which the rebels had a very strong garrison. As soon as he came thither, he called a council of war, and having no intelligence that the earl of Essex was within any distance, it was resolved " the king and the army should rest in those quarters the next day, only that sir Nicholas Byron should march with his brigade, and attempt the taking in of Banbury." And with this resolution the council brake up, and all men went to their quarters, which were at a great distance, without any apprehension of an enemy. But that night, about twelve of the clock, prince Rupert sent the king word, "that the body of the rebels' army was within seven or eight miles, and that the head quarter was at a village called Keinton on the edge of Warwickshire ; and that it would be in his majesty's power, if he thought fit, to fight a battle the next day ;" which his majesty liked well, and therefore immediately despatched orders to cross the design for Banbury, "and that the whole army should draw to a rendezvous on the top of Edge-hill ;" which was a very high hill about two miles from Keinton, where the head quarters of the earl was, and which had a clear prospect of all that valley.

In the morning, being Sunday the twenty-third of October, when the rebels were beginning their march, (for they suspected not the king's forces to be near,) they perceived a fair body of horse on the top of that hill, and easily concluded their march was not then to be far. It is certain they were exceedingly surprised, having never had any other confidence of their men, than by the disparity they concluded would be still between their numbers and the king's, the which they found themselves now deceived in. For two of their strongest and best regiments of foot, and one regiment of horse, was a day's march behind with their ammunition. So that, though they were still superior in number, yet that difference was not so great as they promised themselves. However, it cannot be denied that the earl, with great dexterity, performed whatsoever could be expected from a wise general. He chose that ground which best liked him. There was between the hill and the town a fair campaign, save that near the town it was narrower, and on the right hand some hedges, and inclosures: so that there he placed musketeers, and not above two regiments of horse; where the ground was narrowest; but on his left wing he placed a body of a thousand horse, commanded by one Ramsey a Scotsman; the reserve of horse, which was a good one, was commanded by the earl of Bedford, general of their horse, and sir William Balfour with him. The general himself was with the foot, which were ordered as much to advantage as might be. And in this posture they stood from eight of the clock in the morning.

On the other side, though prince Rupert was early in the morning with the greatest part of the horse on the top of the hill, which gave the first alarm of the necessity of fighting to the other party, yet the foot were quartered at so great a distance, that many regiments marched seven or eight miles to the rendezvous: so that it was past one of the clock, before the king's forces marched down the hill; the general himself alighted at the head of his own regiment of foot, his son the lord Willoughby being next to him, with the king's regiment of guards, in which was the king's standard, carried by sir Edmund Verney, knight marshal. The king's right wing of horse was commanded by prince Rupert, the left wing by Mr. Wilmot, commissary general of the horse, who was assisted by sir Arthur Aston with most of the dragoons, because that left wing was opposed to the enemy's right, which had the shelter of some hedges lined with musketeers: and the reserve was committed to sir John Byron, and consisted indeed only of his own regiment. At the entrance into the field, the king's troop of guards, either provoked by some unseasonable scoffs among the soldiery, or out of desire of glory, or both, besought the king, " that he would give them leave to be absent that day from his person, and to charge in the front among the horse;" the which his majesty consented to. They desired prince Rupert "to give them that honour which belonged to them;" who accordingly assigned them the first place ; which, though they performed their parts with admirable courage, may well be reckoned among the oversights of that day.

It was near three of the clock in the afternoon, before the battle began ; which, at that time of the year, was so late, that some were of opinion, "that the business should be deferred till the next day." But against that there were many objections ; "the king's numbers could not increase, the enemy's might;" for they had not only their garrisons, Warwick, Coventry, and Banbury, within distance, but all that country so devoted to them, that they had all provisions brought to them without the least trouble ; whereas, on the other side, the people were so disaffected to the king's party, that they had carried away, or hid, all their provisions, insomuch as there was neither meat for man or horse ; and the very smiths hid themselves, that they might not be compelled to shoe horses, of which in those stony ways there was great need. This proceeded not from any radical malice, or disaffection to the king's cause, or his person ; though it is true, that circuit in which this battle was fought, being between the dominions of the lord Say and the lord Brooke, was the most eminently corrupted of any county in England ; but by the reports, and infusions which the other very diligent party had wrought into the people's belief; "that the cavaliers were of a fierce, bloody, and licentious disposition, and that they committed all manner of cruelty upon the inhabitants of those places where they came, of which robbery was the least;" so that the poor people thought there was no other way to preserve their goods, than by hiding them out of the way ; which was confessed by them, when they found how much that information had wronged them, by making them so injurious to their friends. And therefore where the army rested a day they found much better entertainment at parting, than when they came ; for it will not be denied, that there was no person of honour or quality, who paid not punctually and exactly for what they had ; and there was not the least violence or disorder among the common soldiers in their march, which scaped exemplary punishment; so that at Bromicham, a town so generally wicked, that it had risen upon small parties of the king's, and killed or taken them prisoners, and sent them to Coventry, declaring a more peremptory malice to his majesty than any other place, two soldiers were executed, for having taken some small trifle of no value out of a house, whose owner was at that time in the rebels' army. So strict was the discipline in this army; when the other, without control, practised all the dissoluteness imaginable. But the march was so fast, that the leaving a good reputation behind them, was no harbinger to provide for their better reception in the next quarters. So that their wants were so great, at the time when they came to Edge-hill, that there were very many companies of the common soldiers, who had scarce eaten bread in eight and forty hours before. The only way to cure this was a victory; and therefore the king gave the word, though it was late, the enemy keeping their ground to receive him without advancing at all.

In this hurry, there was an omission of somewhat, which the king intended to have executed before the beginning of the battle. He had caused many proclamations to be printed of pardon to all those soldiers who would lay down their arms, which he resolved, as is said before, to have sent by a herald to the earl of Essex, and to have found ways to have scattered and dispersed them in that army, as soon as he understood they were within any distance of him. But all men were now so much otherwise busied, that it was not soon enough remembered; and when it was, the proclamations were not at hand; which, by that which follows, might probably have produced a good effect. For as the right wing of the king's horse advanced to charge the left wing, which was the gross of the enemy's horse, sir Faithful Fortescue, (whose fortune and interest being in Ireland, he had come out of that kingdom to hasten supplies thither, and had a troop of horse raised for him for that service; but as many other of those forces were, so his troop was likewise disposed into that army, and he was now major to sir William Wal-

ler; he) with his whole troop advanced from the gross of
their horse, and discharging all their pistols on the ground,
within little more than carabine shot of his own body, presented himself and his troop to prince Rupert; and immediately, with his highness, charged the enemy. Whether this
sudden accident, as it might very well, and the not knowing
how many more were of the same mind, each man looking·
upon his companion with the same apprehension as upon the
enemy, or whether the terror of prince Rupert, and the
king's horse, or all together, with their own evil consciences,
wrought upon them,¹ I know not, but that whole wing, having unskilfully discharged their carabines and pistols into the
air, wheeled about, our horse charging in the flank and rear,
and having thus absolutely routed them, pursued them flying;
and had the execution of them above two miles.

The left wing, commanded by Mr. Wilmot, had as good
success, though they were to charge in worse ground, among
hedges, and through gaps and ditches, which were lined
with musketeers.   But sir Arthur Aston, with great courage
and dexterity, beat off those musketeers with his dragoons;
and then the right wing of their horse was as easily routed
and dispersed as their left, and those followed the chase as
furiously as the other.   The reserve seeing none of the
enemy's horse left, thought there was nothing more to be
done, but to pursue those that fled; and could not be contained by their commanders; but with spurs, and loose
reins, followed the chase, which their left wing had led them.
And by this means, whilst most men thought the victory unquestionable, the king was in danger of the same fate which
his predecessor Henry the Third felt at the battle of Lewes
against his barons; when his son the prince, having routed
their horse, followed the chase so far, that, before his return
to the field, his father was taken prisoner; and so his victory
served only to make the misfortunes of that day the more
intolerable.   For all the king's horse having thus left the

¹ This might be truly said of the grandees of the house, but could
with no pretence of reason or justice be said of this wing of horse.—
W.

field, many of them only following the execution, others intending the spoil in the town of Keinton, where all the baggage was, and the earl of Essex's own coach, which was taken, and brought away ; their reserve, commanded by sir William Balfour, moved up and down the field in good order, and marching towards the king's foot pretended to be friends, till observing no horse to be in readiness to charge them, brake in upon the foot, and did great execution.   Then was the general the earl of Lindsey, in the head of his regiment, being on foot, shot in the thigh ; with which he fell, and was presently encompassed by the enemy ; and his son, the lord Willoughby, piously endeavouring the rescue of his father, taken prisoner with him.   Then was the standard taken, (sir Edmund Verney, who bore it, being killed,) but rescued again by captain John Smith, an officer of the lord Grandison's regiment of horse, and by him brought off.   And if those horse had bestirred themselves, they might with little difficulty have destroyed, or taken prisoner, the king himself, and his two sons, the prince and the duke of York, being with fewer than one hundred horse, and those without officer or command, within half musket shot of that body, before he suspected them to be enemies.

When prince Rupert returned from the chase, he found this great alteration in the field, and his majesty himself with few noblemen, and a small retinue about him, and the hope of so glorious a day quite vanished.   For though most of the officers of horse were returned, and that part of the field covered again with the loose troops, yet they could not be persuaded, or drawn to charge either the enemy's reserve of horse, which alone kept the field, or the body of their foot, which only kept their ground.   The officers pretending, " that their soldiers were so dispersed, that there were not ten of any troop together ;" and the soldiers, " that their horses were so tired, that they could not charge."   But the truth is, where many soldiers of one troop or regiment were rallied together, there the officers were wanting ; and where the officers were ready, there the soldiers were not together ; and neither officers or soldiers desired to move without those who properly belonged to them.   Things had now so ill an aspect, that many were of opinion, that the king should leave the field, though it was not easy to advise whither he should have gone ; which if he had done, he had left an absolute victory to those, who even at this time thought themselves overcome. But the king was positive against that advice, well knowing, that as that army was raised by his person and presence only, so it could by no other means be kept together ; and he thought it unprincely, to forsake them who had forsaken all they had to serve him : besides, he observed the other side looked not as if they thought themselves conquerors ; for that reserve, which did so much mischief before, since the return of his horse, betook themselves to a fixed station between their foot, which at best could but be thought to stand their ground, which two brigades of the king's did with equal courage, and gave equal volleys ; and therefore he tried all possible ways to get the horse to charge again ; easily discerning by some little attempts which were made, what a notable impression a brisk one would have made upon the enemy. And when he saw it was not to be done, he was content with their only standing still. Without doubt, if either party had known the constitution of the other, they had not parted so fairly ; and, very probably, which soever had made a bold offer, had compassed his end upon his enemy. This made many believe, though the horse vaunted themselves aloud to have done their part, that the good fortune of the first part of the day, which well managed would have secured the rest, was to be imputed rather to their enemy's want of courage, than to their own virtue, (which, after so great a victory, could not so soon have forsaken them,) and to the sudden and unexpected revolt of sir Faithful Fortescue with a whole troop, no doubt much to the consternation of those he left ; which had not so good fortune as they deserved ; for by the negligence of not throwing away their orange-tawny scarfs, which they all wore as the earl of Essex's colours, and being immediately engaged in the charge, many of them, not fewer than seventeen or eighteen, were suddenly killed by those to whom they joined themselves.

In this doubt of all sides, the night, the common friend to wearied and dismayed armies, parted them ; and then the king caused his cannon, which were nearest the enemy, to be drawn off; and with his whole forces himself spent the night in the field, by such a fire as could be made of the little wood, and bushes which grew thereabouts, unresolved what to do the next morning; many reporting, " that the enemy was gone :" but when the day appeared, the contrary was discovered ; for then they were seen standing in the same posture and place in which they fought, from whence the earl of Essex, wisely, never suffered them to stir all that night ; presuming reasonably, that if they were drawn off never so little from that place, their numbers would lessen, and that many would run away ; and therefore he caused all manner of provisions, of which the country supplied him plentifully, to be brought thither to them for their repast, and reposed himself with them in the place ; besides, that night he received a great addition of strength, not only by rallying those horse and foot, which had run out of the field in the battle, but by the arrival of colonel Hambden, and colonel Grantham, with two thousand fresh foot, (which were reckoned among the best of the army,) and five hundred horse, which marched a day behind the army for the guard of their ammunition, and a great part of their train, not supposing there would have been any action that would have required their presence. All the advantage this seasonable recruit brought them, was to give their old men so much courage as to keep the field, which it was otherwise believed, they would hardly have been persuaded to have done.[1]　After a very cold night spent in the field, without any refreshment of victual, or provision for the soldiers, (for the country was so disaffected, that it not only not sent in provisions, but many soldiers, who straggled into the villages for relief, were knocked in the head by the common people,) the king found his troops very thin ; for though, by conference with the officers, he might reasonably conclude, that there were not many slain in the battle, yet a third part of his foot were not upon the place, and of the horse many missing; and they that were in the field were so

---

[1] i. e. those who had been in the battle, so distinguished from the *new comers.*

tired with duty, and weakened with want of meat, and shrunk up with the cruel cold of the night, (for it was a terrible frost, and there was no shelter of either tree or hedge,) that though they had reason to believe, by the standing still of the enemy, whilst a small party of the king's horse, in the morning, took away four pieces of their cannon very near them, that any offer towards a charge, or but marching towards them, would have made a very notable impression in them, yet there was so visible an averseness from it in most officers, as well as soldiers, that the king thought not fit to make the attempt; but contented himself to keep his men in order, the body of horse facing the enemy upon the field where they had fought.

Towards noon the king resolved to try that expedient, which was prepared for the day before; and sent sir William le Neve, Clarencieux king at arms, to the enemy, with his proclamation of pardon to such as would lay down arms; believing, though he expected then little benefit by the proclamation, that he should, by that means, receive some advertisement of the condition of the army, and what prisoners they had taken, (for many persons of command and quality were wanting,) giving him order likewise to desire to speak with the earl of Lindsey, who was known to be in their hands. Before sir William came to the army, he was received by the out-guards, and conducted, with strictness, (that he might say or publish nothing amongst the soldiers,) to the earl of Essex; who, when he offered to read the proclamation aloud, and to deliver the effect of it, that he might be heard by those who were present, rebuked him, with some roughness, and charged him, "as he loved his life, not to presume to speak a word to the soldiers;" and, after some few questions, sent him presently back well guarded through the army, without any answer at all. At his return he had so great and feeling a sense of the danger he had passed, that he made little observation of the posture or numbers of the enemy. Only he seemed to have seen, or apprehended so much trouble and disorder in the faces of the earl of Essex, and the principal officers about him, and so much dejection in the common soldiers, that they looked like men who had no far-

ther ambition, than to keep what they had left.   He brought
word of the death of the earl of Lindsey; who, being carried
out of the field a prisoner, into a barn of the next village, for
want of a surgeon, and such accommodations as were necessary, within few hours died with the loss of blood, his wound
not being otherwise mortal or dangerous.   This was imputed
to the inhumanity of the earl of Essex, as if he had purposely neglected, or inhibited the performing any necessary offices
to him, out of the insolence of his nature, and in revenge of
some former unkindnesses, had passed between them.   But,
I presume, it may be with more justice attributed to the hurry and distraction of that season, when, being so unsecure
of their friends, they had no thoughts vacant for their enemies.   For it is not to be denied at the time when the earl
of Lindsey was taken prisoner, the earl of Essex thought
himself in more danger; and among his faults want of civility and courtesy was none.   The loss of the general was a
great grief to the army, and, generally, to all who knew him;
for he was a person of great honour, singular courage, and of
an excellent nature.   He took little delight in the office of
general from the time that prince Rupert came, finding his
highness to pass him by too much in his command; yet having so much reverence to the king's sister's son, and so tender a regard of the present service, that he seemed only to
his friends to take notice of it; and seeing the battle that day
set without advising with him, and in a form that he liked
not, he said, since he was not fit to be a general, he would
die a colonel in the head of his regiment; and was as good
as his word.   There were more lost of the king's side of
note; the lord Aubigney, brother to the duke of Richmond,
a young man of great expectation, who was killed in the
charge with the left wing of horse, in which he commanded
a troop; where there were so few lost, that it was believed
that he fell by his own men, not without the suspicion of an
officer of his own; and he was the only person of name or
command who perished of the horse.   Among the foot, many good officers were lost, and amongst them, sir Edward
Verney was the chief, who that day carried the king's standard, a very honest gentleman, and an old true servant of the

king's, of which he had so very few just to him, that that single person could be ill spared. There fell two or three lieutenant colonels, and some good officers of inferior quality.

The number of the slain, by the testimony of the minister, and others of the next parish, who took care for the burying of the dead, and which was the only computation that could be made, amounted to above five thousand ; whereof two parts were conceived to be of those of the parliament party, and not above a third of the king's. Indeed the loss of both sides was so great, and so little of triumph appeared in either, that the victory could scarce be imputed to the one or the other. Yet the king's keeping the field, and having the spoil of it, by which many persons of quality, who had lain wounded in the field, were preserved, his pursuing afterwards the same design he had when he was diverted to the battle, and succeeding in it, (as shall be touched anon,) were greater ensigns of victory on that side, than the taking the general prisoner, and the taking the standard, which was likewise recovered, were on the other. Of the king's the principal persons, who were lost, were the earl of Lindsey, general of the army, the lord George Stewart, lord Aubigney, son to the duke of Lenox, and brother to the then duke of Richmond and Lenox, sir Edmund Verney, knight marshal of the king's horse, and standard bearer, and some others of less name, though of great virtue, and good quality.

The earl of Lindsey was a man of very noble extraction, and inherited a great fortune from his ancestors ; which though he did not manage with so great care, as if he desired much to improve, yet he left it in a very fair condition to his family, which more intended the increase of it. He was a man of great honour, and spent his youth and vigour of his age in military actions and commands abroad ; and albeit he indulged to himself great liberties of life, yet he still preserved a very good reputation with all men, and a very great interest in his country, as appeared by the supplies he and his son brought to the king's army ; the several companies of his own regiment of foot being commanded by the principal knights and gentlemen of Lincolnshire, who engaged themselves in the service principally out of their personal affection to him.

He was of a very generous nature, and punctual in what he undertook, and in exacting what was due to him; which made him bear that restriction so heavily, which was put upon him by the commission granted to prince Rupert, and by the king's preferring the prince's opinion, in all matters relating to the war, before his.   Nor did he conceal his resentment : the day before the battle, the earl of Dorset and Mr. Hyde conferred with him together, when he used great freedom, as to friends he loved well, and said, "that he did not look upon himself as general; and therefore he was resolved, when the day of battle should come, that he would be in the head of his regiment as a private colonel, where he would die."   He was carried out of the field to the next village ; and if he could then have procured surgeons, it was thought his wound would not have proved mortal.   And it was imputed to the earl of Essex's too well remembering former grudges, that he never sent any surgeon to him, nor performed any other offices of respect towards him ; but it is most certain that the disorder the earl of Essex himself was in at that time, by the running away of the horse, and the confusion he saw the army in, and the plundering the carriages in the town where the surgeons were to attend, was the cause of all the omissions of that kind.   And as soon as the other army was composed by the coming on of the night, the earl of Essex, about midnight, sent sir William Balfour, and some other officers, to see him, and to offer him all offices, and meant himself to have visited him.   They found him upon a little straw in a poor house, where they had laid him in his blood, which had run from him in great abundance, no surgeon having been yet with him ; only he had great vivacity in his looks; and told them, " he was sorry to see so many gentlemen, some whereof were his old friends, engaged in so foul a rebellion :" and principally directed his discourse to sir William Balfour, whom he put in mind of " the great obligations he had to the king ; how much his majesty had disobliged the whole English nation by putting him into the command of the Tower; and that it was the most odious ingratitude in him to make him that return." He wished them to tell my lord Essex, " that he ought to cast himself at the king's feet to beg his pardon ; which if he did not speedily do, his memory would be odious to the nation;" and continued this kind of discourse with so much vehemence, that the officers by degrees withdrew themselves; and prevented the visit the earl of Essex intended him, who only sent the best surgeons to him; who in the very opening of his wounds died before the morning, only upon the loss of blood. He had very many friends, and very few enemies; and died generally lamented.

The lord Aubigney was a gentleman of great hopes, of a gentle and winning disposition, and of very clear courage : he was killed in the first charge with the horse; where, there being so little resistance, gave occasion to suspect that it was done by his own lieutenant, who being a Dutchman, had not been so punctual in his duty, but that he received some reprehension from his captain, which he murmured at. His body was brought off, and buried at Christ-church in Oxford; his two younger brothers, the lord John and the lord Bernard Stewart, were in the same battle, and were both killed afterwards in the war, and his only son is now duke of Richmond. Sir Edmund Verney hath been mentioned before[1] upon his discourse at Nottingham, which was very ominous. He was a person of great honour and courage, and lost his life in that charge, when Balfour, with that reserve of horse, which had been so long undiscerned, broke into those regiments; but his body was not found.

Of the parliament party that perished, the lord Saint-John of Bletnezo, and Charles Essex, were of the best quality. The last had been bred up a page under the earl of Essex, who afterwards, at his charge, preferred him to a command in Holland; where he lived with very good reputation, and preserved the credit of his decayed family; and as soon as the earl unfortunately accepted this command, he thought his gratitude obliged him to run the fortune of his patron,

[1] This implies he had been characterized before; and so indeed he was: but in that part of the MS. from whence this history was extracted, which was thought rather belonging to the life of the noble historian. Those parts have since been collected and published under that title, in which we find a curious anecdote relating to Verney.— W.

and out of pure kindness to the person of the earl, as many other gentlemen did, engaged himself against the king without any malice or rebellion in his heart towards the crown. He had the command of a regiment of foot, and was esteemed the best and most expert officer of the army, and was killed by a musket shot in the beginning of the battle.   The lord Saint-John was eldest son to the earl of Bullingbroke, and got himself so well beloved by the reputation of courtesy and civility, which he expressed towards all men, that though his parts of understanding were very ordinary at best, and his course of life licentious and very much depraved, he got credit enough, by engaging the principal gentlemen of Bedfordshire and Hertfordshire to be bound for him, to contract a debt of fifty or threescore thousand pounds ; for the payment whereof the fortune of the family was not engaged, nor in his power to engage.   So that the clamour of his debts growing importunate, some years before the rebellion, he left the kingdom, and fled into France ; leaving his vast debt to be paid by his sureties, to the utter ruin of many families, and the notable impairing of others.   In the beginning of the parliament, the king was prevailed with to call him to the house of peers, his father being then alive, upon an assurance, " that by his presence and liberty, which could by no other way be secured, means would be found out to pay his debts, and free so many worthy persons from their engagements : besides that the times being like to be troublesome, the king might be sure of a faithful servant, who would always advance his service in that house."   But the king had very ill fortune in conferring those graces, nor was his service more passionately and insolently opposed by any men in that house than by those, who upon those professions were redeemed by him from the condition of commoners.[1] And this gentleman, from the first hour of his sitting in that

[1] He conferred them knowingly on undeserving men ; so it was more his fault than his misfortune.   But their ingratitude was attended with this inconvenience to the king.   The people concluded, that the court must needs have very ruinous views, when the king's most obliged creatures fell from him.   Whereas in truth that worthless tribe ran naturally, like rats, from distress.—W.

house by the king's so extraordinary grace, was never known to concur in any one vote for the king's service, that received any opposition: and, as soon as it was in his power, he received a commission with the first to command a troop of horse against him, in which he behaved himself so ill, that he received some wounds in running away; and being taken prisoner, died before the next morning, without any other signs of repentance, than the canting words, "that he did not intend to be against the king, but wished him all happiness:" so great an influence the first seeds of his birth and mutinous family had upon his nature, that how long so-ever they were concealed, and seemed even buried in a very different breeding and conversation, they sprung up, and bore the same fruit upon the first occasion. And it was an observation of that time, that the men of most licentious lives, who appeared to be without any sense of religion, or reverence to virtue, and the most unrestrained by any obli-gations of conscience, betook themselves to that party, and pretended an impulsion of religion out of fear of popery; and, on the other side, very many persons of quality, both of the clergy and laity, who had suffered under the imputation of puritanism, and did very much dislike the proceedings of the court, and opposed them upon all occasions, were yet so much scandalized at the very approaches to rebellion, that they renounced all their old friends, and applied themselves[1] with great resolution, courage, and constancy to the king's service, and continued in it to the end, with all the disad-vantages it was liable to.

Prisoners were taken by the enemy, the lord Willough-by, hastily and piously endeavouring the rescue of his father; sir Thomas Lunsford, and sir Edward Stradling, both colo-nels; and sir William Vavasour, who commanded the king's regiment of guards under the lord Willoughby; and some other inferior commanders. There were hurt, sir Jacob Ashley, and sir Nicholas Byron, and more dangerously, colo-

---

[1] They understood, and truly, that the king in this parliament had by his concurrence with many good acts, made a reasonable satisfac-tion for his former errors.—W.

nel Charles Gerrard, who, being shot in the thigh, was
brought off the field without any hopes of life, but recovered
to act a great part afterwards in the war ; sir George Strode,
and some other gentlemen who served among the foot; for
of the horse there was not an officer of name, who received
a wound, the lord Aubigney only excepted ; so little resistance did that part of the enemy make.   Of the rebels was
slain, the lord Saint-John, son and heir apparent of the earl
of Bullingbroke, a man known by nothing, but the having
run into a vast debt, to the ruin of his own and many families whom he procured to be engaged for him, whom the
king, shortly after the beginning of this parliament, at the
importunity of the earl of Bedford and some others, unhappily created a peer, and by that rendered his person free
from the arrest of his creditors, and added one to the number of those lords, who most furiously revolted from their
allegiance.   He had at this battle a regiment of horse, and
was taken prisoner after he had received some hurts, of
which he died the next day.   On the field was slain also,
colonel Charles Essex, the soldier of whom they had the
best opinion, and who had always, till this last action, preserved a good reputation in the world, which was now the
worse, over and above the guilt of rebellion, by his having
sworn to the queen of Bohemia, by whose intercession he
procured leave from the prince of Orange to go into England,
"that he would never serve against the king:" and many
other of obscure names, though officers of good command.
There were a good number of their officers, especially of
horse, taken prisoners, but (save that some of them were
parliament men) of mean quality in the world, except only
sir William Essex, the father of the colonel, whose wants,
from having wasted a very great fortune, and his son's invitation, led him into that company ; where he was a private
captain of his regiment.   .

When the armies had thus only looked one upon another
the whole day, and it being discerned that the enemy had
drawn off his carriages, the king directed all his army to retire into their old quarters, presuming (as it proved) that many of those who were wanting would be found there.   And

so himself with his two sons went to Edgecot, where he lay the night before the battle, resolving to rest the next day, both for the refreshing his wearied, and even tired men,[1] and to be informed of the motion and condition of the enemy, upon which some troops of the king's horse attended. The earl of Essex retired with his to Warwick castle, whither he had sent all his prisoners; so that, on the Tuesday morning, the king was informed, that the enemy was gone, and that some of his horse had attended the rear of the enemy almost to Warwick, and that they had left many of their carriages, and very many of their wounded soldiers, at the village next the field; by which it appeared that their remove was in haste, and not without apprehension.

After the horse had marched almost to Warwick, and found the coast clear from the enemy, they returned to the field to view the dead bodies, many going to inquire after their friends who were missing, where they found many not yet dead of their wounds, but lying stripped among the dead; among whom, with others, young Mr. Scroop brought off his father, sir Gervas Scroop; who, being an old gentleman of great fortune in Lincolnshire, had raised a foot company among his tenants, and brought them into the earl of Lindsey's regiment, out of devotion and respect to his lordship, as well as duty to the king; and had, about the time that the general was taken, fallen with sixteen wounds in his body and head; and had lain stripped among the dead, from that time, which was about three of the clock in the afternoon on Sunday, all that cold night, all Monday, and Monday night, and till Tuesday evening, for it was so late before his son found him; whom with great piety he carried to a warm lodging, and afterwards in the march to Oxford; where he wonderfully recovered. The next morning after, being Wednesday, there was another gentleman, one Bellingham, of an ancient extraction in Sussex, and the only son of his father, found among the dead, and brought off by his friends, with twenty wounds; who, after ten days, died at Oxford, by the negligence of his surgeons, who left a wound in his thigh, of itself not danger-

---

[1] Not only *wearied* in this action, but *tired* of the service.—W.

ous, undiscerned, and so by festering destroyed a body very hopefully recovered of those which were only thought mortal. The surgeons were of opinion, that both these gentlemen owed their lives to the inhumanity of those who stripped them, and to the coldness of the nights, which stopped their blood, better than all their skill and medicaments could have done ; and that, if they had been brought off within any reasonable distance of time after their wounds, they had undoubtedly perished.

On Wednesday morning, the king drew his army to a rendezvous, where he found his numbers greater than he expected ; for, in the night after the battle, very many of the common soldiers, out of cold and hunger, had found their old quarters. So that it was really believed upon this view, when this little rest had recovered a strange cheerfulness into all men, that there were not in that battle lost above three hundred men at the most.[1] There the king declared general Ruthen general of his army in the place of the earl of Lindsey ; and then marched to Ayno, a little village two miles distant from Banbury, of which his majesty that day took a view, and meant to attempt it the next day following. There was at that time in Banbury castle a regiment of eight hundred foot, and a troop of horse, which, with spirits proportionable, had been enough to have kept so strong a place from an army better prepared to have assaulted it, than the king's then was, and at a season of the year more commodious for a siege. And therefore many were of opinion, that the king should have marched by it, without taking notice of it, and that the engaging before it might prove very prejudicial to him. That which prevailed with him to stay there, besides the courage of his soldiers, who had again recovered their appetite to action, was that he could not well resolve whither to go ; for till he was informed what the earl of Essex did, he knew not how to direct his march ; and if the enemy advanced upon him, he could not fight in a place of

[1] How is this to be reconciled with what is said in page 1128, where it is said five thousand fell in the action, of which one third were the king's? It is no wonder this should occasion, as the historian expresses it, *a strange cheerfulness.*—W.

more advantage. And therefore, having sent a trumpet to summon the castle, and having first taken the lord Say's house at Broughton, where there was some show of resistance, and in it a troop of horse, and some good arms, the cannon were planted against the castle, and the army drawn out before it; but, upon the first shot made, the castle sent to treat, and, upon leave to go away without their arms, they fairly and kindly delivered the place; and half the common soldiers at the least readily took conditions, and put themselves into the king's army; the rest of the arms came very seasonably to supply many soldiers of every regiment, who either never had any before, or had lost them at the battle.

This last success declared where the victory was before at Edgehill; for, though the routing of their horse, the having killed more on the place, and taken more prisoners, the number of the colours won from the enemy, (which were near forty in number,) without the loss of above three or four, and lastly the taking four pieces of their cannon the next morning after the battle, were so many arguments that the victory inclined to the king: on the other side, the loss of the general himself, and so many men of name either killed or taken prisoners, who were generally known over the kingdom, (whereas, besides the lord Saint-John's, and colonel Essex, the names of the rest of that party were so obscure, that neither the one side seemed to be gainers by having taken or killed them, nor the other side to be losers by being without them,) the having kept the field last, and taking the spoil of it, were sufficient testimonies at the least that they were not overcome. But now the taking of Banbury, which was the more signal, by the circumstances of that part of the army's being, before the battle, designed for that service, then recalled to the field, and after that field fought, and the retreat of the enemy, the readvancing upon it, and taking it, was so undeniable an argument that the earl of Essex was more broken and scattered than at first he appeared to be, that the king's army was looked upon as victorious. A garrison was put into Banbury, and the command thereof committed to the earl of Northampton, and then the king marched to his own house to Woodstock ; and the next day with the whole army to Oxford, which was the only city of England, that he could say was entirely at his devotion ; where he was received by the university, to whom the integrity and fidelity of that place is to be imputed, with all joy and acclamation, as Apollo should be by the muses.

The earl of Essex continued still at Warwick,[1] repairing his broken regiments and troops, which every day lessened and impaired ; for the number of his slain men was greater than it was reported to be, there being very many killed in the chase, and many who died of their wounds after they were carried off, and, of those, who run away in the beginning, more stayed away than returned ; and, which was worse, they who run fastest and farthest told such lamentable stories of the defeat, and many of them shewed such hurts, that the terror thereof was even ready to make the people revolt to their allegiance in all places. Many of those who had stood their ground, and behaved themselves well in the battle, either with remorse of conscience, horror of what they had done, and seen, or weariness of the duty and danger, withdrew themselves from their colours, and some from their commands. And it is certain many engaged themselves first in that service, out of an opinion, that an army would procure a peace without fighting ; others out of a desire to serve the king, and resolving to go away themselves, and to carry others with them, as soon as they should find themselves within a secure distance to do it; both these being, contrary to their expectation, brought to fight, the latter not knowing how to get to the king's army in the battle, discharged themselves of the service as soon as they came to Warwick ; some with leave, and some without.

[1] The reason of this unaccountable conduct in Essex was owing to the old soldiers of fortune, by whom he was governed. In the beginning of the war, they hindered the parliamentarians from coming to a decisive action for the sake of their trade. When the war was become more serious, the king's counsellors hindered a decisive action for the sake of public liberty. Yet till one or other conquered, *peace* was a visionary thing.—W.

But that which no doubt most troubled his excellency, was the temper and constitutions of his new masters; who, he knew, expected no less from him than a victory complete, by his bringing the person of the king alive or dead to them; and would consider what was now fallen out, as it was so much less than they looked for, not as it was more than any body else could have done for them. However, he gave them a glorious account of what had passed,[1] and made as if his stay at Warwick were rather to receive new orders and commands from them, than out of any weakness or inability to pursue the old, and that he attended the king's motion as well as if he had been within seven miles of him.

It is certain the consternation was very great at London, and in the two houses, from the time that they heard, that the king marched from Shrewsbury with a formed army, and that he was resolved to fight, as soon as he could meet with their army. However, they endeavoured to keep up confidently the ridiculous opinion among the common people, that the king did not command, but was carried about in that army of the cavaliers, and was desirous to escape from them; which they hoped the earl of Essex would give him opportunity to do. The first news they heard of the army's be-

[1] In the year 1741, or thereabout, I had a conversation with the duke of Argyle and lord Cobham, concerning the conduct of Essex and the king after the battle of Edge-hill. They said Essex, instead of retiring to Coventry, should either have pushed the king, or attended him closely: that since he neglected that, and went back so far north, the king should have marched hastily to London, and ended the war at a blow: that as lord Clarendon represents it, the conduct of both is incomprehensible. I think the matter very clear. Essex's views and principles would not suffer him to destroy the king, because the constitution would fall with him; and this he loved. This appears evidently from Whitlock, who says, that the next day after the battle, three fresh regiments, one of horse and two of foot, commanded by lord Willoughby of Parham, Hollis, and Hambden, joined him, who all urged him to pursue the king; but he took Dalbier's advice to the contrary. On the other hand, the king's best friends dreaded his ending the war by conquest, as knowing his despotic disposition. And these dissuaded the marching up to London, which lord Clarendon tells us was debated in council.—W.

ing engaged, was by those who fled upon the first charge; who made marvellous haste from the place of danger, and thought not themselves safe, till they were gotten out of any possible distance of being pursued. It is certain, though it was past two of the clock before the battle begun, many of the soldiers, and some commanders of no mean name, were at St. Alban's, which was near thirty miles from the field, before it was dark. These men, as all runaways do for their own excuse, reported all for lost, and the king's army to be so terrible, that it could not be encountered. Some of them, that they might not be thought to come away before there was cause, or whilst there was any hope, reported the progress of the battle, and presented all those lamentable things, and the circumstances by which every part of the army was defeated, which their terrified fancies had suggested to them whilst they run away; some had seen the earl of Essex slain, and heard his dying words; "That every one should shift for himself, for all resistance was to no purpose:" so that the whole city was, the Monday, full of the defeat; and though there was an express, from the earl of Essex himself, of the contrary, there was not courage enough left to believe it, and every hour produced somewhat to contradict the reports of the last. Monday in the afternoon, the earl of Holland produced a letter in the house of peers, which was written the night before by the earl of Essex, in which all particulars of the day were set down, and "the impression that had in the beginning been made upon his horse, but that the conclusion was prosperous." Whilst this was reading, and every man greedily digesting the good news, the lord Hastings, who had a command of horse in the service, entered the house with frighted and ghastly looks, and positively declared "all to be lost, against whatsoever they believed or flattered themselves with." And though it was evident enough that he had run away from the beginning, and only lost his way thither,[1] most men looked upon him as the last messenger, and even shut their ears against any possible comfort; so that without doubt very many, in

[1] Exquisitely satirical.

72*

the horror and consternation of eight and forty hours, paid
and underwent a full penance and mortification for the hopes
and insolence of three months before.   At the last, on Wednesday morning, the lord Wharton, and Mr. William Strode,
the one a member of the house of lords, the other of the
commons, arrived from the army, and made so full a relation
of the battle, "of the great numbers slain on the king's part,
without any considerable loss on their side, of the miserable
and weak condition the king's army was in, and of the earl
of Essex's resolution to pursue him," that they were not
now content to be savers, but voted "that their army had
the victory ;" and appointed a day for a solemn thanksgiving
to God for the same ; and, that so great a joy might not be
enjoyed only within those walls, they appointed those two
trusty messengers to communicate the whole relation with
all circumstances to the city ; which was convened together
at the guildhall to receive the same.   But by this time, so
many persons, who were present at the action, came to the
town of both sides, (for there was yet a free intercourse
with all quarters,) and some discourses were published, how
little either of these two messengers had seen themselves of
that day's business, that the city seemed not so much exalted at their relations, as the houses had done ; the king's
taking Banbury, and marching afterwards to Oxford, and the
reports from those quarters of his power, with the earl of
Essex's lying still at Warwick, gave great argument of discourse ; which grew the greater by the commitment of several persons, for reporting, " that the king had the better of the
field ;" which men thought would not have been, if the success had been contrary ; and therefore there was nothing so
generally spoken of, or wished for, as peace.

   They who were really affected to the king, and from the
beginning opposed all the extravagances, for of such there
were many in both houses, who could not yet find in their
hearts to leave the company, spake now aloud, " that an humble address to the king for the removal of all misunderstandings, was both in duty necessary, and in policy convenient."
The half-hearted and half-witted people, which made much
the major part of both houses, plainly discerned there must

be a war, and that the king at least would be able to make
resistance, which they had been promised he could not do,
and so were equally passionate to make any overtures for accommodation.   They only who had contrived the mischief,
and already had digested a full change and alteration of government, and knew well, that all their arts would be discovered, and their persons odious, though they might be secured,[1]
violently opposed all motions of this kind.   These men pressed earnestly " to send an express to their brethren of Scotland, to invite and conjure them to come to their assistance,
and to leave no way unthought of for suppressing, and totally destroying, all those who had presumed to side with the
king."   This overture of calling the Scots in again was as
unpopular a thing, as could be mentioned ; besides that it implied a great and absolute diffidence in their own strength,
and an acknowledgment that the people of England stood not
so generally affected to their desires, which they had hitherto published, and urged, as the best argument to justify those
desires.   Therefore the wise managers of that party, by whose
conduct they had been principally governed, seemed fully to
concur with those who desired peace, " and to send an humble address to the king, which they confessed to be due from
them as subjects, and the only way to procure happiness for
the kingdom."   And having hereby rendered themselves
gracious, and gained credit, they advised them " so to endeavour peace, that they might not be disappointed of it,"
and wished them " to consider that the king's party were high
upon the success of having an army, (of which they had reasonably before despaired,) though not upon any thing that
army had yet done.   That it was apparent, the king had ministers stirring for him in the north, and in the west, though
hitherto with little effect ; and therefore if they should make
such an application for peace, as might imply the giving over
the thoughts of war, they must expect such a peace, as the
mercy of those whom they had provoked would consent to.
But if they would steadily pursue those counsels as would

---

[1] This is loosely expressed.   Did these grandees believe they might
be secured, or does the historian assure us that they would ?   If the
first, it is certain they did not confide in the king's security offered to
them, as appears throughout their whole conduct.—W.

make their strength formidable, they might then expect such moderate conditions, as they might, with their own, and the kingdom's safety, securely submit to. That therefore the proposition of sending into Scotland was very seasonable ; not that it could be hoped, or was desired, that they should bring an army into England, of which there was not like to be any need ; but that that kingdom might make such a declaration of their affections, and readiness to assist the parliament, that the king might look upon them with the more consideration, as a body not easily to be oppressed, if he should insist upon too high conditions."

By this artifice, whilst they who pressed a treaty thought, that, that being once consented to, a peace would inevitably be concluded, the same day that a committee was appointed, " to prepare heads of an humble address unto his majesty, for composing the present differences and distractions, and settling the peace of the kingdom," (which was a great condescension,) they made no scruple to declare, " that the preparations of forces, and all other necessary means for defence, should be prosecuted with all vigour ;" and thereupon required " all those officers and soldiers, who had left their general, of which the town was then full, upon pain of death, to return to him ;" and, for his better recruit, solemnly declared, " that, in such times of common danger and necessity, the interest of private persons ought to give way to the public ; and therefore they ordained, that such apprentices, as would be listed to serve as soldiers, for the defence of the kingdom, the parliament, and city, (with their other usual expressions of religion, and the king's person,) their sureties, and such as stood engaged for them, should be secured against their masters ; and that their masters should receive them again, at the end of their service, without imputing any loss of time to them, but the same should be reckoned as well spent, according to their indentures, as if they had been still in their shops." And by this means many children were engaged in that service,[1] not only against the consent, but against the

---

[1] Had this been done in the distresses which followed, it might have been pardoned by candid men ; but to do it now, although they gained by making things and persons desperate, yet it must appear to all dispassionate observers to be a throwing off the mask too soon.

persons, of their fathers, and the earl received a notable supply thereby.

Then, for their consent that a formal and perfunctory message should be sent to his majesty, whereby they thought a treaty would be entered upon, they procured at the same time, and as an expedient for peace, this material and full declaration of both houses to the subjects of Scotland, which they caused with all expedition to be sent into that kingdom.

" We the lords[1] and commons, assembled in the parliament of England, considering with what wisdom, and public affection, our brethren of the kingdom of Scotland did concur with the endeavours of this parliament, and the desires of the whole kingdom, in procuring and establishing a firm peace and amity between the two nations, and how lovingly they have since invited us to a nearer and higher degree of union in matters concerning religion and church-government, which we have most willingly and affectionately embraced, and intend to pursue, cannot doubt but they will, with as much forwardness and affection, concur with us in settling peace in this kingdom, and preserving it in their own ; that so we may mutually reap the benefit of that amity and alliance, so happily made, and strongly confirmed betwixt the two nations.   Wherefore, as we did about a year since, in the first appearance of trouble then beginning among them, actually declare, that, in our sense and apprehension of the national alliance betwixt us, we were thereby bound to apply the authority of parliament, and power of this kingdom, to the preservation and maintenance of their peace : and, seeing now that the troubles of this kingdom are grown to a greater height, and the subtle practices of the common enemy of the religion and liberty of both nations do appear with more evident strength and danger than they did at that time, we hold it necessary to declare, that, in our judgment, the same obligation lies upon our brethren, by the aforementioned act, with the power and force of that kingdom, to assist us in repressing those among us, who are now in arms, and make war, not only without consent of parliament, but even against the parliament, and for the destruction thereof.

[1] *In the handwriting of Lord Clarendon's amanuensis.*

" Wherefore we have thought good to make known unto our brethren, that his majesty hath given commission to divers eminent and known papists, to raise forces, and to compose an army in the north, and other parts of this kingdom, which is to join with divers foreign forces, intended to be transported from beyond the seas, for the destruction of this parliament, and of the religion and liberty of the kingdom : and that the principal part of the clergy and their adherents have likewise invited his majesty to raise another army, which, in his own person, he doth conduct against the parliament, and the city of London, plundering and robbing sundry well affected towns within their power; and, in prosecution of their malice, they are so presumptuous, and predominant of his majesty's resolutions, that they forbear not those outrages in places to which his majesty hath given his royal word and protection ; a great cause and incentive of which malice proceeds from the design they have to hinder the reformation of ecclesiastical government in this kingdom, so much longed for by all the true lovers of the protestant religion.

" And hereupon we farther desire our brethren of the nation of Scotland, to raise such forces as they shall think sufficient for securing the peace of their own borders, against the ill affected persons there, as likewise to assist us in suppressing the army of papists and foreigners ; which, as we expect, will shortly be on foot here, and, if they be not timely prevented, may prove as mischievous and destructive to that kingdom, as to ourselves.   And though we seek nothing from his majesty that may diminish his just authority, or honour, and have, by many humble petitions, endeavoured to put an end to this unnatural war and combustion in the kingdom, and to procure his majesty's protection, and security for our religion, liberty, and persons, (according to that great trust which his majesty is bound to by the laws of the land,) and shall still continue to renew our petitions in that kind ; yet, to our great grief, we see the papistical and malignant council so prevalent with his majesty, and his person so engaged to their power, that we have little hope of better success of our petitions than we formerly had ; and are thereby necessitated to stand upon our just defence, and to seek this speedy and powerful assistance of our brethren of Scotland, according to that act agreed upon in the parliament of both kingdoms, the common duty of Christianity, and the particular interests of their own kingdom: to which we hope God will give such a blessing, that it may produce the preservation of religion, the honour, safety, and peace of his majesty, and all his subjects, and a more strict conjunction of the counsels, designs, and endeavours of both nations, for the comfort and relief of the reformed churches beyond sea."

It will not be here unseasonable, having, according to my weak abilities and observation, described the general temper and disposition of that time, and the particular state of affairs in the several parts of the kingdom, to take some short survey of the affections and inclinations of Scotland ; the ordering and well disposing whereof, either side sufficiently understood, would be of moment, and extraordinary importance in the growing contention.   From the time of the king's being last there, when he had so fully complied with all they had desired, both for the public government, and their private advancements, that kingdom within itself enjoyed as much quiet and tranquillity as they could desire; having the convenience of disburdening themselves of their late army into Ireland, whither their old general Leslie, then made earl of Leven, was employed in his full command by the king and the two houses, at the charge of England.   So that many believed they had been so abundantly satisfied with what they had already gotten from England, that they had no farther projects upon this kingdom, but meant to make their fortunes by a new conquest in Ireland, where they had a very great part of the province of Ulster planted by their own nation.   So that, according to their rules of good husbandry, they might expect whatsoever they got from the rebels to keep for themselves.   And the king himself was so confident that the affections of that people could not be corrupted towards him, as to make a farther attempt upon him, that he believed them, to a degree, sensible of their former breach of duty, and willing to repair it by any service.   Leslie himself had made great acknowledgments, and great professions to him, and had told him, " That it was nothing to promise him, that he would never more bear arms against him; but he promised he would serve his majesty upon any summons, without asking the cause." The earl of Lowden, and all the rest, who had misled the people, were possessed of whatsoever they could desire, and the future fortune of that nation seemed to depend wholly upon the keeping up the king's full power in this.

His majesty had, from time to time, given his council of that kingdom full relations of all his differences with the parliament, and had carefully sent them the declarations, and public passages of both sides; and they had always returned very ample expressions of their affections and duty, and expressed a great sense of the parliament's proceedings towards him. And since the time of his being at York, the lord chancellor of Scotland, in whose integrity and loyalty he was least secure, had been with him; and seemed so well satisfied with the justice and honour of his majesty's carriage towards the parliament, that he writ to the Scottish commissioners at London, in the name, and as by the direction of the lords of the secret council of that kingdom, " that they should present to the two houses the deep sense they had of the injuries and indignities, which were offered to the king, whose just rights they were bound to defend; and that they should conjure them to bind up those wounds which were made, and not to widen them by sharpness of language; and to give his majesty such real security for his safety among them, by an effectual declaring against tumults, and such other actions as were justly offensive to his majesty, that he might be induced to reside nearer to them, and comply with them in such propositions as should be reasonably made;" with many such expressions, as together with his return into Scotland without coming to London, where he was expected, gave them so much offence and jealousy, that they never communicated that letter to the houses, and took all possible care to conceal it from the people.

The marquis Hamilton had been likewise with his majesty at York, and finding the eyes of all men directed towards him with more than ordinary jealousy, he offered the king to go into Scotland, with many assurances and undertakings, confident, " that he would at least keep that people from doing any thing, that might seem to countenance the carriage of the parliament." Upon which promises, and to be rid of him at York, where he was by all men looked upon with marvellous prejudice, the king suffered him to go, with full assurance that he would, and he was sure he could, do him very good service there ; as, on the other side, in his own court he was so great an offence, that the whole gentry of Yorkshire, who no doubt had infusions to that purpose from others, had a design to have petitioned the king, that the marquis might be, sequestered from all councils, and presence at court, as a man too much trusted by them who would not trust his majesty.

Lastly, the king had many of the nobility of Scotland then attending him, and among those the earl of Calander, who had been lieutenant-general of the Scotch army, when it invaded England, and had freely confessed to his majesty, upon what errors and mistakes he had been corrupted, and by whom, and pretended so deep a sense of what he had done amiss, that it was believed he would have taken command in the king's army ; which he declined, as if it might have been penal to him in Scotland by some clause in the act of the pacification, but especially upon pretence it would disable him from doing him greater service in that kingdom : whither, shortly after the standard was set up, he repaired, with all solemn vows of asserting and improving his majesty's interest in those parts.

The parliament on the other hand assured themselves, that that nation was entirely theirs, having their commissioners residing with them at London ; and the chief managers and governors in the first war, by their late intercourse, and communication of guilt, having a firm correspondence with the marquis of Argyle, the earl of Lowden, and that party, who, being not able to forgive themselves, thought the king could never in his heart forgive them, when it should be in his power to bring them to justice. And they undertook that when there should be need of that nation, (which the other thought there would never be,) they should be as forward to second them as they had been ; in the mean time returned as fair and respective answers to all their messages, and upon their declarations, which were constantly sent to them, as they did to the king; assisting them in their design against the church, which was not yet grown popular, even in the two houses, by declaring "that the people of that nation could never be engaged on any other ground, than the reformation of religion." And therefore, about the beginning of August, the assembly of the kirk of Scotland published a declaration; "how exceedingly grieved they were, and made heavy, that in so long a time, against the professions both of king and parliament, and contrary to the joint desires and prayers of the godly in both kingdoms, to whom it was more dear and precious than what was dearest to them in the world, the reformation of religion had moved so slowly, and suffered so great interruption."

The ground of which reproach was this; in the late treaty of peace, the commissioners for Scotland had expressed a desire or wish warily couched in words, rather than a proposition, "that there were such an unity of religion, and uniformity of church government agreed on, as might be a special means for conserving of peace betwixt the two kingdoms:" to which there had been a general inclination to return a rough answer, and reproof for their intermeddling in any thing that related to the laws of England. But, by the extraordinary industry and subtlety of those, who saw that business was not yet ripe, and who alleged, that it was only wished, not proposed, and therefore that a sharp reply was not merited, this gentle answer, against the minds of very many, was returned :

" That his majesty, with the advice of both houses of parliament, did approve of the affection of his subjects of Scotland, in their desire of having conformity of church-government between the two nations ; and as the parliament had already taken into consideration the reformation of church-government, so they would proceed therein in due time, as should best conduce to the glory of God, the peace of the church, and of both kingdoms."

Which was consented to by most, as a civil answer, signifying, or concluding nothing ; by others, because it admitted an interpretation of reducing the government of the church in Scotland to this of England, as much as the contrary. But it might have been well discerned, that those men asked nothing without a farther design than the words naturally imported, nor ever rested satisfied with a general formal answer, except they found, that they should hereafter make use, and receive benefit by such answer.   So they now urged the matter of this answer, as a sufficient title to demand the extirpation of prelacy in England, and demolishing the whole fabric of that glorious church ; urging his majesty's late practice, while he was in person in Scotland, in resorting frequently to their exercises of public worship ; and his royal actions, in establishing the worship and government of that kirk in parliament.   And therefore they desired the parliament " to begin their work of reformation at the uniformity of kirk-government ; for that there could be no hope of unity in religion, of one confession of faith, one form of worship, and one catechism, till there were first one form of church-government; and that the kingdom, and kirk of Scotland, could have no hope of a firm and durable peace, till prelacy, which had been the main cause of their miseries and troubles, first and last, were plucked up root and branch, as a plant which God had not planted, and from which no better fruits could be expected, than such sour grapes, as at that day set on edge the kingdom of England."

Which declaration the lords of the secret council, finding, as they said, " the reasons therein expressed to be very pregnant, and the particulars desired, much to conduce to the glory of God, the advancement of the true Christian faith, his majesty's honour, and the peace and union of his dominions," well approved of ; and concurred in their earnest desires to the two houses of parliament, " to take to their serious considerations those particulars, and to give favourable hearing to such desires and overtures, as should be found most conducible to the promoting so great and so good a work."

This being sent to the parliament at the time they were forming their army, and when the king was preparing for his defence, they who, from the beginning, had principally intended this confusion of the church, insinuated "how neces-

sary it was, speedily to return a very affectionate and satisfactory reply to the kingdom of Scotland ; not only to preserve the reputation of unity and consent between them,
which, at that time, was very useful to them, but to hinder
the operations of the disaffected in that kingdom ; who, upon
infusions that the parliament only aimed at taking his majesty's regal rights from him, to the prejudice of monarchique
government, without any thought of reforming religion, endeavoured to pervert the affections of that people towards
the parliament.   Whereas, if they were once assured there
was a purpose to reform religion, they should be sure to have
their hearts ; and, if occasion required, their hands too ;
which possibly might be seduced for the king, if that purpose were not manifested.   Therefore, for the present, they
should do well to return their hearty thanks for, and their
brotherly acceptance and approbation of the desires and advice of that Christian assembly, and of the lords of the council ; and that though, for the present, by reason of the king's
distance from the parliament, they could not settle any conclusion in that matter, that for their parts they were resolved
to endeavour it."

By this artifice and invention, they procured a declaration
from the two houses of parliament, of wonderful kindness,
and confession of many inconveniences and mischiefs the
kingdom had sustained by bishops; and therefore they declared, "that that hierarchical government was evil, and
justly offensive, and burdensome to the kingdom ; a great
impediment to reformation and growth of religion ; very
prejudicial to the state and government of the kingdom ; and
that they were resolved, that the same should be taken
away ; and that their purpose was to consult with godly and
learned divines, that they might not only remove that, but
settle such a government, as might be most agreeable to
God's holy word ; most apt to procure and conserve the
peace of the church at home, and happy union with the
church of Scotland, and other reformed churches abroad ;
and to establish the same by a law, which they intended to
frame for that purpose, to be presented to his majesty for
his royal assent ; and in the mean time to beseech him, that

a bill for the assembly might be passed in time convenient for their meeting;" the two houses having extra-judicially and extravagantly nominated their own divines to that purpose, as is before remembered.

It was then believed by many, and the king was persuaded to believe the same, that all those importunities from Scotland concerning the government of the church were used only to preserve themselves from being pressed by the parliament, to join with them against the king ; imagining that this kingdom would never have consented to such an alteration ; and they again pretending, that no other obligation could unite that people in their service.   But it is most certain, this last declaration was procured by persuading men, " that it was for the present necessary, and that it was only an engagement to do their best to persuade his majesty, who they concluded would be inexorable in the point," (which they seemed not to be sorry for,) and that a receding from such a conclusion would be a means to gratify his majesty in a treaty."   At worst, they all knew, that there would be room enough, when any bill should be brought in, to oppose what they had, for this reason of state, seemed generally to consent to.   And so by these stratagems, thinking to be too hard for each other, they grew all so entangled, that they still wound themselves deeper into those labyrinths, in which the major part meant not to be involved.   And what effect that declaration of the two houses, after the battle of Edgehill, which is mentioned before, wrought, will very shortly appear.

He was received there (*viz. Oxford*) with all the demonstrations of joy as could be expected from the affection of so loyal a university, where care was taken for providing for the sick and wounded soldiers, and for the accommodation of the army, which was, in a short time, recruited there in a good measure ; and the several colleges presented his majesty with all the money they had in their treasuries, which amounted to a good sum, and was a very seasonable supply, as they had formerly sent him all their plate.   It had been very happy, if the king had continued his resolution of sitting still during the winter, without making farther attempts ;

for his reputation was now great, and his army believed to be much greater than it was, by the victory they had obtained, and the parliament grew more divided into factions, and dislike of what they done, and the city appeared fuller of discontent, and less inclined to be imposed upon, than they had been: so that on all hands nothing was pressed, but that some address might be made to the king for an accommodation; which temper and disposition might have been cultivated, as many men thought, to great effects, if no farther approaches had been made to London, to shew them how little cause they had for their great fear. But the weather growing fair again, as it often is about Allhollantide, and a good party of horse having been sent out from Abingdon, where the head quarter of the horse was, they advanced farther than they had order to do, and upon their approach to Reading, where Harry Martin was governor for the parliament, there was a great terror seized upon them, insomuch as governor and garrison fled to London, and left the place to the party of horse; which gave advertisement to the king, "that all fled before them; that the earl of Essex remained still at Warwick, having no army to march; and that there were so great divisions in the parliament, that, upon his majesty's approach, they would all fly; and that nothing could interrupt him from going to Whitehall. However, Reading itself was so good a post, that if the king should find it necessary to make his own residence in Oxford, it would be much the better by having a garrison at Reading."

Upon these and other motives, besides the natural credulity in men, in believing all they wish to be true, the king was prevailed with to march with his army to Reading, but could not overtake his horse; which was still before, and his majesty followed to Colebrooke; whither a message from the parliament was sent to him, to desire him to advance no farther, before they sent persons to treat with him; which they were ready to do. And he did return such an answer as made them believe that he would expect them there, without moving nearer towards London. And if he had then stopped any farther advance, and himself upon that address retired to his castle at Windsor, it would have been delivered to

him, by the order of the parliament, which had then some
troops in it : and being possessed of so considerable a place,
the treaty would very probably have been concluded with
good success.   But the fate of that poor kingdom contradict-
ed that blessing.   All things were in a hurry, and the horse
still engaged the king to follow, so that he advanced with the
whole army to Brentford, and cut off some regiments of foot,
which the earl of Essex had sent thither, himself being the
night before entered London.   It was now evident to all men,
that there had [been] great oversight in making so great
haste; all thoughts of treaty were dashed; they who most
desired it, did not desire to be in the king's mercy ; and
they now believed, by his majesty's making so much haste
towards them, after their offer of a treaty, that he meant to
have surprised and taken vengeance of them without distinction.   All people prepared for a vigorous defence ; and, beside the earl of Essex's army, all the city and nobility that
remained there marched out with him to Hounslow Heath,
with all things proportionable, or that could be of use or convenience to so numerous an army.   Where they quickly had
a view of the whole miserable forces which had given them
that alarum, which they found cause enough to despise, and
so recovered easily their own courage.   And the king found
it necessary, after he had rested one night at Hampton court,
to make a hasty retreat to Reading; where he left a garrison
of about three thousand men under the command of sir Arthur Aston, who undertook to fortify it: and having likewise
left colonel Blake with his regiment to fortify Wallingford
castle, his majesty, towards the end of November, returned
to Oxford, unsatisfied with the progress he had made, which
had likewise raised much faction and discontent amongst the
officers, every man imputing the oversights which had been
committed, to the rashness and presumption of others ; and
prince Rupert, in the march, contracted an irreconcilable prejudice to Wilmot, who was then lieutenant-general of the
horse, and was not fast in the king's favour.

As soon as the king returned to Oxford, his first care was
to publish such declarations and proclamations as might best
compose the minds of the people, by assuring them of the

king's impatient desire of peace, which his hasty march from Colebrooke to Brentford, after the receipt of the parliament message, had made much doubted, and the managers there lost no time in the improving those jealousies; and therefore his majesty caused a declaration to be published concerning that affair, and the ground of his advancement to Brentford; which declaration was prepared by the lord Falkland, through whose hands that address, and the answer to it, had passed. That declaration, and the answer to the nineteen propositions, which is mentioned before, were the two only declarations of the king's which were not prepared and drawn up by Mr. Hyde, who at that time was busy in other things, as drawing proclamations, and other declarations and writings, by which the king thought his service to be much advanced. The fame of the great distractions at London, and the advices from unskilful persons thence, who believed that the appearance of his majesty with his forces near London would so terrify the disaffected, and give such life and courage to those who wished well to him, that the gates would be open to him, prevailed with his majesty, when all armies used to betake themselves to their winter quarters, to lead his again into the field; and therefore having rested himself at Oxford only three days, he marched towards Reading, prince Rupert with his horse and dragoons having so frighted that garrison, (for there was a garrison planted in it by the parliament,) that the chief officers, upon the fame of his coming, fled, that the town willingly received the king's forces, and delivered all their arms and ammunition to his disposal. This alarum quickly came to London, and was received with the deepest horror: they now unbelieved all which had been told them from their own army; that army, which, they were told, was well beaten and scattered, was now advanced within thirty miles of London; and the earl of Essex, who pretended to the victory, and who they supposed was watching the king, that he might not escape from him, could not be heard of, and continued still at Warwick. Whilst the king was at Nottingham, and Shrewsbury, they gave orders magisterially for the war: but now it was come to their own doors, they took not that delight in it.

Before they were resolved what to say, they despatched a messenger, who found the king at Reading, only to desire, " a safe conduct from his majesty for a committee of lords and commons, to attend his majesty with an humble petition from his parliament." The king presently returned his answer, " that he had always been, and was still, ready to receive any petition from them; that their committee should be welcome, provided it consisted of persons, who had not been by name declared traitors by his majesty, and excepted as such in his declarations or proclamations." The cause of this limitation was as well the former rule his majesty had set down at Shrewsbury, (from whence he thought not fit now to recede, after a battle,) as that he might prevent the lord Say's being sent to him, from whom he could expect no entire and upright dealing.

The next day another letter came from the speaker of the house of peers to the lord Falkland, one of his majesty's principal secretaries, to desire " a safe conduct for the earls of Northumberland and Pembroke, and four members of the house of commons, to attend his majesty with their petition;" which safe conduct was immediately signed by his majesty, excepting only for sir John Evelyn, who was by name excepted in his majesty's proclamation of pardon to the county of Wilts; which proclamation was then sent to them with a signification, " that if they would send any other person in his place, not subject to the same exception, he should be received as if his name were in the safe conduct." Though this was no more than they had cause to look for, yet it gave them opportunity for a time to lay aside the thought of petitioning, as if his majesty had rejected all overtures of peace : " For he might every day proclaim as many of their members traitors, and except them from pardon, as he pleased; and therefore it was to no purpose to prepare petitions, and appoint messengers to present them, when it was possible those messengers might, the hour before, be proclaimed traitors: that to submit to such a limitation of the king's was, upon the matter, to consent to and approve the highest breach of privilege, that had been yet offered to them."

So that, for some days, all discourse of peace was waved,

73*

and all possible preparations for defence and resistance made;
for which they had a stronger argument than either of the
other, the advancing of their general, the earl of Essex, who
was now on his march towards London ; and a great fame
came before him of the strength and courage of his army ;
though in truth it was not answerable to the report : however, it served to encourage and inflame those whose fear only
inclined them to peace, and to awe the rest. The king, who
had every night an account of what was transacted in the
houses all day, (what the close committee did, who guided all
private designs, was not so soon known,) resolved to quick-
en them ; and advanced with his whole army to Colebrook.
This indeed exalted their appetite to peace ; for the clamour
of the people was importunate, and somewhat humbled their
style ; for at Colebrook, the 11th of November, his majesty
was met by the two earls of Northumberland and Pembroke,
with those three of the house of commons whose names were
in the safe conduct ; they satisfying themselves, that the leaving sir John Evelyn behind them, without bringing another
in his room, was no submission to the king's exception : and
this petition was by them presented to him.

"We your majesty's[1] most loyal subjects, the lords and
commons in parliament assembled, being affected with a deep
and piercing sense of the miseries of this kingdom, and of the
dangers to your majesty's person, as the present affairs now
stand ; and much quickened therein with the sad consideration of the great effusion of blood at the late battle, and of
the loss of so many eminent persons ; and farther weighing
the addition of loss, misery, and danger to your majesty, and
your kingdom, which must ensue, if both armies should again
join in another battle, as without God's especial blessing, and
your majesty's concurrence with your houses of parliament,
will not probably be avoided : we cannot but believe that a
suitable impression of tenderness and compassion is wrought
in your majesty's royal heart, being yourself an eyewitness
of the bloody and sorrowful destruction of so many of your
subjects ; and that your majesty doth apprehend what dimi-

---

[1] *This petition is in the handwriting of lord Clarendon's amanuensis.*

nution of your own power and greatness will follow, and that all your kingdoms will thereby be so weakened as to become subject to the attempts of any ill-affected to this state.

" In all which respects we assure ourselves, that your majesty will be inclined graciously to accept this our humble petition ; that the misery and desolation of this kingdom may be speedily removed, and prevented. For the effecting whereof, we humbly beseech your majesty to appoint some convenient place, not far from the city of London, where your majesty will be pleased to reside, until committees of both houses of parliament may attend your majesty with some propositions for the removal of these bloody distempers and distractions, and settling the state of the kingdom in such a manner as may conduce to the preservation of God's true religion, your majesty's honour, safety, and prosperity ; and to the peace, comfort, and security of all your people."

The king, within two or three hours after the receipt of this petition, delivered to the same messengers this ensuing answer, with which they returned the same night to London.

" We[1] take God to witness, how deeply we are affected with the miseries of this kingdom, which heretofore we have stroven as much as in us lay to prevent ; it being sufficiently known to all the world that, as we were not the first that took up arms, so we have shewed our readiness of composing all things in a fair way, by our several offers of treaty, and shall be glad now at length to find any such inclinations in others. The same tenderness to avoid the destruction of our subjects, (whom we know to be our greatest strength,) which would always make our greatest victories bitter to us, shall make us willingly hearken to such propositions, whereby these bloody distempers may be stopped, and the great distractions of this kingdom settled to God's glory, our honour, and the welfare and flourishing of our people : and to that end shall reside at our own castle at Windsor, (if the forces there shall be removed,) till committees may have time to attend us with the same, (which, to prevent the in-

---

[1] *This answer is in the same handwriting as the preceding petition.*

conveniences that will intervene, we wish be hastened,) and shall be ready there, or, if that be refused us, at any place where we shall be, to receive such propositions as aforesaid, from both our houses of parliament. Do you your duty, we will not be wanting in ours. God of his mercy give a blessing."

It was then believed by many, that if the king had, as soon as the messengers returned to London, retired with his army to Reading, and there expected the parliament's answer, that they would immediately have withdrawn their garrison from Windsor, and delivered that castle to his majesty for his accommodation to have treated in : and without doubt those lords who had been with the petition, and some others who thought themselves as much overshadowed by the greatness of the earl of Essex, and the chief officers of the army, as they could be by the glory of any favourite, or power of any counsellors, were resolved to merit as much as they could of the king, by advancing an honourable peace ; and had it in their purpose to endeavour the giving up of Windsor to the king ; but whether they would have been able to have prevailed that so considerable a strength, in so considerable a place, should have been quitted, whilst there was only hope of a peace, I much doubt. But certainly the king's army carried great terror with it ; and all those reports, which published the weakness of it, grew to be peremptorily disbelieved. For, besides that every day's experience disproved somewhat which was as confidently reported, and it was evident great industry was used to apply such intelligence to the people as was most like to make impression upon the passions and affections of the vulgar-spirited, it could not be believed that a handful of men could have given battle to their formidable army, and, after taking two or three of their garrisons, presume to march within fifteen miles of London : so that, if from thence the king had drawn back again to Reading, relying upon a treaty for the rest, it is probable his power would have been more valued, and consequently his grace the more magnified. And sure the king resolved to have done so, or at least to have staid at Colebrook (which was not so convenient) till he heard again from

the parliament.   But prince Rupert, exalted with the terror
he heard his name gave to the enemy, trusting too much to
the vulgar intelligence every man received from his friends
at London, who, according to their own passions and the affections of those with whom they corresponded, concluded
that the king had so great a party in London, that, if his army drew near, no resistance would be made, and too much
neglecting the council of state (which from the first hour the
army overmuch inclined to) without any direction from the
king,[1] the very next morning after the committee returned to
London, advanced with the horse and dragoons to Hounslow,
and then sent to the king to desire him that the army might
march after ; which was, in that case, of absolute necessity ;
for the earl of Essex had a part of his army at Brentford, and
the rest at Acton, and Kingston.   So that if the king had
not advanced with his body, those who were before might
very easily have been compassed in, and their retreat very
difficult.

So the king marched with his whole army towards Brentford, where were two regiments of their best foot, (for so
they were accounted, being those who had eminently behaved themselves at Edge-hill,) having barricadoed the narrow
avenues to the town, and cast up some little breastworks at
the most convenient places.   Here a Welsh regiment of the
king's, which had been faulty at Edge-hill, recovered its honour, and assaulted the works, and forced the barricadoes
well defended by the enemy.   Then the king's forces entered the town after a very warm service, the chief officers and
many soldiers of the other side being killed ; and took there

---

[1] He seems to have done it for no other reason than to break off the
treaty.   He was a soldier of fortune, and loved the service, and his
whole conduct was conformable to that character.   In a word, the
king was ruined by his ministers in peace, and by his officers in war.
But he who certainly most contributed to the ill success of his arms
was prince Rupert ; and this was one of the most mischievous as well
as barbarous of his exploits.   In this affair, if the king's sole purpose
was to disengage prince Rupert's horse on Hounslow heath, why did
he advance to Hounslow with his foot, and force the barricades of the
town defended by the parliament's foot ?   I doubt he was not so clear
in his purpose as his historian represents him.—W.

above five hundred prisoners, eleven colours, and fifteen pieces of cannon, and good store of ammunition. But this victory (for considering the place it might well be called so) proved not at all fortunate to his majesty.

The two houses were so well satisfied with the answer their committee had brought from the king, and with the report they made of his majesty's clemency, and gracious reception of them, that they had sent order to their forces, " that they should not exercise any act of hostility towards the king's forces ;" and, at the same time, despatched a messenger, to acquaint his majesty therewith, and to desire " that there might be the like forbearance on his part." The messenger found both parties engaged at Brentford, and so returned without attending his majesty, who had no apprehension that they intended any cessation ; since those forces were advanced to Brentford, Acton, and Kingston, after their committee was sent to Colebrook. However they looked upon this entering of Brentford as a surprise contrary to faith, and the betraying their forces to a massacre, under the specious pretence of a treaty for peace. The alarum came to London, with the same dire yell as if the army were entered their gates, and the king accused " of treachery, perfidy, and blood ; and that he had given the spoil and wealth of the city as pillage to his army, which advanced with no other purpose."

They who believed nothing of those calumnies, were not yet willing the king should enter the city with an army, which, they knew, would not be governed in so rich quarters ; and therefore, with unspeakable expedition, the army under the earl of Essex was not only drawn together, but all the trained bands of London led out in their brightest equipage upon the heath next Brentford ; where they had indeed a full army of horse and foot, fit to have decided the title of a crown with an equal adversary. The view and prospect of this strength, which nothing but that sudden exigent could have brought together, (so that army was really raised by king and parliament) extremely puffed them up ; not only as it was an ample security against the present danger, but as it looked like a safe power to encounter any exigent. They had then before their eyes the king's little handful of men, and then began to wonder and blush at their own fears ; and all this might be without excess of courage ; for without doubt their numbers then, without the advantage of equipage, (which to soldiers is a great addition of mettle,) were five times greater than the king's harassed, weather-beaten, and half-starved troops.

I have heard many knowing men, and some who were then in the city regiments, say, " That if the king had advanced, and charged that massive body, it had presently given ground; and that the king had so great a party in every regiment, that it would have made no resistance."[1]　But it had been madness, which no success could have vindicated, to have made that attempt : and the king easily discerned that he had brought himself into straits and difficulties, which would be hardly mastered, and exposed his victorious army to a view, at too near a distance off his two enemies, the parliament and the city.　Yet he stood all that day in battalia to receive them, who only played upon him with their cannon, to the loss only of four or five horses, and not one man.　That being a good argument to them not to charge the king, which had been an ill one to him to charge them, the constitution of their forces, where there were very many not at all affected to the company they were in.[2]

When the evening drew on, and it appeared that great body stood only for the defence of the city, the king appointed his army to draw off to Kingston, which the rebels had kindly quitted; which they did without the loss of a man ; and himself went to his own house at Hampton-court ; where he rested the next day, as well to refresh his army, even tired with watching and fasting, as to expect some propositions from the houses.　For, upon his advance to Brentford,

[1] Those who read how the city train-bands behaved in the second battle of Newbury will hardly be of this opinion.—W.

[2] The observation is just.　Inclination to the opposite party would make soldiers charge weakly and unwillingly; but when they were charged, both honour and safety would make them defend themselves with vigour.—W

he had sent a servant of his own, one Mr. White, with a message to the parliament, containing the reasons of that motion, (there being no cessation offered on their part,) and desiring "the propositions might be despatched to him with all speed."   But his messenger, being carried to the earl of Essex, was by him used very roughly, and by the houses committed to the Gate-house, not without the motion of some men, " that he might be executed as a spy."

After a day's stay at Hampton-court, the king removed himself to his house at Oatlands, leaving the gross of his army still at Kingston, and thereabouts; but being then informed of the high imputations they had laid upon him ; " of breach of faith, by his march to Brentford ; and that the city was really inflamed with an opinion, that he meant to have surprised them, and to have sacked the town; that they were so possessed with that fear and apprehension, that their care and preparation for their safety would at least keep off all propositions for peace, whilst the army lay so near London;" he gave direction for all his forces to retire to Reading ; first discharging all the common soldiers, who had been taken prisoners at Brentford, (except such who voluntarily offered to serve him,) upon their oaths that they would no more bear arms against his majesty.

The king then sent a message to the houses, in which " he took notice of those unjust and unreasonable imputations raised on him ; told them again of the reasons and circumstances of his motion towards Brentford; of the earl of Essex's drawing out his forces towards him, and possessing those quarters about him, and almost hemming him in, after the time that the commissioners were sent to him with the petition ; that he had never heard of the least overture of the forbearing all acts of hostility, but saw the contrary practised by them by that advance ; that he had not the least thought or intention of mastering the city by force, or carrying his army thither : that he wondered to hear his soldiers charged with thirsting after blood, when they took above five hundred prisoners in the very heat of the fight.   He told them such were most apt and likely to maintain their power by blood and rapine, who had only got it by oppression and injustice; that his was vested in him by the law, and by that only (if the dèstructive counsels of others did not hinder such a peace, in which that might once again be the universal rule, and in which only religion and justice could flourish) he desired to maintain it: that he intended to march to such a distance from his city of London, as might take away all pretence of apprehension from his army, that might hinder them from preparing their propositions, in all security, to be presented to him; and there he would be ready to receive them, or, if that expedient pleased them not, to end the pressures and miseries, which his subjects, to his great grief, suffered through this war, by a present battle."

But as the army's being so near London was an argument against a present treaty, so its remove to Reading was a greater with very many not to desire any. The danger, which they had brought themselves for some days together to look upon at their gates, was now to be contemned at the distance of thirty miles; and this retreat imputed only to the fear of their power, not to the inclinations to peace. And therefore they, who during the time that the major part did really desire a good peace, and whilst overtures were preparing to that purpose, had the skill to intermingle acts more destructive to it, than any propositions could be contributory, (as the inviting the Scots to their assistance by that declaration, which is before mentioned; and the publishing a declaration at the same time, which had lain long by them, in reply to one set forth by the king long before in answer to theirs of the 26th of May, in which they used both his person and his power with more irreverence than they had ever done before,) now only insisted on the surprise, as they called it, of Brentford; published, by the authority of both houses, a relation of the carriage of the king's soldiers in that town after their victory, (which they framed upon the discourses of the country people, who possibly, as it could not be otherwise, had received damage by their licence then,) to make the king and his army odious to the kingdom; " as affecting nothing but blood and rapine;" and concluded, "that there could not be reasonably expected any good conditions of a tolerable peace from the king, whilst he was in such company; and therefore that all particular propositions were to be resolved into that one, of inviting his majesty to come to them;" and got a vote from the major part of both houses, " that no other thought of accommodation or treaty should be thought on."

Their trusty lord mayor of London, Isaac Pennington, who was again chosen to serve another year, so bestirred himself, having to assist him two such sheriffs, Langham and Andrews, as they could wish, that there was not only no more importunity or interposition from the city for peace; but, instead thereof, an overture and declaration from divers, under the style of well-affected persons, " that they would advance a considerable number of soldiers, for the supply and recruit of the parliament forces; and would arm, maintain, and pay them for several months, or during the times of danger and distractions; provided that they might have the public faith of the kingdom for repayment of all such sums of money, which they should so advance by way of loan."   This wonderful kind proposition was presently declared " to be an acceptable service to the king, parliament, and kingdom, and necessarily tending to the preservation of them;" and therefore an ordinance, as they call it, was framed and passed both houses;

" That all such as should furnish men, money, horse, or arms for that service, should have the same fully repaid again, with interest for the forbearance thereof, from the times disbursed.   And for the true payment thereof, they did thereby engage to all, and every such person, and persons, the public faith of the kingdom."   And ordered the lord mayor, and sheriffs of London, by themselves, or such sub-committees as they should appoint, to take subscriptions, and to intend the advancement of that service.   Upon this voluntary, general proposition, made by a few obscure men, probably such who were not able to supply much money, was this ordinance made; and from this ordinance the active mayor, and sheriffs, appointed a committee of such persons whose inclinations they well knew, to press all kind of people, especially those who were not forward, to new subscriptions; and by degrees, from this unconsidered passage, grew the monthly tax of six thousand pounds to be set upon the city for the payment of the army.

As they provided, with this notable circumspection, to raise men and money; so they took not less care, nor used less art and industry, to raise their general; and lest he might suppose himself fallen in their good grace and confidence, by bringing an army back shattered, poor, and discomforted, which he had carried out in full numbers, and glorious equipage, they used him with greater reverence and submission than ever. They had before appointed another distinct army to be raised under the command of the earl of Warwick, and not subject to the power of the earl of Essex; and of this, several regiments and troops were raised : these they sent to the old army, and the earl of Warwick gave up his commission, upon a resolution, " that there should be only one general, and he, the earl of Essex." Then the two houses passed, and presented, with great solemnity, this declaration to his excellency, the same day that their committee went to the king with their petition :

" That, as they had, upon mature deliberation, and assured confidence in his wisdom, courage, and fidelity, chosen and appointed him their captain-general; so they did find, that the said earl had managed that service, of so high importance, with so much care, valour, and dexterity, as well by the extremest hazard of his life, in a bloody battle near Keinton in Warwickshire, as by all the actions of a most excellent and expert commander, in the whole course of that employment, as did deserve their best acknowledgment : and they did therefore declare, and publish, to the lasting honour of the said earl, the great and acceptable service, which he had therein done to the commonwealth : and should be willing and ready, upon all occasions, to express the due sense they had of his merits, by assuring and protecting him, and all others employed under his command in that service, with their lives and fortunes, to the uttermost of their power : that testimony and declaration to remain upon record, in both houses of parliament, for a mark of honour to his person, name, and family, and for a monument of his singular virtue to posterity."

When they had thus composed their army and their general, they sent this petition to the king to Reading, who staid still there in expectation of their propositions.

" May it please[1] your majesty :

" It is humbly desired by both houses of parliament, that your majesty will be pleased to return to your parliament, with your royal, not your martial, attendance ; to the end that religion, laws, and liberties, may be settled and secured by their advice; finding by a sad and late accident, that your majesty is environed by some such counsels, as do rather persuade a desperate division, than a joining and a good agreement with your parliament and people : and we shall be ready to give your majesty assurances of such security, as may be for your honour, and the safety of your royal person."

As soon as the king received this strange address, he returned them by the same messenger a sharp answer : He told them, " he hoped all his good subjects would look upon that message with indignation, as intended, by the contrivers thereof, as a scorn to him ; and thereby designed by that malignant party, (of whom he had so often complained, whose safety and ambition was built upon the divisions and ruins of the kingdom, and who had too great an influence upon their actions,) for a wall of separation betwixt his majesty and his people. He said, he had often told them the reasons, why he departed from London; how he was chased thence, and by whom ; and as often complained, that the greatest part of his peers, and of the members of the house of commons, could not, with safety to their honours and persons, continue, and vote freely among them ; but, by violence, and cunning practices, were debarred of those privileges, which their birthrights, and the trust reposed in them by their counties, gave them : that the whole kingdom knew that an army was raised, under pretence of orders of both houses, (an usurpation never before heard of in any age,)

[1] *This petition is in the handwriting of lord Clarendon's amanuensis.*

which army had pursued his majesty in his own kingdom; given him battle at Keinton; and now, those rebels being recruited, and possessed of the city of London, he was courteously invited to return to his parliament there, that is, to the power of that army.

" That, he said, could signify nothing but that, since the traitorous endeavours of those desperate men could not snatch the crown from his head, it being defended by the providence of God, and the affections and loyalty of his good subjects, he should now tamely come up, and give it them; and put himself, his life, and the lives, liberties, and fortunes of all his good subjects into their merciful hands. He said, he thought not fit to give any other answer to that part of their petition: but as he imputed not that affront to both his houses of parliament, nor to the major part of those who were then present there, but to that dangerous party his majesty and the kingdom must still cry out upon; so he would not (for his good subjects' sake, and out of his most tender sense of their miseries, and the general calamities of the kingdom, which must, if the war continued, speedily overwhelm the whole nation) take advantage of it: but if they would really pursue the course they seemed, by their petition at Colebrook, to be inclined to, he should make good all he then promised; whereby the hearts of his distressed subjects might be raised with the hopes of peace; without which, religion, the laws, and liberties, could by no ways be settled and secured.

" For the late and sad accident they mentioned, if they intended that of Brentford, he desired them once again to deal ingenuously with the people, and to let them see his last message to them, and his declaration concerning the same," (both which his majesty had sent to his press at London, but were taken away from his messenger, and not suffered to be published,) " and then he doubted not, but they would be soon undeceived, and easily find out those counsels, which did rather persuade a desperate division, than a good agreement betwixt his majesty, his two houses, and people."

This answer being delivered, without any farther consideration whether the same were reasonable or not reasonable, they declared "the king had no mind to peace;" and thereupon laid aside all farther debates to that purpose; and ordered their general to march to Windsor with the army, to be so much nearer the king's forces; for the better recruiting whereof, two of their most eminent chaplains, Dr. Downing and Mr. Marshall, publicly avowed,[1] "that the soldiers lately taken prisoners at Brentford, and discharged, and released by the king upon their oaths that they would never again bear arms against him, were not obliged by that oath;" but, by their power, absolved them thereof, and so engaged again those miserable wretches in a second rebellion.

When the king discerned clearly that the enemies to peace had the better of him, and that there was now no farther thought of preparing propositions to be sent to him; after he had seen a line drawn about Reading, which he resolved to keep as a garrison, and the works in a reasonable forwardness, he left sir Arthur Aston, whom he had lately made commissary-general of the horse, (Mr. Wilmot being at the same time constituted lieutenant-general,) governor thereof, with a garrison of above two thousand foot, and a good regiment of horse: and himself with the rest of his army marched to Oxford, where he resolved to rest that winter, settling at the same time a good garrison at Wallingford, a place of great importance within eight miles of Oxford; another at the Brill upon the edge of Buckinghamshire; a third being before settled at Banbury; Abingdon being the head quarters for his horse; and by this means he had all Oxfordshire entire, all Berkshire, but that barren division about Windsor; and from the Brill, and Banbury, a good influence upon Buckinghamshire and Northamptonshire.

The king was hardly settled in his quarters, when he heard

[1] This, if true, was a most villanous profanation of their ministry. The king and parliament were now on the footing of civil enemies. And such an oath, taken by prisoners of war, in consideration of liberty, has always been held binding by the law of nations, and by the law of arms so sacred, that the violators of it are held by military men to be ignominious.

that the parliament was fixing a garrison at Marlborough in Wiltshire, a town the most notoriously disaffected of all that county ; otherwise, saving the obstinacy and malice of the inhabitants, in the situation of it very unfit for a garrison. Thither the earl of Essex had sent one Ramsey, (a Scotsman, as most of their officers were of that nation,) to be governor; who, with the help of the factious people there, had quickly drawn together five or six hundred men. This place, the king saw, would prove quickly an ill neighbour to him ; not only as it was in the heart of a rich county, and so would straiten, and even infest his quarters, (for it was within twenty miles of Oxford,) but as it did cut off his line of communication with the west : and therefore, though it was December, a season, when his tired and almost naked soldiers might expect rest, he sent a strong party of horse, foot, and dragoons, under the command of Mr. Wilmot, the lieutenant-general of his horse, to visit that town ; who, coming thither on a Saturday, found the place strongly manned : for, besides the garrison, it being market-day, very many country people came thither to buy and sell, and were all compelled to stay and take arms for the defence of the place ; which, for the most part, they were willing to do, and the people peremptory to defend it. Though there was no line about it, yet there were some places of great advantage, upon which they had raised batteries, and planted cannon, and so barricadoed all the avenues, which were through deep narrow lanes, that the horse could do little service.

When the lieutenant-general was, with his party, near the town, he apprehended a fellow, who confessed, upon examination, " that he was a spy, and sent by the governor to bring intelligence of their strength and motion." When all men thought, and the poor fellow himself feared, he should be executed, the lieutenant-general caused his whole party to be ranged in order in the next convenient place, and bid the fellow look well upon them, and observe them, and then bid him return to the town, and tell those that sent him, what he had seen, and withal that he should acquaint the magistrates of the town, " that they should do well to treat with the garrison, to give them leave to submit to the king ; that

if they did so, the town should not receive the least prejudice ; but if they compelled him to make his way, and enter the town by force, it would not be in his power to keep
his soldiers from taking that which they should win with
their blood :" and so dismissed him. This generous act
proved of some advantage ; for the fellow, transported with
having his life given him ; and the numbers of the men he
had seen, besides his no experience in such sights, being
multiplied by his fear, made notable relations of the strength,
gallantry, and resolution of the enemy, and of the impossi-
bility of resisting them ; which, though it prevailed not with
those in authority to yield, yet it strangely abated the hopes
and courage of the people. So that when the king's soldiers
fell on, after a volley or two, in which much execution was
done, they threw down their arms, and run into the town ;
so that the foot had time to make room for the horse, who
were now entered at both ends of the town, yet were not
so near an end as they expected ; for the streets were in many
places barricadoed, which were obstinately defended by some
soldiers and townsmen, who killed many men out of the windows of the houses ; so that, it may be, if they had trusted
only to their own strength, without compelling the country
men to increase their number, and who being first frighted,
and weary, disheartened their companions, that vile place
might have cost more blood. Ramsey the governor was
himself retired into the church with some officers, and from
thence did some hurt ; upon this, there being so many killed
out of windows, fire was put to the next houses, so that a
good part of the town was burned, and then the soldiers entered, doing less execution than could reasonably be expected ; but what they spared in blood, they took in pillage, the
soldiers inquiring little who were friends or foes.

This was the first garrison taken on either side; (for I
cannot call Farnham castle in Surry one, whither some gentlemen who were willing to appear for the king had repaired, and were taken with less resistance than was fit, by sir
William Waller, some few days before, and before it deserved the name of a garrison;) in which were taken, besides
the governor, and other officers, who yielded upon quarter,

above one thousand prisoners; great store of arms, four pieces of cannon, and a good quantity of ammunition, with all which the lieutenant-general returned safe to Oxford: though this victory was a little shadowed, by the unfortunate loss of a very good regiment of horse within a few days after; for the lord Grandison, by the miscarriage of orders, was exposed, at too great a distance from the army, with his single regiment of horse consisting of three hundred horse, and a regiment of two hundred dragoons, to the unequal encounter of a party of the enemy of five thousand horse and dragoons; and so was himself, after a retreat made to Winchester, there taken with all his party; which was the first loss the king sustained; and was without the least fault of the commander; who lessened the misfortune much by making an escape himself with two or three of his principal officers, who were very welcome to Oxford.

The first thing the king applied himself to consult upon, after he was settled in his winter quarters, and despaired of any honest overtures for a peace, was, how to apply some antidote to that poison, which was sent into Scotland, in that declaration we mentioned before; the which he had not only seen, as an act communicated abroad and in many hands, but the Scottish earl of Lindsey, who was then a commissioner lieger at London for Scotland, had presented to him. And there was every day some motion in the house of commons to press the Scots, to invade the kingdom for their assistance, upon the growth of the earl of Newcastle's power in the north. And therefore, after full thoughts, the king writ to his privy-council of Scotland, (who, by the laws enacted when he was last there, had the absolute, indeed regal, power of that kingdom,) and took notice of that declaration, which had been sent to them, earnestly inviting, and in a manner challenging assistance from that his native kingdom of men and arms, for making a war against him, and making claim to that assistance by virtue of the late act of pacification.

He told them, " that, as he was at his soul afflicted, that it had been in the power of any factious, ambitious, and malicious persons, so far to possess the hearts of many of his

subjects of England, as to raise this miserable distemper
and distraction in this kingdom against all his real endeavours
and actions to the contrary; so he was glad, that that rage
and fury had so far transported them, that they applied
themselves, in so gross a manner, to his subjects of Scotland; whose experience of his religion, justice, and love of
his people, would not suffer them to believe those horrid
scandals, laid upon his majesty: and their affection, loyalty,
and jealousy of his honour, would disdain to be made instruments to oppress their native sovereign, by assisting an
odious rebellion." He remembered them, "that he had
from time to time acquainted his subjects of that kingdom
with the accidents and circumstances which had disquieted
this; how, after all the acts of justice, grace, and favour,
performed on his part, which were or could be desired to
make a people completely happy, he was driven, by the
force and violence of rude and tumultuous assemblies, from
his city of London, and his houses of parliament; how attempts had been made to impose laws upon his subjects,
without his consent, and contrary to the foundation and constitution of the kingdom; how his forts, goods, and navy,
had been seized, and taken from him by force, and employed
against him; his revenue, and ordinary subsistence, wrested
from him: how he had been pursued with scandalous and
reproachful language; bold, false, and seditious pasquils, and
libels, publicly allowed against him; and had been told that
he might, without want of modesty and duty, be deposed:
that after all this, before any force raised by him, an army
was raised, and a general appointed to lead that army against
his majesty, with a commission to kill, slay, and destroy all
such who should be faithful to him: that when he had been,
by these means, compelled, with the assistance of his good
subjects, to raise an army for his necessary defence, he had
sent divers gracious messages, earnestly desiring that the
calamities and miseries of a civil war might be prevented by
a treaty; and so he might know the grounds of that misunderstanding: that he was absolutely refused to be treated
with, and the army, (raised, as was pretended, for the defence of his person,) brought into the field against him, gave

him battle ; and, though it pleased God to give his majesty the victory, destroyed many of his good subjects, with as eminent danger to his own person, and his children, as the skill and malice of desperate rebels could contrive.

" Of all which, and the other indignities, which had been offered to him, he doubted not the duty and affection of his Scottish subjects would have so just a resentment, that they would express to the world the sense they had of his sufferings : and he hoped, his good subjects of Scotland were not so great strangers to the affairs of this kingdom, to believe that this misfortune and distraction was begot and brought upon him by his two houses of parliament ; though, in truth, no unwarrantable action against the law could be justified even by that authority; but that they well knew how the members of both houses had been driven thence, insomuch that, of above five hundred members of the house of commons, there were not then there above fourscore; and, of above one hundred of the house of peers, not above fifteen or sixteen ; all which were so awed by a multitude of anabaptists, Brownists, and other persons, desperate, and decayed in their fortunes, in and about the city of London, that, in truth, their consultations had not the freedom and privilege which belong to parliament.

" Concerning any commissions granted by his majesty to papists to raise forces, he referred them to a declaration, lately set forth by him upon the occasion of that scandal, which he likewise then sent them. And for his own true and zealous affection to the protestant religion, he would give no other instance than his own constant practice, on which malice itself could lay no blemish ; and those many protestations he had made in the sight of Almighty God, to whom he knew he should be dearly accountable, if he failed in the observation.

" For that scandalous imputation of his intention of bringing in foreign force, as the same was raised without the least shadow or colour of reason, and solemnly disavowed by his majesty, in many of his declarations ; so there could not be a clearer argument to his subjects of Scotland that he had no such thought, than that he had hitherto forborne to re-

quire the assistance of that his native kingdom ; from whose
obedience, duty, and affection, he should confidently expect
it, if he thought his own strength here too weak to preserve
him ; and of whose courage and loyalty he should look to
make use, before he should think of any foreign aid to succour him.   And he knew no reasonable or understanding
man could suppose that they were obliged, or enabled, by
the late act of parliament in both kingdoms, to obey the invitation that was made to them by that declaration, when it
was so evidently provided for by that act, that as the kingdom of England should not war against the kingdom of Scotland, without consent of the parliament of England, so the
kingdom of Scotland should not make war against the kingdom of England without the consent of the parliament of
Scotland."

He told them, " if the grave counsel and advice, which
they had given, and derived to the houses of parliament
here, by their act of the 22d of April last, had been followed in a tender care of his royal person, and of his princely
greatness and authority, there would not that face of confusion have appeared, which now threatened this kingdom :
and therefore he required them to communicate what he
then writ to all his subjects of that kingdom, and to use
their utmost endeavours to inform them of the truth of his
condition ; and that they suffered not the scandals and imputations laid on his majesty by the malice and treason of
some men, to make any impression in the minds of his people, to the lessening or corrupting their affections and loyalty
to him ; but that they assured them all, that the hardness he
then underwent, and the arms he had been compelled to
take up, were for the defence of his person and safety of his
life ; for the maintenance of the true protestant religion, for
the preservation of the laws, liberties, and constitution of
the kingdom, and for the just privileges of parliament ; and
that he looked no longer for a blessing from heaven, than he
endeavoured the defence and advancement of all these : and,
he could not doubt, a dutiful concurrence in his subjects of
Scotland, in the care of his honour, and just rights, would
draw down a blessing upon that nation too."

Though his majesty well knew all the persons, to whom he directed this letter, to be those who were only able and willing to do him all possible disservice, yet he was sure by other instruments, if they neglected, which, for that reason, they were not like to do, to publish it to the people there ; which he believed might so far operate upon them, as the others would not be able to procure them to invade England ; and other fruit of their allegiance he expected not, than that they should not rebel.

His majesty's next care was the procuring money for the payment of his army ; that the narrow circuit which contained his quarters might not be so intolerably oppressed with that whole burden. And this was a very difficult matter ; for the soldiery already grew very high, and would obey no orders or rules but of their own making ; and prince Rupert considered only the subsistence, and advance of the horse, as his province, and indeed as if it had been a province apart from the army ; and therefore would by no means endure that the great contributions, which the counties within command willingly submitted to, should be assigned to any other use than the support of the horse, and to be immediately collected, and received by the officers. So that the several garrisons, and all the body of foot, were to be constantly paid, and his majesty's weekly expense for his house borne, out of such money as could be borrowed. For, of all his own revenue, he had not yet the receiving a penny within his power ; neither did he think fit to compel any one, even such who were known to have contributed freely to the parliament, to supply him : only by letters, and all other gentle ways, he invited those who were able, to consider how much their own security and prosperity was concerned, and depended upon the preservation of his rights ; and offered to sell any of his lands, or to give any personal security for whatsoever money would be lent to him at interest : for he had directed a grant to be prepared of several parks, and forests, and other crown-lands, to many persons of honour and great fortune about him, whose estates and reputation were well known ; who were ready to be personally bound for whatsoever sums could be borrowed.

The affection of the university of Oxford was most eminent : for, as they had before, when the troubles first broke out, sent the king above ten thousand pounds out of the several stocks of the colleges, and the purses of particular persons, many whereof lent him all they had ; so now they presented to him all the plate belonging to all their corporations, which being coined, (for a mint was shortly erected there) amounted to about ten thousand pounds. By these means, and the loan of particular persons, especially from London, (for from thence, notwithstanding all the strict watch to the contrary, considerable sums were drawn,) the king, even above his hopes, was able to pay his foot, albeit it amounted to above three thousand pounds weekly, in such manner, that during that whole winter there was not the least disorder for want of pay. Then he used all possible care to encourage and countenance new levies of horse and foot, for the recruiting his army against the next spring.

The army being now about London, the members of it who were members of parliament attended that council diligently, upon which the army alone depended ; and, though they still seemed very desirous of peace, they very solemnly and severely prosecuted all those who really endeavoured it. Their partiality and injustice was so notorious, that there was no rule or measure of right in any matter depending before them, but consideration only of the affections and opinions of the persons contending ; neither could any thing be more properly said of them, than what Tacitus once spoke of the Jews, *apud ipsos fides obstinata, misericordia in promptu, adversus omnes alios hostile odium.* Volumes would not contain the instances. But they found the old arguments of popery, the militia, and delinquents, for the justification of the war, grew every day of less reverence with the people ; and that as the king's own religion was above any scandal they could lay upon it, so the regal power seemed so asserted by law, and the king, on all occasions, cited particular statutes for the vindication of his right, that whilst they confessed the sovereign power to be vested in him, all legal ministers had that dependence on him, that their authority would by degrees grow into contempt.

ffection of the university of Oxford was most emi-
, as they had before, when the troubles first broke
the king above ten thousand pounds out of the se-
cks of the colleges, and the purses of particular per-
y whereof lent him all they had; so now they pre-
him all the plate belonging to all their corporations,
ing coined, (for a mint was shortly erected there)
to about ten thousand pounds. By these means,
oan of particular persons, especially from London,
thence, notwithstanding all the strict watch to the
considerable sums were drawn,) the king, even
hopes, was able to pay his foot, albeit it amounted
three thousand pounds weekly, in such manner, that
at whole winter there was not the least disorder for
pay. Then he used all possible care to encourage
tenance new levies of horse and foot, for the recruit-
rmy against the next spring.

army being now about London, the members of it
e members of parliament attended that council dili-
pon which the army alone depended; and, though
seemed very desirous of peace, they very solemnly
erely prosecuted all those who really endeavoured it.
artiality and injustice was so notorious, that there was
or measure of right in any matter depending before
ut consideration only of the affections and opinions of
sons contending; neither could any thing be more
said of them, than what Tacitus once spoke of the
ud ipsos fides obstinata, misericordia in promptu, ad-
mnes alios hostile odium. Volumes would not con-
instances. But they found the old arguments of
the militia, and delinquents, for the justification of
, grew every day of less reverence with the people;
t as the king's own religion was above any scandal
uld lay upon it, so the regal power seemed so assert-
law, and the king, on all occasions, cited particular
for the vindication of his right, that whilst they con-
the sovereign power to be vested in him, all legal mi-
had that dependence on him, that their authority would
rees grow into contempt.

him battle; and, though it pleased God to give his majesty
the victory, destroyed many of his good subjects, with as
eminent danger to his own person, and his children, as the
skill and malice of desperate rebels could contrive.

" Of all which, and the other indignities, which had been
offered to him, he doubted not the duty and affection of his
Scottish subjects would have so just a resentment, that they
would express to the world the sense they had of his sufferings: and he hoped, his good subjects of Scotland were not
so great strangers to the affairs of this kingdom, to believe
that this misfortune and distraction was begot and brought
upon him by his two houses of parliament; though, in truth,
no unwarrantable action against the law could be justified
even by that authority; but that they well knew how the
members of both houses had been driven thence, insomuch
that, of above five hundred members of the house of commons, there were not then there above fourscore; and, of
above one hundred of the house of peers, not above fifteen
or sixteen; all which were so awed by a multitude of anabaptists, Brownists, and other persons, desperate, and decayed in their fortunes, in and about the city of London,
that, in truth, their consultations had not the freedom and
privilege which belong to parliament.

" Concerning any commissions granted by his majesty to
papists to raise forces, he referred them to a declaration,
lately set forth by him upon the occasion of that scandal,
which he likewise then sent them. And for his own true
and zealous affection to the protestant religion, he would
give no other instance than his own constant practice, on
which malice itself could lay no blemish; and those many
protestations he had made in the sight of Almighty God, to
whom he knew he should be dearly accountable, if he failed
in the observation.

" For that scandalous imputation of his intention of bringing in foreign force, as the same was raised without the least
shadow or colour of reason, and solemnly disavowed by his
majesty, in many of his declarations; so there could not be
a clearer argument to his subjects of Scotland that he had
no such thought, than that he had hitherto forborne to re-

quire the assistance of that his native kingdom ; from whose obedience, duty, and affection, he should confidently expect it, if he thought his own strength here too weak to preserve him ; and of whose courage and loyalty he should look to make use, before he should think of any foreign aid to succour him. And he knew no reasonable or understanding man could suppose that they were obliged, or enabled, by the late act of parliament in both kingdoms, to obey the invitation that was made to them by that declaration, when it was so evidently provided for by that act, that as the kingdom of England should not war against the kingdom of Scotland, without consent of the parliament of England, so the kingdom of Scotland should not make war against the kingdom of England without the consent of the parliament of Scotland."

He told them, " if the grave counsel and advice, which they had given, and derived to the houses of parliament here, by their act of the 22d of April last, had been followed in a tender care of his royal person, and of his princely greatness and authority, there would not that face of confusion have appeared, which now threatened this kingdom : and therefore he required them to communicate what he then writ to all his subjects of that kingdom, and to use their utmost endeavours to inform them of the truth of his condition ; and that they suffered not the scandals and imputations laid on his majesty by the malice and treason of some men, to make any impression in the minds of his people, to the lessening or corrupting their affections and loyalty to him ; but that they assured them all, that the hardness he then underwent, and the arms he had been compelled to take up, were for the defence of his person and safety of his life ; for the maintenance of the true protestant religion, for the preservation of the laws, liberties, and constitution of the kingdom, and for the just privileges of parliament ; and that he looked no longer for a blessing from heaven, than he endeavoured the defence and advancement of all these : and, he could not doubt, a dutiful concurrence in his subjects of Scotland, in the care of his honour, and just rights, would draw down a blessing upon that nation too."

Though his majesty v
he directed this letter, to
willing to do him all possi
other instruments, if they
they were not like to do,
which he believed might
others would not be able to
and other fruit of their alle
they should not rebel.

His majesty's next care
payment of his army ; tha
tained his quarters might nc
that whole burden. And
for the soldiery already gre
orders or rules but of their
considered only the subsiste
as his province, and indeed
from the army ; and therefor
the great contributions, whic
willingly submitted to, shoul
than the support of the horse
ed, and received by the offic
sons, and all the body of foo
and his majesty's weekly exp
such money as could be borrc
venue, he had not yet the rece
neither did he think fit to co
were known to have contribut
supply him : only by letters,
invited those who were able,
own security and prosperity
upon the preservation of his ri
of his lands, or to give any per
money would be lent to him at
a grant to be prepared of sev
other crown-lands, to many per
tune about him, whose estate
known ; who were ready to be
soever sums could be borrowed.

The a
nent : fo
out, sent
veral sto
sons, ma
sented to
which b
amountec
and the
(for fron
contrary
above hi
to above
during th
want of
and cour
ing his
The
who we
gently,
they stil
and sev
Their p
no rule
them, b
the per
properl
Jews, a
versus
tain th
popery
the wa
and tha
they cc
ed by
statute
fessed
nisters
by deg

And of this disadvantage the season of the year put them in mind : for the king now, according to course, pricked sheriffs, and made such choice in all counties, that they foresaw the people were not like to be so implicitly at their disposal. Therefore, as they had before craftily insinuated the same in some particulars, they now barefaced avow, " that the sovereign power was wholly and entirely in them ; and that the king himself, severed from them, had no regal power in him." Their clergy had hitherto been their champions, and wrested the scripture to their sense ; their lawyers were now to vindicate their title, and they were not more modest in applying their profession to their service.   As all places of scripture, or in the fathers, which were spoken of the church of Christ, are by the papists applied to the church of Rome ; so whatsoever is written in any of the books of the law, or mentioned in the records, of the authority and effects of the sovereign power, and of the dignity and jurisdiction of parliament, was, by these men, alleged and urged for the power of the two houses, and sometimes for the single authority of the house of commons.   Being supplied with the learning of these gentlemen, they declared, that " the sheriffs, then constituted by the king, were not legal sheriffs, nor ought to execute, or be submitted to in that office ;" and ordered, whomsoever the king made sheriff in any county, to be sent for as a delinquent :" and because it seemed unreasonable, that the counties should be without that legal minister, to whom the law had intrusted its custody, it was proposed, " that they might make a new great seal, and by that authority make sheriffs, and such other officers as they should find necessary ;" but for the present that motion was laid aside.

The king had appointed some of those prisoners who were taken in the battle of Keinton-field, and others apprehended in the act of rebellion, to be indicted of high treason, upon the statute of the 25th year of king Edward the Third, before the lord chief justice, and other learned judges of the law, by virtue of his majesty's commission of oyer and terminer : they declared " all such indictments, and all proceedings thereupon, to be unjust and illegal ;" and inhibited the judges to proceed farther therein ; declaring, (which was

a stronger argument,) that if any man were executed, or
suffered hurt, for any thing he had done by their order, the
like punishment should be inflicted, by death or otherwise,
upon such prisoners as were, or should be, taken by their
forces :" and in none of these cases ever asked the judges
what the law was. By the determination of the statute, and
the king's refusal, which hath been mentioned before, to pass
any new law to that purpose, there was no farther duty of
tonnage and poundage due upon merchandise, and the statute
made this very parliament involved all men in the guilt and
penalty of a præmunire, who offered to receive it. The king
published a proclamation upon that statute, " and required all
men to forbear paying that duty, and forbid all to receive it."
They again declared, " that no person, who received those
duties by virtue of their orders, was within the danger of a
præmunire, or any other penalty whatsoever ; because the
intent and meaning of that penal clause was only to restrain
the crown from imposing any duty or payment upon the subjects, without their consent in parliament ; and was not intended to extend to any case whereunto the lords and commons give their assent in parliament."

And that this sovereignty might be farther taken notice of
than within the limits of this kingdom, they sent, with all
formality, letters of credence, and instructions, and their
agents, into foreign states and kingdoms.

By their agent to the United Provinces, where the queen
was then residing, they had the courage, in plain terms, to
accuse the prince of Orange " for supplying the king with
arms and ammunition ; for licensing divers commanders, officers, and soldiers, to resort into this kingdom to his aid."
They remembered them " of the great help that they had received from this kingdom, when heretofore they lay under the
heavy oppression of their princes; and how conducible the
friendship of this nation had been to their present greatness
and power ; and therefore they could not think, that they
would be forward to help to make them slaves, who had
been so useful, and assistant in making them free men ; or
that they would forget, that their troubles and dangers issued
from the same fountain with their own ; and that those who

were set awork to undermine religion and liberty in the kingdom, were the same who by open force did seek to bereave
them of both." They told them, " it could not be unknown
to that wise state, that it was the jesuitical faction in this kingdom, that had corrupted the counsels of the king, the consciences of a great part of the clergy ; which sought to destroy the parliament, and had raised the rebellion in Ireland."
They desired them therefore, " not to suffer any more ordnance, armour, or any other warlike provision, to be brought
over to strengthen those, who, as soon as they should prevail
against the parliament, would use that strength to the ruin of
those from whom they had it."

They desired them, " they would not send over any of
their countrymen to further their destruction, who were sent
to them for their preservation ; that they would not antici-
pate the spilling of English blood, in an unnatural civil war,
which had been so cheerfully and plentifully hazarded, and
spent, in that just and honourable war by which they had
been so long preserved, and to which the blood of those persons, and many other subjects of this kingdom, was still in
a manner dedicated ; but rather that they would cashier, and
discard from their employment, those that would presume to
come over for that purpose." They told them, " the question between his majesty and the parliament was not whether
he should enjoy the same prerogative and power, which had
belonged to their former kings, his majesty's royal predecessors ; but whether that prerogative and power should be employed to their defence, or to their ruin ; that it could not
be denied by those, who look indifferently on their proceedings and affairs, that it would be more honour and wealth,
safety and greatness to his majesty, in concurring with his
parliament, than in the course in which he now is : but so
unhappy had his majesty and the kingdom been, in those
who had the greatest influence upon his counsels, that they
looked more upon the prevailing of their own party, than
upon any those great advantages, both to his crown and
royal person, which he might obtain by joining with his people : and so cunning were those factors for popery, in prosecution of their own aims, that they could put on a counter-

feit visage of honour, peace, and greatness, upon those courses and counsels, which had no truth and reality, but of weakness, dishonour, and miseries to his majesty, and the whole
kingdom."

They said, " they had lately expressed their earnest inclinations to that national love and amity with the united
provinces, which had been nourished and confirmed by so
many civil respects, and mutual interests, as made it so natural to them, that they had, this parliament, in their humble
petition, desired, that they might be joined with that state in
a more near and strait league and union : and they could
not but expect some returns from them, of the like expressions ; and that they would be far from blowing the fire,
which began to kindle among them, that they would rather
endeavour to quench it, by strengthening and encouraging
them who had no other design but not to be destroyed, and
to preserve their religion, save themselves, and the other
reformed churches of Christendom, from the massacres and
extirpations, with which the principles of the Roman religion
did threaten them all ; which were begun to be acted in Ireland, and in the hopes, and endeavours, and intentions of that
party had long since been executed upon them, if the mercy,
favour, and blessing of Almighty God had not superabound-
ed, and prevented the subtilty and malignity of cruel, wicked, and bloodthirsty men."

With this specious despatch, in which were many other
particulars to render the king's cause ungracious, and their
own very plausible, their agent, one Strickland, an obscure
gentleman, was received by the States ; and, notwithstanding the queen was then there, and the prince of Orange visibly inclined to assist the king with all his interests, and the
interposition of the king's resident, did not only hinder the
States from giving the least countenance to the king's cause,
but really so corrupted the English in the army, and in the
court, that there was nothing designed to advance it by the
prince of Orange himself, (who with great generosity supplied the king with arms and ammunition to a very considerable value,) or by the private activity and dexterity of particular persons, out of their own fortune, or by the sale or

pawning of jewels, but intelligence was given soon enough to the parliament, either to get stops, and seizures upon it, by order of the state, or to intercept the supply by their navy at sea. So that much more was in that manner, and by that means, taken and intercepted at sea, than ever arrived at any port within his majesty's obedience : of which at that time he had only one, the harbour of Newcastle. With the same success they sent another agent to Brussels, who prevailed with don Francisco de Melos, then governor of Flanders, to discountenance always, and sometimes to prevent, the preparations which were there making by the king's ministers. And in France they had another agent, one Aulgier, a man long before in the constant pay of the crown ; who, though he was not received, and avowed, (to put the better varnish upon their professions to the king,) by that crown, did them more service than either of the other; by how much more that people had an influence upon the distempers of the three kingdoms.

And as the parliament made all these addresses to foreign states and princes, which no parliament had ever done before, so it will be fit here to take notice how other princes appeared concerned on the king's behalf. The Spaniard was sufficiently incensed by the king's reception of the ambassadors of Portugal, and, which was more, entering into terms of amity and league with that crown, and had therefore contributed notable assistance to the rebellion in Ireland, and sent both arms and money thither. And since the extravagances of this parliament, the ambassador of that king had made great application to them.

The French, according to their nature, were much more active, and more intent upon blowing the fire. The former commotions in Scotland had been raised by the special encouragement, if not contrivance, of the cardinal Richelieu ; who had carefully kept up and enlarged the old franchises of the Scots under that crown ; which made a very specious show of wonderful grace and benefit, at a distance, to that nation, and was of little burden to the French ; and, in truth, of little advantage to those who were in full possession of all those relations. Yet, by this means, the French have

always had a very great influence upon the affections of that
people, and opportunities to work great prejudice to that
crown : as nothing more was visible than that, by that cardinal's activity, all those late distempers in Scotland were
carried on till his death, and, by his rules and principles, afterwards : the French ministers always making their correspondence with, and relation to those who were taken notice
to be of the puritan party; which was understood to be in
order only to the opposition of those counsels, which should
at any time be offered on the behalf of Spain.

Since the beginning of this parliament, the French ambassador, monsieur la Ferté, dissembled not to have notable
familiarity with those who governed most in the two houses;
discovered to them whatsoever he knew, or could reasonably
devise to the prejudice of the king's counsels and resolutions ;
and took all opportunities to lessen and undervalue the king's
regal power, by applying himself on public occasions of state,
and in his master's name, and to improve his interest, to the
two houses of parliament, (which had in no age before been
ever known,) as in the business of transportation of men out
of Ireland, before remembered ; in which he caused, by the
importunity of the two houses, his majesty's promise and engagement to the Spanish ambassador to be rendered of no effect.   And, after that, he formally exhibited, in writing, a
complaint to the two houses against sir Thomas Rowe, his
majesty's extraordinary ambassador to the emperor, and princes of Germany, upon the treaty of an accommodation on the
behalf of the prince elector and restitution of the palatinate,
confidently avowing, " that sir Thomas Rowe had offered, on
the king's part, to enter into a league offensive and defensive
with the house of Austria, and to wed all their interests ;"
and, in plain terms, asked them, " whether they had given
him instructions to that purpose ?" expressing a great value
his master had of the affection of the parliament of England ;
which drew them to a return of much and unusual civility,
and to assure the French king, " that sir Thomas Rowe had
no such instructions from them ; and that they would examine
the truth of it ; and would be careful that nothing should be
done and perfected in that treaty, which might reflect upon

the good of the French king." Whereas in truth there was not the least ground or pretence for that suggestion ; sir Thomas Rowe having never made any such offer, or any thing like it. And when, after his return out of Germany, he expostulated with the French ambassador, for such an injurious, causeless information, he answered, "that since his master had received such advertisement, and had given him order to do what he did." So that it easily appeared, it was only a fiction of state, whereby they took occasion to publish, that they would on any occasion resort to the two houses, and thereby to flatter them in their usurpation of any sovereign authority.

There is not a sadder consideration (and I pray God the almighty justice be not angry with, and weary of the government of kings and princes, for it is a strange declension monarchical government is fallen to, in the opinion of the common people within these late years) than this passion and injustice, in Christian princes, that they are not so solicitous that the laws be executed, justice administered, and order preserved within their own kingdoms, as they are that all three may be disturbed and confounded amongst their neighbours. And therefore there is no sooner a spark of dissension, a discomposure in affections, a jealousy in understandings, discerned to be in or to be easy to be infused into a neighbour province, or kingdom, to the hazarding of the peace thereof, but they, though in league and amity, with their utmost art and industry, make it their business to kindle that spark into a flame, and to contract and ripen all unsettled humours, and jealous apprehensions, into a peremptory discontent, and all discontent to sedition, and all sedition to open and professed rebellion. And have never so ample satisfaction in their own greatness, or so great a sense and value of God's blessing upon them, as when they have been instruments of drawing some notorious calamity upon their neighbours. As if the religion of princes were nothing but policy, enough to make all other kingdoms but their own miserable : and that because God hath reserved them to be tried only within his own jurisdiction, and before his own tribunal, that he means to try them too by other laws, and rules, than

he hath published to the world for his servants to walk by.
Whereas they ought to consider, that God hath placed them
over his people as examples, and to give countenance to his
laws by their own strict observation of them; and that as
their subjects are to be defended and protected by them, so
themselves are to be assisted and supported by one another;
the function of kings being a classis by itself: and as a contempt and breach of every law is, in the policy of states, an
offence against the person of the king, because there is a kind
of violence offered to his person in the transgression of that
rule without which he cannot govern; so the rebellion of
subjects against their prince ought to be looked upon, by all
other kings, as an assault of their own sovereignty, and a
design against monarchy itself; and consequently to be suppressed, and extirpated, in what other kingdom soever it
is, with the same concernment as if it were in their own
bowels.

Besides these indirect artifices, and activity in the French
ambassador, the Hugonots in France from whom this crown
heretofore received wonderful advantages were declared enemies to the king; and, in public and in secret, gave all possible assistance to those whose business was to destroy the
church. And as this animosity proved of unspeakable inconvenience and damage to the king, throughout all these
troubles, and of equal benefit to his enemies; so the occasion, from whence those disaffections grew, was very unskilfully and imprudently administered by the state here.
Not to speak of the business of Rochelle, which, though it
stuck deep in all, yet most imputed the counsels of that
time to men that were dead, and not to a fixed design of the
court; but they had a greater quarrel, which made them believe, that their very religion was persecuted by the church
of England.

When the reformation of religion first began in England,
in the time of king Edward the Sixth, very many, out of
Germany and France, left their countries, where the reformation was severely persecuted, and transplanted themselves, their families, and estates, into England, where they
were received very hospitably; and that king, with great

piety and policy, by several acts of state, granted them many indemnities,[1] and the free use of churches in London for
the exercise of their religion: whereby the number of them
increased ; and the benefit to the kingdom, by such an access of trade, and improvement of manufactures, was very
considerable.   The which queen Elizabeth finding, and well
knowing that other notable uses of them might be made, enlarged their privileges by new concessions; drawing, by all
means, greater numbers over, and suffering them to erect
churches, and to enjoy the exercise of their religion after
their own manner, and according to their own ceremonies,
in all places, where, for the conveniency of their trade, they
chose to reside.   And so they had churches in Norwich,
Canterbury, and other places of the kingdom, as well as in
London; whereby the wealth of those places marvellously
increased: And, besides the benefit from thence, the queen
made use of them in her great transactions of state in France,
and the Low Countries, and, by the mediation and interposition of those people, kept an useful interest in that party,
in all the foreign dominions where they were tolerated.
The same charters of liberty were continued and granted to
them, during the peaceable reign of king James, and in the
beginning of this king's reign, although, it may be, the politic considerations in those concessions, and connivances,
were neither made use of, nor understood.[2]

Some few years before these troubles, when the power
of churchmen grew more transcendent, and indeed the faculties and understandings of the lay-counsellors more dull,
lazy, and unactive, (for, without the last, the first could
have done no hurt,)[3] the bishops grew jealous 'that the
countenancing another discipline of the church here, by order of the state, (for those foreign congregations were govern-

[1] Immunities.—W.

[2] The historian could never have made this observation without
having a very poor opinion of Charles's ministers of state, whether
ecclesiastical or lay.—W.

[3] This is a true observation, which might be carried through all the
ages of the church.—W.

ed by a presbytery, according to the custom and constitution of those parts of which they had been natives : for the French, Dutch, and Walloons had the free use of several churches according to their own discipline,) would at least diminish the reputation and dignity of the episcopal government, and give some hope and countenance to the factious and schismatical party in England to hope for such a toleration.

Then there wanted not some fiery, turbulent, and contentious persons of the same congregations, who, upon private differences and contests, were ready to inform against their brethren, and to discover what, they thought, might prove of most prejudice to them ; so that, upon pretence that they far exceeded the liberties which were granted to them, and that, under the notion of foreigners, many English separated themselves from the church, and joined themselves to those congregations, (which possibly was in part true,) the council-board connived, or interposed not, that the bishops did some acts of restraint, with which that tribe grew generally discontented, and thought the liberty of their consciences to be taken from them ; and so in London there was much complaining of this kind, but much more in the diocese of Norwich ; where Dr. Wren, the bishop there, passionately and furiously proceeded against them : so that many left the kingdom, to the lessening the wealthy manufacture there of kerseys, and narrow cloths, and, which was worse, transporting that mystery into foreign parts.

And, that this might be sure to look like more than what was necessary to the civil policy of the kingdom,[1] whereas, in all former times, the ambassadors, and all foreign ministers of state, employed from England into any parts where the reformed religion was exercised, frequented their churches, gave all possible countenance to their profession, and held correspondence with the most active and powerful persons of that relation, and particularly the ambassador lieger

[1] He means, that the world might see that this new policy was for the sake of the church, not the state ; the English ambassador at Paris broke communion with them.—W.

at Paris from the time of the reformation had diligently and
constantly frequented the church at Charenton, and held a
fair intercourse with those of that religion throughout the
kingdom, by which they had still received advantage, that
people being industrious and active to get into the secrets
of the state, and so deriving all necessary intelligence to
those whom they desired to gratify: the contrary whereof
was now with great industry practised, and some advertisements, if not instructions, given to the ambassadors there,
" to forbear any extraordinary commerce with that tribe."
And the lord Scudamore, who was the last ordinary ambassador there, before the beginning of this parliament, whether
by the inclination of his own nature, or by advice from
others, not only declined going to Charenton, but furnished
his own chapel, in his house, with such ornaments, (as
candles upon the communion-table, and the like,) as gave
great offence and umbrage to those of the reformation, who
had not seen the like : besides that he was careful to publish, upon all occasions, by himself, and those who had the
nearest relation to him, " that the church of England looked
not on the Hugonots as a part of their communion ;" which
was likewise too much and too industriously discoursed at
home.

They who committed the greatest errors this way, had,
no doubt, the least thoughts of making any alterations in the
church of England, as hath been uncharitably conceived :
but (having too just cause given them to dislike the passion,[1]
and licence, that was taken by some persons in the reformed
churches, under the notion of conscience and religion, to the
disturbance of the peace of kingdoms) unskilfully believed,
that the total declining the interest of that party,[2] where it
exceeded the necessary bounds of reformation, would make
this church of England looked upon with more reverence ;
and that thereby the common adversary, the papist, would
abate somewhat of his arrogance and superciliousness ; and

[1] The doctrine of resistance.—W.

[2] i. e. persecuting them.—W.

75*

so all parties,[1] piously considering the charity which religion
should beget, might, if not unite, yet refrain from the bitterness[2] and uncharitableness of contention in matters of opinion,
severed from the practical duties of Christians and subjects.
And so, contracting their considerations in too narrow a compass, contented themselves with their pious intentions, without duly weighing objections, or the circumstances of policy.
And they who differed with them in opinion in this point,
though they were in the right, not giving, and, it may be,
not knowing the right reasons, rather confirmed than reformed them in their inclinations : neither of them discerning the
true and substantial grounds of policy,[3] upon which those
conclusions had been founded, which they were now about
to change: it were therefore to be wished, that in all great
acts of state some memorials should be kept, and always reserved in the archives of the crown, of the true motives and
grounds of such acts, (which are seldom the same that appear
publicly;) whereby posterity may duly discern, before any
alteration or revocation, the policy thereof, and so take heed
that that may not be looked upon as indifferent, which, rightly understood, is of a substantial consideration.   This was
the state of the king's affairs at home and abroad, when his
standard was erected at Nottingham.

After all discourses and motions for peace were, for a
time, laid aside ; and new thoughts of victory, and utterly
subduing the king's party, again entertained ; they found
one trouble falling upon them, which they had least suspected, want of money; all their vast sums collected, upon any
former bills, passed by the king for the relief of Ireland, and
payment of the debt to the Scots, and all their money upon
subscriptions of plate, and loans upon the public faith, which
amounted to incredible proportions, were even quite wasted ;
and their constant expense was so great, that no ordinary

---

[1] Papists and church of England.—W.

[2] In other words, a comprehension between popery and the church
of England.—W.

[3] All this while the true religious policy of toleration (on which
doubtless the first reformers went) is forgot.—W.

supply would serve their turn ; and they easily discerned, that their money only, and not their cause, procured them soldiers of all kinds ; and that they could never support their power, if their power was not able to supply them. All voluntary loans were at an end, and the public faith thought a security not to be relied on, by how much greater the difficulty was, by so much the more fatal would the sinking under it prove; and therefore it was with the more vigour to be resisted. In the end, they resolved upon the full execution of their full sovereign power, and to let the people see what they might trust to; in which it is necessary to observe the arts and degrees of their motion.

They first ordered, "that committees should be named in all counties, to take care for provisions of victuals for the army, and also for the taking up of horses for service in the field, dragooners and draught horses, and for borrowing of money and plate to supply the army : and upon certificate from these committees," (who had power to set what value or rates they pleased upon these provisions of any kind,) "the same should be entered with their treasurer, who should hereafter repay the same." It was then alleged, "that this would only draw supplies from their friends, and the well affected ; and that others, who either liked not their proceedings, or loved their money better than the liberty of their country, would not contribute." Upon this it was ordered, "that in case the owners refused to bring in money, provisions, plate, and horse, upon the public faith, for the use of the army; for the better preventing the spoil, and embezzling of such provisions of money, plate, and horses, by the disorder of the soldiers, and that they may not come into the hands of the enemies, that the committees, or any two of them, should be authorized, and enabled to send for such provisions, money, plate, and horses; and to take the same into their custody, and to set indifferent value and rate upon them ; which value they should certify to the treasurers, for the proportions to be repaid at such time, and in such manner, as should be ordered by both houses of parliament."

This was done only to shew what they meant to do over

all England, and as a stock of credit to them.   For at present
it would neither supply their wants ; neither was it seasonable for them, or indeed possible to endeavour the execution
of it in many counties.   London was the place from whence
only their present help must come.   To them therefore they
declared, " that the king's army had made divers assess-
ments upon several counties, and the subjects were compelled, by the soldiers, to pay the same ; which army, if it continued, would soon ruin and waste the whole kingdom ; and
overthrow religion, law, and liberty : that there was no probable way, under God, for the suppressing that army, and
other ill affected persons, but by the army raised by the authority of the parliament ; which army could not be maintained, without great sums of money ; and for raising such
sums, there could be no act of parliament passed with his
majesty's assent, albeit there was great justice that such
money should be raised : that, hitherto, the army had been,
for the most part, maintained by the voluntary contributions
of well affected people, who had freely contributed according
to their abilities : that there were divers others within the
cities of London and Westminster, and the suburbs, that had
not contributed at all towards the maintenance of that army,
or if they had, yet not answerable to their estates ; who
notwithstanding received benefit and protection by the same
army, as well as any others; and therefore it was most just,
that they should, as well as others, be charged to contribute
to the maintenance thereof."

Upon these grounds and reasons, it was ordained, " by the
authority of parliament, that Isaac Pennington, the then lord
mayor of London, and some other aldermen, and citizens, or
any four of them, should have power and authority to nominate, and appoint, in every ward, within the city of London,
six such persons as they should think fit, who should have
power to inquire of all who had not contributed upon the
propositions concerning the raising of money, plate, &c. and
of such able men who had contributed, yet not according to
their estates and abilities ; and those persons so substituted,
or any four of them, within their several wards and limits,
should have power to assess all persons of ability who had

not contributed, and also those who had contributed, yet not according to their ability, to pay such sums of money, according to their estates, as the assessors, or any four of them, should think reasonable, so as the same exceeded not the twentieth part of their estates; and to nominate fit persons for the collection thereof. And if any person so assessed should refuse to pay the money so assessed upon him, it should be lawful for the assessors and collectors to levy that sum by way of distress, and sale of the goods of persons so refusing. And if any person distrained should make resistance, it should be lawful for the assessors and collectors to call to their assistance any of the trained bands of London, or any other his majesty's subjects; who were required to be aiding and assisting to them. And the burgesses of Westminster and Southwark, and a committee appointed to that purpose, were to do the same within those limits, as the other in London."

And that there might be no stratagem to avoid this tax, (so strange and unlooked for,) by a second ordinance in explanation of the former, they ordained, " that, if no sufficient distress could be found for the payment of what should be assessed, the collectors should have power to inquire of any sum of money due to those persons so assessed, from what persons soever, for rents, goods, or debts, or for any other thing or cause whatsoever. And the collectors had power to receive all such debts, until the full value of the sums so assessed, and the charges in levying or recovering the same, should be satisfied : and lest the discovery of those debts might be difficult, the same collectors had power to compound for any rents, goods, or debts, due to such persons so assessed, with any person by whom the same was due, and to give full discharges for the money so compounded for, which should be good and effectual to all purposes. And if the money assessed could not be levied by any of these ways, then the persons assessed should be imprisoned in such places of the kingdom, and for so long time, as the committee of the house of commons for examinations should appoint, and order ; and the families of all such persons so imprisoned should no longer remain within the cities of London or West-

minster, the suburbs, or the counties adjacent. And all
assessors and collectors should have the protection of both
houses of parliament, for their indemnity in that service, and
receive allowance for their pains and charges." Several ad-
ditional and explanatory orders they made for the better
execution of this grand one, by every of which some clause
of severity, and monstrous irregularity, was added; and, for
the complement of all, they ordered that themselves, the
members of either house, should not be assessed by any body.

The truth is, the king was not sorry to see this ordinance,
which he thought so prodigious, that he should have been a
greater gainer by it than they that made it; which he thought
so palpable and clear a demonstration of the tyranny the people were to live under, that they would easily have discerned the change of their condition: yet he took so much pains,
to awaken his subjects to a due apprehension of it, and to
apply the thorough consideration of it to them, that he published a declaration upon that ordinance; the which, present-
ing many things to them, which have since fallen out, may
be, in this place, fit to be inserted in the king's own words,
which were these:

"It would not' be believed, (at least great pains have
been taken that it might not,) that the pretended ordinance
of the militia, (the first attempt that ever was, to make a law
by ordinance, without our consent,) or the keeping us out of
Hull, and taking our arms and ammunition from us, could
any way concern the interest, property, or liberty of the
subject: and it was confessed, by that desperate declaration
itself of the 26th of May, that if they were found guilty of
that charge of destroying the title and interest of our subjects
to their lands and goods, it were indeed a very great crime.
But it was a strange fatal lethargy which had seized our good
people, and kept them from discerning that the nobility, gentry, and commonalty of England were not only stripped of
their preeminence and privileges, but of their liberties and
estates, when our just rights were denied us; and that no
subject could from thenceforth expect to dwell at home,

---

[1] *This declaration is in the handwriting of lord Clarendon's secretary.*

when we were driven from our houses and our towns. It was not possible, that a commission could be granted to the earl of Essex, to raise an army against us, and, for the safety of our person, and preservation of the peace of the kingdom, to pursue, kill, and slay us, and all who wish well to us, but that, in a short time, inferior commanders, by the same authority, would require our good subjects, for the maintenance of the property of the subject, to supply them with such sums of money as they think fit, upon the penalty of being plundered with all extremity of war, (as the title of sir Edward Bainton's warrant runs, against our poor subjects in Wiltshire,) and by such rules of unlimited arbitrary power as are inconsistent with the least pretence or shadow of that property, it would seem to defend.

" If there could be yet any understanding so unskilful and supine to believe, that these disturbers of the public peace do intend any thing but a general confusion, they have brought them a sad argument to their own doors to convince them. After this ordinance and declaration, it is not in any sober man's power to believe himself to be worth any thing, or that there is such a thing as law, liberty, or property, left in England, under the jurisdiction of these men. And the same power that robs them now of the twentieth part of their estates, hath, by that, but made a claim, and entitled itself to the other nineteen, when it shall be thought fit to hasten the general ruin. Sure, if the minds of all men be not stubbornly prepared for servitude, they will look on this ordinance, as the greatest prodigy of arbitrary power and tyranny, that any age hath brought forth in any kingdom. Other grievances[1] (and the greatest) have been conceived intolerable, rather by the logic and consequence, than by the pressure itself : this at once sweeps away all that the wisdom and justice of parliaments have provided for them. Is their property in their estates, (so carefully looked to by their ancestors, and so amply established by us, against any possibility of invasion from the crown,) which makes the meanest subject as much a lord of his own as the greatest peer, to be

---

[1] Ship-money.—W.

valued, or considered? Here is a twentieth part of every man's estate, or so much as four men will please to call the twentieth part, taken away at once, and yet a power left to take a twentieth still of that which remains ; and this to be levied by such circumstances of severity, as no act of parliament ever consented to.

"Is their liberty, which distinguishes subjects from slaves, and in which this freeborn nation hath the advantage of all Christendom, dear to them?   They shall not only be imprisoned in such places of this kingdom, (a latitude of judgment no court can challenge to itself in any cases,) but for so long time as the committee of the house of commons for examination shall appoint and order: the house of commons itself having never assumed, or in the least degree pretended to, a power of judicature; having no more authority to administer an oath, the only way to discover and find out the truth of facts, than to cut off the heads of any of our subjects : and this committee being so far from being a part of the parliament, that it is destructive to the whole, by usurping to itself all the power of king, lords, and commons.   All who know any thing of parliaments know that a committee of either house ought not, by the law, to publish their own results ; neither are their conclusions of any force, without the confirmation of the house, which hath the same power of controlling them, as if the matter had never been debated. But that any committee should be so contracted, (as this of examination, a style no committee ever bore before this parliament,) as to exclude the members of the house, who are equally trusted by their country, from being present at the counsels, is so monstrous to the privileges of parliament, that it is no more in the power of any man to give up that freedom, than of himself to order, that, from that time, the place for which he serves shall never more send a knight or burgess to the parliament; and in truth is no less than to alter the whole frame of government, to pull up parliaments by the roots, and to commit the lives, liberties, and estates, of all the people of England to the arbitrary power of a few unqualified persons, who shall dispose thereof according to their discretion, without account to any rule or authority whatsoever.

"Are their friends, their wives, and children, the greatest blessings of peace, and comforts of life, precious to them? Would their penury and imprisonment be less grievous by those cordials? They shall be divorced from them, banished, and shall no longer remain within the cities of London and Westminster, the suburbs and the counties adjacent; and how far those adjacent counties shall extend no man knows. Is there now any thing left to enjoy but the liberty to rebel, and destroy one another? Are the outward blessings only of peace, property, and liberty, taken and forced from our subjects? Are their consciences free and unassaulted by the violence of these firebrands? Sure the liberty and freedom of conscience cannot suffer by these men. Alas! all these punishments are imposed upon them, because they will not submit to actions contrary to their natural loyalty, to their oaths of allegiance and supremacy, and to their late voluntary protestation, which obliges them to the care of our person, and our just rights.

"How many persons of honour, quality, and reputation, of the several counties of England, are now imprisoned, without any objections against them, but suspicion of their loyalty! How many of the gravest and most substantial citizens of London, by whom the government and discipline of that city was preserved, are disgraced, robbed, and imprisoned, without any process of law, or colour of accusation, but of obedience to the law and government of the kingdom! whilst anabaptists and Brownists, with the assistance of vicious and debauched persons of desperate fortunes, take upon them to break up and rifle houses, as public and avowed ministers of a new-invented authority. How many godly, pious, and painful divines, whose lives and learning have made them of reverend estimation, are now slandered with inclination to popery, discountenanced, and imprisoned, for discharging their consciences, instructing the people in the christian duty of religion and obedience! whilst schismatical, illiterate, and scandalous preachers fill the pulpits and churches with blasphemy, irreverence,[1] and treason; and incite their auditory to nothing but murder and rebellion.

[1] Irreligion.—W.

" We pass over the vulgar charm, by which they have captivated such who have been contented to dispense with their consciences for the preservation of their estates, and by which they persuade men cheerfully to part with this twentieth part of their estates to the good work in hand. For whosoever will give what he hath may escape robbing. They shall be repaid upon the public faith, as all other monies lent upon the propositions of both houses. It may be so. But men must be condemned to a strange unthriftiness, who will lend upon such security. The public faith indeed is as great an earnest as the state can give, and engages the honour, reputation, and honesty of the nation, and is the act of the kingdom: it is the security of the king, the lords, and commons, which can never need an executor, can never die, never be bankrupt;[1] and therefore we willingly consented to it for the indemnity of our good subjects of Scotland, (who, we hope, will not think the worse of it for being so often and so cheaply mentioned since.) But that a vote of one, or both houses, should be an engagement upon the public faith, is as impossible as that the committee of the house of commons for examination should be the high court of parliament.

" And what is or can be said, with the least shadow of reason, to justify these extravagances? We have not heard lately of the fundamental laws, which used to warrant the innovations: these need a refuge even below those foundations. They will say, they cannot manage their great undertakings without such extraordinary ways. We think so too. But that proves only, they have undertaken somewhat they ought not to undertake, not that it is lawful for them to do any thing that is convenient for those ends. We remembered them long ago, and we cannot do it too often, of that excellent speech of Mr. Pym's. The law is that which puts a difference betwixt good and evil, betwixt just and unjust: if you take away the law, all things will be in a confusion, every man will become a law unto himself; which, in the depraved condition of human nature, must

---

[1] This state aphorism will now, since the debt of one hundred and fifty millions sterling, begin to be brought in question.—W.

needs produce many great enormities. Lust will become a law, and envy will become a law, covetousness and ambition will become laws ; and what dictates, what decision, such laws will produce, may easily be discerned : it may indeed by these sad instances over the whole kingdom.

" But will posterity believe, that, in the same parliament, this doctrine was avowed with that acclamation, and these instances after produced ? That, in the same parliament, such care was taken that no man should be committed in what case soever, without the case of his imprisonment expressed ; and that all men should be immediately bailed in all cases bailable; and, during the same parliament, that alderman Pennington, or indeed any body else, but the sworn ministers of justice, should imprison whom they would, and for what they would, and for as long time as they would ? That the king should be reproached with breach of privilege, for accusing sir John Hotham of high treason, when with force of arms he kept him out of Hull, and despised him to his face, because in no case a member of either house might be committed, or accused without leave of that house of which he is a member ; and yet that, during the same parliament, the same alderman shall commit the earl of Middlesex, a peer of the realm, and the lord Buckhurst, a member of the house of commons, to the counter, without reprehension ? That to be a traitor (which is defined, and every man understands) should be no crime ; and to be called malignant, which nobody knows the meaning of, should be ground enough for close imprisonment ? That a law should be made, that whosoever should presume to take tonnage and poundage without an act of parliament, should incur the penalty of a præmunire ; and, in the same parliament, that the same imposition should be laid upon our subjects, and taken by order of both houses, without and against our consent ? Lastly, that, in the same parliament, a law should be made to declare the proceedings and judgment upon ship-money to be illegal, and void : and, during that parliament, that an order of both houses shall, upon pretence of necessity, enable four men to take away the twentieth part of their estates from all their neighbours, according to their discretion.

" But our good subjects will no longer look upon these
and the like results, as upon the counsels and conclusions of
both our houses of parliament ; (though all the world knows,
even that authority can never justify things unwarrantable
by the law.)   They well know how few of the persons
trusted by them are trusted at their consultations, of above
five hundred of the commons' not 'fourscore; and of the
house of peers, not a fifth part : that they who are present
enjoy not the privilege and freedom of parliament, but are
besieged by an army, and awed by the same tumults which
drove us and their fellow members from thence, to consent
to what some few seditious, schismatical persons among them
do propose.   These are the men, who, joining with the anabaptists and Brownists of London, first changed the government and discipline of that city ; and now, by the pride and
power of that city, would undo the kingdom : whilst their
lord mayor, a person accused and known to be guilty of high
treason, by a new legislative power of his own, suppresses
and reviles the Book of Common Prayer, robs and imprisons
whom he thinks fit ; and, with the rabble of his faction,
gives laws to both houses of parliament, and tells them, *They
will have no accommodation :* whilst the members sent, and
intrusted by their countries, are expelled the house, or committed, for refusing to take the oath of association to live
and die with the earl of Essex, as very lately sir Sydney
Mountague.   These are the men who have presumed to
send ambassadors, and to enter into treaties with foreign states
in their own behalfs, having all this time an agent of their
own with the states of Holland, to negociate for them upon
private instructions : these are men who, not thinking they
have yet brought mischief enough unto this kingdom, at this
time invite and solicit our subjects of Scotland, to enter this
land with an army against us : in a word, these are the men
who have made this last devouring ordinance to take away
all law, liberty, and property from our people, and have by
it really acted that upon our people, which with infinite ma-

¹ *These words are inserted by lord Clarendon himself; which shews
that his lordship revised this transcript of his amanuensis.*

lice, and no colour or ground, was laboured to be infused into them, to have been our intention by the commissions of array.

" We have done : What power and authority these men have, or will have, we know not : for ourself, we challenge none such. We look upon the pressures and inconveniences our good subjects bear, even by us, and our army, (which the army raised by them enforced us to levy in our defence, and their refusal of all offers and desires of treaty enforceth us to keep,) with very much sadness of heart. We are so far from requiring a twentieth part of their estates, though for their own visible preservation, that, as we have already sold or pawned our own jewels, and coined our own plate, so we are willing to sell all our own lands and houses for their relief : yet we do not doubt but our good subjects will seriously consider our condition, and their own duties, and think our readiness to protect them with the utmost hazard of our life, deserves their readiness to assist us with some part of their fortunes ; and, whilst other men give a twentieth part of their estates to enable them to forfeit the other nineteen, that they will extend themselves to us in a liberal and free proportion, for the preservation of the rest, and for the maintenance of God's true religion, the laws of the land, the liberty of the subject, and the safety and very being of parliaments, and this kingdom : for if all these ever were, or can be, in manifest danger, it is now in this present rebellion against us.

" Lastly, we will and require all our loving subjects, of what degree or quality soever, as they will answer it to God, to us, and to posterity, by their oaths of allegiance and supremacy ; as they would not be looked upon now, and remembered hereafter, as betrayers of the laws and liberties they were born to ; that they in no degree submit to this wild pretended ordinance, and that they presume not to give any encouragement or assistance to the army now in rebellion against us ; which if notwithstanding they shall do, they must expect from us the severest punishment the law can inflict, and a perpetual infamy with all good men."

Whatsoever every man could say to another against that

ordinance, and whatsoever the king said to them all against
it, it did bring in a great supply of money, and gave them a
stock of credit to borrow more; so that the army was again
drawn out, though but to winter quarters, twenty miles from
London, and the earl of Essex fixed his head quarters at
Windsor, to straiten the king's new garrison at Reading,
and sent strong parties still abroad, which got as much
ground as, at that time of the year, could reasonably be expected; that is, brought those adjacent counties entirely
under the obedience of the parliament, which would at least
have kept themselves neutral: and still persuaded the people " that their work was even at an end, and that the
king's forces would be swallowed up in a very short time :"
so that there was no day, in which they did not publish
themselves to have obtained some notable victory, or taken
some town, when in truth each party wisely abstained from
disturbing the other: yet the bulk of their supply came
only from the city of London. For though their ordinances extended over the whole kingdom, yet they had power
to execute them only there ; for it was not yet time to try
the affections of all places within their own verge, with the
severe exercise of that authority.

And therefore divers of the wealthiest and most substantial citizens of London, observing liberty to be taken by all
men to petition the houses, and the multitude of the petitioners to carry great authority with them, and from those
multitudes, and that authority, the brand to have been laid
upon the city, " of being an enemy to peace," met together,
and prepared a very modest and moderate petition to the
houses ; in which they desired " that such propositions and
addresses might be made by them to his majesty, that he
might with his honour comply with them, and thereby a
happy peace ensue;" the which, being signed by many
thousand hands, was ready to be presented, but was rejected by the house of commons, for no other reason publicly
given, but " that it was prepared by a multitude ;" and objections were framed against the principal promoters of it,
upon other pretences of delinquency ; that they were compelled to forsake the town, and so that party was, for the
present, discountenanced.

At the same time the inhabitants of Westminster, St. Martin's, and Covent-garden, who always underwent the imputation of being well affected to the king, prepared the like petition, and met with the same reproach, being strictly inhibited to approach the houses with more than six in company. This unequal kind of proceeding added nothing to their reputation, and they easily discerned those humours, thus obstructed, would break out the more violently : therefore they again resumed all professions of a desire of peace, and appointed a committee to prepare propositions to be sent to the king to that purpose ; and because they found that would be a work of time, (for the reasons which will be anon remembered,) and that many arts were to be applied to the several affections, and to wipe out the imagination that the city desired peace upon any other terms than they did, and the disadvantage that accrued to them by such imagination, and also to stay the appetite of those who were importunate to have any advance made towards peace, having procured, by the activity of their agents and ministers, to have such a common-council chosen for the city, as would undoubtedly comply with their desires and designs, they underhand directed their own mayor to engage that body in such a petition to his majesty, as, carrying the sense and reputation of the whole city, might yet signify nothing to the prejudice of the two houses ; and so a petition was framed in these words :

To the king's[1] most excellent majesty ;

The humble petition of the mayor, aldermen, and commons of the city of London,

" Sheweth,

" That the petitioners, your majesty's most humble and loyal subjects, being much pierced with the long and great divisions between your majesty and both your houses of parliament, and with the sad and bloody effects thereof, both

---

[1] *This petition is in the handwriting of lord Clarendon's amanuensis.*

209409

here and in Ireland, are yet more deeply wounded by the misapprehension, which your majesty seemeth to entertain of the love and loyalty of this your city, as if there were some cause of fear, or suspicion of danger to your royal person, if your majesty should return hither; and that this is made the unhappy bar to that blessed reconciliation with your great and most faithful council for preventing that desolation, and destruction, which is now most apparently imminent to your majesty, and all your kingdoms.

" For satisfaction therefore of your majesty, and clearing of the petitioners' innocency, they most humbly declare, as formerly they have done, that they are no way conscious of any disloyalty, but abhor all thoughts thereof; and that they are resolved to make good their late solemn protestation, and sacred vow, made to Almighty God; and, with the last drop of their dearest bloods, to defend and maintain the true reformed protestant religion, and, according to the duty of their allegiance, your majesty's royal person, honour, and estate, (whatsoever is maliciously and falsely suggested to your majesty to the contrary,) as well as the power and privilege of parliament, and the lawful rights and liberties of the subject: and do hereby engage themselves, their estates, and all they have, to their uttermost power, to defend and preserve your majesty, and both houses of parliament, from all tumults, affronts, and violence, with as much loyalty, love, and duty, as ever citizens expressed towards your majesty, or any of your royal progenitors in their greatest glory.

" The petitioners therefore, upon their bended knees, do most humbly beseech your majesty, to return to your parliament, (accompanied with your royal, not martial attendance,) to the end that religion, laws, and liberties, may be settled and secured, and whatsoever is amiss in church and commonwealth reformed by their advice, according to the fundamental constitutions of this kingdom : and that such a peace may thereby be obtained, as shall be for the glory of God, the honour and happiness of your majesty and posterity, and welfare of all your loyal subjects; who, (the petitioners are fully assured,) whatsoever is given out to the contrary, do unanimously desire the peace herein expressed."

Though this petition was in effect no other than to desire the king to disband his army, and to put himself into the absolute disposal of the parliament, and therefore all wise men concluded that no great progress would be made by it towards peace ; yet so sotted and infatuated were the people, that, upon this very petition, they prevailed with the people to submit to another subscription for money and plate, for the necessary provision of arms, ammunition, and pay of their army, until their disbanding and return home to their several counties : that so they might not be occasioned, through want of pay, to plunder, rob, or pillage by the way homewards, after their discharge and dismission.   So that men were persuaded that this was now the last tax they should be invited to, though every one of those ordinances and declarations loaded the king with some new calumnies and reproaches, that it was plain the authors of them meant not so soon to put themselves under his subjection.

This petition was, about the tenth of January, 1642–3, presented to the king at Oxford, by some aldermen, and others of the common council, who were for the most part of moderate inclinations.   The king considered sadly what answer to return ; for, albeit it appeared that the petition had been craftily framed by those who had no thoughts of peace, and that there was no argument in it to hope any good from that people ; yet there were, to vulgar understandings, very specious and popular professions of great piety, and zeal to his service, and care of his security ; and he was to be very tender in seeming to doubt the inclinations and affections of that city, by whose strength alone the war was supported, and that strength procured by corrupting those affections : and therefore the king was not sorry to have this opportunity of saying somewhat, and communicating himself freely to the city, being persuaded, that the ill they did, proceeded rather from misinformation, than any general and habitual malice in them.   All his proclamations, messages, and declarations, had been with so much industry suppressed there, that they were not in truth generally informed of the matter of fact, and the justice of the king's cause ; and therefore he was persuaded that if he enlarged himself, in his answer to

76*

this petition, and exposed those few men who were most notoriously malignant against the government of the church and state, and who were generally known to be so, to the knowledge of the people, that it would at least lessen their power and ability to do hurt : and so he resolved to return an answer to them in these words :

" That his majesty[1] doth not entertain any misapprehension of the love and loyalty of his city of London ; as he hath always expressed a singular regard and esteem of the affections of that city, and is still desirous to make it his chief place of residence, and to continue, and renew many marks of his favour to it ; so he believes, much the better and greater part of that his city is full of love, duty, and loyalty to his majesty ; and that the tumults which heretofore forced his majesty, for his safety, to leave that place, though they were contrived and encouraged by some principal members thereof, (who are since well known, though they are above the reach of justice,) consisted more of desperate persons of the suburbs, and the neighbouring towns, (who were misled too by the cunning and malice of their seducers,) than of the inhabitants of that city.   He looks on his good subjects there as persons groaning under the same burden which doth oppress his majesty, and awed by the same persons who begat those tumults, and the same army which gave battle to his majesty : and therefore, as no good subject can more desire, from his soul, a composure of the general distractions ; so no good citizen can more desire the establishment of the particular peace and prosperity of that place, by his majesty's access thither, than his majesty himself doth.

" But his majesty desires his good subjects of London seriously to consider, what confidence his majesty can have of security there, whilst the laws of the land are so notoriously despised, and trampled under foot, and the wholesome government of that city, heretofore so famous over all the world, is now submitted to the arbitrary power of a few desperate persons, of no reputation, but for malice and disloyalty to him ; whilst arms are taken up, not only without, but against

[1] *In the handwriting of Lord Clarendon's amanuensis.*

his consent and express command, and collections publicly made, and contributions avowed, for the maintenance of the army which hath given him battle, and therein used all possible means treason and malice could suggest to them, to have taken his life from him, and to have destroyed his royal issue ; whilst such of his majesty's subjects, who, out of duty and affection to his majesty, and compassion of their bleeding country, have laboured for peace, are reviled, injured, and murdered, even by the magistrates of that city, or by their directions : lastly, what hopes his majesty can have of safety there, whilst alderman Pennington, their pretended lord mayor, the principal author of those calamities which so nearly threaten the ruin of that famous city, Ven, Foulke, and Manwairing, all persons notoriously guilty of schism and high treason, commit such outrages, in oppressing, robbing, and imprisoning, according to their discretion, all such his majesty's loving subjects, whom they are pleased to suspect but for wishing well to his majesty.

"And his majesty would know, whether the petitioners believe, that the reviling and suppressing the book of common prayer, established in this church ever since the reformation, the discountenancing and imprisoning godly, learned, and painful preachers, and the cherishing and countenancing of Brownists, anabaptists, and all manner of sectaries, be the way to defend and maintain the true reformed protestant religion ?   That to comply with and assist persons who have actually attempted to kill his majesty, and to allow and favour libels, pasquils, and seditious sermons against his majesty, be to defend his royal person, and honour, according to the duty of their allegiance ?   Whether to imprison men's persons, and to plunder their houses, because they will not rebel against his majesty, nor assist those that do ; whether to destroy their property by taking away the twentieth part of their estates from them, and, by the same arbitrary power, to refer to four standers-by, of their own faction, to judge what that twentieth part is, be to defend the lawful rights and liberties of the subject ?   And if they think these actions to be instances of either ; whether they do not know the persons before named to be guilty of them all ? or whether they think it possible, that Almighty God can bless that city, and preserve it from destruction, whilst persons of such known guilt and wickedness are defended, and justified among them, against the power of that law, by which they can only subsist.

" His majesty is so far from suffering himself to be incensed against the whole city, by the actions of these ill men, though they have hitherto been so prevalent, as to make the affections of the rest of little use to him; and is so willing to be with them, and to protect them, that the trade, wealth, and glory thereof, so decayed and eclipsed by these public distractions, may again be the envy of all foreign nations, that he doth once more graciously offer his free and general pardon to all the inhabitants of that his city of London, the suburbs and city of Westminster, (except the persons formerly excepted by his majesty,) if they shall yet return to their duty, loyalty, and obedience. And if his good subjects of that his city of London shall first solemnly declare, that they will defend the known laws of the land, and will submit to, and be governed by, no other rule; if they shall first manifest, by defending themselves, and maintaining their own rights, liberties, and interests, and suppressing any force and violence unlawfully raised against those and his majesty, their power to defend and preserve him from all tumults, affronts, and violence : lastly, if they shall apprehend, and commit to safe custody, the persons of those four men who enrich themselves by the spoil and oppression of his loving subjects, and the ruin of the city, that his majesty may proceed against them by the course of law, as guilty of high treason ; his majesty will speedily return to them with his royal, and without his martial attendance, and will use his utmost endeavour, that they may hereafter enjoy all the blessings of peace and plenty; and will no longer expect obedience from them, than he shall, with all the faculties of his soul, labour in the preserving and advancing the true reformed protestant religion, the laws of the land, the liberty and property of the subjects, and the just privileges of parliament.

" If, notwithstanding all this, the art and interest of these men can prevail so far, that they involve more men in their guilt, and draw that his city to sacrifice its present happiness, and future hopes, to their pride, fury, and malice, his majesty shall only give them this warning : that whosoever shall henceforward take up arms, without his consent, contribute any money or plate, upon what pretence of authority soever, for maintenance of the army under the command of the earl of Essex, or any other army in rebellion against him, or shall pay tonnage and poundage, till the same shall be settled by act of parliament, every such person must expect the severest punishment the law can inflict ; and, in the mean time, his majesty shall seize upon any part of his estate within his power, for the relief and support of him and his army, raised and maintained for the defence of his person, the laws, and this his kingdom : and since he denies to his majesty the duty and benefit of his subjection, by giving assistance to rebels, which, by the known laws of the land, is high treason ; his majesty shall likewise deny him the benefit of his protection, and shall not only signify to all his foreign ministers, that such persons shall receive no advantage by being his subject, but shall, by other ways and means, proceed against him as a public enemy to his majesty and this kingdom.

" But his majesty hopes, and doubts not, but his good subjects of London will call to mind the acts of their predecessors, the duty, affection, loyalty, and merit towards their princes, the renown they have had with all posterity for, and the blessing of Heaven which always accompanied, those virtues ; and will consider the perpetual scorn and infamy which unavoidably will follow them and their children, if infinitely the meaner part in quality, and much the lesser part in number, shall be able to alter the government so admirably established, destroy the trade so excellently settled, and to waste the wealth so industriously gotten, of that flourishing city : and then they will easily gather up the courage and resolution to join with his majesty in defence of that religion, law, and liberty, which hitherto hath, and only can, make themselves, his majesty, and his kingdom, happy.

" For concurring with the advice of his two houses of

parliament, which, with reference to the commonwealth, may be as well at this distance, as by being at Whitehall, his majesty doubts not, but his good subjects of London well know, how far, beyond the example of his predecessors, his majesty hath concurred with their advice, in passing of such laws, by which he willingly parted with many of his known rights, for the benefit of his subjects ; which the fundamental constitutions of this kingdom did not oblige him to consent unto ; and hath used all possible means to beget a right understanding between them : and will therefore apply themselves to those who, by making just, peaceable, and honourable propositions to his majesty, can only beget that concurrence."

This answer the king sent by a servant of his own, supposing, that if he sent by the messengers who brought the petition, it might either be suppressed, or not communicated in that manner as he desired. Besides, the messengers themselves, after the king had caused it to be read to them, were very well contented that it should be delivered by other hands than theirs. So they promised his majesty, that they would procure a common hall, (which is the most general assembly of the city, the meanest person being admitted,) to be called as soon as they returned ; where his messenger might deliver it : and having been graciously used by the king and the court, after two days' stay, they returned from Oxford together with the gentleman sent by his majesty. When they came to London, the contents of the answer were quickly known, though not delivered; and the two houses made an order, " that the lord mayor should not call a common hall, till he received farther direction from them." So that, though the gentleman sent by the king often solicited the lord mayor, " that he would call a common hall, at which he was to deliver a message from the king," many days passed before any orders were issued to that purpose.

At last, a day was appointed ; and, at the same time, a committee of the lords and commons were sent to be present, to see that it might not have such a reception, as might render their interest suspected. As soon as the gentleman sent by the king had read his majesty's answer, the earl of North-

umberland told them, " of the high value the parliament had
of the city ; that they had considered of those wounding
aspersions, which, in that answer, were cast upon persons
of such eminent affection in their city, and upon others, of
great fidelity and trust among them : that they owned themselves equally interested in all things that concerned them,
and would stand by them with their lives and fortunes, for
the preservation of the city in general, and those persons in
particular who had been faithful, and deserved well both of
the parliament and kingdom. And they would pursue all
means with their lives and fortunes, that might be for the
preservation of that city, and for the procuring of safety, happiness, and peace, to the whole kingdom."

As soon as his lordship had finished his oration, which
was received with marvellous acclamations, Mr. Pym enlarged himself upon the several parts of the king's answer, (for
it was so long before it was delivered, that the printed copies
from Oxford, which were printed there after the messenger
was gone so long that all men concluded it was delivered,
were public and in all hands,) and told them the sense of
the two houses of parliament, upon every part of it. Among
the rest, " that the demanding the lord mayor, and the other
three citizens, was against the privilege of parliament, (two
of them being members of the house of commons,) and most
dishonourable to the city, that the lord mayor of London
should be subjected to the violence of every base fellow ;
and that they should be commanded to deliver up their chief
magistrates, and such eminent members of the city, to the
king's pleasure, only because they had done their duty, in
adhering to the parliament, for the defence of the kingdom."

He told them, " that, to the objection that the government of the city had been managed by a few desperate persons, and that they did exercise an arbitrary power, the two
houses gave them this testimony, that they had, in most of
the great occasions concerning the government of the city,
followed their direction ; and that direction which the parliament had given, they had executed ; and they must and
would maintain to be such, as stood with their honour in
giving it, and the others' trust and fidelity in performing it."

To the objection, "that the property of the subject was destroyed, by taking away the twentieth part by an arbitrary power," he told them, "that that ordinance did not require a twentieth part, but did limit the assessors that they should not go beyond a twentieth part, and that was done by a power derived from both houses of parliament ; the lords, who had an hereditary interest in making of laws in this kingdom ; and the commons, who were elected and chosen to present the whole body of the commonalty, and trusted, for the good of the people, whenever they see cause to charge the kingdom." He said farther, "that the same law which did enable the two houses of parliament to raise forces to maintain and defend the safety of religion, and of the kingdom, did likewise enable them to require contributions whereby those forces might be maintained; or else it were a vain power to raise forces, if they had not a power like-wise to maintain them in that service for which they were raised." He observed, "that it was reported, that the king declared that he would send some messengers to observe their carriage in the city, and what was done among them : the parliament had just cause to doubt, that those would be messengers of sedition and trouble, and therefore desired them to observe and find them out, that they might know who they were." He concluded with "commending unto their consideration the great danger that they were all in ; and that that danger could not be kept off, in all likelihood, but by the army that was then on foot ;" and assured them, " that the lords and commons were so far from being fright-ed by any thing that was in that answer, that they had, for themselves, and the members of both houses, declared a far-ther contribution towards the maintenance of that army ; and could not but hope, and desire, that the city, which had shewed so much good affection in the former necessities of the state, would be sensible of their own, and of the condi-tion of the whole kingdom, and add to that which they had already done, some farther contribution, whereby that army might be maintained for all their safeties."

Whether the solemnity for the reception of this message after it was known what the contents were, and the bring-

ing so great a guard of armed men to the place where it
was to be delivered, frighted the well affected party of the
city from coming thither, or frighted them, when they were
there, from expressing those affections, I know not. But it
is certain, these speeches and discourses were received and
entertained with all imaginable applause, and that meeting
was concluded with a general acclamation, " that they would
live and die with the houses," and other expressions of that
nature. So that all thoughts of farther address, or compliance with his majesty were so entirely and absolutely laid
aside, that the licence of seditious and treasonable discourses
daily increased; insomuch, that complaint being made to
the then lord mayor, that a certain desperate person had
said, " that he hoped shortly to wash his hands in the king's
blood," that minister of justice refused to send any warrant,
or to give any direction to any officer, for the apprehension
of him. And this was the success of that petition and
answer.

The houses now began to speak themselves of sending
propositions to the king for peace. For, how great soever
the compliance seemed with them from the city, or the
country, they well enough discerned that that compliance
was generally upon the hope and expectation that they
would procure a speedy peace. And they had now procured that to pass both houses, which they only wanted, the
bill for the extirpation of episcopacy : in the doing whereof,
they used marvellous art and industry. They who every
day did somewhat, how little soever then taken notice of, to
make peace impossible, and resolved, that no peace could
be safe for them, but such a one as would be unsafe for the
king, well enough knew that they should never be able to
hold up, and carry on the war against the king in England,
but by the help of an army out of Scotland ; which they had
no hope to procure but upon the stock of alteration of the
government of the church; to which that nation was violently inclined. But to compass that was very difficult ;
very much the major part, even of those members who still
continued with them, being cordially affected to the government established, at least not affected to any other. To

those therefore, who were so far engaged as to desire to have it in their power to compel the king to consent to such a peace as they desired, they presented " the consequence of getting the Scots to declare for them ; which would more terrify the king, and keep the northern parts in subjection, than any forces they should be able to raise : that it was impossible to draw such a declaration from them, without first declaring themselves that they would alter the government by the bishops ; which that people pretended to believe the only justifiable ground to take up arms." To others, which was indeed their public, and avowed, and current argument in debates, they alleged, " that they could not expect that any peace would be effected by the king's free concurrence to any message they could send to him, but that it must arise and result from a treaty between them, upon such propositions as either party would make upon their own interest : that it could not be expected that such propositions would be made on either side, as would be pertinaciously insisted on by them who made them ; it being the course, in all affairs of this nature, to ask more than was expected to be consented to ; that it concerned them as much, to make demands of great moment to the king, from which they meant to recede, as others upon which they must insist : that all men knew the inclination and affection the king had to the church, and therefore if he saw that in danger, he would rescue it at any price, and very probably their departing from their proposition of the church, might be the most powerful argument to the king, to gratify them with the militia."

By these artifices, and especially by concluding obstinately, "that no propositions should be sent to the king for peace, till the bill for extirpation of bishops was passed the lords' house," (where it would never otherwise have been submitted to,) they had their desire, and, about the end of January, they sent the earls of Northumberland, Pembroke, Salisbury, and Holland, with eight members of the commons, to Oxford, with their petition and propositions. And here I cannot omit one stratagem, which, at that time, occasioned some mirth. The common people of London were persuad-

ed, " that there was so great scarcity of victual and provisions at Oxford, and in all the king's quarters, that they
were not without danger of starving; and that, if all other
ways failed, that alone would in a short time bring the king
to them." To make good this report, provisions of all
kinds, even to bread, were sent in waggons, and on horses,
from London to Oxford, for the supply of this committee :
when, without doubt, they found as great plenty of all things
where they came, as they had left behind them. The petition presented to his majesty with the propositions were,
in these words, at the presentation, read by the earl of
Northumberland.

*The humble desires[1] and propositions of the lords and com-
mons in parliament, tendered to his majesty.*

" We your majesty's most humble and faithful subjects,
the lords and commons in parliament assembled, having in
our thoughts the glory of God, your majesty's honour, and
the prosperity of your people, and being most grievously
afflicted with the pressing miseries, and calamities, which
have overwhelmed your two kingdoms of England and Ireland, since your majesty hath, by the persuasion of evil counsellors, withdrawn yourself from the parliament, raised an
army against it, and, by force thereof, protected delinquents
from the justice of it, constraining us to take arms for the
defence of our religion, laws, liberties, privileges of parliament, and for the sitting of the parliament in safety; which
fears and dangers are continued, and increased, by the raising,
drawing together, and arming of great numbers of papists,
under the command of the earl of Newcastle ; likewise by
making the lord Herbert of Ragland, and other known papists, commanders of great forces, whereby many grievous
oppressions, rapines, and cruelties have been and are daily
exercised upon the persons and estates of your people, much
innocent blood hath been spilt, and the papists have attained
means of attempting, with hopes of effecting, their mischievous designs of rooting out the reformed religion, and des-

---

[1] *This petition is in the handwriting of lord Clarendon's secretary.*

troying the professors thereof: in the tender sense and compassion of these evils, under which your people and kingdom lie, (according to the duty, which we owe to God, your majesty, and the kingdom, for which we are trusted,) do most earnestly desire, that an end may be put to these great distempers and distractions, for the preventing of that desolation which doth threaten all your majesty's dominions.   And as we have rendered, and still are ready to render to your majesty, that subjection, obedience, and service, which we owe unto you; so we most humbly beseech your majesty, to remove the causes of this war, and to vouchsafe us that peace and protection, which we and our ancestors have formerly enjoyed under your majesty, and your royal predecessors, and graciously to accept and grant these our most humble desires and propositions:

1. "That your majesty will be pleased to disband your armies, as we likewise shall be ready to disband all those forces which we have raised ; and that you will be pleased to return to your parliament.

2. "That you will leave delinquents to a legal trial, and judgment of parliament.

3. "That the papists may not only be disbanded, but disarmed according to law.

4. "That your majesty will be pleased to give your royal assent unto the bill for taking away the superstitious innovations; to the bill for the utter abolishing and taking away of all archbishops, bishops, their chancellors, and commissaries, deans, sub-deans, and chapters, archdeacons, canons, and prebendaries, and all chanters, chancellors, treasurers, sub-treasurers, succentors, and sacrists, and all vicars choral, and choristers, old vicars, and new vicars of any cathedral or collegiate church, and all other their under-officers, out of the church of England : to the bill against scandalous ministers : to the bill against pluralities; and to the bill for consultation to be had with godly, religious, and learned divines. That your majesty will be pleased to promise to pass such other good bills for settling of church-government, as, upon consultation with the assembly of the said divines, shall be resolved on by both houses of parliament, and by them presented to your majesty.

5. " That your majesty having expressed, in your answer to the nineteen propositions of both houses of parliament, an hearty affection and intention for the rooting out of popery out of this kingdom; and that, if both the houses of parliament can yet find a more effectual course to disable Jesuits, priests, and popish recusants, from disturbing the state, or eluding the laws, that you would willingly give your consent unto it ; that you would be graciously pleased, for the better discovery and speedier conviction of recusants, that an oath may be established by act of parliament, to be administered in such manner as by both houses shall be agreed on; wherein they shall abjure and renounce the pope's supremacy, the doctrine of transubstantiation, purgatory, worshipping of the consecrated host, crucifixes, and images : and the refusing the said oath, being tendered in such manner as shall be appointed by act of parliament, shall be a sufficient conviction in law of recusancy.   And that your majesty will be graciously pleased to give your royal assent unto a bill, for the education of the children of papists by protestants in the protestant religion.[1]   That, for the more effectual execution of the laws against popish recusants, your majesty will be pleased to consent to a bill, for the true levying of the penalties against them; and that the same penalties may be levied, and disposed of in such manner as both houses of parliament shall agree on, so as your majesty be at no loss; and likewise to a bill, whereby the practice of papists against the state may be prevented, and the law against them duly executed.

6. " That the earl of Bristol may be removed from your majesty's councils ; and that both he, and the lord Herbert, eldest son to the earl of Worcester, may likewise be restrained from coming within the verge of the court; and that they may not bear any office, or have any employments concerning state or commonwealth.

7. " That your majesty will be graciously pleased, by act

[1] There cannot be a stronger proof that all their pretence of taking up arms for the preservation of the rights of subjects and citizens was a mere farce, than this wicked request, the violation of all law, divine and human. For these leaders in parliament were well acquainted with the rights of conscience.—W.

of parliament, to settle the militia both by sea and land, and for the forts and ports of the kingdom, in such a manner as shall be agreed on by both houses.

8. " That your majesty will be pleased, by your letters patents, to make sir John Brampston, chief justice of the court of king's bench; William Lenthall, esquire, the now speaker of the commons' house, master of the rolls; and to continue the lord chief justice Banks, chief justice of the court of common pleas; and likewise to make Mr. Sergeant Wild, chief baron of your court of exchequer; and that Mr. Justice Bacon may be continued; and Mr. Sergeant Rolls, and Mr. Sergeant Atkins, made justices of the king's bench: that Mr. Justice Reeves, and Mr. Justice Foster, may be continued; and Mr. Sergeant Pheasant made one of the justices of your court of common pleas; that Mr. Sergeant Creswell, Mr. Samuel Brown, and Mr. John Puleston, may be barons of the exchequer; and that all these, and all the judges of the same courts, for the time to come, may hold their places by letters patents under the great seal, *quamdiu se bene. gesserint :*[1] and that the several persons not before named, that do hold any of these places before mentioned, may be removed.

9. " That all such persons, as have been put out of the commissions of peace, or oyer and terminer, or from being *custodes rotulorum*, since the first day of April, 1642, (other than such as were put out by desire of both or either of the houses of parliament,) may again be put into those commissions and offices; and that such persons may be put out of those commissions and offices, as shall be excepted against by both houses of parliament.

10. " That your majesty will be pleased to pass the bill now presented to your majesty, to vindicate and secure the privileges of parliament, from the ill consequence of the late precedent in the charge and proceeding against the lord Kim-

---

[1] Had they really not been factious, and resolved to change the regal power, they would have been content to make that reasonable demand, that the judges should hold their places, *quamdiu se bene gesserint*, and confined themselves to that only in this 8th article.—W.

bolton, now earl of Manchester, and the five members of the house of commons.

11. " That your royal assent may be given unto such acts as shall be advised by both houses of parliament, for the satisfying and paying the debts and damages, wherein the two houses of parliament have engaged the public faith of the kingdom.

12. " That your majesty will be pleased, according to a gracious answer heretofore received from you, to enter into a more strict alliance with the States of the United Provinces, and other neighbour princes and states of the protestant religion, for the defence and maintenance thereof against all designs and attempts of the popish and jesuitical faction, to subvert and suppress it; whereby your subjects may hope to be free from the mischiefs which this kingdom hath endured, through the power which some of that party have had in your counsels; and will be much encouraged, in a parliamentary way, for your aid and assistance in restoring your royal sister, and the prince elector, to those dignities and dominions which belong unto them; and relieving the other protestant princes who have suffered in the same cause.

13. " That in the general pardon, which your majesty hath been pleased to offer to your subjects, all offences and misdemeanours committed before the 10th of January, 1641, which have been or shall be questioned, or proceeded against in parliament, upon complaint in the house of commons, before the 10th of January, 1643, shall be excepted; which offences and misdemeanours shall nevertheless be taken, and adjudged to be fully discharged against all other inferior courts. That likewise there shall be an exception to all offences committed by any person or persons, which hath, or have had, any hand or practice in the rebellion of Ireland; which hath, or have given, any counsel, assistance, or encouragement to the rebels there, for the maintenance of that rebellion; as likewise exception of William earl of Newcastle, and George lord Digby.

14. " That your majesty will be pleased to restore such members of either house of parliament to their several places of services, and employment, out of which they have been

put since the beginning of this parliament; that they may receive satisfaction, and reparation for those places, and for the profits which they have lost by such removals, upon the petition of both houses of parliament : and that all others may be restored to their offices and employments, who have been put out of the same upon any displeasure conceived against them, for any assistance given to both houses of parliament, or obeying their commands, or forbearing to leave their attendance upon the parliament without licence ; or for any other occasion, arising from these unhappy differences betwixt your majesty and both houses of parliament, upon the like petition of both houses.

" These things being granted, and performed, as it hath always been our hearty prayer, so shall we be enabled to make it our hopeful endeavour, that your majesty, and your people, may enjoy the blessings of peace, truth, and justice ; the royalty and greatness of your throne may be supported by the loyal and bountiful affections of your people ; their liberties and privileges maintained by your majesty's protection and justice ; and this public honour, and happiness of your majesty, and all your dominions, communicated to other churches and states of your alliance, and derived to your royal posterity, and the future generations of this kingdom for ever."

They who brought this petition and propositions, spake to their friends at Oxford with all freedom of the persons from whom they came ; inveighed against " their tyranny and unreasonableness," and especially against the propositions themselves had brought; but positively declared, " that if the king would vouchsafe so gracious an answer (which they confessed they had no reason to expect) as might engage the two houses in a treaty, it would not be then in the power of the violent party to deny whatsoever his majesty could reasonably desire." However (though the king expected little from those private undertakings, well knowing that they who wished best were of least power, and that the greatest among them, as soon as they were but suspected to incline to peace, immediately lost their reputation) his majesty, within two days, graciously dismissed those messengers with this answer :

"If his majesty[1] had not given up all the faculties of his soul to an earnest endeavour of peace and reconciliation with his people ; or if he would suffer himself, by any provocation, to be drawn to a sharpness of language, at a time when there seems somewhat like an overture of accommodation, he could not but resent the heavy charges upon him in the preamble of these propositions; would not suffer himself to be reproached, with protecting of delinquents, by force, from justice, (his majesty's desire having always been, that all men should be tried by the known law, and having been refused it,) with raising an army against his parliament, and to be told that arms have been taken up against him for the defence of religion, laws, liberties, and privileges of parliament, and for the sitting of the parliament in safety, with many other particulars in that preamble so often and so fully answered by his majesty, without remembering the world of the time and circumstances of raising those arms against him ; when his majesty was so far from being in a condition to invade other men's rights, that he was not able to maintain and defend his own from violence; and without telling his good subjects, that their religion, (the true protestant religion, in which his majesty was born, hath faithfully lived, and to which he will die a willing sacrifice,) their laws, liberties, privileges, and safety of parliament, were so amply settled, and established, or offered to be so by his majesty,[2] before any army was raised against him, and long before any raised by him for his defence, that if nothing had been desired but that peace and protection which his subjects, and their ancestors, had in the best times enjoyed, under his majesty, or his royal predecessors, this misunderstanding and distance between his majesty and his people, and this general misery and distraction upon the face of the whole kingdom, had not been now the discourse of all Christendom.

[1] *This answer is in the handwriting of lord Clarendon's secretary.*

[2] Nothing was more true than this assertion. And to estimate the merits in this quarrel, this truth must be always kept in mind. —W.

77*

" But his majesty will forbear any expressions of bitterness, or of a sense of his own sufferings, that, if it be possible, the memory thereof may be lost to the world. And therefore, though many of the propositions, presented to his majesty by both houses, appear to him very derogatory from, and destructive to, his just power and prerogative, and no way beneficial to his subjects, few of them being already due to them by the laws established, (and how unparliamentary it is by arms to require new laws, all the world may judge,) yet (because these may be waved, or mollified, and many things, that are now dark and doubtful in them, cleared, and explained upon debate) his majesty is pleased, such is his sense of the miseries this kingdom suffers by this unnatural war, and his earnest desire to remove them by an happy peace, that a speedy time and place be agreed upon, for the meeting of such persons as his majesty and both houses shall appoint to discuss these propositions, and such others here following as his majesty doth propose to them.

1. " That his majesty's own revenue, magazine, towns, forts, and ships, which have been taken or kept from him by force, be forthwith restored unto him.

2. " That whatsoever hath been done, or published, contrary to the known laws of the land, or derogatory to his majesty's legal and known power and rights, be renounced, and recalled, that no seed may remain for the like to spring out of for the future.

3. " That whatsoever illegal power hath been claimed and exercised by or over his subjects, as imprisoning their persons without law, stopping their *Habeas Corpus's*, and imposing upon their estates without act of parliament, &c. either by both, or either house, or any committee of both, or either, or by any persons appointed by any of them, be disclaimed ; and all such persons so committed forthwith discharged.

4. " That as his majesty will readily consent (having done so heretofore) to the execution of all laws already made, and to any good acts to be made for the suppressing of popery, and for the firm settling of the protestant religion

now established by law ; so he desires, that a good bill may be framed, for the better preserving the Book of Common Prayer from the scorn and violence of Brownists, anabaptists, and other sectaries, with such clauses for the ease of tender consciences, as his majesty hath formerly offered.[1]

5. " That all such persons, as, upon the treaty, shall be excepted out of the general pardon, shall be tried *per pares*, according to the usual course, and known laws of the land; and that it be left to that, either to acquit or condemn them.

6. " And, to the intent this treaty may not suffer interruption by any intervening accidents, that a cessation of arms, and free trade for all his majesty's subjects, may be first agreed upon.

" This offer and desire of his majesty, he hopes, will be so cheerfully entertained, that a speedy and blessed peace may be accomplished. If it shall be rejected, or, by insisting upon unreasonable circumstances, be made impossible, (which, he hopes, God in his mercy to this nation will not suffer,) the guilt of the blood which will be shed, and the desolation which must follow, will lie upon the heads of the refusers. However, his majesty is resolved, through what accidents soever he shall be compelled to recover his rights, and with what prosperous success soever it shall please God to bless him, that by his earnest, constant endeavours to propagate and promote the true protestant religion, and by his governing according to the known laws of the land,[2] and

[1] How much hath the king in this article the advantage of the parliament in their 5th, in which is the execrable clause of *educating the children of papists !*—W.

[2] The king, in all his papers of appeal to the people against this faction of a parliament, carefully avoids touching upon his preceding arbitrary government, but appears willing the people should believe that he always governed by law. This seems to have been ill policy in his council. The people both saw and felt his ill government. The confessing it would have gone a great way to persuade them, that now he had seen his error, he would be disposed to govern better ; whereas the acknowledging no fault, gave no room for hopes of amendment.—W.

upholding the just privileges of parliament, according to his frequent protestations made before Almighty God, (which he will always inviolably observe,) the world shall see, that he hath undergone all these difficulties and hazards, for the defence and maintenance of those, the zealous preservation of which, his majesty well knows, is the only foundation and means for the true happiness of him and his people."

Whilst these overtures and discourses were made of peace, the kingdom, in all parts, felt the sad effects of war; neither the king nor the parliament being slack in pursuing the business by the sword; and the persons of honour and quality in most counties more vigorously declaring themselves than they had done. Among the rest, upon the king's retreat from Brentford, whilst he yet staid about Reading, some of the well affected gentry of Sussex, upon the confidence of their interests in those parts, offered the king to raise forces there; and presumed they should be able to seize some place of security and importance for their retreat, if the enemy should attempt upon them; which, at that time of the year, was not conceived could be with any notable success. And being armed with such authority and commissions, as they desired, and seconded with a good number of considerable officers, their first success was answerable to their own hopes, and they possessed themselves, partly by force, and partly by stratagem, of the city of Chichester; which, being encompassed with a very good old wall, was very easy to be so fortified, that, with the winter, they might well think themselves secure against any forcible attempt could be made upon them. And no doubt they had been so, if the common people of the county (out of which the soldiers were to rise) had been so well affected as was believed.

But, before they could draw in men or provisions into the city, the earl of Essex sent sir William Waller with horse, foot, and cannon, to infest them; who, with the assistance of the country, quickly shut them up within their walls. They within the town were easily reduced to straits they could not contend with; for, besides the enemy without, against which the walls and the weather seemed of equal power, and the small stock of provisions, which, in so short time, they were able to draw thither, they had cause to apprehend their friends would be weary before their enemies ; and that the citizens would not prove a trusty part of the garrison ; and their number of common men was so small, that the constant duty was performed by the officers, and gentlemen of quality, who were absolutely tired out.   So that, after a week or ten days' siege, they were compelled, upon no better articles than quarter, to deliver that city, which could hardly have been taken from them ; by which (with the loss of fifty or three score gentlemen of quality, and officers of name, whose very good reputation made the loss appear a matter of abso- lute and unavoidable necessity)[1] the king found that he was not to venture to plant garrisons so far from his own quarters, where he could not, in reasonable time, administer succour or supply.

This triumph of the enemy was shortly after abated, and the loss on the king's part repaired, by the winning of Ci- rencester, a good town in Glocestershire, which the rebels were fortifying, and had in it a very strong garrison ; and, being upon the edge of Wiltshire, Berkshire, and Oxford- shire, shrewdly straitened the king's quarters.   The marquis of Hertford bringing with him, out of Wales, near two thous- and foot, and one regiment of horse, intended, with the as- sistance of prince Rupert, who appointed to join with him with some regiments from Oxford, to take in that town ; but by the extreme foulness of the ways, the great fall of rain at that time, (being about Christmas,) and some mistake in or- ders between the two generals, that design was disappointed ; and the alarm gave the enemy so much the more courage and diligence to provide for an assault.

In the beginning of February, prince Rupert went upon the same design with better success ; and at one and the same time, storming the town in several places, their works being not yet finished, though pertinaciously enough defend- ed, entered their line with some loss of men, and many hurt,

[1] i. e. their military reputation was so good, as to make it be believed that it was impossible for them to hold out longer than they did.—W.

but with a far greater of the enemy; for there were not so
few as two hundred killed upon the place, and above one
thousand taken prisoners, whereof Warneford[1] and Fetty-
place, (two gentlemen of good quality and fortune near that
town, and very active in the service,) Mr. George, a member of parliament who served for that borough, and two or
three Scottish officers of the field, whereof Carr the governor was one, were the chief.   The town yielded much plunder, from which the undistinguishing soldier could not be
kept,[2] but was equally injurious to friend and foe ; so that
many honest men, who were imprisoned by the rebels for
not concurring with them, found themselves at liberty and
undone together: amongst whom John Plot, a lawyer of very
good reputation, was one ; who being freed from the hard and
barbarous imprisonment in which he had been kept, when he
returned to his own house, found it full of soldiers, and twelve
hundred pounds in money taken from thence, which could
never be recovered.   The prince left a strong garrison there,
that brought almost all that whole county into contribution,
which was a great enlargement to the king's quarters, which
now, without interruption, extended from Oxford to Worcester; which important city, with the other of Hereford, and
those counties, had, some time before, been quitted by the
rebels; the earl of Stamford, who was left in those parts by
the earl of Essex, being called from thence, by the growth
of the king's party in Cornwall, to the securing the west.

We remembered before, when the marquis of Hertford
transported himself and his few foot into Wales from Minhead, that sir Ralph Hopton, and the other gentlemen, mentioned before, with their small force, consisting of about one
hundred horse, and fifty dragoons, retired into Cornwall,
neglected by the earl of Bedford, as fit and easy to be suppressed by the committees.   And, in truth, the committees
were entirely possessed of Devonshire, and thought themselves equally sure of Cornwall, save that the castle of
Pendennis was in the custody of one they had no hope of.

[1] Of Bibury.--W.   [2] A curious and well chosen and well
related instance of the miseries attending civil distractions.—W.

They were welcomed into Cornwall by sir Bevil Greenvil, who marched with them towards the west of that county, as being best affected, where they might have leisure to refresh their wearied and almost tired horse and men, and to call the well disposed gentry together; for which they chose Truro as the fittest place, the east part of the county being possessed by sir Alexander Carew, and sir Richard Buller, two members of the house of commons, and active men for the settling of the militia.   There was in this county, as throughout the whole kingdom, a wonderful and superstitious reverence towards the name of a parliament, and a prejudice to the power of the court; yet a full submission, and love of the established government of church and state,[1] especially to that part of the church as concerned the liturgy, or Book of Common Prayer, which was a most general object of veneration with the people.   And the jealousy, and apprehension that the other party intended to alter it, was a principal advancement of the king's service.   Though the major and most considerable part of the gentry, and men of estate, were heartily for the king, many of them being of the house of commons, and so having seen and observed by what spirit the distemper was begot, and carried on; yet there were others of name, fortune, and reputation with the people, very solicitous for the parliament, and more active than the other. There was a third sort (for a party they cannot be called) greater than either of the other, both in fortune and number, who, though they were satisfied in their consciences of the justice of the king's cause, had yet so great a dread of the power of the parliament, that they sat still as neuters, assisting neither.   So that they who did boldly appear, and declare for the king, were compelled to proceed with all wariness and circumspection; by the known and well understood rules of the law and justice; and durst not oppose the most extravagant act of the other side but with all the formality

[1] It was impossible for the historian to give a stronger proof of the king's ill government, and the endeavours of the several parliaments to maintain the people's rights, than this prejudice of a brave and honest people, which at the same time bore a reverence for the constitution both of church and state.—W.

that was used in full peace : which must be an answer to all
those oversights and omissions, which posterity will be apt
to impute to the king, in the morning of these distractions.[1]

The committee of the parliament, who were entirely possessed of Devonshire, and believed themselves masters of
Cornwall, drew their forces of the country to Launceston,
to be sure that sir Ralph Hopton and his adherents (whose
power they thought contemptible) might not escape out of
their hands.   This was before the battle of Edge-hill, when
the king was at lowest, and when the authority of parliament found little opposition in any place.   The quarter sessions came, where they caused a presentment to be drawn,
in form of law, " against divers men unknown, who were
lately come armed into that county *contra pacem,* &c."
Though none were named, all understood who were meant ;
and therefore sir Ralph Hopton, who well understood those
proceedings, voluntarily appeared ; took notice of the presentment, and produced the commission granted by the king,
under the great seal of England, to the marquis of Hertford,
by which he was constituted general of the west ; and a
commission, from his lordship, to sir Ralph Hopton, of lieutenant general of the horse ; and told them, " he was sent
to assist them, in the defence of their liberties, against all
illegal taxes and impositions."   Hereupon, after a full and
solemn debate, the jury, which consisted of gentlemen of
good quality, and fortunes in the county, not only acquitted
sir Ralph Hopton, and all the other gentlemen his companions, of any disturbance of the peace ; but declared, " that
it was a great favour and justice of his majesty, to send
down aid to them who were already marked out to destruction ; and that they thought it the duty of every good subject, as well in loyalty to the king, as in gratitude to those
gentlemen, to join with them with any hazard of life and fortune."

---

[1] The observance of this rule hindered the king from making a sufficient provision for his defence in the beginning of the war ; and the
violation of it towards the conclusion, presently destroyed that provision that had been made.—W.

As this full vindication was thus gotten on the king's part, so an indictment was preferred against sir Alexander Carew, sir Richard Buller, and the rest of the committee, " for a rout and unlawful assembly at Launceston ; and for riots and misdemeanours committed against many of the king's good subjects, in taking their liberties from them ;" (for they had intercepted and apprehended divers messengers, and others of the king's party, and employed by them.)   This indictment and information was found by the grand jury, and thereupon, according to a statute in that case provided, an order of sessions was granted to the high sheriff, a person well affected to the king's service, " to raise the *posse comitatus,* for the dispersing that unlawful assembly at Launceston, and for the apprehension of the rioters."   This was the rise and foundation of all the great service that was after performed in Cornwall, by which the whole west was reduced to the king.   For, by this means, there were immediately drawn together a body of three thousand foot, well armed ; which by no other means that could have been used could have been done : with which sir Ralph Hopton, whom they all willingly obeyed, advanced towards Launceston, where the committee had fortified, and from thence had sent messages of great contempt upon the proceedings of the sessions ; for, besides their confidence in their own Cornish strength, they had a good body of horse to second them upon all occasions, in the confines of Devon.

Sir George Chudleigh, a gentleman of good fortune and reputation in that county, and very active for the militia, being then at Tavistock, with five or six full troops of horse, raised in that county to go to their army, but detained till Cornwall could be settled ; and upon the news of sir Ralph Hopton's advancing, these drew to Litton, a village in Devonshire, but within three miles of Launceston.   Sir Ralph Hopton marched within two miles of the town, where he refreshed his men, intending, the next morning early, to fall on the town : but sir Richard Buller, and his confederates, not daring to abide the storm, in great disorder quitted the town that night, and drew into Devonshire, and so towards Plymouth ; so that in the morning sir Ralph Hopton found the gates of Launceston open, and entered without resistance. As the submission to, and reverence of, the known practised laws had, by the sheriff's authority, raised this army within very few days, so the extreme superstition to it as soon dissolved it.[1] For when all the persons of honour and quality, who well knew the desperate formed designs of the other party, earnestly pressed the pursuing the disheartened and dismayed rebels into Devon, by which they should quickly increase their numbers, by joining with the well affected in that large and populous county, who were yet awed into silence; it was powerfully objected, "that the sheriff, by whose legal authority only that force was drawn together, might not lawfully march out of his own county; and that it was the principal privilege of the trained bands, that they might not be compelled to march farther than the limits of their shire."

How grievous and inconvenient soever this doctrine was discerned to be, yet no man durst presume so far upon the temper of that people, as to object policy or necessity to their notions of law. And therefore, concealing, as much as was possible, the true reasons, they pretended their not following the enemy proceeded from apprehension of their strength, by joining with sir George Chudleigh, and of want of ammunition, (either of which were not unreasonable,) and so marched to Saltash, a town in Cornwall upon an arm of the sea; which only divided it from Plymouth and Devon, where was a garrison of two hundred Scots; who, upon the approach of sir Ralph Hopton, as kindly quit Saltash, as the others had Launceston before. So that being now entirely masters of Cornwall, they fairly dismissed those who could not be kept long together, and retired with their own handful of horse and dragoons, till a new provocation from the enemy should put fresh vigour into that county.

In the mean time, considering the casualty of those trained

[1] But by all this it appears that these loyal Cornish men, with all their reverence for the constitution of church and state, had little regard to the general quarrel. They only wanted to provide for themselves in peace in that sequestered corner. But they were soon wakened from this flattering dream.—W.

bands, and that strength, which on a sudden could be raised by the *posse comitatus*, which, though it made a gallant show in Cornwall, they easily saw would be of no use towards the quenching the general rebellion over England, they entered upon thoughts of raising voluntary regiments of foot; which could be only done by the gentlemen of that country among their neighbours, and tenants, who depended on them. Sir Bevil Greenvil, (the generally most loved man of that county,) sir Nicholas Slanning, the gallant governor of Pendennis castle, John Arundel, and John Trevannion, two young men of excellent hopes, and heirs to great fortunes in that country, (all four of them members of the house of commons, and so better informed, and acquainted with the desperate humours of the adverse party,) undertook the raising regiments of volunteers; many young gentlemen, of the most considerable families of the county, assisting them as inferior officers. So that, within a shorter time than could be expected, from one single small county, there was a body of foot, of near fifteen hundred, raised, armed, and well disciplined for action. But there was then an accident, that might have discomposed a people which had not been very well prepared to perform their duties.

The lord Mohun, (who had departed from York from the king with all professions of zeal and activity in his service) had, from the time of the first motion in Cornwall, forborne to join himself to the king's party ; staying at home at his own house, and imparting himself equally to all men of several constitutions, as if he had not been yet sufficiently informed which party to adhere to. But after all the adverse party was driven out of Cornwall, and the fame of the king's marching in the head of an army, and having fought the battle at Edge-hill, (the event whereof was variously reported,) without acquainting any body with his intention, he took a journey towards London, at the time when the king marched that way, and presented himself to his majesty at Brentford, as sent from sir Ralph Hopton and the rest of those gentlemen engaged in Cornwall ; though many men believed that his purpose was in truth for London, if he had not then found the king's condition better than it was generally believed. Upon his lordship's information of the state of those western parts, and upon a supposition that he spake the sense and desires of those from whom he pretended to come, the king granted a commission jointly to his lordship, sir Ralph Hopton,[1] sir John Berkley, and colonel Ashburnham, to govern those forces, in the absence of the lord marquis of Hertford; with which he returned into Cornwall, and immediately raised a regiment of foot; behaving him as actively, and being every way as forward in the advancing the great business, as any man; so that men imputed his former reservedness, only to his not being satisfied in a condition of command.

On the other side, they who were concerned in that alteration were not at all well contented. For before, those gentlemen of Cornwall, upon whose interest and activity the work depended, had, with great readiness, complied with the other, both out of great value of their persons, with whom they had good familiarity and friendship, and in respect of their authority and commissions, with which they came qualified in that county: for, as was remembered before, sir Ralph Hopton had a commission from the marquis of Hertford, to be lieutenant general of the horse; sir John Berkley, to be commissary general; and colonel Ashburnham, to be major general of the foot; so that there was no dispute of commands. But now, the lord Mohun's coming into an equal command with any, and superior to those who thought their reputation and interest to be superior to his, (for he had not the good fortune to be very gracious in his own country,) and this by his own solicitation and interposition, gave them some indignation. However their public-heartedness, and joint concernment in the good cause, so totally suppressed all animosities, or indeed indispositions, that a greater concurrence could not be desired in whatsoever could contribute to the work in hand; so that they not only preserved Cornwall entire, but made bold incursions into Devon, even to the walls of Plymouth and Exeter; though the season of the year, being the deep winter,[2] and the want of ammunition, forced them to retire into Cornwall.

[1] This was of a piece with all the rest of the court conduct throughout the prosecution of the war.—W.

[2] Deep of winter.—W.

The reputation of their being masters of that one county, and the apprehension of what they might be shortly able to do, making the parliament think it time to take more care for their suppression.   And therefore they sent their whole forces out of Dorset and Somerset, to join with those of Devon, to make an entire conquest of Cornwall.   With these, Ruthen (a Scotchman, then governor of Plymouth) advanced into Cornwall, by a bridge over the Tamar, six miles above Saltash, (where he had before endeavoured to force his passage by water, but had been beaten off with loss,) having mastered the guard there ; the earl of Stamford following him, two or three days' march behind, with a new supply of horse and foot ; albeit those the Scotchman had with him were much superior to those of the king's ; which, upon this sudden invasion, were forced to retire with their whole strength to Bodmin ; whither, foreseeing this storm some few days before it came, they had again summoned the *posse comitatus,* which appeared in considerable numbers.

They had scarce refreshed themselves there, and put their men in order, when Ruthen, with his horse, foot, and cannon, was advanced to Liskard, within seven miles of Bodmin ; from whence they moved towards the enemy with all alacrity, knowing how necessary it was for them to fight before the earl of Stamford, who was at that time come to Launceston with a strong party of horse and foot, should be able to join with the rebels.   And as this consideration was of importance to hasten the one, so it prevailed with the other party too ; for Ruthen, apprehending that his victory, of which he made no question, would be clouded by the presence of the earl of Stamford, who had the chief command, resolved to despatch the business before he came.   And so sir Ralph Hopton (to whom the other commissioners, who had a joint authority with him, willingly devolved the sole command for that day, lest confusion of orders might beget distraction) was no sooner known to be drawing towards him, (to whom a present battle was so necessary, that it was resolved, upon all disadvantages, to have fallen on the enemy in the town rather than not fight,) but Ruthen likewise drew out his forces, and, choosing his ground upon the east

side of Bradock-Down near Liskard, stood in battalia to expect the enemy: sir Ralph Hopton, having likewise put his
men in order, caused public prayers to be said, in the head
of every squadron, (which the rebels observing, told their
fellows, "they were at mass," to stir up their courages in
the cause of religion,) and having winged his foot with his
horse and dragoons, he advanced within musket-shot of the
enemy, who stood without any motion.   Then perceiving
that their cannon were not yet come up from the town, he
caused two small iron minion drakes (all the artillery they
had) to be drawn, under the cover of little parties of horse,
to a convenient distance from the body of the enemies ; and
after two shots of those drakes, (which being not discerned,
and doing some execution, struck a great terror into them,)
advanced with his body upon them ; and, with very easy
contention, beat them off their ground ; they having lined
the hedges behind them with their reserve, by which they
thought securely to make their retreat into the town.   But
the Cornish so briskly bestirred themselves, and pressed
them so hard on every side, being indeed excellent at hedge-
work, and that kind of fight, that they quickly won that
ground too, and put their whole army in a rout, and had the
full execution of them as far as they would pursue.   But,
after that advantage, they were always more sparing than is
usually known in civil wars, shedding very little blood after
resistance was given over, and having a very noble and
Christian sense of the lives of their brethren : insomuch as
the common men, when they have been pressed by some
fiercer officer, to follow the execution, have answered, "they
could not find in their hearts to hurt men who had nothing
in their hands."

In this battle, without the loss of any officer of name, and
very few common men, they took twelve hundred and fifty
prisoners, most of their colours, all their cannon, being four
brass guns, (whereof two were twelve pounders,) and one
iron saker, all their ammunition, and most of their arms.
Ruthen himself, and those few who could keep pace with
him, fled to Saltash ; which he thought to fortify, and by
the neighbourhood of Plymouth, and assistance of the ship-

ping, to defend ; and thereby still to have an influence upon a good part of Cornwall.   The earl of Stamford, receiving quick advertisement of this defeat, in great disorder retired to Tavistock, to preserve the utmost parts of Devon from incursions.   Hereupon, after a solemn thanksgiving to God for this great victory, (which was about the middle of January,) and a little refreshing their men at Liskard, the king's forces divided themselves ; sir John Berkley, and colonel Ashburnham, with sir Bevil Greenvil, sir Nicholas Slanning's and colonel Trevannion's voluntary regiments, and such a party of horse and dragoons as could be spared, advanced to Tavistock to visit the earl of Stamford ; the lord Mohun and sir Ralph Hopton, with the lord Mohun's and colonel Godolphin's voluntary regiments, and some of the trained bands, marched towards Saltash, to dislodge Ruthen ; who in three days (for there was no more between his defeat at Bradock-Down, and his visitation at Saltash) had cast up such works, and planted such store of cannon upon the narrow avenues, that he thought himself able, with the help of a goodly ship of four hundred tons, in which were sixteen pieces of cannon, which he had brought up the river to the very side of the town, to defend that place against any strength was like to be brought against him.   But he quickly found that the same spirit possessed his enemies that drove him from Liskard, and the same that possessed his own men when they fled from thence ; for as soon as the Cornish came up, they fell upon his works, and in a short time beat him out of them ; and then out of the town, with a good execution upon them ; many being killed, and more drowned : Ruthen himself hardly getting into a boat, by which he got into Plymouth, leaving all his ordnance behind him, which, together with the ship, and sevenscore prisoners, and all their colours, which had been saved at Liskard, were taken by the conquerors, who were now again entire masters of Cornwall.

The earl of Stamford had not the same patience to abide the other party at Tavistock, but, before their approach, quitted the town ; some of his forces making haste into Plymouth, and the rest retiring into Exeter.   And so, though the old superstition, of not going out of the county, again disbanded the trained bands, the Cornish, with all their voluntary forces, drew into Devon, and fixed quarters within less than a mile of Plymouth, and kept guards even within musket-shot of their line. Sir John Berkley in the mean time with a good party volant, of horse and dragoons, with great diligence and gallantry, visiting all places in Devon, where their people were gathered together, and dissolving them, took many prisoners of name ; and so kept James Chudleigh, the major general of the parliament forces, from raising a body there; which he industriously intended.

In those necessary and brisk expeditions falling upon Chagford[1] (a little town in the south of Devon) before day, the king lost Sidney Godolphin, a young gentleman of incomparable parts; who, being of a constitution and education more delicate, and unacquainted with contentions, upon his observation of the wickedness of those men in the house of commons, of which he was a member, out of the pure indignation of his soul, and conscience to his country, had, with the first, engaged himself with that party in the west: and though he thought not fit to take command in a profession he had not willingly chosen, yet as his advice was of great authority with all the commanders, being always one in the council of war, and whose notable abilities they had still use of in their civil transactions, so he exposed his person to all action, travel, and hazard ; and by too forward engaging himself in this last, received a mortal shot by a musket,[2] a little above the knee, of which he died in the instant ; leaving the ignominy of his death upon a place, which could never otherwise have had a mention to the world.

After this, which happened about the end of January, in respect of the season of the year, and the want of ammunition, finding that they could make no impression upon the strong holds of the enemy, they retired, with their whole forces, to Tavistock ; where they refreshed and rested themselves many days, being willing to ease their fast friends of Cornwall, as much as was possible, from the trouble and

[1] Midway between Tavistock and Exeter.—W.

[2] By his will he left Hobbes, with whom he was intimate, 200l. in esteem of his great parts, not his principles.—W.

charge of their little army.   The difficulties they were entangled with were very prodigious ; of which one was, that
the west were so entirely possessed by the enemy, that they
could have no correspondence, or receive any intelligence
from the king, not one messenger in ten arriving at his journey's end.   Then though the justice and piety of the cause
added much power to particular persons in raising an army ;
yet the money, that was raised for the maintenance and payment of that army, was entirely upon the reputation, credit,
and interest of particular men : and how long that spring
would supply those streams, the most sanguine among them
could not presume ; but the want of ammunition troubled
them most of all : they had yet had none but what had been
taken out of the low store of Pendennis castle, and what they
had won from the enemy ; the first wanted a supply for its
own provision, but which way to procure that supply they
could not imagine ; and the fear and apprehension of such
straits, against which no probable hope occurs, is more grievous and insupportable than any present want.

In this instant, as if sent by Providence, an opportunity
found them they had scarce courage to hope for : captain
Carteret, the controller of the king's navy, having in the beginning of the troubles, after he had refused to have command in their fleets, had without noise withdrawn himself
and his family out of England to Jersey, and being there impatient to be quiet, whilst his master was in the field, he
transported himself into Cornwall with a purpose to raise a
troop of horse, and to engage in that service : when he came
thither, he was unanimously importuned by the commanders,
after they had acquainted him with their hopeless and desperate want of powder, to assist them in that manner, that
the many good ports in their power might be made of some
use to them in the supply of powder : whereupon he shortly
returned into France ; and first upon his own credit, and then
upon return of such commodities out of Cornwall as they
could well spare, he supplied them with such great proportions of all kinds of ammunitions, that they never found want
after.

In the mean time, when they were clouded with that want
78*

at Tavistock, some gentlemen of Cornwall who adhered to the rebels, and were thereby dispossessed of their county, made some overtures, " that a treaty might be entered into, whereby the peace of those two counties of Cornwall and Devon might be settled, and the war be removed into other parts." They who had most experience of the humours and dispositions of the factious party, easily concluded the little hope of peace by such a treaty ; yet the proposition was so specious and popular, that there was no rejecting it; and therefore they agreed to a meeting between persons chosen of either side ; and the earl of Stamford himself seemed so ingenuous,[1] that, at the very first meeting, to show their clear intentions, it was mutually agreed, that every person employed and trusted in the treaty should first make a pro-testation in these words: " I do solemnly vow and protest, in the presence of Almighty God, that I do not only come a commissioner to this treaty, with an hearty and fervent de-sire of concluding an honourable and firm peace between the two counties of Cornwall and Devon ; but also will, to the utmost of my power, prosecute and really endeavour to ac-complish and effect the same, by all lawful ways and means I possibly can; first by maintaining the protestant religion established by law in the church of England, the just rights and prerogative of our sovereign lord the king, the just pri-vileges and freedom of parliaments; together with the just rights and liberty of the subjects; and that I am without any intention (by fomenting this unnatural war) to gain, or hope to advantage myself with the real or personal estate of any person whatsoever, or obtaining any office, command, title of honour, benefit, or reward, either from the king's majesty, or either or both houses of parliament now assembled. And this I take, in the presence of Almighty God, and as I shall answer the same at his tribunal, according to the literal sense

[1] This was politicly done of the earl of Stamford and his party, for they were distressed by the successes of those of Cornwall. But the gentlemen there on the other side would certainly never have consent-ed to a neutrality at this juncture, could they have overcome what lord Clarendon calls the *superstition,* and I the *absurdity,* of the common people of Cornwall.—W.

and meaning of the foregoing words, without any equivoca-
tion, mental reservation, or other evasion whatsoever. So
help me God."

The taking this protestation with that solemnity, and the
blessed sacrament thereupon, made even those, who before
expected little fruit from the treaty, believe, that men, being
so engaged, would not be liable to those passions and affections, which usually transported that party; and so to hope
that some good might proceed from it: and therefore the
king's party were easily induced to retire with their forces
into Cornwall; and thereupon a truce and cessation was
agreed upon, that the treaty might proceed without interruption. In which treaty, the same continuing beyond the expiration of the present year 1642, we shall for the present
leave them; that we may take a short survey of the northern parts, and remember by what degrees they came to feel
the calamities, and to bear their burden in the civil war.

When the king left Yorkshire, he appointed sir Thomas
Glemham, at the desire of the gentlemen of that county, as
was before remembered, to stay in York, to order and command those forces, which they should find necessary to raise,
to defend themselves from the excursions of Hull, whence
young Hotham infested the country more than his father; who
was willing enough to sit still in his garrison, where he believed
he could make advantage upon the success of either party :
and they who were most inclined to the parliament (whereof the lord Fairfax and his son were the chief; from whom
the king was so far from expecting any notable mischief, that
he left them all at their own houses, when he went thence;
and might, if he had thought it requisite, have carried them
away prisoners with him) were rather desirous to look on,
than engage themselves in the war; presuming that one battle would determine all disputes, and the party which prevailed in that would find a general submission throughout the
kingdom. And truly, I believe,[1] there was scarce one con-

---

[1] The historian's reason for his belief could be only this, that, if all
the king's friends had appeared ready for service together, so formidable a power would have confined the parliament within peaceful limits. But he did not consider the friends of parliament were as back-

clusion, that hath contributed more to the continuance and
length of the war, than that generally received opinion in the
beginning, that it would be quickly at an end.   Hereupon,
there being but one visible difference like to beget distractions in the country, which was about the militia, the king
appointing it to be governed and disposed by the commission
of array, and the parliament by its ordinance; for the composing whereof, the gentlemen of the several opinions proposed, between themselves, " that neither the one nor the
other should be meddled with ; but that all should be contented to sit still, without engagement to either party."   This
seemed very reasonable to the parliament party, who were
rather carried away with an implicit reverence to the
name of a parliament (the fatal disease[1] of the whole kingdom) than really transported with the passion and design of
the furious part of it ; and who plainly discerned, that by
much the greatest part of the persons of honour, quality, and
interest in the county would cordially oppose their proceedings: for, besides the lord Fairfax, there were in truth few
of good reputation and fortune, who run that way.   On the
other hand, the king's party thought their work done by it;
for they having already sent two good regiments of foot, the
one under colonel John Bellasis, younger son to the lord viscount Falconbridge, and the other under sir William Penny-
man ; and two regiments of dragoons, the one under colonel
Duncomb; the other, colonel Gowre ; besides three or four
good troops of horse ; and the king being at that distance,
that they could not send him farther supply ; they thought
they had nothing to do, but to keep the country in such a
peace, that it might do the king no harm by sending men to
the earl of Essex, or adhering to the garrison of Hull ; and
concluding, as the other did,[2] that the decision between the

ward, and that the appearance of their enemies would have brought
them likewise forward, so the balance would soon have been even.—
W.

  [1] But a disease arising from the long preceding corruptions of the
court.—W.

  [2] The noble historian confesses this was the case of both parties ;

king and parliament would be at the first encounter. Upon these deliberations, articles were solemnly drawn up, consented to and subscribed by the lord Fairfax, and Harry Bellasis, the heir apparent of the lord Falconbridge, who were the two knights who served in parliament for Yorkshire, nearly allied together, and of great kindness till their several opinions and affections had divided them in this quarrel: the former adhering to the parliament; the latter, with great courage and sobriety, to the king.

With them, the principal persons of either party subscribed the articles, and gave their mutual faiths to each other, that they would observe them; being indeed no other than an engagement of neutrality, and to assist neither party. Of all the gentry of Yorkshire, there were only two dissenters on the parliament side; young Hotham, and sir Edward Rhodes; who, though of the better quality, was not so much known, or considered, as the other. But they quickly found seconds enough; for the parliament no sooner was informed of this transaction, than they expressed their detestation of it, and gently in words (though scornfully in matter) reprehending the lord Fairfax,[1] and his party, " for being cozened and overreached by the other;" they declared, " that none of the parties to that agreement had any authority to bind that country to any such neutrality, as was mentioned in that agreement; it being a peculiar and proper power and privilege of parliament, where the whole body of the kingdom is represented, to bind all, or any part thereof: that it was very

he says that they concluded alike, that *the decision between the king and parliament would be at the first encounter.*—W.

[1] The general argument in this reprehension is very solid; nothing being more unjust and absurb than such partial neutralities in a quarrel that concerns the whole. It is true, the parliament was much more concerned to discountenance them than the king, since the cause of the parliament could be only supported by extraordinary measures, which an inflamed and enthusiastic temper only will engage in; and when this is suffered to cool by a neutrality, all is in danger. Whereas the other party following and relying upon established law and custom, a neutrality gives new force to their operations, which had been weakened by the bold impingments on them.—W.

prejudicial and dangerous to the whole kingdom, that one county should withdraw themselves from the assistance of the rest, to which they were bound by law, and by several orders and declarations of parliament: that it was very derogatory to the power and authority of parliament, that any private men should take upon them to suspend the execution of the ordinance of the militia, declared by both houses to be according to law, and very necessary, at that time, for the preservation of the peace and safety of the kingdom. And therefore, they said, they thought themselves bound in conscience to hinder all farther proceedings upon that agreement; and ordered, that no such neutrality should be observed in that county. For if they should suffer particular counties to divide themselves from the rest of the kingdom, it would be a means of bringing all to ruin and destruction." And therefore they farther declared, that "neither the lord Fairfax, nor the gentlemen of Yorkshire, who were parties to those articles, nor any other inhabitants of that county, were bound by any such agreement; but required them to pursue their former resolutions, of maintaining and assisting the parliament, in defence of the common cause, according to the general protestation wherein they were bound with the rest of the kingdom, and against the particular protestation by themselves lately made; and according to such orders and commissions as they should receive from both houses of parliament, from the committee of the lords and commons appointed for the safety of the kingdom, or from the earl of Essex, lord general." And, lest this their declaration should not be of power enough to dissolve this agreement, they published their resolution, and directed that "Mr. Hotham and sir Edward Rhodes should proceed upon their former instructions; and that they should have power to seize and apprehend all delinquents that were so voted by the parliament, and all such others, as delinquents, as had, or did show themselves opposite and disobedient to the orders and proceedings of parliament."

Upon this declaration, and vote, not only young Hotham fell to the practice of acts of hostility, with all licence, out of the garrison at Hull: but the lord Fairfax himself, and all

the gentlemen of that party, who had, with that protestation, signed the articles, instead of resenting the reproach to
themselves, tamely submitted to those unreasonable conclusions; and, contrary to their solemn promise and engagement, prepared themselves to bear a part in the war, and
made all haste to levy men.

Upon so great a disadvantage were the king's party in all
places;[1] who were so precise in promises, and their personal
undertakings, that they believed they could not serve the
king, and his cause, if their reputation and integrity were
once blemished, though some particular contract proved to
his disadvantage : whilst the others exposed their honours
for any present temporary conveniencies, and thought themselves absolved by any new resolution of the houses, to
whose custody their honour and ingenuity was committed.
The present disadvantage of this rupture[2] was greater to the
king's party there, than to the other. For (besides that
many, who concurred with them very frankly and solicitous-
ly in the neutrality, separated themselves from them now
there was a necessity of action) they had neither money to
raise men, nor arms to arm them; so that the strength consisted in the gentlemen themselves, and their retinue ; who,
by the good affections of the inhabitants of York, were
strong enough to secure one another within the walls of that
city.   Then the earl of Cumberland, in whom the chief
power of command was to raise men and money in a case of
necessity, though he was a person of entire devotion to the
king, was in his nature unactive, and utterly unexperienced
in affairs and exigents of that nature.

On the other hand, the opposite party was strengthened
and enabled by the strong garrison of Hull, whence young
Hotham, on all occasions, was ready to second them with
his troop of horse, and to take up any well affected person

---

[1] This might be true in fact, but it makes nothing against what I
here say of these neutralities.—W.

[2] The rupture was more disadvantageous to the royalists than to
the parliamentarians, for the reason given above, as well as for the
reasons here urged by the noble historian.—W.

who was suspected to be loyal; which drove all resolved men from their houses into York, where they only could be safe. They could have what men more they desired from London, and both ready money from thence to Hull, and ordinances to raise what they would in the county to pay them. Leeds, Halifax, and Bradford, three very populous and rich towns, (which depending wholly upon clothiers naturally maligned the gentry,) were wholly at their disposition.[1] Their neighbours in Lincolnshire were in a body to second them, and sir John Gell was on the same behalf possessed of Derby, and all that county, there being none that had the hardiness yet, to declare there for the king. So that, if sir John Hotham's wariness had not kept him from being active, and his pride, and contempt of the lord Fairfax, upon whom the country chiefly depended, hindered him from seconding and assisting his lordship; or if any man had had the entire command of those parts and forces, to have united them, the parliament had, with very little resistance, been absolute masters of all Yorkshire ; and, as easily, of the city itself. But their want of union in the by, though they agreed too well in the main, gave the king's party time to breathe, and to look about for their preservation. Thereupon they sent to the earl of Newcastle for assistance; offering, " if he would march into Yorkshire, they would join with him, and be entirely commanded by him ;" the earl of Cumberland willingly offering to wave any title to command.

It was before remembered, that, when the king left York, he had sent the earl of Newcastle, as a person of great honour and interest in those parts, to be governor of Newcastle; and so to secure that port, that the parliament might neither seize it, nor the Scots be bribed by it to come to the assistance of their brethren. Which commission from

---

[1] It is true, this is too much the general disposition of rich manufacturers; but I believe in civil dissensions, men take their party on more substantial and affecting motives. Nothing is more baleful to trade and commerce than arbitrary government. It is no wonder then that the trading communities should think those pretended patrons of liberty in parliament were their natural protectors.—W.

the king his lordship no sooner executed, without the least hostility, (for that town received him with all possible acknowledgments of the king's goodness in sending him,) but he was impeached by the house of commons of high treason. From his going thither, (which was in August,) till toward the end of November, the earl spent his time in disposing the people of Northumberland, and the bishopric of Durham, to the king's service, and to a right understanding of the matters in difference; in the fortifying Newcastle, and the river; whereby that harbour might only be in the king's obedience; in raising a garrison for that place, and providing arms for a farther advance of the king's service. Then he provided for the assistance of his friends in Yorkshire, whose condition grew every day more desperate. For the parliament, finding the inconveniencies of having no commander in chief in those parts, had caused their generalissimo, the earl of Essex, to send a commission to the lord Fairfax, " to command all the forces of Yorkshire, and the adjacent counties, in chief;" by which, in less time than could be reasonably imagined, he was able to draw together an army of five or six thousand horse and foot; so that York must presently have been swallowed up.

But, in the beginning of December, the earl of Newcastle marched to their relief; and having left a good garrison in Newcastle, and fixed such small garrisons in his way, as might secure his communication with that port, to which all his ammunition was to be brought; and with a body of near three thousand foot, and six or seven hundred horse and dragoons, without any encounter with the enemy, (though they had threatened loud,) he entered York; having lessened the enemy's strength, without blood, both in territories and men. For, as soon as he entered Yorkshire, two regiments raised in Richmondshire and Cleveland dissolved of themselves; having it yet in their choice to dwell at home, or to leave their houses to new comers. The earl being now master of the north as far as York, thought rather of forming an army, and providing money to pay it, than of making any farther progress in the winter; and therefore suffered the lord Fairfax to enjoy the southern part of that large rich county, till the spring, and his improved posture, should enable him to advance : yet few days passed without blows, in which the parliament forces had usually the worst.

Shortly after the earl's coming to York, general King repaired to him, whom he made lieutenant general of his army ; who, notwithstanding the unavoidable prejudice of his being a Scotchman, ordered the foot with great wisdom and dexterity : the charge of the horse being at the same time committed to general Goring ; who, by the queen's favour,[1] notwithstanding all former failings, was recommended to that province, and quickly applied himself to action : so that, though the lord Fairfax kept Selby and Cawood, both within a small distance from York, the earl was absolute master of the field.　And now the north yielding secure footing for those who had been unreasonably persecuted for their obedience to the king, the queen herself thought of returning into England.

Her majesty had, from her first going into Holland, dexterously laboured to advance the king's interest, and sent very great quantities of arms and ammunition to Newcastle, (though, by the vigilance of the parliament agents in those parts, and the power of their ships, too much of it was intercepted,) with some considerable sums of money, and good store of officers ; who, by the connivance of the prince of Orange, came over to serve their own king.　And from this extraordinary care of her majesty's, and her known grace and favour to the person of the earl of Newcastle, who she well knew had contracted many enemies by the eminency of his devotion to the king, that army was by the parliament styled the *queen's army*, and the *catholic army*, thereby to expose her majesty the more to the rude malice of the people, and the army to their prejudice ; persuading them " that it consisted of none but professed papists, who intended nothing but the extirpation of the protestants, and establishing their own profession."

About the middle of February, the queen took shipping

---

[1] This was not one of the least of the mischiefs she caused to the king by her pragmatic temper, always busy and overbearing.—W.

from Holland, in a States man of war, assigned by the prince of Orange with others for her convoy, and arrived safely in Burlington Bay, upon the coast of Yorkshire; where she had the patience to stay on shipboard at anchor, the space of two days, till the earl had notice, " to draw such a part of his forces that way, as might secure her landing, and wait on her to York;" which he no sooner did, (and he did it with all imaginable expedition,) but her majesty came on shore; and, for the present, was pleased to refresh herself in a convenient house upon the very key, where all accommodations were made for her reception; there being many things of moment to be unshipped before she could reasonably enter upon her journey towards York.

The second day after the queen's landing, Batten, vice-admiral to the earl of Warwick, (who had waited to intercept her passage,) with four of the king's ships, arrived in Burlington Road; and, finding that her majesty was landed, and that she lodged upon the key, bringing his ships to the nearest distance, being very early in the morning, discharged above a hundred cannon (whereof many were laden with cross-bar-shot) for the space of two hours upon the house where her majesty was lodged: whereupon she was forced out of her bed, some of the shot making way through her own chamber; and to shelter herself under a bank in the open fields; which barbarous and treasonable act was so much the more odious, in that the parliament never so far took notice of it, as to disavow it. So that many believed it was very pleasing to, if not commanded by them; and that, if the ships had encountered at sea, they would have left no hazard unrun to have destroyed her majesty.

The queen shortly after removed to York, and the king's affairs prospered to that degree, that, as the earl of Newcastle had before fixed a garrison at Newark in Nottinghamshire, which kept the forces of Lincoln from joining entirely with the lord Fairfax, and had with great courage beaten off a formed body of the rebels who attempted it; so he now sent Charles Cavendish, the younger brother of the earl of Devonshire, with a party volant of horse and dragoons, into Lincolnshire; where, about the middle of March, he assaulted Grantham, a new garrison of the rebels ; which he took, and in it above three hundred prisoners, with all their officers, arms, and ammunition : and, about the same time, sir Hugh Cholmondley, who had done very notable service to the parliament, and oftener defeated the earl of Newcastle's troops (though he had been in truth hurried to that party, rather by the engagement of sir John Hotham, with whom he had long friendship, than by his own inclination) than any officer of those parts, very frankly revolted to his allegiance ; and waiting on her majesty for her assurance of his pardon, delivered up the castle of Scarborough (a place of great importance) to the king ; the command and government whereof was again by the earl committed to him ; which he discharged with courage and singular fidelity. By this means, and those successes, the lord Fairfax quitted Selby, Cawood, and Tadcaster, and retired to Pomfret and Halifax ; whereby the earl was, upon the matter, possessed of that whole large county, and so able to help his neighbours. This was the state of that part of the north which was under the earl of Newcastle's commission : for Lancashire, Cheshire, and Shropshire, were in a worse condition ; of which, and the neighbour counties, it will be necessary in the next place to say somewhat ; and of those first which lie farthest off.

We have said before, that when the king left Shrewsbury, and marched to meet the earl of Essex, (which he did at Edge-hill,) all his designs being to come to a battle ; and the opinion of most, that a battle would determine all ; he was to apply all the strength and forces he could possibly raise, to the increasing his army ; so that he left no one garrison behind him, but relied upon the interest and authority of the lord Strange, (who was, by the death of his father, now earl of Derby,) to suppress all commotions and insurrections, which might happen in the counties of Lancashire and Cheshire ; which his lordship was confident he should be able to do, and was then generally believed to have a greater influence upon those two counties, and a more absolute command over the people in them, than any subject in England had, in any other quarter of the kingdom. The town of Shrewsbury, and that good county, where the king had been so prosperous, (and by which the people were more engaged,) he intrusted only to that good spirit that then possessed it, and to the legal authority of the sheriffs and justices of the peace. And it fared in those counties as in all other parts of the kingdom, that the number of those who desired to sit still was greater than of those who desired to engage in either party; so that they were generally inclined to articles of neutrality.[1] And in Cheshire, the active people of both sides came to those capitulations, with as much solemnity as had been in Yorkshire, and with the same declaration (so much the same, that there was no other difference but alterations of names and place) were absolved from the observation of them. And then sir William Bruerton, a gentleman of a competent fortune in that county, and knight for that shire in parliament, but most notorious for a known aversion to the government of the church, bringing with him from London a troop of horse, and a regiment of dragoons, marched thither to protect those who were of that party, and, under such a shelter, to encourage them to appear.

The city of Chester was firm to the king, by the virtue of the inhabitants, and interest of the bishop, and cathedral men; but especially by the reputation and dexterity of Mr. Bridgman, son to the bishop, and a lawyer of very good estimation; who not only informed them of their duties, and encouraged them in it, but upon his credit and estate, both which were very good, supplied them with whatsoever was necessary for their defence; so that they were not put to be honest and expensive together. But as they had no garrison of soldiers, so they had no officer of skill and experience to manage and direct that courage which, at least, was willing to defend their own walls; which they were now like to be put to. Therefore the king sent thither sir Nicholas Byron, a soldier of very good command, with a commission to be " colonel general of Cheshire and Shropshire ; and to be go-

---

[1] There cannot be a stronger proof than this, that the body of the people of England thought that the king had made ample amends for his ill government, by his passing so many salutary laws before the two parties had recourse to arms.---W.

vernor of Chester ;" who being a person of great affability and dexterity, as well as martial knowledge, gave great life to the designs of the well affected there ; and, with the encouragement of some gentlemen of North Wales, in a short time raised such a power of horse and foot, as made often skirmishes with the enemy; sometimes with notable advantage, never with any signal loss. So that sir William Bruerton fortified Nantwich, as the king's party did Chester : from which garrisons, which contained both their forces, they contended which should most prevail upon, that is most, subdue, the affections of the county, to declare for and join with them. But the fair expectation of Cheshire was clouded by the storms that arose in Lancashire, where men of no name, and contemned interest, by the mere credit of the parliament, and frenzy of the people, on a sudden snatched that large and populous county from their devotion to the great earl of Derby.

The town of Manchester had, from the beginning, (out of that factious humour which possessed most corporations, and the pride of their 'wealth,) opposed the king, and declared magisterially for the parliament. But as the major part of the county consisted of papists, of whose insurrections they had made such use in the beginning of the parliament, when they had a mind to alarm the people with dangers ; so it was confidently believed, that there was not one man of ten throughout that county, who meant not to be dutiful and loyal to the king : yet the restless spirit of the seditious party was so sedulous and industrious, and every one of the party so ready to be engaged, and punctually to obey ; and, on the other hand, the earl of Derby so unactive, and through greatness of mind so uncomplying with those who were fuller of alacrity, and would have proceeded more vigorously against the enemy ; or, through fear so confounded, that, instead of countenancing the king's party in Cheshire, which was expected from him, the earl, insensibly, found Lancashire to be almost possessed against him ; the rebels every day gaining and fortifying all the strong towns, and surprising his troops,

---

[1] In other words, love of liberty for the sake of trade.

without any considerable encounter.   And yet, so hard was the king's condition, that, though he knew those great misfortunes proceeded from want of conduct, and of a vigorous and expert commander, he thought it not safe to make any alteration, lest that earl might be provoked, out of disdain to have any superior in Lancashire, to manifest how much he could do against him, though it appeared he could do little for him.   Yet it was easily discerned, that his ancient power there depended more upon the fear than love of the people; there being very many, now in this time of liberty, engaging themselves against the king, that they might not be subject to that lord's commands.

However, the king committing Lancashire still to his lordship's care, (whose fidelity, without doubt, was blameless, whatever his skill and courage was,) he sent the lord Capel to Shrewsbury, with a commission of "lieutenant general of Shropshire, Cheshire, and North Wales;" who, being a person of great fortune and honour, quickly engaged those parts in a cheerful association; and raised a body of horse and foot, that gave sir William Bruerton so much trouble at Nantwich, that the garrison at Chester had breath to enlarge its quarters, and to provide for its own security; though the enemy omitted no opportunity of infesting them, and gave them as much trouble as was possible.   And it cannot be denied but sir William Bruerton, and the other gentlemen of that party, albeit their education and course of life had been very different from their present engagements, and for the most part were very unpromising to matters of courage, and therefore were too much contemned enemies, executed their commands with notable sobriety, and indefatigable industry, (virtues not so well practised in the king's quarters,) insomuch as the best soldiers who encountered with them had no cause to despise them.   It is true, they had no other straits and difficulties to struggle with, than what proceeded from their enemy; being always supplied with money to pay their soldiers, and with arms to arm them; whereby it was in their power not to grieve and oppress the people. And thereby (besides the spirit of faction that much governed) the common people were more devoted to them, and gave them all intelligence of what might concern them; whereas they who were intrusted to govern the king's affairs had intolerable difficulties to pass through; being to raise men without money, to arm them without weapons, (that is, they had no magazine to supply them,) and to keep them together without pay; so that the country was both to feed and clothe the soldiers; which quickly inclined them to remember only the burden, and forget the quarrel.

And the difference in the temper of the common people of both sides was so great,[1] that they who inclined to the parliament left nothing unperformed that might advance the cause; and were incredibly vigilant and industrious to cross and hinder whatsoever might promote the king's: whereas they who wished well to him thought they had performed their duty in doing so, and that they had done enough for him, in that they had done nothing against him.

Though, by this sending the lord Capel, those counties of Shropshire and Cheshire, with the assistance of North Wales, kept those parts so near their obedience, that their disobedience was not yet pernicious to the king, in sending assistance to the earl of Essex against his majesty, or to the lord Fairfax against the earl of Newcastle; yet those counties which lay in the line between Oxford and York were, upon the matter, entirely possessed by the enemy. The garrison of Northampton kept that whole county in obedience to the parliament, save that from Banbury the adjacent parishes were forced to bring some contribution thither. In Warwickshire the king had no footing; the castle of Warwick, the city of Coventry, and his own castle of Killingworth, being fortified against him. The lord Grey, son to the earl of Stamford, had the command of Leicestershire, and had put a garrison into Leicester. Derbyshire, without any visible

---

[1] The reason of this different temper is evident; the royalists had the constitution and the established laws on their side, so all they had to fear in adhering to them was, not to irritate the parliament by an over active prosecution of them; whereas the parliamentarians acting in an extraordinary [way], not authorized by the established laws, had no other way to save themselves harmless but by subduing the constitution, which required vigour and activity.—W.

party in it for the king, was under the power of sir John
Gell, who had fortified Derby.   And all these counties, with
Staffordshire, were united in an association against the king
under the command of the lord Brook ; who was, by the
earl of Essex, made general of that association; a man cordially disaffected to the government of the church, and upon
whom that party had a great dependence.   This association
received no other interruption from, or for the king, than
what colonel Hastings gave; who, being a younger son to the
earl of Huntingdon, had appeared eminently for the king from
the beginning; having raised a good troop of horse with the
first, and, in the head thereof, charged at Edge-hill.

After the king was settled at Oxford, colonel Hastings, with
his own troop of horse only, and some officers which he easily
gathered together, went with a commission into Leicestershire, of " colonel general of that county," and fixed himself at
Ashby de la Zouch, the house of the earl of Huntingdon, his
father, who was then living; which he presently fortified ;
and, in a very short time, by his interest there, raised so
good a party of horse and foot, that he maintained many skirmishes with the lord Grey : the king's service being the
more advanced there, by the notable animosities between the
two families of Huntingdon and Stamford; between whom
the county was divided passionately enough, without any
other quarrel.   And now the sons fought the public quarrel,
with their private spirit and indignation.   But the king had
the advantage in his champion, the lord Grey being a young
man of no eminent parts, and only backed with the credit
and authority of the parliament : whereas colonel Hastings,
though a younger brother, by his personal reputation, had supported his decaying family ; and, by the interest of his family,
and the affection that people bore to him, brought, no doubt,
an addition of power to the very cause.   Insomuch as he not
only defended himself against the forces of the parliament in
Leicestershire, but disquieted sir John Gell in Derbyshire,
and fixed some convenient garrisons in Staffordshire.

About the same time, some gentlemen of that county,
rather well affected than well advised, before they were well
enough provided to go through their work, seized of the

Close in Lichfield for the king; a place naturally strong, and defended with a moat, and a very high and thick wall; which in the infancy of the war was thought a good fortification. To suppress this growing force, within the limits of his association, the lord Brook advanced with a formed body of horse, foot, and cannon ; part drawn from the earl of Essex's army, and the rest out of the garrisons of Coventry and Warwick ; and, without any resistance, entered the city of Lichfield ; which, being unfortified, was open to all comers. The number in the Close was not great, nor their provisions such as should have been, and very well might have been, made ; so that he made no doubt of being speedily master of it ; sir John Gell having brought up a good addition of strength to him from Derby. He was so far from apprehending any danger from the besieged, that himself lodged in a house within musket-shot of the Close ; where, the very day he meant to assault it, sitting in his chamber, and the window open, he was, from the wall of the Close, by a common soldier, shot with a musket in the eye ; of which he instantly died without speaking a word.

There were many discourses and observations upon his death, that it should be upon St. Chad's day,[1] (being the second day of March,) by whose name, he being a bishop shortly after the planting of Christianity in this island, that church had been anciently called. And it was reported, that in his prayer, that very morning, (for he used to pray publicly, though his chaplain were in the presence,) he wished, " that, if the cause he were in were not right and just, he might be presently cut off." They who were acquainted with him believed him to be well natured and just ; and rather seduced and corrupted in his understanding, than perverse and malicious. Whether his passions or conscience swayed him, he was undoubtedly one of those who could have been with most difficulty reconciled to the government of church or state :[2] and therefore his death was

[1] Unworthy of the historian's remembrance.—W.

[2] i. e. whether resentment of the injustice of ruling churchmen and arbitrary ministers, or the persuasion that episcopacy in the church,

looked upon as no ill omen to peace, and was exceedingly lamented by that party; which had scarce a more absolute confidence in any man than in him. However, it brought not that relief to the besieged in the Close as was believed it would; for the same forces, under sir John Gell, proceeded so vigorously in the work, and they within so faintly or unskilfully, that without any of that distress which men thought it might bear, and which it did, within a short time after, bear against the king, the place was yielded without other conditions than of quarter; by which many persons became prisoners, of too good quality to have their names remembered.[1]

By this prize, the spirits of that party were much exalted, and the king's party in those parts as much cast down. Yet some gentlemen betook themselves to the town of Stafford, and having too much declared for the king, when they thought Lichfield would have been of strength to secure them, to hope to live unhurt at their houses, resolved to defend that place; against which the triumphant Gell drew his late fleshed troops. But the earl of Northampton (who intended the relief of Lichfield, if they had had any patience to expect it) with a strong party of horse and dragoons, from his garrison of Banbury, came seasonably to their succour, and put himself into the town; and, the same night, beat up a quarter of the enemy's, in which he killed and took above an hundred of their horse. Sir John Gell retired so far as to meet with sir William Bruerton, who, from Nantwich, was coming to join with him for the subduing of Stafford; and, having done that, resolved to march in a body for the clearing the other counties. When they were joined, being near three thousand foot and horse, with a good train of artillery, they moved back towards Stafford, imagining the earl of Northampton would meet them without the walls:

and monarchy in the state, were not the best forms of government to procure those blessings of which society is productive.—W.

[1] This was only said as a mark of indignation, not seriously, as if there was any solid reason why an impartial historian should have his scruples to mention their names.—W.

and it so fell out; for the earl no sooner heard that the rebels were drawing towards the town, but he drew out his party to encounter them; imagining it could be only Gell, whose numbers he understood, and whose courage he much undervalued.

It was on a Sunday, about the middle of March, when, in the afternoon, he marched out of Stafford; his party consisting of horse, and dragoons, and some few foot, the whole number being under one thousand, and found the enemy, in very good order, expecting them upon a place called Hopton-Heath, some two miles from Stafford. Though the number was more than double to the earl's, yet the heath seeming very fair, the breadth of it being more than musket-shot from enclosure on each side, and the number of his horse being at least equal to the other, he resolved to charge them; and accordingly did, with so good success, that he totally routed that part of their horse; and, rallying again his men, he charged the other part of their horse, which stood more in shelter of their foot; and so totally routed and dispersed them, that the enemy had scarce a horse left upon the field; and took likewise from them eight pieces of cannon.

In this second charge, the earl of Northampton, being engaged on the execution, very near or among their foot, had his horse killed under him. So that his own horse (according to their unhappy practice) with too much fury pursuing the chase, he was left encompassed by his enemy;[1] so that what his behaviour was afterwards, and their carriage towards him, can be known only by the testimony of the rebels; who confessed, that, after he was on his feet, he killed with his own hand the colonel of foot who made first haste to him; and that, after his headpiece was stricken off with the butt-end of a musket, they offered him quarter; which, they say, he refused; answering, "that he scorned to take quarter from such base rogues and rebels, as they

[1] In this practice the *courage* was as questionable as the *discipline* was faulty: for it was to avoid returning to the charge against unbroken bodies of the enemy.—W.

were." After which, he was slain by a blow with a halbert on the hinder part of his head, receiving, at the same time, another deep wound in his face.

All this time the enemy's foot stood, which (after their horse were dispersed) sir Thomas Byron, who commanded the prince of Wales's regiment, a gentleman of great courage, and of very good conduct, charged with good execution. But the night came on apace, and the field, which they thought so fair, was found full of coal-pits and holes dangerous for their horse ; so that they thought fit to forbear farther action, till they might have the morning's light ; and stood all that night in the field. When the morning appeared, there was no enemy to be seen. For as soon as the fight ended, and the night drew on, that they were unperceived, they had left the field, in hope that their scattered horse would find them in quarters more remote from the danger. But the victorious party was so harassed with duty, and tired with the fight, so cast down with the loss of their general, and so destitute of officers to direct and command what was next to be done, (for the lord Compton, the earl's eldest son, had received a shot in the leg; sir Thomas Byron a shot in the thigh, whereby they were not able to keep the field ; and many other officers hurt,) that they retired to refresh themselves at Stafford, after they had taken the spoil of the field, and buried their dead.

In this fight, which was sharp and short, there were killed, and taken prisoners, of the parliament party, above two hundred, and more than that number wounded. For, the horse charging among their foot, more were hurt than killed. Eight pieces of their cannon, and most of their ammunition was likewise taken. Of the earl's party were slain but five and twenty, whereof there were two captains, some inferior officers, and the rest common men ; but there were as many hurt, and those of the chief officers. They who had all the ensigns of victory, but their general, thought themselves undone ; whilst the other side, who had escaped in the night, and made a hard shift to carry his dead body with them, hardly believed they were losers :

> *Et, velut æquali bellatum sorte fuisset,*
> *Componit cum classe virum————*

The truth is, a greater victory had been an unequal recompense for a less loss. He was a person of great courage, honour, and fidelity, and not well known till his evening; having, in the ease, and plenty, and luxury of that too happy time, indulged to himself, with that licence which was then thought necessary to great fortunes : but from the beginning of these distractions, as if he had been awakened out of a lethargy, he never proceeded with a lukewarm temper. Before the standard was set up, he appeared in Warwickshire against the lord Brook, and as much upon his own reputation as the justice of the cause (which was not so well then understood)[1] discountenanced, and drove him out of that county. Afterwards he took the ordnance from Banbury castle, and brought them to the king. As soon as an army was to be raised, he levied, with the first, upon his own charge, a troop of horse, and a regiment of foot, and (not like some other men, who warily distributed their family to both sides, one son to serve the king, whilst his father, or another son, engaged as far for the parliament) entirely dedicated all his children to the quarrel; having four sons officers under him, whereof three charged that day in the field : and, from the time he submitted himself to the profession of a soldier, no man more punctual upon command, no man more diligent and vigilant in duty. All distresses he bore like a common man, and all wants and hardnesses, as if he had never known plenty or ease ; most prodigal of his person to danger ; and would often say, " that if he outlived these wars, he was certain never to have so noble a death." So that it is not to be wondered, if, upon such a stroke, the body that felt it, thought it had lost more than a limb.

As soon as it was known where the enemy rested after their retreat, the young earl of Northampton sent a trumpet to sir John Gell, to desire the body of his father, that he might give it such decent burial as became him. Gell and Bruerton jointly, by letter, demanded, " in exchange for the dead

---

[1] By this the historian seems to suppose, that the papers he wrote in the king's name, and for the king's cause, while at York, had opened the people's eyes, and he did not judge too partially of the effects of them.—W.

body, all their ammunition, prisoners, and cannon, they had lost at the battle ;" which demands being so unreasonable, and against the law of arms, the earl sent again to them, to desire, " that if they would not return the corpse, that his chirurgeon might have leave to embalm it, whereby it might be preserved to receive those rites, when they should be willing to gratify him, which, he presumed, upon more dispassionate thoughts, they would be." Their answer to this was as unreasonable as the other ; " that they would neither send the body, nor permit his chirurgeons to come to embalm it ;"[1] presuming, it is probable, that the piety of the son would have prevailed to have their unheard of propositions complied with.

And so we shall, for the present, leave these parts, and visit the principality of Wales ; of which, hitherto, very little hath been said ; and from the affection whereof, the king had, from the beginning, a very great benefit ; it having supplied him with three or four good regiments of foot, in which many of their gentry were engaged, before the battle of Edge-hill.

It hath been before remembered, that the marquis of Hertford drew with him out of Wales, and brought to Oxford, about Christmas, near two thousand men ; leaving Wales guarded only with the courage and fidelity of the gentry and inhabitants. After that, North Wales lying most convenient to back Chester and Shrewsbury, which places, whilst the enemy was master of the field, received their chief supplies of men and provisions from thence ; the king always put it under the government of those to whom he committed those parts. South Wales, which is much the larger and richer part of that dominion, he committed to the charge of the lord Herbert, eldest son to the marquis of Worcester ; whom he made his lieutenant general, adding Monmouthshire to his commission.

There were, in the opinion of many, great objections against committing that employment to that noble lord, whose person many men loved, and very few hated. First, he had no knowledge or experience in the martial profession ; then his reli-

[1] Incredibly base.

gion, being of that sort of catholics the people rendered odious, by accusing it to be most jesuited, men apprehended would not only produce a greater brand upon the king, of favouring papists and popery, than he had been yet reproached with ; (for, though he had some papists entertained in his armies, yet all men trusted by him in superior commands were men of unblemished integrity in the protestant religion ; and in all his armies he had but one general officer of the contrary religion, sir Arthur Aston, whom the papists notwithstanding would not acknowledge for a papist ;) this gave opportunity and excuse to many persons of quality, and great interest in those counties, (between whom and that lord's family there had .been perpetual feuds and animosities,) to lessen their zeal to the king's cause, out of jealousy of the other's religion ; and those contestations had been lately improved with some sharpness, by the lord Herbert's carriage towards the lord marquis of Hertford, during the time of his residence there ; when, out of vanity to magnify his own power, he had not shewed that due regard to that of the other, which he should have had. And no doubt, if he had been of that mind, it would much more have advanced the king's service, if he would have contributed his full assistance to another, who more popularly might have borne the title of such a command.

But, on the other side, the necessity of disposing those parts, divided from the rest of the kingdom, under the command of some person of honour and interest, was very visible ; and the expedition in doing it was as penal and necessary ; the parliament being possessed of Gloucester and Bristol, and so having such an influence upon the trade and livelihood of that people, by their absolute command of the Severn, that, except there were extraordinary care of keeping them, they would be quickly lost. Besides that, at the same time, there was discourse, in the houses, " of sending the earl of Pembroke thither," whose estate was very great in those parts, and his reputation equal. Then the parliament had already such a footing in Pembrokeshire, that many of the principal gentlemen had declared for them ; and the harbour of Milford-Haven gave their fleet opportunity to

give them all supplies and relief. This being the state of
those parts, the lord Herbert not only offered, but desired to
receive that command ; and engaged himself, "not only to
secure it from the opposition and malignity of the other party, but, before the spring, to raise such a strength of horse
and foot, and to provide such an equipage to march with,
that might reduce Gloucester, and be then added to the king's
army, when he should be ready to take the field ; and all
this so much at his own charge," (for his father, who was
well able, would furnish money, as was pretended, upon the
king's promise to repay him, when he should be restored to
his own,) " that he would receive no part of the king's revenue, or of such money as he could be able to draw for the
supply of his own more immediate occasions."

This was a very great offer,[1] and such as no man else
could so reasonably make. For the marquis of Worcester
was generally reputed the greatest monied man of the kingdom ; and, probably, might not think it an unthrifty thing,
rather to disburse it for the king, who might be able to repay it, than to have it taken from him by the other party ;
which would be hardly questionable if they prevailed. The
lord Herbert himself was a man of more than ordinary affection and reverence to the person of the king, and one, who,
he was sure, would neither deceive nor betray him. For
his religion, it might work upon himself, but could not disquiet other men. For though he were a papist, he was
never like to make others so ; and his reputation and interest
was very great with many gentlemen of those counties, who
were not at all friends to his religion. It was not possible

---

[1] As *great* as it was, it should in common prudence have been refused at this juncture, when the king had fairly divided the kingdom with
his enemies. After the fatal battle of Naseby indeed, when the king
was forced to fly for refuge into Wales, and was received by the marquis of Worcester, such an acceptance of service from the papists
might be excused. But till such an extremity, the king's council
should have considered there was an extreme great difference between
taking an able officer of that persuasion into his service, and receiving
the assistance, of what his enemies, without much violation of truth or
candour, might call a *popish army.*—W.

to employ any person of interest and power in those parts, (and there were many objections, from the nature and manners of that people, against a mere stranger,) against whom there would not be some faction and animosity; for the emulations, and dissension between families was general, and notorious; and therefore it would be best to choose such a one, who was like to have a greater faction for him, than against him. And it was to be hoped that the old grudges and prejudices, which had been rather against the house of Worcester, and the popish religion professed there, than against the person of this lord, would have been composed and declined by his fair and gentle carriage towards all men, (as in truth he was of a civil and obliging nature,) and by the public-heartedness of those, who, for the cause, and conscience sake, would, it was hoped, sacrifice all trivial and private contentions to a union that must vindicate the religion, honour, and justice of the kingdom.

Upon these reasons, and these presumptions, the king granted such a commission, as is before mentioned, to the lord Herbert; who, with more expedition than was expected by any, or by others believed possible, raised a body of above fifteen hundred foot, and near five hundred horse, very well and sufficiently armed; which increased the merit of the service.

The horse he put under the command of his brother, the lord John Somerset, a maiden soldier too; and the foot under colonel Lawly, whom he made his major general, a bold and a sprightly officer. About the middle of February he marched towards Gloucester, with an ill omen at his setting out; for a rabble of country people being got together, without order, or officer of name, barricadoed a little village in the forest of Deane, called Cover, (through which he was to pass,) and refused to give him entrance; and out of a window killed colonel Lawly, and two officers more, without hurting a common soldier; whereby that body was destitute of any person of experience to command them. However the lord Herbert, who was himself seldom with his forces, shortly after placed colonel Brett in that command; who, without any skirmish of importance, marched through the

forest of Deane, and fixed a quarter, which contained his
whole body, at the Vineyard, the bishop of Gloucester's
palace, within less than half a mile of Gloucester.   And by
that means, there being only a long bridge over the Severn,
by which men could come out or go in to Gloucester, he
fully blocked up the town on that side, expecting that prince
Maurice from Cirencester should take equal care to distress
it on the other ; which he did to a good degree.

But sir William Waller, with a light party of horse, and
dragoons, near two thousand, from the earl of Essex's army,
had made a quick march through Wiltshire, (after his taking
of Chichester,) and taking, with little loss and trouble, a
small garrison of the king's, consisting of about six or seven
score, at Malmsbury, before it was fortified, or provided,
made a face of looking towards Cirencester; where when he
found he was expected, by a sudden night march, in which
he was very dexterous and successful, he posted to the river
of Severn, six miles west of Gloucester, from whence he
had appointed many flat boats to meet him ; and in them, in
the light day, the guard of the river being either treacherously or sottishly neglected by the lord Herbert's forces, transported his whole body, which, upon the advantage of that
pass, might have been resisted by a hundred men.   Hereupon the consternation was so great among the new Welsh
soldiers, very few of their officers having ever seen an enemy, that though their works were too good to be entered
by horse and dragoons; though the avenues were but narrow, in all which they had cannon planted, and their numbers very near, if not fully, equal to the enemy ; upon the
advance of sir William Waller upon them, without giving or
receiving blow, they fairly sent out to treat ; and as kindly
delivered up themselves, and their arms, upon the single
grant of quarter: a submission so like a stratagem, that the
enemy could hardly trust it.   Yet, in the end, they made a
shift to put near thirteen hundred foot, and three troops of
horse, prisoners into Gloucester, the lord Herbert himself
being at that time at Oxford, and the lord John Somerset
with three or four troops at a safe distance from the rest.

This was the end of that mushroom-army, which grew up

and perished so soon, that the loss of it was scarce apprehended at Oxford, because the strength, or rather the number, was not understood. But if the money, which was laid
out in raising, arming, and paying that body of men, which
never advanced the king's service in the least degree, had
been brought into the king's receipt at Oxford, to have been
employed to the most advantage, I am persuaded the war
might have been ended the next summer. For I have heard
the lord Herbert say, " that those preparations, and the other,
which by that defeat were rendered useless, cost above three
score thousand pounds ;" whereof, though much came from
the marquis's coffers, yet, no doubt, the general contributions
from the catholics made a good part; and very considerable
sums were received by him of the king's revenue upon ward-
ships, and other ways: for it was a common practice in those
times, for men to get into employments upon promises, that
they would not do this or that, without which nobody else
would undertake that service ; and being, upon those terms,
received into it, they immediately did the other, because no
other man could do the service without it.

The fame of this prodigious victory so subdued all those
parts, that sir William Waller, with the same spirit of celerity,
and attended with the same success, flew to Hereford ; and
being a walled town, and replenished with a garrison, had
that likewise delivered to him upon the same terms as the
other was; and from thence (being with more confidence refused to be admitted into Worcester, than he thought reasonable to require it) passed to Tewkesbury; which he likewise surprised, being newly garrisoned ; his motion being so
quick, that though prince Maurice attended him with all possible diligence, he could never farther engage him than in
light skirmishes ; and, having taken this progress, returned
safe to Gloucester ; and from thence to the earl of Essex's
army ; having made no other use of his conquests, than the
dishonouring so many places,[1] which had so quietly yielded
to him ; into which (for he fixed no one garrison) the king's

---

[1] This doubtless was of considerable use to the parliament, at a time
when the king's horse were thought to be irresistible.—W.

forces immediately entered again. So that his majesty's quarters continued the same they were, harassed only, and discountenanced, nothing straitened by this incursion; and the lord Herbert again intended new levies.

Having now, with as much clearness as I could, remembered the true state of the king's affairs, and the condition of the kingdom, at the end of this year 1642, with which I intend to conclude this sixth book; I shall, before I return to Oxford, to conclude the year, briefly call to remembrance the disconsolate state of Ireland; of which, advantage was always taken against the king, to render him odious to the people, as if he countenanced, at least not sufficiently abhorred, that wicked and unnatural rebellion. And this imputation was with so great art insinuated, that it got credit with many; insomuch as I have heard some, who could make no other excuse for adhering to the parliament, than " they were persuaded that the king favoured those rebels;" which, they said, " could not be without some design upon the religion, liberty, and prosperity of England." Whereas I can aver truly, upon as good grounds as ever any man spoke the heart of another, that the king always looked upon it, as the most groundless, bloody, and wicked rebellion, that ever possessed the spirits of that people;[1] and was not more grieved at any one circumstance of the domestic distraction, than as it hindered him from chastising and taking vengeance upon the other : which from his soul he desired.

But in this discourse of Ireland, it cannot be imagined, neither do I intend to mention all the memorable actions, (in which were as great instances of God's own detestation of those inhuman rebels, by the signal victories he gave against them,) or other transactions within that kingdom; but shall remember no more of that business, than had immediate reference to, and dependence on, the difference between the king and the two houses of parliament.

It is said before, that when the first visible rupture was

---

[1] This I verily believe, nor is it at all inconsistent with his first drawing out of Ireland many of the forces then fighting against the Irish rebels ; and afterwards bringing over the rebels themselves to support his cause against his English rebels.—W.

declared between them, which was in the business of Hull,
(which the king understood to be a direct levying of war
against him,) in the protestation made by his majesty, "that
he would no farther treat or concur with them in any acts
proposed by them, till he first received reparation or satisfaction in that particular;" he always excepted what should
any way concern Ireland : in which he offered to consent
to whatsoever might reasonably conduce to the reducing
those rebels; and did, after that, concur in some propositions
of that nature.   Yet it is certain that, from that time, the two
houses were so busy in preparing the war for England, that
they did very little advance the war of Ireland ; save only
by some small supplies of money and provisions.   The
king objected to them, " the employing the monies, raised,
by acts of parliament, for the preservation and reduction of
Ireland, with a special clause that the same should not be diverted to any other use whatsoever, in the supporting the
unnatural war and rebellion against his majesty; particularly
one hundred thousand pounds at one time ; and that many
soldiers, raised under pretence of being sent into Ireland,
were, contrary to their expectation and engagement, forced
to serve under the earl of Essex against the king;" of which
he named sir Faithful Fortescue's regiment of horse, and the
lord Wharton's and the lord Kerry's regiment of foot.

To this they answered, " that albeit they had, upon the
urgent occasions of this kingdom, sometimes made use of monies raised and collected for Ireland ; yet, that they had in
due time repaid it, and that the other affairs had never suffered by the loan : and for the men, that it proceeded from his
majesty's own default; for after they had raised them, with a
serious intention to send them into Ireland, under the command of the lord Wharton, the king refused to grant a commission to him to transport them, and so they had been compelled to use them in their own service here."

The king replied, " that it appeared, they had diverted that
money to other uses than those for which it was provided ;
which was manifestly unlawful ; and that it did not appear
they had again reimbursed it, because very little supply was
sent thither, and very much wanted : and for the soldiers,

that they first levied them, without his majesty's leave ; which they had always before asked, for their other levies ; and being levied, they desired a commission for the lord Wharton to command them absolutely, without any dependence upon the lord lieutenant of Ireland ; which had been never heard of, and which his majesty refused ; but offered such a commission as was granted to other men."

On the other hand, they objected to the king, " the seizing some cart-horses at Chester, provided for the train of artillery for Ireland ; that his forces had taken many clothes and provisions on the road, which were going to Chester to be transported thither for the relief of the soldiers ; and that he entertained and countenanced men in his court, which were favourers or actors in that rebellion ;" naming the lord viscount Costeloe, and the lord Taffe, which gave great umbrage to those who were well affected, and as great encouragement to the rebels there.

To the first, the king confessed, " he found about six score horses at Chester, which had long lain there ; and, at his remove from Nottingham, knowing the other horse and men raised for Ireland were then marching with the earl of Essex against him, he knew not that these likewise might be so likewise employed, and therefore in his own necessity took them for his own draughts.   For the clothes, which had been taken by his soldiers, that it proceeded by the default of the parliament ; who, after the war was begun, had sent those carriages through his quarters, without sending to his majesty for a safe conduct, or giving any notice to him of it, till after they were taken : that it was within two miles of Coventry (which was then in rebellion) that those clothes were taken ; and that, as soon as he knew they were designed for Ireland, his majesty had used the best means he could to recover them ; but that the soldiers, who were almost naked, had divided them for their own supplies; and his majesty offered to give a safe conduct at all times for whatsoever should be designed for Ireland."

The occasion of the other reproach, " for countenancing persons who adhered to the rebels," was this.   The lords Dillon (viscount Costeloe) and Taffe had, four months be-

fore, passed out of Ireland into England, having never been
in consort with the rebels, but so much trusted by them, that
they desired, by their hands, tó address a petition to the king;
humble enough, desiring " only to be heard, and offering to
submit to his majesty's single judgment." With this petition, and all other instructions, as they pretended, these lords
acquainted the lords justices and council of Ireland; who were
so well satisfied with the persons employed, that they granted their safe pass, and sent letters by them of testimony.
They were no sooner landed in England, but they were apprehended, and sent prisoners to the parliament, and by them
committed with all strictness, " as agents employed by the
rebels of Ireland to the king;" and that circumstance enforced, and spread among the people, with all licentious glosses
against the king; who, for that reason, took no notice of their
restraint, though from his ministers he received advertisement
of the truth of the whole business. After some time was
spent in close imprisonment, these lords, by petition, and all
other addresses they could make, pressed to be brought to
any kind of examination and trial; of which they found no
other benefit, than that, upon this importunity, their imprisonment was less close; and, by degrees, under a formal restraint, (which, though more pleasant, was not less costly,)
had the liberty of London, and from thence, after four months'
restraint, without being formally charged with any crime, or
brought to any trial, which they often desired, they escaped,
and came to York; whither a messenger from the house of
commons followed them, and demanded them as prisoners.

Many were of opinion, that they should have been delivered back; foreseeing that the parliament would press the
scandal of sheltering them much to the king's disadvantage;
and any imputations, " of countenancing the rebels of Ireland," found more credit, and made deeper impression with
the people, than any other discourses of " protecting malignants and delinquents." On the other side, it was thought
unreasonable to remit men to an imprisonment, which appeared to have been unjust, by their not being proceeded
against in so long time; especially when their coming to the
king would be declared such a crime, that it would be now

in their enemies' power to cause them to be punished; which before they could not do ; at best, it were to deliver them up to the sergeant of the house of commons, from whence no innocence could redeem them, without paying such vast fees, as would amount to a greater sum than they could probably be supplied with.   So that the king, who wished that they had rather gone any whither than where he was, resolved to take no notice of their escape.   And so they continued in his quarters, and put themselves into the troops ;[1] where they behaved themselves with good courage, and frankly engaged their persons in all dangerous enterprises.

In these jealousies and contests, the king being visibly and confessedly unable to send succours of any kind thither, and the parliament having enough else to do, and, in truth, not taking so much pains to preserve it, as to impute the loss of it to the king, poor Ireland got very small relief.   The earl of Leicester, lord lieutenant of that kingdom, had received his despatch from the king, before he went to Shrewsbury.   But when the king thought he would have gone directly to Chester, and so to Ireland, his lordship returned to London ; which increased the king's jealousy and prejudice to him ; which his former carriage, and a letter writ lately by him from Nottingham to the earl of Northumberland, and by order of parliament printed, had begot to a great degree.   Shortly after his return to London; the house of commons demanded, " to see the instructions he had received from the king ;" which, as it was unreasonable in them, so he had received express command from the king, " not to communicate them."   However, after he had avoided it as long as he could, and they continued peremptory in the demand, in the end, he produced them to be perused by the committee of both houses. The truth is, the earl's condition was very slippery, and almost impossible to be safely managed by the most dexterous person.

He was designed to that employment by the king, short-

[1] It had surely at this time been more prudent to have banished them his presence, or confined them prisoners in his garrisons, than to employ them in his armies.—W.

ly upon the death of the earl of Strafford, (or rather before;
not without some advice from that earl,) with as great circumstances of grace and favour, as could be; and as a person, of whom entirely the king assured himself, being then
so ungracious to the parliament, that as there were some
sharp glances at him in that time, (which are before remembered,) so nothing preserved him from a public exception,
but the interest of the earl of Northumberland, whose sister
he had married; whom that party was not willing to irre-
concile.   After the rebellion was broke out in Ireland, and
the king had committed the carrying on the war to the
houses, he thought it absolutely necessary for his province,
to render himself as gracious to that people as was possible;
and laboured that with so good effect and industry, that he
omitted that care which should have been observed in continuing his interest at court.   For the king and queen grew
every day less satisfied with him;[1] which sure he did not
with wariness enough provide against; though, I believe,
he had never unfaithful purposes towards either of them;
but did sadly project, by his demeanour and interest in the
houses, to provide so well for Ireland, and to go thither in
so good a condition, that, being once there, he might be able
to serve the king as he should be required.

But one man is rarely able to act both those parts: for
his shewing his instructions, he gave a reason, which, if he
had been free from all other objections, might appear no ill
excuse: "He knew his instructions were such, that, being
perused by the committee, could by no misconstruction, or
possible perversion, be wrested to the king's disadvantage;"
as indeed they never were able, nor ever attempted, to fix
any reproach from them upon the king.   "Whereas, after
they were so peremptorily required, if he should have as
peremptorily refused to submit, they would have concluded
that there had been somewhat unjustifiable in them, and
upon that jealousy made no scruple of publishing the worst
reproaches upon his majesty."   And it may be, he was not

---

[1] A language well adapted to the uxorious temper and conduct of
the king.—W.

without an imagination, that if by this contest he had drawn
the displeasure of the two houses upon him, as could not be
avoided, his misfortune at court [1] might have suffered that
contest to have depressed him, and revenged itself upon the
choler of the other.   And when he left the king between
Nottingham and Shrewsbury, his condition was so low, that
a man might have imagined his interest would be best preserved by being within the verge of the parliament's protection.   As his return to London was besides the king's expectation, so his stay there was longer than seemed to be
by his own proposal ; for he staid there above two months,
till after the battle of Edge-hill, and both parties being fixed
in their winter quarters ; and then, without waiting again
on the king,[2] though Oxford was very few miles out of his
way, about the end of November, he went to Chester, with
a purpose of transporting himself for Ireland, but without the
least appearance of addition of strength, or provisions from
the parliament ; neither were their ships there ready to
transport him.

About the end of November, four officers of the army in
Ireland, sir James Montgomery, sir Hardress Waller, colonel
Arthur Hill, and colonel Audly Mervin, having been employed from Ireland to solicit the parliament for succours,
came from London to Oxford, and delivered a petition to
the king ; in which they told him, " that they had addressed
themselves to the parliament for supplies, whose sense of
their miseries, and inclination to redress, appeared very tender to them ; but the present distempers of the kingdom of
England were grown so great, that all future passages, by
which comfort and life should be conveyed to that gasping
kingdom, seemed totally to be obstructed ; so that, unless
his majesty, out of his singular wisdom and fatherly care,

[1] i. e. want of credit.—-W.

[2] He must have ill consulted his safety in so doing, if what the historian says of his interest at court (just above) be true, when he left
the king between Nottingham and Shrewsbury. And yet he had
given fresh offence after that by staying so long in the enemy's quarters. —W.

applied some speedy care, his loyal and distressed subjects of that kingdom must inevitably perish. They acknowledged his princely favour and goodness since this rebellion, so abundantly expressed in a deep sense and lively resentment of their bleeding condition ; and therefore they besought him, among his other weighty cares, so to reflect upon the bleeding condition of that perishing kingdom, that timely relief might be afforded. Otherwise his loyal subjects there must yield their fortunes, as a prey ; their lives, a sacrifice ; and their religion, a scorn to the merciless rebels, powerfully assisted from abroad."

And indeed the condition of the protestants, in that kingdom, was very miserable : for, whilst the distractions of England kept them from receiving succours, the rebels had arms, ammunition, money, and commanders, from Rome, Spain, and France ; the pope having sent a formal avowed nuncio, to whose jurisdiction the Irish submitted ; and the kings of France and Spain having sent great supplies, and their agents, to countenance and foment the rebellion ; who gave notable countenance to the assembly and formed council for the rebels, settled at Kilkenny.

The king, who well knew this petition was sent by the permission of those at Westminster, and that the agents employed were men of notorious disaffection to him, who looked for some such answer as might improve the envy of the people, used the messengers with all possible grace, and returned them as gracious an answer : " That, from the beginning of that monstrous rebellion, he had had no greater sorrow, than for the bleeding condition of that his kingdom. That he had, by all means, laboured, that timely relief might be afforded to it, and consented to all propositions, how disadvantageous soever to himself, that had been offered to him to that purpose ; and, not only at first recommended their condition to both his houses of parliament, and immediately, of his own mere motion, sent over several commissions, and caused some proportion of arms and ammunition (which the petitioners well knew to have been a great support to the northern parts of that kingdom) to be conveyed to them out of Scotland, and offered ten thousand volunteers to undertake that war; but had often pressed, by many several messages, that sufficient succours might be hastened thither, and other matters of smaller importance laid by, which did divert it; and offered, and most really intended, in his own royal person, to have undergone the danger of that war, for the defence of his good subjects, and the chastisement of those perfidious and barbarous rebels; and in his several expressions of his desires of treaty and peace, he had declared the miserable present condition and certain future loss of Ireland, to be one of the principal motives most earnestly to desire, that the present distractions of this kingdom might be composed, and that others would concur with him to the same end."

He told them, " He was well pleased, that his offers, concurrence, actions, and expressions, were so rightly understood by the petitioners, and those who had employed them, (notwithstanding the groundless and horrid aspersions which had been cast upon him;) but he wished, that, instead of a mere general complaint, to which his majesty could make no return but of compassion, they could have digested, and offered to him any such desires, by consenting to which, he might convey, at least in some degree, comfort and life to that gasping kingdom; preserve his distressed and loyal subjects of the same from inevitably perishing, and the true protestant religion from being scorned and trampled on by those merciless rebels. And, if the petitioners could yet think of any such, and propose them to his majesty, he assured them, that by his readiness to consent, and his thanks to them for the proposal, he would make it appear to them, that their most pressing personal sufferings could not make them more desirous of relief, than his care of the true religion, and of his faithful subjects, and of his duty, which obliged him, to his power, to protect both, rendered him desirous to afford it to them."

The king being fully informed now, as well by this committee, as from his ministers of state in that kingdom, of the growing power of the rebels in Ireland, and of the weak resistance his good subjects were like to make, whose only hopes depended upon those succours which they presumed the lord lieutenant would bring over with him, and that he was now going thither without the least addition of strength, or probable assurance that any would be sent after him ; his majesty considered likewise, that, besides the damp this naked arrival of the lord lieutenant there must cast upon the minds of all, it would make likewise a great alteration in the conduct of affairs there.   For, upon his landing, the commission to the earl of Ormond, of lieutenant general of the army, would be determined ; and there had those jealousies and disrespects passed between the earl of Leicester and him, that the earl of Ormond was resolved, no more to continue that command, but immediately to transport himself out of that kingdom ; by which the king should lose the service of a person much the most powerful, most able, and most popular within that province; and who had, with wonderful courage and conduct, and almost miraculous success, hitherto restrained the rage and fury of the rebels, and indeed a man so accomplished, that he had either no enemies, or such who were ashamed to profess they were so.[1]

Upon these considerations, the king thought fit, for some time, till he might farther weigh the whole business, to suspend the earl of Leicester's journey : and therefore sent to him to Chester (where he had lain, in some indisposition of health, above a fortnight ; and the ships being not yet come for his transportation) " to attend his majesty at Oxford ;" which he did shortly after Christmas, and continued there; the king directing the earl of Ormond (whom about this time he made a marquis) " to carry on the war as he had done; and, during the absence of the lord lieutenant, to dispose of all places and offices in the army which became void," and likewise making an alteration in the civil power ; for whereas sir William Parsons and sir John Burlacy had continued lords justices from and before the death of the earl of Strafford, the king finding that sir William Parsons (who was a man of long experience in that kingdom, and confessed abili-

---

[1] And yet this accomplished man (for indeed he was such) acted by his old friend in his distresses, when ruined by Charles the Second's wicked crew of courtiers, in so paltry a manner, as was a disgrace to his character.   See Carte's Collection of Letters, written at that time. —W.

ties, but always of suspected reputation) did him all imaginable disservice, and combined with the parliament in England, about this time removed sir Will. Parsons from that trust; and, in his room, deputed sir Harry Tichborne, a man of so excellent a fame, that though the parliament was heartily angry at the remove of the other, and knew this would never be brought to serve their turn, they could not fasten any reproach upon the king for this alteration.

Another circumstance must not be forgotten. After the war broke out in England, the parliament had sent over a couple of their members of the commons (Mr. Raynolds and Mr. Goodwyn) as a committee into Ireland, to reside at Dublin, and had given directions to the lords justices, " that they should have leave to be present at all their consultations;" which they had; and were no other than spies upon those, who should presume to deliver any opinions there not agreeable to the sense of the houses. When the king made that alteration in the government, he likewise took notice, that strangers were admitted to be present at their debates, which had never been before practised; and therefore required them, " that it might be so no more." Hereupon, the committee, who had carried themselves very insolently and seditiously there, and with notable contempt of the king, and his authority, were, by the lords justices and council, inhibited from being present at the council; and thereupon they quickly left the kingdom, and returned to London; the parliament unreasonably and impudently accusing the king of a new breach of privilege, for this disrespect to their members. This was the state of Ireland, the war being that spring prosperously carried on by the marquis of Ormond, and the earl of Leicester still staying at Oxford with the title of lord lieutenant. And so we will return to Oxford and London.

Many days being past since the return of the committee of lords and commons from Oxford, with the king's answer to their propositions, and no reply being made by the houses, or indeed any solemn debate entered thereupon, (for his majesty had every day information of what passed among them, even in their most secret councils,) and, on the contrary, preparations more vigorously intended for the war, than had

been before, in sending out strong parties to infest the king's
quarters, (for, besides the incursions and progress of sir
William Waller, which are before remembered, Mr. Hambden had made some attempts upon the Brill, a garrison of
the king's upon the edge of Buckinghamshire, but without
effect, and with some considerable loss,) in levying great
numbers of men, for the recruiting the earl of Essex's army;
and designing new extraordinary ways for the raising of
money, and associating several counties of the kingdom, towards the raising new armies : the king, as well to have the
conveniency of sending to London, (of which journeys he
made good use,) as to quicken and necessitate them to some
reply, sent another message to them, putting them in mind
of " the proposition he had made for a cessation of arms ;"
and desired " that if they approved of a cessation, that the
day upon which they thought fit it should begin, and such
particulars, limits, and conditions of it, as were necessary to
be understood, and agreed on, before the cessation itself
could actually begin, might be proposed by them.   Since,"
his majesty said, " he supposed, by the present great preparations of several forces to march several ways, that, till all
that should be agreed upon, they did not conceive themselves obliged to an actual cessation ; so neither, till then,
did his majesty conceive himself obliged to it: however, he
wished it might be clearly understood between them, that no
such imputations, as had been formerly, might be laid upon
him, upon occasion of any thing that might intervene."

This message put a necessity upon them, of entering again
upon the argument, and gave them, who desired peace and
accommodation, an opportunity to press for the debate,
which had been craftily laid aside for the despatch of other
matters ; that party, which was most deeply engaged in the
war, and resolved to carry it on, having a notable dexterity in keeping those things from being debated, in which
they found their sense would not prevail.   And at this time,
the number of those in both houses, who really desired the
same peace the king did,' was (if they had not been over-

¹ Insinuating that the king desired a peace upon terms by which the

witted by them) superior to the other. For, besides that many persons, who from the beginning had always dissented from them, for their ease and conveniency had staid among them, very many were convinced in their understandings, that they had been misled ; and discerned, in what a bottomless gulph of misery the kingdom would be plunged, if an immediate composure were not made ; and some of those who had been as fierce as any, and given as great countenance to the kindling the fire, either out of conscience that they had done amiss, or fear that the king would prevail by power, or anger that they found other men valued above them ; in their present distraction, or their natural inconstancy even in ill,[1] were most solicitous for a treaty. So that, within few days after the receipt of this message, both houses agreed, " that there should be a treaty, in which so much of the king's propositions as concerned the magazines, forts, and ships, and the proposition of both houses for the disbanding the armies, should be first treated on, and concluded, before the proceeding to treat upon any of the other propositions ; and that the treaty should begin the fourth of March, or sooner if it might be ; and that, from the beginning, the time should not exceed twenty days."

The persons they made choice of to treat, were the earl of Northumberland, the lord Say, Mr. Pierrepoint, sir William Armyn, sir John Holland, and Mr. Whitlock, for whose safe conduct they despatched a messenger to his majesty ; this resolution being taken but the last day of February. As soon as the request was presented, the king returned a safe conduct for the earl of Northumberland and the four commoners ; but refused to admit the lord Say to his presence, upon the same exception he had formerly refused sir John Evelyn at Colebrook ; his lordship being personally excepted from pardon by a former proclamation ; but signified, " that if they would employ any other person not with-

public liberty might be secured. This is true, if by the king was meant the king's council.—W.

[1] This was the true character of many ; at the head of which class was earl Holland.—W.

in the same rule, he should as freely come as if he were in the safe conduct."

Whether the lord Say was nominated by those who believed they should be able, upon the refusal of him, (which they could not but foresee,) to break off all overtures of farther treaty; or whether they believed, they had so far prevailed by underhand negociations at Oxford, that he should be admitted, and that he would have been able to persuade the king to yield to what they proposed, or at least to have engaged the king to those who would have yielded to him, I know not; but as it was not so insisted on at Westminster as to break the treaty, so many were of opinion at Oxford, that the king should have admitted him. They said, "he was a wise man, and could not but know, that it would not be possible for him to make any impression upon his majesty's judgment in the propositions in debate; and therefore, that he would never have suffered himself to be designed to that negociation, (which, without doubt, by his interest in both houses he might have prevented,) if he did not purpose to do some signal service to his majesty." And indeed many believed, "that if he had come, and found the king's goodness inclined to pardon and trust him, that he would have done the best he could, to redeem his former breaches." Others were of opinion, "that he was so far from being inclined to serve the king, or advance the treaty, that he should have been sent as a spy, lest others should;" and these were the thoughts both at Oxford and London. But the king, who knew the lord Say as well as any of them, believed, that it was not in his power to do any good, and if it had, that it was not in his will; was resolved not to break his rule, lest such a remission might give advantage against him in the future: and so sent the answer above remembered. Together with this desire of a safe conduct, they sent his majesty word, "that they had likewise consented, that there should be a cessation of arms on either side, under the restrictions and limitations hereafter following.

1. " That all manner of arms, ammunition, victuals, money, bullion, and all other commodities, passing without such

a safe conduct as may warrant their passage, may be stayed and seized on, as if no cessation was agreed on.

2. " That all manner of persons, passing without such a safe conduct as is mentioned in the article next going before, shall be apprehended, and detained, as if no such cessation were agreed on at all.

3. " That his majesty's forces in Oxfordshire should advance no nearer to Windsor than Wheatley, and in Buckinghamshire no nearer to Aylesbury than Brill ; and that in Berkshire, the forces respectively shall not advance nearer the one to the other than now they are : and that the parliament forces in Oxfordshire shall advance no nearer to Oxford than Henley, and those in Buckinghamshire no nearer to Oxford than Aylesbury : and that his majesty's forces shall make no new quarters, above twelve miles from Oxford, any way ; and the parliament forces shall take no new quarters, above twelve miles from Windsor, any way.

4. " That no siege shall be begun or continued against Gloucester ; and that his majesty's forces, now employed in the siege, shall return to Cirencester and Malmsbury, or to Oxford, as shall be most for their convenience ; and the parliament forces, which are in Gloucestershire, shall remain in the cities of Gloucester, Bristol, and the castle and town of Berkley, or retire nearer to Windsor, as they shall see cause ; and that those of Wales, which are drawn to Gloucester, shall return to their quarters where they were before they drew down to Gloucestershire.

5. " That, in case it be pretended on either side, that the cessation is violated, no act of hostility is immediately to follow, but first the party complaining is to acquaint the lord general on the other side, and to allow three days, after notice, for satisfaction ; and in case satisfaction be not given, or accepted, then five days' notice to be given, before hostility begin, and the like to be observed in the remoter armies, by the commanders in chief.

6. " Lastly, that all other forces in the kingdom of England, and dominion of Wales, not before mentioned, shall remain in the same quarters, and places, as they are at the time of publishing this cessation, and under the same condi-

tions as are mentioned in the articles before. And that this cessation shall not extend, to restrain the setting forth or employing of any ships, for the defence of his majesty's dominions."

All which they desired " his majesty would be pleased to ratify and confirm ; and that this cessation might begin upon the fourth of March next, or sooner if it might be ; and continue until the five and twentieth of the same month ; and in the mean time to be published on either side ; and that the treaty might likewise commence upon the same day ; and the continuance thereof not to exceed twenty days."

These propositions were delivered to his majesty on the first of March, which was almost a month after the cessation had been proposed by him, (for his propositions were made on the third of February,) which administered cause of doubt, that the overture was not sincere ; since it was hardly possible, that the cessation could begin so soon as the fourth, by which time, though the king should consent to the terms proposed, upon sight, his answer could very hardly be returned to them. But the articles themselves were such as occasioned much debate, and difference of opinion, among those who desired the same thing. The king, after the examination of them with his privy-council, and at a council of war, made a committee out of each, to consider the inconvenience his consent to them might produce to his party, if that cessation and treaty did not produce a peace ; and the inequality in them, if the overture passed from an equal enemy according to the rules of war. Some were of opinion, " that the cessation should be consented to by the king, upon the articles proposed, though they should be thought unequal, not only because it would be an act of great grace and compassion to the people, to give them some respite, and taste of peace, and the not consenting to it (the reason not being so easy to be understood) would be as impopular and ungracious ; but that, they believed, it would at least cast the people into such a slumber, that much of their fury and madness would be abated ; and that they would not be easily induced to part with the ease they felt, and would look upon that party as an enemy, that robbed them of it ;

that it would give an opportunity of charitable intercourse, and revive that freedom of conversation, which, of itself, upon so great advantage of reason, as they believed the king's cause gave, would rectify the understanding of many who were misled ; but especially, that it would not only hinder the recruit of the earl of Essex's army, (for that no man would be so mad to declare themselves against the king, when they saw a cessation, in order to restoring the king to his rights,) but would lessen the forces he had already ; in that the army consisted most of men engaged by the pay, not affection to the cause ; who, upon such a remission of duty as would necessarily attend a cessation, would abandon a party which they foresaw, upon a peace, must be infamous, though it might be secure : and whereas all overtures of a treaty hitherto had advanced their levies upon pretence of being in a posture not to be contemned, they believed, a real cessation would render those levies impossible."

Others thought " any cessation disadvantageous enough to the king; and therefore, that the terms, upon which it was to be made, were to be precisely looked to : that the articles proposed would only produce a suspension of present acts of hostility and blood among the soldiers ; but not give the least taste of peace, or admit the least benefit to the people ; for that all intercourse and conversation was inhibited, insomuch as no person of the king's party, though no soldier, had liberty to visit his wife, or family, out of the king's quarters, during this cessation ; and the hindering recruits could only prejudice the king, not at all the earl of Essex, who had at present a greater army than ever before ; and the city of London was such a magazine of men, as could supply him upon very small warning. Besides, though the state of the king's army and quarters about Oxford was such as might receive some advantage by a cessation ; yet, in the west, it was hoped his affairs were in the bud ; and the earl of Newcastle was so much master in the north, that if a peace ensued not, (which wise men did not believe was seriously intended on the parliament's part, by reason the propositions to be treated on were so unreasonable, and impossible to be consented to,) such a cessation would hinder the motion and progress of the earl's good fortune, and give time to the lord Fairfax, who was at present very low, to put himself into such a posture as might give new trouble." And it is certain the northern forces had then great dread of this cessation.

To these considerations was added another of greater moment, and which could be less answered and poized by any access of benefit or advantage on the king's party. Hitherto the parliament had raised their vast sums of money, for the support of their army, (which could only be supported by constant great pay,) and the discharge of their other immense expenses, incident to such a rebellion, from the city of London, and principally from their friends, not daring so rigidly to execute their ordinances generally, but contented themselves with some severe judgments upon particular men, whom they had branded with some extraordinary mark of malignancy, out of London, save only that they gleaned among their own zealots upon voluntary collections, and plundered by their army, which brought no supply to their common stock : and what they imposed upon cities and towns, in which they had garrisons, (in which they had been likewise very tender,) they had received very little ; not venturing yet, by any general tax and imposition upon the people, to inflame them, and inform them how far they meant to invade their liberty and their property, with the jealousy whereof they had blown them up to all those swellings and seditious humours against the king ; and apprehending, that if they should attempt that, any encouragement of strength from any of the king's armies would make the whole kingdom rise against them.

But now, after they had agreed to a treaty, and framed even articles for a cessation, they passed an ordinance for a weekly assessment throughout the kingdom, towards the support of a war ; by which was imposed upon the city of London the weekly sum of ten thousand pounds, and upon the whole kingdom no less than a weekly payment of thirty-three thousand five hundred and eighteen pounds, amounting in the year to one million seven hundred forty-two thousand nine hundred thirty-six pounds ; a prodigious sum for a people to bear, who, before this war, thought the payment of two subsidies in a year, which, in the best times, never amounted to above two hundred thousand pounds, and never in our age to above a hundred and fifty, an insupportable burden upon the kingdom : and indeed had scarce borne the same, under all the kings that ever reigned.

For the speedy and exact collection whereof, they appointed, by the same ordinance, commissioners in each county, such as were sufficiently inclined to, and engaged in their designs. To this they added other ordinances, for exacting the twentieth part, and other payments, throughout the kingdom ; which had been only undergone (and that not generally) in London ; and, above all, for the sequestering and seizing of the estates of all who adhered to the king. " Now if a cessation were consented to by the king, on the articles proposed, and thereby the king's forces locked up within the several limits and narrow bounds, in which they were contained, these ordinances might be executed throughout all their quarters ; and thereby vast sums be raised. Their great association of Norfolk, Suffolk, Cambridge, Huntingdon, Bedford, and Essex, (in neither of which the king had any visible party, or one fixed quarter,) upon which, the apprehension of the earl of Newcastle's advance upon them, kept them from notable pressures, would by this means yield them a great supply of men and money. In Somersetshire and Devonshire, whilst sir Ralph Hopton might hereby be kept from advancing, they might raise what they would, and might dispose of the stocks and personal estates of those, whom they had, and would declare to be malignant ; and so this cessation, besides the damage and prejudice to the loyal party, would probably fill the rebels' coffers, the emptiness whereof was the most, if not only, probable way and means to determine the war."

These considerations made a deep impression upon those, who believed the treaty was not like to produce a peace ; the number of which was increased by a new resolution, at this time entered upon, and vigorously prosecuted, " to fortify the city of London, and to draw a line about it ;" which was executed with marvellous expedition ; which, many be-

lieved, would not have been then done, both for the charge
and jealousy of it, if it had not been resolved it should not
yet return to the king's obedience.   And many persons of
honour and quality about the king, who had given great life
to his affairs, were so startled with the sense of it, that they
addressed themselves together to his majesty, and besought
him, " that they might not lose that now, by an unequal
cessation, which had been preserved for them, during the
licence of hostility ; and that his and their enemies might
not be that way enabled to destroy them, which yet they
durst not attempt to do."   The king hereupon, after solemn
debates in council, the chief officers of his army being present, resolved to make such alterations in the articles, as
might make the terms a little more equal, at least prevent
so intolerable disadvantages.

1. " To the first article as it was proposed by them, his
majesty fully and absolutely consented.

2. " To the second likewise fully, as far as it concerned
all officers and soldiers of the army ; but he proposed, that
all other his subjects, of what quality or condition soever,
might, during the cessation, pass to and from the cities of
Oxford or London, or any other parts of his majesty's dominions, without any search, stay, or imprisonment of their
persons, or seizure and detention of their goods or estates :
and that all manner of trade and commerce might be open
and free between all his subjects, except between the officers and soldiers of either army, or for arms, ammunition,
money, bullion, or victuals for the use of either army, without a pass, or safe conduct ;" which, his majesty told them,
" would be a good beginning to renew the trade and correspondence of the kingdom, and whereby his subjects might be
restored to that liberty and freedom they were born to, and
had so happily enjoyed till these miserable distractions ; and
which, even during this war, his majesty had, to his utmost,
laboured to preserve, opening the way, by most strict proclamations, to the passage of all commodities, even to the city
of London itself."

3, 4, 5, 6. To these the king likewise consented, with
two provisions : first, " that such ships, as were necessary

to be set forth, should be commanded by such persons as his majesty should approve of. Secondly, that, during the cessation, none of his subjects should be imprisoned otherwise than according to the known laws of the land, and that there should be no plundering, or violence offered to any of his subjects." The first of these was inserted, (without purpose of insisting on it,) lest by the king's consent to the article, in the terms it was proposed, he might be thought to consent in any degree to their usurpation of the naval authority. And the second was, to prevent the execution of the ordinances before mentioned.

And his majesty told them, " he hoped, these small alterations would sufficiently manifest, how solicitous he was for the good of his people, for whose liberties he should insist, when, in matters merely concerning himself, he might descend to easier conditions ; and how desirous he was, that, in this unnatural contention, no more blood of his subjects might be spilt, upon which he looked with much grief, compassion, and tenderness of heart, even of those, who had lifted up their hands against him. And therefore he doubted not, but both houses would consent to them. However, if any scruples should be made, he was willing that the commissioners for the treaty might nevertheless immediately come to him, and so all matters concerning the cessation might be there settled between them."

After this answer returned by the king, many days passed without any return to him ; and in the mean time another address was made to his majesty, upon which the great managers at London had set their hearts, more than upon the treaty ; and for which indeed they deferred their treaty. They had still a great dependence and confidence upon their brethren of Scotland, and yet that people moved very slowly ; and, since the earl of Essex had been settled in his winter quarters, there had been high quarrels between the English and Scotch officers, insomuch as, upon some reproachful words which had been cast out, many swords were one day drawn in Westminster-hall, when the houses were sitting, between them ; and a little blood drawn, which (though the houses industriously laboured to compose with declara-

81*

tions " of their joint value and respect of that nation with
their own, and that their deserts could only distinguish
them") gave so great umbrage, that many of the Scots, some
of eminent command, quitted the service ; and it was hoped
it would have broke any farther national combination in mischief.

But the general inclination to rebellion mastered those
particular considerations and disobligations ; and, about the
end of February, to facilitate the king's consent to the grand
proposition for the extirpation of episcopacy, (which the two
houses had been, by the arts before mentioned, wrought to
make; when, in truth, there were very few of themselves
desired it ; as, when it passed the house of peers, there were
but five lords present,) there arrived at Oxford the earl of
Lowden, lord chancellor of Scotland, and Mr. Alexander
Henderson, a man of equal fame in the distractions that arose
in that kingdom : the former came as a commissioner from
the lords of the secret council of that kingdom, or, as they
then thought fit to call themselves, " the conservators of the
peace between the two kingdoms ;" and desired to pass as a
mediator in the differences between the king and the two
houses, and that the king would give them leave upon the
matter to be umpires between them.   The other, Mr. Henderson, had a special employment from the assembly of the
kirk of Scotland, to present a petition from that body to the
king ; the which, because it was then thought of a very
strange nature and dialect, and because I shall always report
the acts of that nation (as far as I am obliged to mention
them) in their own words, I think very convenient to insert
in this place.

But it will be first necessary, for the better understanding
one angry clause in it, to remember, that, when the earl of
Newcastle marched into Yorkshire, upon occasion of some
aspersions published against him by the lord Fairfax, " that
his army consisted only of papists, and that his design was to
extirpate the protestant religion," the earl set forth a declaration of the reasons of his marching into that country, which
was, " upon the desire of the principal gentlemen, to rescue
and protect them from the tyranny of the parliament ;" and

then, taking notice of " the scandalous imputations upon him in point of religion," after he had vindicated himself from the least suspicion of inclination to popery, he confessed " he had granted commissions to many papists, which, as he knew, was, in this case, agreeable to the laws of the kingdom, so he believed it very agreeable to the present policy ; and that the quarrel between the king and the two houses being not grounded upon any matter of religion, the rebels professing themselves to be of the same of which his majesty was clearly known to be, and the papists generally at this time appearing very loyal to him, which too many protestants were not, he thought their assistance might very fitly be made use of, to suppress the rebellion of the other." And from thence these zealous Scots concluded, that he preferred the papists, in point of loyalty, before the protestants ; which was a calumny of so public a concernment, that they could not be silent in.   Their petition follows in these words.

To the king's[1] most excellent majesty.

The humble petition of the commissioners of the general assembly of the kirk of Scotland, met at Edinburgh, Jan. 4, 164$\frac{2}{3}$.

" Our silence, and ceasing to present before your majesty our humble thoughts and desires, at this time of common danger to religion, to your majesty's sacred person, your crown, and posterity, and to all your majesty's dominions, were impiety against God, unthankfulness and disloyalty against your majesty, and indirect approbation and hardening of the adversaries of truth and peace in their wicked ways, and cruelty against our brethren, lying in such depths of affliction and anguish of spirit ; any one of which crimes were, in us above all others, unexcusable, and would prove us most unworthy of the trust committed unto us. The flame of this common combustion hath almost devoured Ireland, is now wasting the kingdom of England, and we cannot tell how soon it shall enter upon ourselves, and set this your

[1] *This petition is in the handwriting of lord Clarendon's amanuensis.*

majesty's most ancient and native kingdom on fire. If in
this woful case, and lamentable condition of your majesty's
dominions, all others should be silent, it behoveth us to
speak : and if our tongues and pens should cease, our consciences within us would cry out, and the stones in the
streets would answer us.

" Our great grief, and apprehension of danger, is not a little
increased, partly by the insolence and presumption of papists,
and others disaffected to the reformation of religion, who, although for their number and power they be not considerable
among us, yet, through the success of the popish party in Ireland, and the hopes they conceive of the prevailing power of
the popish armies and the prelatical faction in England, they
have of late taken spirit, and begun to speak big words
against the reformation of religion, and the work of God in
this land ; and partly, and more principally, that a chief praise
of the protestant religion (and thereby our not vain, but just
gloriation) is, by the public declaration of the earl of Newcastle, general of your majesty's forces for the northern
parts, and nearest unto us, transferred unto papists; who,
although they be sworn enemies unto kings, and be as infamous for their treasons and conspiracies against princes and
rulers, as for their known idolatry and spiritual tyranny, yet
are they openly declared to be not only good subjects, or
better subjects, but far better subjects than protestants :
which is a new and foul disparagement of the reformed religion, a notable injury to your majesty in your honour, a sensible reflection upon the whole body of this kingdom, which
is impatient that any subjects should be more loyal than
they ; but abhorreth, and extremely disdaineth, that papists,
who refuse to take the oath of allegiance, should be compared with them in allegiance and fidelity ; and which (being
a strange doctrine from the mouth or pen of professed protestants) will suffer a hard construction from all the reformed
kirks.

" We therefore, your majesty's most humble and loving
subjects, upon these and the like considerations, do humbly
entreat, that your majesty may be pleased, in your princely
wisdom, first to consider, that the intentions of papists, di-

rected by the principles of their profession, are no other than they have been from the beginning, even to build their Babel, and to set up their execrable idolatry and antichristian tyranny, in all your majesty's dominions ; to change the face of your two kingdoms of Scotland and England into the similitude of miserable Ireland ; which is more bitter to the people of God, your majesty's good subjects, to think upon, than death ; and whatsoever their present pretences be, for the defence of your majesty's person and authority, yet, in the end, by their arms and power, with a displayed banner, to bring that to pass against your royal person and posterity, which the fifth of November, never to be forgotten, was not able by their subtile and undermining treason to produce ; or, which will be their greatest mercy, to reduce your majesty, and your kingdoms, to the base and unnatural slavery of their monarch, the pope : and next, that your majesty, upon this undeniable evidence, may timely and speedily apply your royal authority, for disbanding their forces, suppressing their power, and disappointing their bloody and merciless projects.

"And for this end, we are, with greater earnestness than before, constrained to fall down again before your majesty, and, in all humility to renew the supplication of the late general assembly, and our own former petition in their name, for unity of religion, and uniformity of church-government in all your majesty's kingdoms, and, to this effect, for a meeting of some divines to be holden in England, unto which, according to the desire of your majesty's parliament, some commissioners may be sent from this kirk ; that, in all points to be propounded and debated, there may be the greater consent and harmony. We take the boldness to be the more instant in this our humble desire, because it concerneth the Lord Jesus Christ so much in his glory, your majesty in your honour, the kirk of England (which we ought to tender as our own bowels, and whose reformation is more dear unto us than our lives) in her happiness, and the kirk of Scotland in her purity and peace ; former experience and daily sense teaching us, that, without the reformation of the kirk of England, there is no hope or possibility of the continuance of reformation here.

"The Lord of heaven and earth, whose vicegerent your majesty is, calleth for this great work of reformation at your hands; and the present commotions and troubles of your majesty's dominions are either a preparation, in the mercy of God, for this blessed reformation and unity of religion, (which is the desire, and expectation of all your majesty's good subjects in this kingdom,) or, which they tremble to think upon, and earnestly deprecate, are (in the justice of God, for the abuse of the gospel, the tolerating of idolatry and superstition, against so clear a light, and not acknowledging the day of visitation) the beginning of such a doleful desolation, as no policy or power of man shall be able to prevent, and as shall make your majesty's kingdoms, within a short time, as miserable as they may be happy by a reformation of religion. God forbid that, whilst the houses of parliament do profess their desire of the reformation of religion in a peaceable and parliamentary way, and pass their bills for that end in the particulars; that your majesty, the nurse-father of the kirk of Christ, to whose care the custody and vindication of religion doth principally belong, shall, to the provoking of the anger of God, the stopping of the influence of so many blessings from Heaven, and the grieving of the hearts of all the godly, frustrate our expectation, make our hopes ashamed, and hazard the loss of the hearts of all your good subjects; which, next unto the truth and unity of religion, and the safety of your kingdoms, are willing to hazard their lives, and spend their blood, for your majesty's honour and happiness.

"We are not ignorant, that the work is great, the difficulties and impediments many; and that there be both mountains and lions in the way; the strongest let, till it be taken out of the way, is the mountain of prelacy: and no wonder, if your majesty consider, how many papists, and popishly affected, have, for a long time, found peace and ease under the shadow thereof; how many of the prelatical faction have thereby their life and being; how many profane and worldly men do fear the yoke of Christ, and are unwilling to submit themselves to the obedience of the gospel; how many there be, whose eyes are dazzled with the external glory and

pomp of the kirk ; whose minds are miscarried with a con-
ceit of the governing of the kirk by the rules of human policy ; and whose hearts are affrighted with the apprehensions
of the dangerous consequences, which may ensue upon alterations.   But when your majesty, in your princely and religious wisdom, shall remember, from the records of former
times, how against the gates of hell, the force and fraud of
wicked and worldly men, and all panic fears of danger, the
Christian religion was first planted ; and the Christian kirk
thereafter reformed : and, from the condition of the present
times, how many, from the experience of the tyranny of the
prelates, are afraid to discover themselves, lest they be revenged upon them hereafter, (whereas prelacy being removed, they would openly profess what they are, and join with
others in the way of reformation,) all obstacles and difficulties shall be but matter of the manifestation of the power of
God, the principal worker ; and means of the greater glory
to your majesty, the prime instrument.

" The intermixture of the government of prelates with the
civil state, mentioned in your majesty's answer to our former
petition, being taken away, and the right government by assemblies, which is to be seen in all the reformed kirks, and
wherein the agreement will be easy, being settled ; the kirk
and religion will be more pure, and free of mixture, and the
civil government more sound and firm.   That government
of the kirk must suit best with the civil state, and be most
useful for kings and kingdoms, which is best warranted by
God, by whom kings do reign, and kingdoms are established.
Nor can a reformation be expected in the common and ordinary way, expressed also in your majesty's answer.   The
wisest and most religious princes have found it impossible,
and implying a repugnancy, since the persons to be reformed,
and reformers, must be diverse ; and the way of reformation
must be different from the corrupt way, by which defection
of workmen, and corruption in doctrine, worship, and government, have entered into the kirk.   Suffer us, therefore,
dread sovereign, to renew our petitions for this unity of religion, and uniformity of kirk-government, and for a meeting
of some divines of both kingdoms, who may prepare matters

for your majesty's view, and for the examination and approbation of more full assemblies. The national assembly of
this kirk, from which we have our commission, did promise,
in their thanksgiving for the many favours expressed in your
majesty's letter, their best endeavour to keep the people
under their charge in unity and peace, and in loyalty and
obedience to your majesty, and your laws ; which, we confess, is a duty well beseeming the preachers of the gospel.

"But we cannot conceal how much both pastors and people are grieved and disquieted with the late reports of the
success, boldness, and strength of popish forces in Ireland and
England ; and how much danger, from the power of so malicious and bloody enemies, is apprehended to the religion
and peace of this kirk and kingdom, conceived by them to be
the spring, whence have issued all their calamities and miseries. Which we humbly remonstrate to your majesty as a
necessity requiring a general assembly, and do earnestly sup-
plicate for the presence and assistance of your majesty's commissioners, and the day to be appointed ; that, by universal
consent of the whole kirk, the best course may be taken for
the preservation of religion, and for the averting of the great
wrath, which they conceive to be imminent to this kingdom.
If it shall please the Lord, in whose hand is the heart of the
king, as the rivers of waters, to turn it whithersoever he will,
to incline your majesty's heart to this through reformation ;
no more to tolerate the mass, or any part of Romish superstition, or tyranny ; and to command that all good means be
used for the conversion of your princely consort, the queen's
majesty, (which is also the humble desire of this whole kirk
and kingdom,) your joint comforts shall be multiplied above
the days of your affliction, to your incredible joy ; your glory
shall shine in brightness, above all your royal progenitors, to
the admiration of the world, and the terror of your enemies :
and your kingdoms so far abound in righteousness, peace, and
prosperity, above all that hath been in former generations,
that they shall say, *It is good for us, that we have been afflicted.*"

This petition was not stranger in itself, than in the circumstances that attended it ; for it was no sooner (if so

soon) presented to the king, than it was sent to London, and printed, and communicated with extraordinary industry to the people; that they might see how far the Scottish nation would be engaged for the destruction of the church; and the messenger who presented it, Mr. Henderson, confessed to his majesty, that he had three or four letters to the most active and seditious preachers about London, from men of the same spirit in Scotland.   Upon this provocation, the king might have very reasonably proceeded against Mr. Henderson, who was neither included in his safe conduct, (as the lord Lowden and the rest of the commissioners were,) nor had any authority from the lords of the council of that kingdom, (who were qualified with large powers,) to countenance his employment; being sent only from the commissioners of the general assembly, (who were not authorized by their own constitutions, to make any such declaration,) and there being then no assembly sitting; which itself, with all their new privileges, could not, with any colour of reason, or authority, have transacted such an instrument. However the king, who well knew the interest and influence the clergy had upon the people of that kingdom; and that, whilst they pretended to remove them from all secular employment, they were the principal instruments and engines, by which the whole nation was wrought to sedition; resolved, not only to use the person of Mr. Henderson very graciously, and to protect him from those affronts, which he might naturally expect in a university, (especially, having used some grave and learned doctors with great insolence, who went civilly to him to be informed, what arguments had prevailed with him, to be so professed an enemy to the church of England, and to give him some information in the argument; with whom he superciliously refused to hold any discourse,) but to return an answer with all possible candour to the petition itself; and so, before he entered upon the other address, made by the lord Lowden and the rest, he returned (after very solemn debates in council, where the earl of Lanerick the secretary for Scotland, and other lords of Scotland, who were of the privy-council, were present, and fully concurred, with many expressions of their

detestation of the manners of their countrymen, yet with assured confidence that they would not be corrupted to any
act of hostility) to Mr. Henderson, and, with all expedition,
by other hands into Scotland, this answer; which likewise
I think fit to insert in the very words, that posterity may
know how tender and provident the king always was, to
prevent any misunderstanding of him and his actions with
that people; and consequently any commotions in that kingdom ; which was the only thing, he feared, might contribute
to, and continue, the distractions in this.

His majesty's answer[1] *to a late petition presented unto
him by the hands of Mr. Alexander Henderson, from
the commissioners of the general assembly of the church
of Scotland.*

" We received lately a petition from you, by the hands of
Mr. Alexander Henderson, to the which we intended to
have given an answer, as soon as we had transacted the business with the other commissioners, addressed to us from
the conservators of the treaty of that our kingdom. But
finding the same to be published in print, and to be dispersed throughout our kingdom, to the great danger of scandal-
ing of our well affected subjects; who may interpret the
bitterness and sharpness of some expressions, not to be so
agreeable to that regard and reverence, which is due to our
person, and the matter itself to be reproachful to the honour
and constitution of this kingdom : we have been compelled,
the more strictly to examine, as well the authority of the
petitioners, as the matter of the petition itself, and to publish our opinion of both, that our subjects of both kingdoms
may see how equally just, and sensible, we are of the laws
and honour of both our kingdoms.
" And first, upon perusal of the petition, we required to
see the commission, by which the messenger who brought
the petition, or the persons who sent him, are qualified to
intermeddle in affairs so foreign to their jurisdiction, and of
so great concernment to this our kingdom of England,

---

[1] *This answer is in the handwriting of lord Clarendon's amanuensis.*

Upon examination whereof, and in defence of the laws and government of this our kingdom, which we are trusted and sworn to defend, we must profess that the petitioners, or the general assembly of our church of Scotland, have not the least authority, or power, to intermeddle or interpose in the affairs of this kingdom, or church; which are settled and established by the proper laws of this land, and, till they be altered by the same competent power, cannot be inveighed against without a due sense of us, and this nation; much less can they present any advice or declaration to our houses of parliament against the same; or, to that purpose, send any letters, as they have now done, to any ministers of our church here; who, by the laws of this land, cannot correspond against the same.

" Therefore, we do believe that the petitioners, when they shall consider how unwarranted it is by the laws of that kingdom, and how contrary it is to the laws of this, to the professions they have made to each other, and how unbecoming in itself, for them to require the ancient, happy, and established government of the church of England to be altered, and conformed to the laws and constitutions of another church, will find themselves misled by the information of some factious persons here, who would willingly engage the petitioners to foment a difference and division between the two kingdoms, which we have, with so much care and industry, endeavoured to prevent; not having laboured more to quench the combustion in this kingdom, than we have to hinder the like from either devouring Ireland, or entering into Scotland; which, if all others will equally labour, will undoubtedly be avoided. But we cannot so easily pass over the mention of Ireland, being moved to it by the scandalous aspersions, that have been often cast upon us, upon that subject, and the use that hath been made of the woful distractions of that kingdom, as of a seminary of fears and jealousies, to beget the like distractions in this; and, which lest they may have farther influence, we are the more willing to make our innocence appear in that particular.

" When first that horrid rebellion began, we were in our

kingdom of Scotland; and the sense we had then of it, the expressions we made concerning it, the commissions, together with some other assistance, we sent immediately into that kingdom, and the instant recommendation we made of it to both our houses of parliament in England, are known to all persons of quality there and then about us. After our return into England, our ready concurring to all the desires of both houses, that might most speedily repress that rebellion, by passing the bill of pressing, and in it a clause, which quitted a right challenged by all, and enjoyed by many of our predecessors, by parting with our rights in the lands escheated to us by that rebellion, for the encouragement of adventurers; by emptying our magazines of arms and ammunition for that service, (which we have since needed for our necessary defence and preservation,) by consenting to all bills for the raising of money for the same, though containing unusual clauses, which trusted both houses without us with the manner of disposing it : our often pressing both houses, not to neglect that kingdom, by being diverted by considerations and disputes less concerning both kingdoms : our offer of raising ten thousand volunteers to be sent thither ; and our several offers to engage our own royal person, in the suppression of that horrid rebellion, are no less known to all this nation, than our perpetual earnestness, by our foreign ministers, to keep all manner of supplies from being transported for the relief of the rebels, is known to several neighbouring princes ; which if all good subjects will consider, and withal how many of the men, and how much of the money raised for that end, and how much time, care, and industry, have been diverted from that employment, and employed in this unnatural war against us, (the true cause of the present misery, and want, which our British armies there do now endure,) they will soon free us from all those imputations, so scandalously and groundlessly laid upon us ; and impute the continuance of the combustion of that miserable kingdom, the danger it may bring upon our kingdoms of England and Scotland, and the beginning of this doleful desolation, to those who are truly guilty of it.

" For unity in religion, which is desired, we cannot but

answer, that we much apprehend, lest the papists may make some advantage of that expression, by continuing that scandal with more authority, which they have ever heretofore used to cast upon the reformation, by interpreting all the differences in ceremony, government, or indifferent opinions between several protestant churches, to be differences in religion ; and lest our good subjects of England, who have ever esteemed themselves of the same religion with you, should suspect themselves to be esteemed by you to be of a contrary ; and that the religion which they and their ancestors have held, ever since the blessed reformation, and in, and for which, they are resolved to die, is taxed, and branded of falsehood, or insufficiency, by such a desire.

" For uniformity in church-government, we conceived the answer formerly given by us (at Bridgenorth, 13th October 1642) to the former petition in this argument, would have satisfied the petitioners ; and is so full, that we can add little to it ; viz. that the government here established by the laws hath so near a relation and intermixture with the civil state, (which may be unknown to the petitioners,) that till a composed, digested form be presented to us, upon a free debate of both houses in a parliamentary way, whereby the consent and approbation of this whole kingdom may be had, and we and all our subjects may discern, what is to be left, or brought in, as well as what is to be taken away ; we know not how to consent to any alteration, otherwise than to such an act for the ease of tender consciences in the matter of ceremonies, as we have often offered ; and that this, and any thing else that may concern the peace of the church, and the advancement of God's true religion, may be soberly discussed, and happily effected, we have formerly offered, and are still willing, that debates of that nature may be entered into by a synod of godly and learned divines, to be regularly chosen according to the laws and customs of this kingdom : to which we shall be willing that some learned divines of our church of Scotland may be likewise sent, to be present, and offer, and debate their reasons.   With this answer the petitioners had great reason to acquiesce, without enlarging the matter of their former petition only with bitter expressions against the established government and laws of their neighbour nation, (as if it were contrary to the word of God,) with whom they have so lately entered into a strict amity and friendship.

"But we cannot enough wonder, that the petitioners should interpose themselves, not only as fit directors and judges between us, and our two houses of parliament, in business so wholly concerning the peace and government of this our kingdom; and in a matter so absolutely intrusted to us, as what new laws to consent, or not to consent to; but should assume, and publish, that the desire of reformation in this kingdom is in a peaceable and parliamentary way; when all the world may know, that the proceedings here have been, and are, not only contrary to all the rules and precedents of former parliaments, but destructive to the freedom, privilege, and dignity of parliaments themselves: that we were first driven by tumults, for the safety of our life, from our cities of London and Westminster; and have been since pursued, fought withal, and are now kept from thence by an army, raised and paid, as is pretended, by the two houses, which consist not of the fourth part of the number they ought to do; the rest being either driven from thence by the same violence, or expelled, or imprisoned, for not consenting to the treasons and unheard of insolencies practised against us. And if the petitioners could believe these proceedings to be in a peaceable and parliamentary way, they were unacquainted with the order and constitution of this kingdom, and not so fit instruments to promote the reformation and peace, they seem to desire.

"We cannot believe the intermixture of the present ecclesiastical government with the civil state, to be other than a very good reason; and that the government of the church should be by the rules of human policy, to be other than a very good rule, unless some other government were as well proved, as pretended, to be better warranted by the word of God.

"Of any bills offered to us, we shall not now speak, they being a part of those articles upon which we have offered, and expect to treat: but cannot but wonder, by what authority you prejudge our judgment herein, by denouncing God's anger upon us, and our hazard of the loss of the hearts of all our good subjects, if we consent not unto them. The influence of so many blessings from Heaven upon the reigns of queen Elizabeth and our father of blessed memory, and the acknowledgment of them by all protestant churches, to have been careful nurses of the church of Christ, and to have excellently discharged their duties, in the custody and vindication of religion ; and the affection of their subjects to them, do sufficiently assure us, that we should neither stop the influence of such blessings, nor grieve the hearts of all the godly, nor hazard the loss of the hearts of our good subjects, although we still maintain, in this kingdom, the same established ecclesiastical government which flourished in their times, and under their special protection.

" We doubt not, but our subjects of Scotland will rest abundantly satisfied with such alterations in their own church, as we have assented unto ; and not be persuaded by a mere assertion, that there is no hope of continuance of what is there settled by law, unless that be likewise altered which is settled here. And our subjects of England will never depart from their dutiful affection to us, for not consenting to new laws, which, by the law of the land, they know we may as justly reject, if we approve not of them, as either house hath power to prepare for, or both, to propound to us. Nor are you a little mistaken, if either you believe the generality of this nation to desire a change of church-government, or that most of those, who desire it, desire by it to introduce that which you will only esteem a reformation ; but are as unwilling to submit to what you call the yoke of Christ, and obedience to the gospel, as those whom you call profane and worldly men ; and so equally averse both to episcopacy and presbytery, that, if they should prevail in this particular, the abolition of the one would be no inlet to the other ; nor would your hearts be less grieved, your expectations less frustrated, your hopes less ashamed, or your reformation more secured. And the petitioners, upon due consideration, will not find themselves less mistaken in the government of all the reformed churches, which, they say,

is by assemblies, than they are in the best way of a reformation ; which sure is best to be in a common and ordinary
way, where the passion or interest of particular men may
not impose upon the public ; but alteration be then only
made, when, upon debates, and evident and clear reason,
and convenience, the same shall be generally consented to
for the peace and security of the people ; and those who are
trusted by the law with such debates, are not divested of
that trust, upon a general charge of corruptions, pretended
to have entered by that way ; and of being the persons to
be reformed, and so unfit to be reformers.   And certainly,
the like logic, with the like charges and pretences, might be
used to make the parliament itself an incapable judge of any
reformation, either in church or state.

" For the general expressions in the petition against papists, in which the petitioners may be understood to charge
us with compliance and even favour to their opinions ; we
have taken all occasions to publish to the world our practice
and resolution in the true protestant reformed religion : and
we are verily persuaded, there is no one subject in either
of our dominions, who at all knows us, and hath observed
our life, but is, in his soul, satisfied of our constant zeal and
unremoveable affection to that religion, and of our true dislike of, and hearty opposition to popery.   And as we willingly consented, at our being in Scotland, to all acts proposed to us, for the discountenancing and the reforming the
papists in that our kingdom ; so, by our proclamations for
the putting of all laws severely in execution against recusants ; and by not refusing any one bill, presented to us to
that purpose, in this kingdom ; and by our perpetual and
public professions of readiness, with the advice of our two
houses of parliament, prepared for us in a deliberate and
orderly way, to find some expedient to perfect so good a
work ; we conceived, we had not left it possible for any
man to believe us guilty of tolerating any part of the Romish tyranny or superstition ; or to suspect, that the conversion of our dearest consort was not so much our desire,
that the accession of as many crowns as God hath already
bestowed on us, would not be more welcome to us than that

day : a blessing, which it is our daily prayer to the Almighty to bestow upon us.

" But we might well have expected from the petitioners, who have, in their solemn national covenant, literally sworn so much care of the safety of our person, and cannot but know in how much danger that hath been, and still is, by the power and threats of rebellious armies, that they would as well have remembered the 23d of October, as the 5th of November ; and as well have taken notice of the army raised, and led against us by the earl of Essex, which hath actually assaulted, and endeavoured to murder us ; which we know to abound in Brownists, anabaptists, and other sectaries ; and in which we have reason (by prisoners we have taken, and the evidence they have given) to believe there are many more papists (and many of those foreigners) than in all our army ; as have advised us, to disband out of the army of the earl of Newcastle, which is raised for our defence, the papists in that army ; who are known to be no such number, as to endanger their obtaining any power of building their Babel, and setting up their idolatry ; and whose loyalty he hath reason to commend (though he was never suspected for favouring their religion) not before that of protestants, but of such as rebel under that title ; and whose assistance is as due to us, by the law of God and man, to rescue us from domestic rebellion, as to defend us from foreign invasion ; which we think no man denies to be lawful for them to do.　But we do solemnly declare, and protest, that God shall no sooner free us from the desperate and rebellious arms taken up against us, but we shall endeavour to free ourselves and kingdom from any fear of danger from the other, by disarming them, according to the laws of this land ; as we shall not fail to send our commissioners to the assembly, at the time appointed for it by the laws of Scotland.

" To conclude, we desire and require the petitioners (as becomes good and pious preachers of the gospel) to use their utmost endeavours, to compose any distraction in opinions, or misunderstandings, which may, by the faction of some turbulent persons, be raised in the minds of our good sub-

jects of that our kingdom ; and to infuse into them a true
sense of charity, obedience, and humility, the great principles of the Christian religion; that they may not suffer themselves to be transported with things that they do not understand, or think themselves concerned in the government of
another kingdom, because it is not according to the customs
of that in which they live ; but that they dispose themselves,
with modesty and devotion, to the service of Almighty God ;
with duty and affection, to the obedience of us, and our laws ;
(remembering the singular grace, favour, and benignity, we
have always expressed to that our native kingdom ;) and
with brotherly and Christian charity one towards another :
and we doubt not but God, in his mercy to us and them,
will make us instruments of his blessings upon each other,
and both of us, of a great measure, of happiness and prosperity to the whole nation."

The lord Lowden and the other lay-commissioners, who
were persons entirely guided by him, and of inferior quality,
gave the precedence to this petition, which they called matter of religion ; and pressed not their own commission, till
the king had declared and published his answer to that : and
though they pretended not to have any authority to say any
thing in that engagement of the commissioners of the assembly; yet the lord Lowden used all importunity, and arguments, to persuade the king in private, to consent to the alteration of the government of the church ; assuring him,
" that it would be a means, not only to hinder his subjects
of Scotland from adhering to the parliament ; but that it
would oblige them to assist his majesty to the utmost, in the
vindication of all his rights."   But he quickly found the king
too strongly fixed to be swayed in a case of conscience, by a
consideration of convenience ; and his lordship undertook to
give no other arguments.

He betook himself then with his companions to their own
proper and avowed errand ; which consisted of two parts :
the one, to offer " the mediation of the conservators of the
peace of that kingdom, for the composure of the differences
between the king and the two houses;" the other, " to de-

sire his majesty, that he would send out his precepts to summon a parliament in Scotland." These desires, and any arguments to enforce them, they always delivered to the king himself in writing; declining any address to his ministers, or any debates with his council, lest it might seem to lessen the grandeur and absoluteness of the kingdom of Scotland. But the king always brought those papers, which he received from them, to his council; and received their advice, what answers to return. For the first, of mediation, they pretended a title and obligation to it, by a clause in the act of pacification made at the beginning of this parliament; which clause was, " That the peace to be then established might be inviolably observed in all time to come, it was agreed, that some should be appointed by his majesty, and the parliaments of both kingdoms, who, in the interim betwixt the sitting of the parliaments, might be careful that the peace then happily concluded might be continued ; and who should endeavour by all means to prevent all troubles and divisions ; and if any debate and difference should happen to arise, to the disturbance of the common peace, they should labour to remove or compose them, according to their power; it being supposed, that, for all their proceedings of this kind, they should be answerable to the king's majesty and the parliament : and if any thing should fall out that should be above their power, and could not be remedied by them, they should inform themselves in the particulars, and represent the same to the king's majesty, and the ensuing parliament; that, by their wisdoms and authority, all occasion and causes of troubles might be removed, and the peace of the kingdom might be perpetual to all posterity. And it was declared, that the power of the commission should be restrained to the articles of peace in that treaty."

This clause, and the whole statute, being carefully perused, and examined before his majesty in his council, the king returned an answer to them in writing.

" That he could not find any colour, or pretence of authority, to be granted by that act of parliament, by which the commissioners for Scotland could conceive themselves interessed in a faculty of mediation ; that the clause mentioned

by them (besides that there was no such commission granted as was mentioned in that clause, nor any commissioners
named for those purposes) related only to the differences
that might grow between the two nations ; and only upon
the articles of that treaty, which, his majesty said, had been,
and should be, inviolably observed by him.   That the differences between his majesty and his two houses of parliament had not the least relation to the peace between the
two kingdoms, but to the unquestionable and long enjoyed
rights of his, which his rebellious subjects endeavoured, by
force, to wrest from him ; and concerned the fundamental
laws of this kingdom ; which, as they could not be supposed
to be known to the conservators of the peace of Scotland, so
they could not have any possible cognizance of them.   That
it might give great umbrage to his subjects of England, if
he should consent to what they now proposed ; and, instead
of confirming and continuing the peace, breed jealousies between the nations; and therefore he could not admit of any
such mediation as they proposed ; but that he hoped the
treaty, which he now expected, would beget so good an understanding between him and his two houses, that a peace
might ensue ; towards which he would expect nothing from
his subjects of Scotland, but their prayers."

This gave them no satisfaction, but they insisted still on
their right by that clause ; which, without any reason or argument to persuade others to be of their mind, they said,
" they conceived; laid that obligation upon them of interposition ;" to which the king still gave the same answer.

For their other demand of a parliament in Scotland, the
case stood thus : The king, at his last being in Scotland, had,
according to the precedent he had made here, granted an act
for triennial parliaments in that kingdom ; and, at the close of
that present parliament, had ratified another act, by which a
certain day was appointed, for the commencement of the
next ; which day was to be on the first Tuesday of June, in
the year 1644, except the king should call one sooner ;
which he had power to do.   So that the question was only, whether the calling a parliament sooner in that kingdom was like to advance his service, and to contribute to the

peace of this ? In the disquisition whereof, there needed no
arguments, that such a convention could not then produce
benefit to the king ; the entire government of that people
being in those persons, who had contrived those dismal alterations.   On the other hand, all men thought it very happy for the king, that, without his consent, there could be no
parliament in Scotland, till June, 1644 ; which was more
than fourteen months from this time : till when, how disinclined soever the whole nation should be, there was as much
assurance as could possibly be, from that people, that the
parliament would not be able to procure any avowed supply
from that kingdom : it being the express words in the late
act of pacification, " that the kingdom of England should not
denounce or make war against the kingdom of Scotland,
without consent of the parliament of England ;" as on the other
part it was enacted, "that the kingdom of Scotland should not
denounce or make war against the kingdom of England,
without the consent of the parliament of Scotland.   And in
case any of the subjects of either of the kingdoms should
rise in arms, or make war against the other kingdom, or
subjects thereof, without consent of the parliament of that
kingdom, whereof they are subjects, or upon which they do
depend, that they should be held, reputed, and demanded, as
traitors to the estates, whereof they are subjects.   And, that
both the kingdoms, in that case, should be bound to concur
in the repressing of those that should happen to arise in
arms, or make war, without consent of their own parliament."

So that whoever believed, that those people could be contained by any obligations, divine or human, thought it impossible, by these clear texts, that any forces could be raised
there to invade England, and disturb his majesty, till June
1644 ; before which time, there was hope the king might so
far prevail, that the spirit of the rebellion might be broken,
and men return again to their understanding and allegiance.
Therefore to that demand the king returned answer, " that
against the time by which they could legally demand a parliament," (naming the day,) " he would issue out his writs,
and there being no emergent cause to do it sooner, he would

forbear to put his subjects there to that trouble, which those
meetings, how necessary soever, would naturally carry with
them."

When they perceived that they should not receive satisfaction in either of their proposals, and (which it may be troubled them more) that the king was so wary in his answers,
and so clearly expressed the reasons and justice of them, that
they should have no arguments to apply to the passion or
interest of their countrymen ; which they expected at least ;
(for in that, in which he was most steadfastly resolved, the
preservation of the government of the church, he expressed
no more to them, than, " that being a matter of so great importance, and having so near relation to the civil government and laws of England, they could not be competent con-
siderers of it ; but that he would do what should be most
safe, and necessary for the peace and welfare of his subjects,
who were most concerned in it ;") at last rather cursorily,
and as matter of ceremony at parting, than of moment, they
desired " the king's leave, and pass to go. to London," having, as they said, " some business there before their return
into their own country."

This was, by many, thought a thing of so small moment,
that the king should readily grant it ; since it was evident,
that it was in their own power to go thither without his
leave ; for they were necessarily to return through the enemy's quarters ; and being once there, they might choose
whether they would go directly home, or visit London. And
therefore that request was thought but an instance of their
modesty, that they might not return without one thing granted to them, at their request.   But the king looked upon it
as no indifferent thing ; and their asking a business that they
needed not ask, was enough to demonstrate, that there was
more in it than appeared.   And he well knew, there was a
great difference between their going to London with his pass
and licence, and without it, which they might easily do.
They had now publicly declared their errand, and claimed a
title, and legal capacity to undertake the business of mediation ; which would be so far from being rejected there, that
they would be thankfully received, and admitted to a power

of umpirage. If upon, or after this claim, the king should grant them his pass, it would, by their logic, more reasonably conclude his assent, than many of those inferences which they drew from more distant propositions ; and having that ground once, his majesty's not consenting to what those grave mediators would propose, and afterwards, as arbitrators, award, should be quarrel sufficient for the whole nation to engage. And therefore the king expressly denied his pass and safe conduct ; and told them plainly the reason why he did so ; and required them, " since he had denied to consent to that, which could be the only ground of their going to London, that they should first return to those that sent them, before they attempted that journey : if they did otherwise, they must run the hazard of persons, whom his majesty would not countenance with his protection." And the truth is, though they might very well have gone to London, they could not have returned thence to Scotland, (except they would have submitted to the inconvenience and hazard of a voyage by sea,) without so much danger from the king's quarters in the north, (York and Newcastle being at his devotion,) that they could not reasonably promise themselves to escape.

Whilst this was in agitation, the committee from the parliament for the treaty, to wit, the earl of Northumberland, Mr. Pierrepoint, sir W. Armyn, sir John Holland, and Mr. Whitlock, came to Oxford ; who shortly took notice of the Scotch commissioners' desires, and also desired on their behalf, " that they might have his majesty's leave to go to London :" but being quickly answered, " that that request would not fall within either of the propositions agreed to be treated of," they modestly gave over the intercession : and in the end, the Lord Lowden and his countrymen returned directly to Scotland, staying only so long in the garrisons of the enemy, through which they were reasonably to pass, as to receive such animadversions, and to entertain such communication, as they thought most necessary.

As soon as the committee arrived at Oxford, they were very graciously received by the king; his majesty always giving them audience in council, and they withdrawing into a pri-

vate chamber prepared for them, whilst their proposals, which
they still delivered in writing, were considered, and debated
before the king. They declared, " that they were first to
treat of the cessation, and till that was concluded, that they
were not to enter upon any of the other propositions;" with
which his majesty was well pleased, presuming that they had
brought, or had power to give, consent to the articles proposed by him ; which he the rather believed, when they
read the preamble to the articles; in which it was declared,
" that the lords and commons being still carried on with a
vehement desire of peace, that so the kingdom might be freed
from the desolation and destruction, wherewith it was like to
be overwhelmed, had considered of the articles of cessation
with those alterations, and additions, offered by his majesty;
unto which they were ready to agree in such manner as was
expressed in the ensuing articles." After which, were inserted the very articles had been first sent to the king, without the least condescension to any one alteration, or addition,
made by him : neither had the committee power to recede,
or consent to any alteration, but only to publish it, if the king
consented in terms, and then, and not till then, to proceed
to treat upon the other propositions.

This the king looked upon as an ill omen ; other men as
a plain contempt, and stratagem, to make the people believe,
by their sending their committee, that they did desire a
treaty and a cessation, yet, by limiting them so strictly, to
frustrate both, and to cast the envy of it upon the king.
Hereupon, the next day, the king sent a message to them,
which he published, to undeceive the people; farther pressing " the weight and consequence of his former exceptions,
and alterations ; and the inconvenience that proceeded from
not granting their committee power to alter so much as ver-
bal expressions: so that, if the king should consent to the
articles as they were proposed, he should not only submit to
great disadvantages ; but some such, as themselves would not
think reasonable to oblige him to. As by that article wherein they reserved a power to send out a fleet, or what ships
they thought good, to sea ; they were not at all restrained
from sending what land forces they pleased, to any part of

the kingdom ; so that, when the cessation ended, they might
have new and greater armies throughout the kingdom, than
they had when it begun ; which, he presumed, they did not
intend ; being a thing so unequal, and contrary to the nature
of a cessation.

"Then in the articles they last sent, they styled their
forces, the army raised by the parliament; the which, if his
majesty should consent to, he must acknowledge, either that
he consented to the raising that army, or that he was no part
of the parliament: neither of which, he conceived, they
would oblige him to do.   And therefore he desired, that
their committee might have liberty to treat, debate, and agree
upon the articles ; upon which they and all the world should
find, that he was less solicitous for his own dignity and greatness, than for his subjects' ease and liberty.   But if that so
reasonable, equal, and just desire of his should not be yielded
unto, but the same articles still insisted upon, though his majesty, next to peace, desired a cessation, yet, that the not
agreeing upon the one might not destroy the hopes of, nor
so much as delay, the other ; he was willing to treat, even
without a cessation, upon the propositions themselves, in that
order that was agreed ; and desired their committee might be
enabled to that effect.   In which treaty he would give," he
said, "all his subjects that satisfaction, that if any security
to enjoy all the rights, privileges, and liberties, due to them
by the law, or that happiness in church and state, which the
best times had seen, with such farther acts of grace, as might
agree with his honour, justice, and duty to his crown, and
which might not render him less able to protect his subjects,
according to his oath, would satisfy them ; his majesty was
confident, in the mercy of God, that no more precious blood
of this nation would be thus miserably spent."

This message produced liberty to the committee to enter
upon the treaty itself, upon the propositions, though the
cessation should not be agreed to : and shortly after they
sent reasons to the king, why they consented not to the
cessation in such manner, and with those limitations, as he
had proposed.   1. They alleged, "that, if they should grant
such a free trade, as the king desired, to Oxford, and other

places, where his forces lay, it would be very difficult, if not impossible, to keep arms, ammunition, money, and bullion, from passing to his army : however, it would be exceeding advantageous to his majesty, in supplying his army with many necessaries, and making their quarters a staple for such commodities, as might be vented in the adjacent counties ; and so draw money thither ; whereby the inhabitants would be better enabled by loans, and contributions, to support his army.   As this advantage to him was very demonstrable, so it was very improbable that it would produce any supply to them ; and, in a treaty for a cessation, those demands could not be thought reasonable that were not indifferent, that is, equally advantageous to both parties.   2. That to demand the approving the commanders of the ships, was, to desire the strength of the one party to the other, before the differences were ended ; against all rules of treaty.   And to make a cessation at sea, was to leave the kingdom naked to foreign forces, and the ports open for his supplies of arms and ammunition.   But for conveying any forces, by those means, from one part to the other, they would observe the articles by which that was restrained.   3. For the expression of the army raised by the parliament, they were contented it should be altered, and the name of the two houses used. 4. For the committing none, but according to the known laws of the land, that is, by the ordinary process of law, it would follow, that no man must be committed by them for supplying the king with arms, money or ammunition ; for, by the law of the land, the subject might carry such goods from London to Oxford : the soldiers must not be committed who do run from their colours, and refuse any duty in the army ; no man should be committed, for not submitting to necessary supplies of money : so that if it should be yielded to, in his majesty's sense, they should be disabled to restrain supplies from their enemies, and to govern and maintain their own soldiers; and so, under a disguise of a cessation, that should admit that which would necessarily produce the dissolving of their army, and destruction of their cause.   And," they said, " it was not probable, that his majesty would suffer the same inconveniences by that clause ;

for that they believed he would interpret, that what his general did by virtue of his commission, was and would be done according to the known laws of the land ; whereas he had denied, that those known laws gave any power to the two houses of parliament to raise armies ; and so, consequently, their general could not exercise any martial laws. So that under the specious show of liberty and law, they should be altogether disabled to defend their liberties and laws ; and his majesty would enjoy an absolute victory and submission, under pretence of a cessation and treaty." They said, " being, by a necessity inevitable, enforced to a defensive war, and therein warranted both by the laws of God and man, it must needs follow, that, by the same law, they were enabled to raise means to support that war; and therefore they could not relinquish that power of laying taxes upon those who ought to join with them in that defence, and the necessary way of levying those taxes upon them, in case of refusal ; for otherwise their army must needs be dissolved."

Though these reasons were capable, in a sad and composed debate, of full answers, and many things would naturally have flowed from them, to disprove the practice and assertions of the framers of them ; yet it was very evident, that they carried such a kind of reason with them, as would prevail over the understandings of the people; and that the king, by not consenting to the cessation, as it was proposed by them, would be generally thought to have rejected any ; which could not but have an ill influence upon his affairs : and therefore his majesty sent them, as soon as he had weighed this late message, which he well discerned was not formed to satisfy him, but to satisfy the people against him, an answer ; in which he explained the ill consequence of many of their assumptions, and enforced the importance of his former demands on the behalf of the people : however, he offered " to admit the cessation upon the matter of their own articles ; so that he might not be understood to consent to any of those unjust and illegal powers, which they exercised upon the subjects." But from henceforward, the houses declined any farther argument and debate concerning the cessation ; and directed their committee, " to expedite the treaty upon the propositions:" the particulars whereof being transacted in the beginning of the year 1643, I shall refer the narrative to the next book ; intending in this, only to comprehend the transactions to the end of 1642.[1]

I am persuaded, if the king had, upon the receipt of the articles for the cessation, when they were first sent to him, frankly consented to it, it would have proved very much to his advantage ; and that his army would very much have increased by it, and the other been impaired ; and that it would have been very difficult for the parliament to have dissolved it, if once begun, or to have determined the treaty. But besides the reasons before mentioned, the consideration of the northern forces, and the restraining them within their old quarters, who seemed to be in a condition of marching even to London itself, prevailed very far with the king ; or rather (which indeed was the grand reason, and rendered every other suggestion of weight) the jealousy that they did not intend to consent to or admit any peace, but such a one as his majesty might not admit, made all the preliminary debates the more insisted on.

Before I conclude this book, I cannot but insert one particular, which by some men may hereafter be thought of some signification. It was now the time of the year, when, by the custom of the kingdom, the king's judges itinerant used to go their circuits throughout England and Wales, to administer justice to the people ; and to inquire into all treasons, felonies, breaches of the peace, and other misdemeanours, which were any where committed contrary to the known laws ; and who were sworn to judge according to those known laws, the study and knowledge whereof was their profession.

The lords and commons now sent to the king a special message, " to advise, and desire him, that, in regard of the present distractions, which might hinder both the judges and the people from resorting to those places where such meetings might be appointed, the assizes and goal-delivery might

[1] *Namely old style.*

not be holden ; but that it might be deferred, until it should please God to restore peace unto his people."

The king returned them answer ; " that the present bloody distractions of the kingdom, which he had used all possible means to prevent, and would still to remove, did afflict his majesty under no consideration more, than of the great interruption and stop it made in the course and proceedings of justice, and the execution of the laws ; whereby his good subjects were robbed of the peace and security they were born to. And therefore, as much as in him lay, he would advance that only means of their happiness-; at least, they should see that their sufferings that way proceeded not from his majesty ; and since they might now expect, by the laws, statutes, and customs of the kingdom, the assizes and general gaol-delivery in every county, his majesty thought not fit to command the contrary ; but would take severe and precise order, that none of his subjects should receive the least prejudice, as they repaired thither, by any of his forces, which rule he should be glad to see observed by others. And then he hoped, by the execution of the laws, even those public calamities might have some abatement, and the kingdom recover its former peace and prosperity."

But this answer was not more satisfactory than they had usually received from him ; and therefore they betook themselves to their old tried weapon, and made an ordinance, " that all judges, and justices of assize and nisi prius, and justices of oyer and terminer, and gaol-delivery, should forbear to execute any of their said commissions, or to hold or keep any assizes, or gaol-delivery, at any time during that Lent vacation ; as they would answer the contempt and neglect thereof before the lords and commons in parliament." And this was the first avowed interruption and suspension of the public justice,' that happened, or that was known ever before in that kind ; and gave the people occasion to believe, that what the parliament did (what pretence soever there was of

' For the parliament to consent to the holding assizes and gaol-delivery, *flagrante bello*, and when the sword was appealed to, was not only confessing the injustice of their cause, but contributing to the punishment of it.—W.

fundamental laws) was not so warrantable by that rule, since
they laboured so much to suppress that inquisition. It was
not in the king's power to help this ; for besides that the example of judge Mallet, who, the circuit before, had been for-
cibly taken from the bench by a troop of horse, as is before
remembered, terrified all the judges, (and there were very
few counties in England, in which they could have been secure from the like violence,) the records, upon which the
legal proceedings were to be, were at London ; and so the
exercise of the law ceased throughout the kingdom, save only
in some few counties, whither the king sent some judges of
assize, and into others, his commissions of oyer and terminer ;
by virtue whereof, the earl of Essex, and many others, were
as legally attainted of high treason, as the wisdom of our ancestors could direct.

We shall in this place, and before we mention the treaty
which shortly ensued, for in the time between the return of
the commissioners to London, and the beginning of the treaty,
this person (whom we shall hereafter mention under the
style of chancellor of the exchequer) was preferred to that
office, and because it was about the end of the year (1642-3),
it being in February when he was sworn a privy-counsellor,
we shall set down the state of the court and the state of the
kingdom at this time, the names of those privy-counsellors
who attended the king, or were in his service, and the names
of those who were likewise of the council, but stayed and
acted with the parliament against the king ; and likewise the
temper of the kingdom at that season, as it was possessed
and made useful to either party ; and then it will easily appear how little motive any man could have from interest or
ambition, who was not carried by the impulsion of conscience
and consideration of duty, to engage himself in the quarrel
on the king's side.

The lord Littleton was keeper of the great seal of England, of whom so much hath been said before, that there is
no need of enlargement upon him in this place. His parts,
which in the profession of the law were very great, were not
very applicable to the business now in hand ; and though,
from the time of the king's coming to Oxford, the king had

confidence enough in him, to leave the seal in his custody, and he would have been glad to have done any service ; his very ill fortune had drawn so great a disesteem upon him from most men, that he gave little reputation to the council, and had little authority in it. He was exceedingly glad that his friend the chancellor of the exchequer was become a member of it.

The duke of Richmond, as he was of the noblest extraction, being nearest allied to the king's person of any man who was not descended from king James ; so he was very worthy of all the grace and favour the king had showed him ; who had taken great care of his education, and sent him into France, Italy, and Spain, where he was created a grandee of that kingdom ; and as soon as he returned, though he was scarce one and twenty years of age, made him a privy-counsellor ; and shortly after, out of his abundant kindness to both families, married him to the sole daughter of his dead favourite, the duke of Buckingham ; with whom he received twenty thousand pounds in portion ; and his majesty's bounty was likewise very great to him ; so that, as he was very eminent in his title, so he was at great ease in his fortune. He was a man of very good parts, and an excellent understanding ; yet, which is no common infirmity, so diffident of himself, that he was sometimes led by men who judged much worse. He was of a great and haughty spirit, and so punctual in point of honour, that he never swerved a tittle. He had so entire a resignation of himself to the king, that he abhorred all artifices to shelter himself from the prejudice of those, who, how powerful soever, failed in their duty to his majesty ; and therefore he was pursued with all imaginable malice by them, as one that would have no quarter, upon so infamous terms, as but looking on whilst his master was ill used. As he had received great bounties from the king, so he sacrificed all he had to his service, as soon as his occasions stood in need of it ; and lent his majesty, at one time, twenty thousand pounds together ; and, as soon as the war begun, engaged his three brothers, all gallant gentlemen, in the service; in which they all lost their lives. Himself lived, with unspotted fidelity, some years after the murder of his master, and was suffered to put him into his grave; and died, without the comfort of seeing the resurrection of the crown.

The marquis of Hertford was a man of great honour and fortune, and interest in the affection of the people; and had always undergone hard measure from the court, where he received no countenance, and had no design of making advantage from it. For, though he was a man of very good parts, and conversant in books, both in the Latin and Greek languages, and of a clear courage, of which he had given frequent evidence; yet he was so wholly given up to a country life, where he lived in splendour, that he had an aversion, and even an unaptness, for business : besides his particular friendship with the earl of Essex, whose sister he had married, his greatest acquaintance and conversation had been with those who had the reputation of being best affected to the liberty of the kingdom, and least in love with the humour of the court ;[1] many of whom were the chief of those who engaged themselves most factiously and furiously against the king. But as soon as he discerned their violent purposes against the government established,[2] before he suspected their blacker designs,[3] he severed himself from them ; and, from the beginning of the parliament, never concurred with them in any one vote dishonourable to the king, or in the prosecution of the earl of Strafford. He did accept the government of the prince of Wales, as is mentioned before, purely out of obedience to the king ; and, no doubt, it was a great service ; though for the performance of the office of a governor, he never thought himself fit, nor meddled with it. He left York, as is remembered, to form an army for the king in the west, where his interest was ; but he found those parts so corrupted, and an army from the parliament was poured down so soon upon him, that there was nothing for the present to be done worthy of his presence; so that he sent the small party, that was with him, farther west to Cornwall ; where, by degrees, they grew able to raise an

[1] i. e. arbitrary power.---W.   [2] Meaning church government.—W.
[3] Meaning against monarchy.—W.

army, with which they joined with him afterwards again ;
and himself returned to the king at Oxford, about the time
when the chancellor of the exchequer was made, who was
much in his favour, and with whom he had corresponded
principally during his absence from the court.

The earl of Southampton was indeed a great man in all
respects, and brought very much reputation to the king's
cause.   He was of a nature much inclined to melancholy,
and being born a younger brother, and his father and his
elder brother dying upon the point together, whilst he was
but a boy, he was much troubled to be called *my lord*, and
with the noise of attendance ; so much he then delighted to
be alone.   Yet he had a great spirit, and exacted the respect
that was due to his quality ; he had never had any conversation in the court, nor obligation to it.   On the contrary,
he had undergone some hardship from it ; which made it
believed, that he would have been ready to have taken all
occasions to have been severe towards it.   And therefore,
in the beginning of the parliament, no man was more courted by the managers of those designs.   He had great dislike
of the high courses,[1] which had been taken in the government, and a particular prejudice to the earl of Strafford, for
some exorbitant proceedings.[2]   But, as soon as he saw the
ways of reverence and duty towards the king declined, and
the prosecution of the earl of Strafford to exceed the limits
of justice, he opposed them vigorously in all their proceedings.   He was a man of a great sharpness of judgment, a
very quick apprehension, and that readiness of expression
upon any sudden debate, that no man delivered himself
more advantageously and weightily, and more efficaciously
with the hearers ; so that no man gave them more trouble
in his opposition, or drew so many to a concurrence with
him in opinion.   He had no relation to, or dependence upon,
the court, or purpose to have any ; but wholly pursued the
public interest.   It was long before he could be prevailed
with to be a counsellor, and longer before he would be admitted to be of the bedchamber ; and received both honours

---

[1] i. e. arbitrary courses.—W.   [2] Tyrannical.—W.

the rather, because, after he had refused to take a protestation, which both houses had ordered to be taken by all their
members, they had likewise voted, " that no man should be
capable of any preferment in church or state, who refused
to take the same;" and he would show how much he contemned those votes.   He went with the king to York; was
most solicitous, as hath been said, for the offer of peace at
Nottingham; and was then with him at Edge-hill; and
came and stayed with him at Oxford to the end of the war,
taking all opportunities to advance all motions towards
peace; and, as no man was more punctual in performing his
own duty, so no man had more melancholy apprehensions of
the issue of the war;[1] which is all shall be said of him in
this place, there being frequent occasions to mention him, in
the continuance of this discourse: there being always a fast
friendship between him and the chancellor of the exchequer,
which lasted to his death.

The earl of Leicester was a man of great parts, very conversant in books, and much addicted to the mathematics; and
though he had been a soldier, and commanded a regiment,
in the service of the States of the United Provinces, and was
afterwards employed in several embassies, as in Denmark and
in France, was in truth rather a speculative, than a practical
man; and expected a greater certitude in the consultation of
business, than the business of this world is capable of: which
temper proved very inconvenient to him through the course
of his life.   He was, after the death of the earl of Strafford,
by the concurrent kindness and esteem both of king and
queen, called from his embassy in France, to be lieutenant
of the kingdom of Ireland; and, in a very short time after,
unhappily lost that kindness and esteem: and being, about

---

[1] This is the state in which the noble historian represents all those
excellent men who adhered to the king after he had given satisfaction
to public liberty, and who before that had either opposed the court,
or been ill used by it.   Now from whence could arise the *melancholy
apprehensions* of these men, but their foreseeing that, which ever side
conquered, public liberty would be destroyed, and therefore were always labouring in vain to end the quarrel by treaty and convention.---
W.

the time of the king's coming to Oxford, ready to embark at
Chester, for the execution of his charge, he was required to
attend his majesty, for further instructions, at Oxford ; where
he remained ; and though he was of the council, and sometimes present, he desired not to have any part in the business ; and lay under many .reproaches and jealousies, which
he deserved not : for he was a man of honour, and fidelity to
the king, and his greatest misfortunes proceeded from the
staggering and irresolution in his nature.

The earl of Bristol was a man of a grave aspect, of a presence that drew respect, and of long experience in affairs of
great importance.   He had been, by the extraordinary favour of king James to his person (for he was a very handsome man) and his parts, which were naturally great, and
had been improved by a good education at home and abroad,
sent ambassador into Spain, before he was thirty years of
age ; and afterwards in several other embassies ; and at last,
again into Spain ; where he treated and concluded the marriage between the prince of Wales and that infanta ; which
was afterwards dissolved.   He was by king James made of
the privy-council, vice-chamberlain of the household, an earl,
and a gentleman of the bedchamber to the prince, and was
then crushed by the power of the duke of Buckingham, and
the prejudice the prince himself had contracted against him,
during his highness's being in Spain ; upon which he was imprisoned upon his return ; and after the duke's death, the
king retained so strict a memory of all his friendships and
displeasures, that the earl of Bristol could never recover any
admission to the court ; but lived in the country, in ease, and
plenty in his fortune, and in great reputation with all who
had not an implicit reverence for the court ; and before, and
in the beginning of the parliament, appeared in the head of
all the discontented party ; but quickly left them, when they
entered upon their unwarrantable violences, and grew so
much into their disfavour, that after the king was gone to
York, upon some expressions he used in the house of peers
in debate, they committed him to the Tower ; from whence
being released, in two or three days, he made haste to York
to the king ; who had before restored him to his place in the

council and the bedchamber. He was with him at Edge-hill, and came with him from thence to Oxford; and, at the end of the war, went into France; where he died; that party having so great an animosity against him, that they would not suffer him to live in England, nor to compound for his estate, as they suffered others to do, who had done them more hurt. Though he was a man of great parts, and a wise man, yet he had been for the most part single, and by himself, in business; which he managed with good sufficiency; and had lived little in consort, so that in council he was passionate, and supercilious, and did not bear contradiction without much passion, and was too voluminous in discourse; so that he was not considered there with much respect; to the lessening whereof no man contributed more than his son, the lord Digby; who shortly after came to sit there as secretary of state, and had not that reverence for his father's wisdom, which his great experience deserved, though he failed not in his piety towards him.[1]

The earl of Newcastle was a person well bred, and of a full and plentiful fortune; and had been chosen by the king to be governor to the prince of Wales, and made of the council, and resigned that office of governor to the marquis of Hertford, for the reasons which have been mentioned. He was not at Oxford, but remained at Newcastle, with the king's commission to be general of those parts; being a man of great courage, and signal fidelity to the crown, of whom there will be more occasion hereafter to enlarge.

The earl of Berkshire was of the council, but not yet at Oxford; having been, about or before the setting up of the standard, taken prisoner in Oxfordshire, and committed to the Tower, upon an imagination that he had some purpose to have executed the commission of array in that county; but they afterwards set him at liberty, as a man that could do them no harm any where; and then he came to Oxford, with the title and pretences of a man, who had been imprisoned for

---

[1] The father had contracted the Spanish gravity, the son was born with the French vivacity; so it was no wonder he had not much reverence for his father's *wisdom*. But that he preserved a filial *piety* to him is to be ascribed to his grandeur of mind.—W.

the king, and thereby merited more than his majesty had to give. His affection for the crown was good, his interest and reputation less than any thing but his understanding.

The lord Dunsmore had been made a privy-counsellor, after so many, who had deserved worse, had been called thither, to make an atonement; which failing, he could not be refused who was ready to do whatever he was directed: he was a man of a rough and tempestuous nature, violent in pursuing what he wished, without judgment, or temper to know the way of bringing it to pass; however, he had some kind of power with froward and discontented men; at least he had credit to make them more indisposed. But his greatest reputation was, that the earl of Southampton married his daughter, who was a beautiful and a worthy lady.

The lord Seymour, being brother to the marquis of Hertford, was a man of interest and reputation; he had been always very popular in the country; where he had always lived out of the grace of the court; and his parts and judgment were best in those things which concerned the good husbandry, and the common administration of justice to the people. In the beginning of the parliament, he served as knight of the shire for Wiltshire, where he lived; and behaving himself with less violence in the house of commons, than many of his old friends did, and having a great friendship for the earl of Strafford, he was, by his interposition, called to the house of peers; where he carried himself very well in all things relating to the crown; and when the king went to York, he left the parliament, and followed his majesty, and remained firm in his fidelity.

The lord Savile was likewise of the council, being first controller, and then treasurer of the household, in recompense of his discovery of all the treasons and conspiracies, after they had taken effect, and could not be punished. He was a man of an ambitious and restless nature; of parts and wit enough; but, in his disposition, and inclination, so false, that he could never be believed, or depended upon. His particular malice to the earl of Strafford, which he had sucked in with his milk, (there having always been an immortal feud between the families; and the earl had shrewdly overborne his father,) had engaged him with all persons who were willing, and like to be able, to do him mischief. And so, having opportunity, when the king was at the Berks, and made the first unhappy pacification, to enter into conversation, and acquaintance, with those who were then employed as commissioners from the Scots, there was a secret intelligence entered into between them from that time ; and he was a principal instrument to engage that nation to march into England with an army ; which they did the next year after. To which purpose, he sent them a letter, signed with the names of several of the English nobility, inviting them to enter the kingdom, and making great promises of assistance; which names were forged by himself, without the privity of those who were named. And when all this mischief was brought to pass, and he found his credit in the parliament not so great as other men's, he insinuated himself into credit with somebody, who brought him to the king or queen, to whom he confessed all he had done to bring in the Scots, and who had conspired with him, and all the secrets he knew, with a thousand protestations " to repair all by future loyalty and service ;" for which he was promised a white staff, which the king had then resolved to take from sir Henry Vane, who held it with the secretary's office; which he had accordingly; though all his discovery was of no other use, than that the king knew many had been false, whom he could not punish; and some, whom he could not suspect. When the king came to York, where this lord's fortune and interest lay, his reputation was so low, that the gentlemen of interest, who wished well to the king's service, would not communicate with him; and, after the king's remove from thence, the earl of Newcastle found cause to have such a jealousy of him, that he thought it necessary to imprison him; and afterwards sent him to Oxford; where he so well purged himself, that he was again restored to his office. But in the end he behaved himself so ill, that the king put him again out of his place, and committed him to prison, and never after admitted him to his presence ; nor would any man of quality ever after keep any correspondence with him.

Of the lord Falkland, and sir John Colepepper, there hath

been so much said before, that there is no occasion to add
to it in this place. There will be reason too soon to lament
the unhappy death of the former ; and the latter, who never
failed in his fidelity, will be very often mentioned throughout
the ensuing discourse.

Secretary Nicholas was a very honest and industrious
man,[1] and always versed in business ; which few of the
others were, or had been. After some time spent in the
university of Oxford, and then in the Middle Temple, he
lived a year or thereabouts in France ; and was then secretary to the lord Zouch, who was a privy-counsellor, and warden of the cinque ports ; and thereby he understood all that
jurisdiction, which is very great, and exclusive to the admiral. And when that lord, many years after, surrendered
that office to that king, to the end that it might be conferred
upon the duke of Buckingham, his secretary was likewise
preferred with the office ; and so, in a short time, became
secretary of the admiralty, as well as of the cinque ports ;
and was entirely trusted, and esteemed by that great favourite. After his death, he continued in the same place, whilst
the office was in commission, and was then made clerk of
the council, from whence the king called him to be secretary of state, after secretary Windebank fled the kingdom ;
upon his own observation of his virtue and fidelity, and
without any other recommendation : and he was in truth,
throughout his whole life, a person of very good reputation,
and of singular integrity.

There remain only two of the council then at Oxford,
who are not yet named, sir John Banks, who had been at-
torney general, and was then chief justice of the common
pleas, a grave and a learned man in the profession of the
law ; and sir Peter Wych, who had been ambassador at Con-

---

[1] Nothing can give one a higher idea of the virtue and integrity of
this great historian (as well as of his incomparable eloquence) than his
characters. Secretary Nicholas was his bosom friend, and never forfeited his good opinion ; yet he would say nothing of his parts, because, in truth, he could not. Yet he is very lavish in the praise of
great parts wherever they were found, though in his greatest personal enemies.—W.

stantinople ; from whence he returned very little before the
troubles, and gratified sir Thomas Jermyn very liberally for
his white staff, when the court was very low, and so was
made a privy-counsellor, and controller of the household.
He was a very honest, plain man; and died very shortly after the treaty, and was succeeded by sir Christopher Hatton,
a person of great reputation at that time, which in few
years he found a way utterly to lose.

This was the state of the king's council at Oxford when
Mr. Hyde was made chancellor of the exchequer; and amongst
them there were not many who had been acquainted with
the transaction of business, at least with business of that kind
which they were then to be incumbent to ; and from the first
entrance into the war, the soldiers did all they could to lessen the reverence that was due to them, thinking themselves
the best judges of all counsels and designs, because they were
for the most part to execute them: but they neither designed well nor executed, and it may be executed the worse,
because they had too great a power in the designing; the
king himself too much inclining to them, out of too little esteem of many of his counsellors. At that time the king's
quarters were only between Oxford and Reading, and some
miles on the other side to Banbury, and the town of Newcastle in the north, and Pendennis in the west of Cornwall;
but in some months after, they were extended as far as Chester upon the Severn; and the earl of Newcastle reduced all
to York, and drove all who professed for the parliament into
Hull; and sir Ralph Hopton, with the assistance of sir Nicholas Slanning, Arundel, and Trevannion, made themselves
masters of Cornwall, and afterwards advanced further towards a conjunction with the king.

And here it will not be amiss to look back, and take a
view of those persons who were of the king's council, and
had deserted his service, and stayed in the parliament to
support the rebellion ; and of the parliament's strength and
power at that time in and over the kingdom. The earl of
Northumberland may well be reckoned the chief of them, in
respect of the antiquity and splendour of his family, his great
fortune and estate, and the general reputation he had among

the greatest men, and his great interest, by being high admiral of England.   Though he was of a family that had lain
under frequent blemishes of want of fidelity to the crown,
and his father had been long a prisoner in the Tower, under
no less a suspicion than of having some knowledge of the
gunpowder treason ; and after he was set at liberty, by the
mediation and credit of the earl of Carlisle, who had, without and against his consent, married his daughter, he continued, to his death, under such a restraint, that he had not
liberty to live and reside upon his northern estate : yet his
father was no sooner dead, than the king poured out his favours upon him in a wonderful measure : he began with conferring the order of the garter upon him, and shortly after
made him of his privy-council ; when a great fleet of ships
was prepared, by which the king meant that his neighbour
princes should discern, that he meant to maintain and preserve his sovereignty at sea, he sent the earl of Northumberland admiral of that fleet, a much greater than the crown
had put to sea since the death of queen Elizabeth, that he
might breed him for that service, before he gave him a more
absolute command.   And after he had, in that capacity, exercised himself a year or two, he made him lord high admiral of England ; which was such a quick succession of bounties and favours, as had rarely befallen any man, who had
not been attended with the envy of a favourite.   He was,
in all his deportment, a very great man, and that which looked like formality, was a punctuality in preserving his dignity
from the invasion and intrusion of bold men, which no man
of that age so well preserved himself from.   Though his notions were not large or deep, yet his temper, and reservedness in discourse, and his unrashness in speaking, got him
the reputation of an able and a wise man ; which he made
evident in the excellent government of his family, where no
man was more absolutely obeyed ; and no man had ever
fewer idle words to answer for ; and in debates of importance, he always expressed himself very pertinently.   If he
had thought the king as much above him, as he thought himself above other considerable men, he would have been a
good subject ; but the extreme undervaluing those, and not

enough valuing the king, made him liable to the impressions, which they who approached him by those addresses of reverence and esteem, which usually insinuate themselves into such natures, made in him. And so after he was first prevailed upon, not to do that which in honour and gratitude he was obliged to, (which is a very pestilent corruption,) he was, with the more facility, led to concur in what, in duty and fidelity, he ought not to have done, and which at first he never intended to have done. And so he concurred in all the counsels which produced the rebellion, and stayed with them to support it; which is as much as is necessary to say of him in this place, since there will be often occasion hereafter to mention him, with some enlargement.

The earl of Pembroke hath been enough mentioned in a better conjuncture of time, when his virtues were thought greater than they were, and his vices very little discerned. Yet, by what was then said, his nature and his parts might be well enough understood; and as neither the one nor the other were improveable, so they were liable to be corrupted by any assaults; his understanding being easy to be imposed upon, and his nature being made up of very strong passions. Whilst there was tranquillity in the kingdom, he enjoyed his full share in pomp and greatness; the largeness and plentifulness of his fortune being attended with reverence and dependence from the people where his estate and interest lay, and where indeed he was a great man; getting an affection and esteem from persons who had no dependence upon him, by his magnificent living, and discoursing highly of justice, and of the protestant religion; inveighing bitterly against popery, and telling what he used to say to the king; and speaking frankly of the oversights of the court, that he might not be thought a slave to it. He had been bred from his cradle in the court; and had that perfection of a courtier, that as he was not wary enough in offending men, so he was forward in acknowledging it, even to his inferiors, and to impute it to his passion, and ask pardon for it; which made him be thought a well-natured man. Besides, he had a choleric office, which entitled him to the exercise of some rudenesses, and the good order of the court had some dependence upon his incivilities.

There were very few great persons in authority, who
were not frequently offended by him, by sharp and scandalous discourses, and invectives against them, behind their
backs ; for which they found it best to receive satisfaction
by submissions, and professions, and protestations, which
was a coin he was plentifully supplied with for the payment
of all those debts : and his infirmities were so generally
known, that men did not think they could suffer in their
reputations by any thing he said; whilst the king retained
only some kindness for him, without any value and esteem
of him.   But, from the beginning of the parliament, when
he saw and heard a people stout enough to inveigh against
the king's authority, and to fall upon those persons, whom
he had always more feared than loved ; and found that there
were two armies in the kingdom, and that the king had not
the entire command of either of them ; when the decrees of
the star-chamber, and the orders and acts of the council, in
all which he had concurred, as his concurrence was all that
he had contributed towards any counsel, were called in
question, and like to be made penal to those who would not
redeem their past errors by future service ; his fear, which
was the passion always predominant in him above all his
choler and rage, prevailed so far over him, that he gave himself up into the hands of the lord Say, to dispose of him as
he thought fit, till he committed so many faults and follies,
that the king was willing to take advantage of a censure of
the house of peers inflicted upon him, for a rash and choleric
action he had committed at a private committee that sat in
the house, when in a debate he had struck or offered to
strike the lord Matravers with his white staff, the other
throwing an ink-horn at him ; for which unusual and inde-
cent behaviour, the house thought itself obliged to send them
both to the Tower, without any imagination that either of
them should undergo any other censure, and discharged both
within few days : but in the mean time the king had sent
for his white staff, declaring, that as he would not suffer it
to remain in the Tower, so he would not put it into the
hands of a man who had deserved so severe a punishment
from the parliament; which they looked upon as no great

compliment to them, and were exceedingly troubled, when they saw the office conferred upon the earl of Essex, being very sure, that the one was removed, whatever was pretended, for his concurrence with them, and fearing that the other would concur the less with them for that promotion : and probably they might not have been deceived in that, if any care and dexterity had been used to keep, as well as to get him.

From this time, he took himself to be absolved from all obligations and dependence upon the court, which he had lived too long in to be willing to quit; and therefore the more closely adhered to them, by whose power he thought he might get thither again ; and, for some time, entertained the hope of obtaining the other superior white staff; which remained then in the king's hand by the departure of the earl of Arundel into the parts beyond the seas.   But when he saw that staff given to the duke of Richmond, who was then made steward of the household, he gave over those weak imaginations, and concurred roundly in all the lord Say proposed : and was so weak still, as to believe they never meant to rebel against the king; or that the king could long subsist, without putting himself into their hands. When they had any thing to do in the west, as the exercise of the militia, or executing any other ordinance, they sent him into the country, and shewed him to the people, under the conduct of two or three members of the house, in whom they could confide ; and he talked "of the king's evil counsellors, who carried him from his parliament ; and of the malignants; and against scandalous ministers ;" whilst none of his old friends came near him.   And when they were resolved no longer to trust the Isle of Wight in the hands of the earl of Portland, who had been long the king's governor there, and had an absolute power over the affections of that people, they preferred the poor earl of Pembroke to it, by an ordinance of parliament ; who kindly accepted it, as a testimony of their favour ; and so got into actual rebellion, which he never intended to do.   It is pity to say more of him, and less could not be said to make him known, if any thing were necessary ; and it cannot be avoided to mention him again hereafter, there being particular passages between him and the chancellor of the exchequer, who had great kindness for him, whilst he had any hope of reclaiming him, and even when that was desperate, was never without a desire to serve him, having been formerly beholden to him for many civilities, when there was so great a distance between their conditions.

The earl of Essex hath been enough mentioned before ; his nature and his understanding have been described ; his former disobligations from the court, and then his introduction into it, and afterwards his being displaced from the office he held in it, have been set forth ; and there will be occasion, hereafter, to renew the discourse of him ; and therefore it shall suffice, in this place, to say, that a weak judgment, and a little vanity, and as much of pride, will hurry a man into as unwarrantable and as violent attempts, as the greatest, and most unlimited, and insatiable ambition will do. He had no ambition of title, or office, or preferment, but only to be kindly looked upon, and kindly spoken to, and quietly to enjoy his own fortune : and, without doubt, no man in his nature more abhorred rebellion than he did, nor could he have been led into it by any open or transparent temptation, but by a thousand disguises and cozenages. His pride supplied his want of ambition, and he was angry to see any other man more respected than himself, because he thought he deserved it more, and did better requite it. For he was, in his friendships, just and constant ; and would not have practised foully against those he took to be enemies. No man had credit enough with him to corrupt him in point of loyalty to the king, whilst he thought himself wise enough to know what treason was. But the new doctrine, and distinction of allegiance, and of the king's power in and out of parliament, and the new notions of ordinances, were too hard for him, and did really intoxicate his understanding, and made him quit his own, to follow theirs, who, he thought, wished as well, and judged better than himself. His vanity disposed him to be his excellency ; and his weakness, to believe that he should be the general in the houses, as well as in the field ; and be able to govern their counsels, and restrain their passions, as well as to fight their battles; and that, by this means, he should become the preserver, and not the destroyer, of the king and kingdom. And with this ill-grounded confidence, he launched out into that sea, where he met with nothing but rocks and shelves, and from whence he could never discover any safe port to harbour in.

The earl of Salisbury had been born and bred in court, and had the advantage of a descent from a father, and a grandfather, who had been very wise men, and great ministers of state in the eyes of Christendom; whose wisdom and virtues died with them, and their children only inherited their titles. He had been admitted of the council to king James; from which time he continued so obsequious to the court, that he never failed in overacting all that he was required to do. No act of power was ever proposed, which he did not advance, and execute his part with the utmost rigour. No man so great a tyrant in his country, or was less swayed by any motives of justice or honour. He was a man of no words, except in hunting and hawking, in which he only knew how to behave himself. In matters of state and council, he always concurred in what was proposed for the king, and cancelled and repaired all those transgressions, by concurring in all that was proposed against him, as soon as any such propositions were made. Yet when the king went to York, he likewise attended upon his majesty; and, at that distance, seemed to have recovered some courage, and concurred in all counsels which were taken to undeceive the people, and to make the proceedings of the parliament odious to all the world. And meeting Mr. Hyde one day, he walking with him to advise and consult how they might draw the earl of Pembroke, with whom he had most friendship, to leave the parliament, and betake himself to serve the king; and within two hours after this conference he caused his horses to attend him out of the town, and having placed fresh ones at a distance, he fled back to London, with the expedition such men use, when they are most afraid; and never after denied to do any thing that was required of him; and when the war was ended, and Cromwell had put down the house of peers, he got himself to be chosen a member of the house of commons; and sat with them, as of their own body ; and was esteemed accordingly. In a word, he became so despicable to all men, that he will hardly ever enjoy the ease which Seneca bequeathed him ; *Hic egregiis majoribus ortus est, qualiscunque est, sub umbra suorum lateat ; ut loca sordida repercussa sole illustrantur, ita inertes majorum suorum luce resplendeant.*

The earl of Warwick was of the king's council too, but was not wondered at for leaving the king, whom he had never served ; nor did he look upon himself as obliged by that honour, which, he knew, was conferred upon him in the crowd of those whom his majesty had no esteem of, or ever purposed to trust ; so his business was to join with those to whom he owed his promotion. He was a man of a pleasant and companionable wit and conversation ; of an universal jollity ; and such a license in his words, and in his actions, that a man of less virtue could not be found out : so that a man might reasonably have believed, that a man so qualified would not have been able to have contributed much to the overthrow of a nation and kingdom. But, with all these faults, he had great authority and credit with that people, who, in the beginning of the troubles, did all the mischief ; and by opening his doors, and making his house the rendezvous of all the silenced ministers, in the time when there was authority to silence them, and spending a good part of his estate, of which he was very prodigal, upon them, and by being present with them at their devotions, and making himself merry with them, and at them, which they dispensed with, he became the head of that party ; and got the style of a godly man. When the king revoked the earl of Northumberland's commission of admiral, he presently accepted the office from the parliament ; and never quitted their service ; and when Cromwell disbanded that parliament, he betook himself to the protection of the protector ; married his heir to his daughter ; and lived in so entire a confidence and friendship with him, that when he died he had the honour to be exceedingly lamented by him ; and left his estate, which before was subject to a vast debt, more improved and repaired, than any man who trafficked in that desperate commodity of rebellion.

The earl of Holland had grown up under the shadow of the court, and had been too long a counsellor before, and contributed too much to the counsels which had most preju- diced the crown, to have declined waiting upon it, when it needed attendance. But he chose to stay with the parlia- ment; and there hath been enough said of him before, and more must be said hereafter. And therefore it shall suffice now, to say, that there was a very froward fate attended all, or most of the posterity of that bed, from whence he and his brother of Warwick had their original; though he, and some others among them, had many very good parts and excellent endowments.

The earl of Manchester,[1] of the whole cabal, was, in a thousand respects, most unfit for the company he kept. He was of a gentle and a generous nature; civilly bred; had re- verence and affection for the person of the king, upon whom he had attended in Spain; loved his country with too unskilful a tenderness;[2] and was of so excellent a temper and disposi- tion, that the barbarous times, and the rough parts he was forced to act in them, did not wipe out, or much deface, those marks: insomuch as he was never guilty of any rude- ness towards those he was obliged to oppress, but performed always as good offices towards his old friends, and all other persons, as the iniquity of the time, and the nature of the employment he was in, would permit him to do; which kind of humanity could be imputed to very few.

And he was at last dismissed, and removed from any trust, for no other reason, but because he was not wicked enough. He married first into the family of the duke of Buckingham, and, by his favour and interest, was called to the house of peers in the life of his father; and made baron of Kimbolton, though he was commonly treated and known by the name of the lord Mandeville; and was as much addicted to the ser- vice of the court as he ought to be. But the death of his lady, and the murder of that great favourite, his second mar- riage with the daughter of the earl of Warwick, and the very

---

[1] Lord Kimbolton.—W.   [2] i. e. was too violent in his resent- ments against a court which was oppressing it.—W.

narrow and restrained maintenance, which he received from his father, and which would in no degree defray the expenses of the court, forced him too soon to retire to a country life, and totally to abandon both the court and London; whither he came very seldom in many years. And in this retirement, the discountenance which his father underwent at court, the conversation of that family into which he was married, the bewitching popularity, which flowed upon him with a wonderful torrent, with the want of those guards which a good education should have supplied him with, by the clear notion of the foundation of the ecclesiastical, as well as the civil government, made a great impression upon his understanding, (for his nature was never corrupted, but remained still in its integrity,) and made him believe that the court was inclined to hurt, and even to destroy the country; and from particular instances to make general and dangerous conclusions.[1] They who had been always enemies to the church prevailed with him to lessen his reverence for it, and having not been well instructed to defend it, he yielded too easily to those who confidently assaulted it; and thought it had great errors, which were necessary to be reformed; and that all means are lawful to compass that which is necessary. Whereas the true logic is, that the thing desired is not necessary, if the ways are unlawful, which are proposed to bring it to pass. No man was courted with more application, by persons of all conditions and qualities; and his person was not less acceptable to those of steady and uncorrupted principles, than to those of depraved inclinations. And in the end, even his piety administered some excuse to him; for his father's infirmities and transgressions had so far exposed him to the inquisition of justice, that he found it necessary to procure the assistance and protection of those who were strong enough to violate justice itself; and so he adhered to those who were best able to defend his father's honour, and thereby to secure his own fortune; and concurred with

[1] Whenever a king attempts to overthrow public liberty, the attempt can never be detected but by *drawing general conclusions from particular instances;* and without reliance on this sort of logic, no opposition to such an attempt can be justified.—W.

them in their most violent designs, and gave reputation to them. And the court as unskilfully took an occasion too soon to make him desperate, by accusing him of high treason, when (though he might be guilty enough) he was, without doubt, in his intentions, at least, as innocent as any of the leading men.

And it is some evidence, that God Almighty saw his heart was not so malicious as the rest, that he preserved him to the end of the confusion ; when he appeared as glad of the king's restoration, and had heartily wished it long before, and very few, who had a hand in the contrivance of the rebellion, gave so manifest tokens of repentance as he did ; and having, for many years, undergone the jealousy and hatred of Cromwell, as one who abominated the murder of the king, and all the barbarous proceedings against the lives of men in cold blood ; the king upon his return received him into grace and favour, which he never after forfeited by any undutiful behaviour.

The last of those counsellors which were made after the faction prevailed in parliament, who were all made to advance an accommodation, and who adhered to the parliament, was the lord Say ; a man, who had the deepest hand in the original contrivance of all the calamities which befell this unhappy kingdom, though he had not the least thought of dissolving the monarchy, and less of levelling the ranks and distinctions of men. For no man valued himself more upon his title, or had more ambition to make it greater, and to raise his fortune, which was but moderate for his title. He was of a proud, morose, and sullen nature ; conversed much with books, having been bred a scholar, and (though nobly born) a fellow of New College in Oxford ; to which he claimed a right, by the alliance he pretended to have from William of Wickham, the founder ; which he made good by such an unreasonable pedigree, through so many hundred years, half the time whereof extinguishes all relation of kindred. However, upon that pretence, that college hath been seldom without one of that lord's family. His parts were not quick,' but so much above those of his own

' His *reading* a long speech of several hours in the house of lords,

rank, that he had always great credit and authority in parliament; and the more, for taking all opportunities to oppose the court; and he had, with his milk, sucked in an implacable malice against the government of the church. When the duke of Buckingham proposed to himself, after his return with the prince from Spain, to make himself popular, by breaking that match, and to be gracious with the parliament, as for a short time he was, he resolved to embrace the friendship of the lord Say; who was as solicitous to climb by that ladder. But the duke quickly found him of too imperious and pedantical a spirit, and to affect too dangerous mutations; and so cast him off; and from that time he gave over any pursuit in court, and lived narrowly and sordidly in the country; having conversation with very few, but such who had great malignity against the church and state, and fomented their inclinations, and gave them instructions how to behave themselves with caution, and to do their business with most security; and was in truth the pilot, that steered all those vessels which were freighted with sedition to destroy the government.

He found always some way to make professions of duty to the king, and made several undertakings to do great services, which he could not, or would not, make good; and made haste to possess himself of any preferment he could compass, whilst his friends were content to attend a more proper conjuncture. So he got the mastership of the wards shortly after the beginning of the parliament, and was as solicitous to be treasurer after the death of the earl of Bedford; and, if he could have satisfied his rancour in any degree against the church, he would have been ready to have carried the prerogative as high as ever it was. When he thought there was mischief enough done, he would have stopped the current, and have diverted further fury; but he then found he had only authority and credit to do hurt; none to heal the wounds he had given; and fell into as much contempt with those whom he had led, as he was with those whom he had undone.

occasioned a standing order that no lord should read a written speech.
—W.

The last of the counsellors who stayed with the parliament was sir Henry Vane ; who had so much excuse for it, that, being thrown out of the court, he had no whither else to go ; and promised himself to be much made of by them, for whose sakes only he had brought that infamy upon himself.[1] He was of very ordinary parts by nature, and had not cultivated them at all by art ; for he was illiterate. But being of a stirring and boisterous disposition, very industrious, and very bold, he still wrought himself into some employment. He had been acquainted with the vicissitudes of court, and had undergone some severe mortification, by the disfavour of the duke of Buckingham, in the beginning of the king's reign. But the duke was no sooner dead, (which made it believed that he had made his peace in his lifetime, for the king was not, in a long time after, reconciled to any man who was eminently in the duke's disfavour,) but he was again brought into the court, and made a counsellor, and controller of the household ; which place he became well, and was fit for ; and if he had never taken other preferment, he might probably have continued a good subject. For he had no inclination to change, and the judgment he had, liked the government both of church and state ; and only desired to raise his fortune, which was not great, and which he found many ways to improve. And he was wont to say, "that he never had desired other preferment ; and believed, that marquis Hamilton," (with whom he had never kept fair quarter,) " when he first proposed to him to be secretary of state, did it to affront him ; well knowing his want of ability for the discharge of that office." But, without doubt, as the fatal preferring him to that place was of unspeakable prejudice to the king, so his receiving it was to his own destruction. His malice to the earl of Strafford, (who had unwisely provoked him, wantonly,[2] and out of contempt) transported him to all imaginable thoughts of revenge ; which is a guest, that naturally disquiets and tor-

[1] i. e. the minutes of the council-board, procured for the managers in the prosecution against the earl of Strafford.—W.

[2] By taking the title of *Raby.*—W.

tures those who entertain it, with all the perplexities they contrive for others; and that disposed him to sacrifice his honour and faith, and his master's interest, that he might ruin the earl, and was buried himself in the same ruin; for which being justly chastised by the king, and turned out of his service, he was left to his own despair.; and, though he concurred in all the malicious designs against the king, and against the church, he grew into the hatred and contempt of those who had made most use of him; and died in universal reproach, and not contemned more by any of his enemies, than by his own son; who had been his principal conductor to destruction.

We now pass to the transactions in the treaty itself, which was in the beginning of the year 1643.

THE HISTORY

OF THE REBELLION, &c.

BOOK VII.

THE sum of the demands and concessions of both sides upon the first article of the treaty—His majesty's message to the two houses of April 12, 1643—The Earl of Essex marches to besiege Redding April 15, being the last day of the treaty—Sir William Waller takes Hereford: comes before Worcester: is repulsed—Prince Rupert marches towards the north: takes Bromicham, and Litchfield, and returns to the king—Reading surrendered upon articles, April 27—Colonel Fielding ordered to be tried for the surrender—The king sends a message to the two houses, May 20—The house of commons commit the messenger—The commons impeach the queen of high treason—A design discovered at London, wherein Mr. Waller, Mr. Tomkins, and others, were concerned—A vow and covenant agreed to be taken by the members of both houses upon discovery of that design—The same vow and covenant taken throughout the city and army—The trial and execution of Mr. Tomkins and Mr. Chaloner—The earl of Essex marches to Thame—Prince Rupert beats up some of his quarters with good success—Mr. Hambden wounded in Chalgrave field, of which he died—The earl of Essex marches from Thame to London; quartering his army about St. Alban's—The king's affairs in the west—The earl of Stamford marches into Cornwall with an army—The earl is beaten near Stratton, May 16—The marquis of Hertford and prince Maurice, with their forces, join the Cornish army at Chard—The parliament sent sir William Waller into the west with an army—The battle of Lansdown, July 5—Sir Bevil Greenvil slain—The battle of Roundway-down, wherein sir William Waller is routed—The king meets the queen near Keinton: she coming with a great recruit—The earl of Essex retires from Thame with his army to Uxbridge—Bristol besieged by prince Rupert—It is surrendered upon articles—The two houses send commissioners into Scotland for relief—The king's declaration after his late successes—Jealousies arise among the king's principal officers about the government of Bristol—The king goes to Bristol to compose the difference—Prince Maurice sent into the west with an army—The king marches towards Gloucester, and summons it, Aug. 10, 1643 —The citizens' and garrison's answer—The king besieges the town —Propositions for peace given by the house of lords to the house of commons in a conference—A petition of the common council of London against peace ; whereupon the house of commons rejected the propositions of the lords—An ordinance for raising an army under the earl of Manchester—The earls of Bedford and Holland put themselves into the king's quarters, as likewise some other of the parliament lords—Debates in the council at Oxford how those lords should be received—The king comes to Oxford to consult about it— —The king's affairs in the west—Dorchester surrendered—Weymouth and Portland surrendered to the king's forces—Prince Maurice comes before Exeter with his army—The earl of Warwick with his fleet attempts the relief of it, but succeeds not—Sir John Digby routs the parliament's forces at Torrington—Barnstable and Bediford yielded to him—Exeter delivered to the prince upon articles, September 4—The prosecution of the siege of Gloucester—The custody of the Tower committed by the two houses to the lord mayor Pennington—The earl of Essex marches out of London to relieve Gloucester—The siege of Gloucester raised—The earl of Essex in his return seizes upon Cirencester—The battle of Newbury—The earl of Essex gets into Reading ; thence to London—The earl of Sunderland slain in this battle : and the earl of Carnarvon ; his character—And the lord viscount Falkland ; his character—The earl of Essex returns to London—The temper of the army and the court at Oxford, upon the return of the king thither—The earl of Holland returns into the parliament's quarters—And likewise the earls of Bedford and Clare—The transactions of the committee of the two houses in Scotland—A covenant proposed by the Scots between the two kingdoms, and agreed to—It is taken and subscribed by the lords and commons and their assembly of divines, Sept. 25—A copy of the covenant—The covenant ordered to be taken by others, especially by the city—A parliament summoned by the covenanters in Scotland—The substance of the treaty between the English com missioners and the Scots—The Scots raise an army under Lesley— Divisions amongst the councils at Oxford—The king's affairs in the west—Sir Alexander Carew treats to surrender the fort of Plymouth to the king's forces, but is surprised—Prince Maurice sits down before Dartmouth ; and takes it—Sits down before Plymouth too late

—The conte d'Harcourt arrives ambassador from France—Returns
into France without any good effect to the king—1 Sam. xxix. 6—
The commons vote a new broad seal : the lords concurred with them
—The seal delivered to six commissioners—Colonel Fiennes tried
for surrendering Bristol, and condemned ; but pardoned by the general—(The Scots enter England in Jan. 1643, 4)—A letter from the
peers on the king's side to the council in Scotland—The king's proclamation for assembling the members of parliament at Oxford—An
address of the lords justices and the council in Ireland to the king
—A cessation of arms concluded for a year in Ireland, Sept. 7, disowned by the two houses at Westminster—A letter concerning it,
from the two houses to the lords justices, July 4, 1643—The lords
justices' answer—The king sends for part of the English army out
of Ireland—The members of both houses met at Oxford—The substance of the king's speech to them—They send a letter to the earl
of Essex—The earl of Essex's answer directed to the earl of Forth,
with the two following declarations—An extract of the declaration
of the kingdom of Scotland—An extract of the declaration of England and Scotland—The king's message to both houses—The two
houses' answer—Means agreed upon by the lords and commons at
Oxford to raise money—The two houses at Westminster impose an
excise—The two houses at Oxford follow the example—The substance of the declaration of the lords and commons at Oxford—The
marquis of Newcastle marches to oppose the Scots—Sir Thomas
Fairfax defeats and takes colonel Bellasis at Selby :—Whereupon
the marquis of Newcastle retires to York—The marquis of Ormond
made lord lieutenant of Ireland, sends the king assistance—The
Irish forces routed by sir Thomas Fairfax at Nantwich—The earl
of Montrose comes to the king, and informs him of the state of Scotland—Duke Hamilton made prisoner at Oxford—Mr. Pym's death—
The prince elector arrives at London—Prince Rupert is sent to relieve Newark, and effects it.

WHEN the treaty was first consented to by the two houses,
they ordered that it should be upon the first proposition
made by his majesty, and the first proposition made by themselves, and that those should be first concluded on, before
they proceeded to treat upon any of the other propositions.
So that the committee, in the first place, applied themselves to
his majesty, upon his own first proposition, which was, " That
his own revenue, magazines, towns, forts, and ships, which
had been taken, or kept from him by force, should be forth-

with restored to him." To which the committee answered,
" That the two houses had made use of his majesty's own
revenue, but in a very small proportion, which in a good
part had been employed in the maintenance of his children,
according to the allowance established by himself. And the
houses would satisfy what should remain due to his majesty
of those sums, which they had received ; and would leave
the same to him for the time to come. And they desired
likewise, that his majesty would restore what had been taken
for his use, upon any of the bills, assigned to other purposes
by several acts of parliament, or out of the provision made
for the war of Ireland : that all the arms and ammunition
taken out of his magazines should be delivered into his
stores, and whatsoever should be wanting, they would supply
in kind, according to the proportions they had received : but
they proposed, the persons, to whose charge those public
magazines should be committed, being nominated by his majesty, might be such, as the two houses of parliament might
confide in, and that his majesty would restore all such arms
and ammunition, as had been taken for his use, from the
several counties, cities, and towns.

" That the two houses would remove the garrisons out of
all towns and forts in their hands, wherein there were no
garrisons before these troubles, and slight all fortifications
made since that time, and those towns and forts to continue
in the same condition they were in before ; and that those
garrisons should not be renewed, or the fortifications repaired, without consent of his majesty, and both houses of parliament. That the towns and forts, which were within the
jurisdiction of the cinque ports, should be delivered into the
hands of such a noble person, as the king should appoint to
be warden of the cinque ports, being such a one as they
should confide in. That Portsmouth should be reduced to
the number of the garrison, as was at that time when the
lords and commons undertook the custody of it ; and that all
other forts, castles, and towns, in which garrisons had been
kept, and had been since the beginning of these troubles
taken into their care and custody, should be reduced to the
same establishment they had in the year 1636, and should

be so continued ; and that all those towns, forts, and castles,
should be delivered up into the hands of such persons of
quality and trust, to be likewise nominated by his majesty, as
the two houses should confide in.   That the warden of the
cinque ports, and all governors and commanders of towns,
castles, and forts, should keep the same towns, castles, and
forts, respectively, for the service of his majesty, and the
safety of the kingdom ; and that they should not admit into
them any foreign forces, or any other forces raised without
his majesty's authority, and consent of the two houses of
parliament ; and they should use their utmost endeavours to
suppress all forces whatsoever raised without such authority
and consent ; and they should seize all arms and ammunition
provided for any such forces.

  " They likewise proposed to the king, that he would remove the garrison out of Newcastle, and all other towns,
castles, and forts, where any garrisons had been placed by him since these troubles ; and that the fortifications
might be likewise slighted, and the towns and forts left in
such state as they were in the year 1636 ; and that all
other towns and castles in his hands, wherein there had been
formerly garrisons, might be committed to such persons nominated by him, as the houses should confide in, and under
such instructions as were formerly mentioned ; and that the
new garrisons should not be renewed, or the fortifications repaired, without the consent of the king and both houses of
parliament.   That the ships should be delivered into the
charge of such a noble person, as the king should nominate
to be lord high admiral of England, and the two houses confide in ; who should receive that office by letters patents,
quam diu se bene gesserit, and should have power to nominate and appoint all subordinate commanders and officers,
and have all other powers appertaining to the office of high
admiral ; which ships he should employ for the defence of
the kingdom, against all foreign forces whatsoever, and for
the safeguard of merchants, securing of trade, and the guarding of Ireland, and the intercepting of all supplies to be carried to the rebels ; and should use his utmost endeavour to
suppress all forces, which should be raised by any person

without his majesty's authority, and consent of the lords and commons in parliament, and should seize all arms and ammunition provided for supply of any such forces."

To this answer, by which they required at least to go whole sharers with him in his sovereignty, the king replied, " That he knew not what proportion of his revenue had been made use of by his two houses, but he had reason to believe, if much of it had not been used, very much remained still in their hands ; his whole revenue being so stopped, and seized on, by the orders of one or both houses, even to the taking of his money out of his exchequer and mint, and bonds (forced from his cofferer's clerk) for the provisions of his household ; that very little had come to his use for his own support ; but he would be well contented to allow whatsoever had been employed in the maintenance of his children, and to receive the arrears due to himself, and to be sure of his own for the future. He was likewise willing to restore all monies taken for his use, by any authority for him, upon any bills assigned to other purposes, being assured he had received very little or nothing that way : and he expected likewise, that satisfaction should be made by them for all those several vast sums, received, and diverted to other purposes, which ought to have been paid by the act of pacification to his subjects of Scotland, or employed for the discharge of the debts of the kingdom ; or, by other acts of parliament, for the relief of his poor protestant subjects in Ireland. For what concerned his magazines, he was content that all the arms and ammunition, taken out of his magazines, which did remain in the hands of both houses, or of persons employed by them, should be, as soon as the treaty was concluded, delivered into the Tower of London ; and that whatsoever should be wanting of the proportions taken by them, should be supplied by them, with all convenient speed, in kind ; which, he said, should be committed to, and continued in, the custody of his sworn officers, to whose places the same belonged : and if any of those officers had already forfeited, or hereafter should forfeit, that trust, by any misdemeanours, his majesty would by no means defend them from the justice of the law. That he always intended to restore such arms and ammunition, which he had been compelled to take from any persons and places, when his own had been taken from him; and would make them recompense as soon as his own stores were restored to him.

" To whatsoever they proposed for the slighting all fortifications, and reducing all garrisons, which had been made since the beginning of the troubles, and leaving them in the state they were before, the king fully and absolutely consented; and that the old castles and garrisons should be reduced to their ancient proportion and establishment : but for the governors and commanders of them, he said, that the cinque ports were already in the custody of a noble person, against whom he knew no just exception, and who had such a legal interest therein, that he could not, with justice, remove him from it, until some sufficient cause were made appear to him : but he was very willing, if he should at any time be found guilty of any thing that might make him unworthy of that trust, that he might be proceeded against according to the rules of justice. That the government of the town of Portsmouth, and all other forts, castles, and towns, as were formerly kept by garrisons, should be put into the hands of such persons, against whom no just exceptions could be made ; all of them being, before these troubles, by letters patents granted to several persons, against any of whom he knew not any exceptions who should be removed, if just cause should be given for the same. The warden of the cinque ports, and all other governors and commanders of the towns and castles, should keep their charges, as by the law they ought to do, and for the king's service, and safety of the kingdom ; and they should not admit into any of them foreign forces, or other forces raised, and brought into them contrary to the law ; but should use their utmost endeavours to suppress such forces, and should seize all arms and ammunition, which, by the laws and statutes of the kingdom, they ought to seize."

To that part which concerned the ships, the king told them, " That he expected his own ships should be delivered to him, as by the law they ought to be ; and that when he should think fit to nominate a lord high admiral of England, it should be such a person against whom no just exception could be made; and if any should be, he would always leave him to his due trial and examination; and he would grant his office to him by such letters patents as had been used. In the mean time he would govern the admiralty by commission, as had been in all times accustomed; and whatsoever ships should be set out by him, or his authority, should be employed for the defence of the kingdom against all foreign forces whatsoever, for the safeguard of merchants, securing of trade, guarding of Ireland, and the intercepting of all supplies to be carried to the rebels; and they should use their utmost endeavours to suppress all forces which should be raised, by any person whatsoever, against the laws and statutes of the kingdom, and to seize all arms and ammunition provided for the supply of any such forces."

It is evident to all men where the difference now lay between them,[1] being whether the king would reserve the disposal of those offices and places of trust to himself, which all kings had enjoyed, and was indeed a part of his regality, or whether he would be content with such a nomination, as, being to pass, and depend upon their approbation, no man should ever be admitted to them, who was nominated by him. The committee, upon his answer, desired to know, " if he did intend, that both houses should express their confidence of the persons, to whose trust those places were to be committed; for that they were directed by their instructions, that, if his majesty was pleased to assent thereunto, and to nominate persons of quality to receive the charge of them, that they should certify it to both houses of parliament, that thereupon they might express their confidence in those persons, or humbly desire his majesty to name others, none of which persons to be removed during three years next ensuing, without just cause to be approved by both houses; and if any should be so removed, or die within that space, the persons, to be put in their places, to be such as the two houses should confide in." The king

---

[1] It is evident that the king treated the parliament as if he had subdued them, only granting them an amnesty.---W.

answered, " That he did not intend, that the houses should express their confidence of the persons, to whose trusts those places should be committed, but only that they should have liberty, upon any just exception, to proceed against any such persons according to law; his majesty being resolved not to protect them against the public justice. When any of the places should be void, he well knew the nomination, and free election, of those who should succeed, to be a right belonging to and inherent in his majesty; and having been enjoyed by all his royal progenitors, he could not believe his well affected subjects desired to limit him in that right; and desired they would be satisfied with this answer, or give him any reasons to alter his resolution, and he would comply with them."

They told him, " there could be no good and firm peace hoped for, if there were not a cure found out for the fears and jealousies: and they knew none sure, but this which they had proposed." The king replied, " That he rather expected reasons grounded upon law, to have shewed him, that by the law he had not that right he pretended, or that they had a right superior to his, in what was now in question; or that they would have shewed him some legal reason, why the persons trusted by him were incapable of such a trust; than that they would only have insisted upon fears and jealousies, of which as he knew no ground, so he must be ignorant of the cure. That the argument they used might extend to the depriving him of, or at least sharing with him in, all his just regal power; since power, as well as forces, might be the object of fears and jealousies, and there would be always a power left to hurt, whilst there was any left to protect and defend." He told them, " If he had as much inclination, as he had more right, to fears and jealousies, he might with more reason have insisted upon an addition of power, as a security to enable him to keep his forts, when he had them, since it appeared it was not so great, but that they had been able to take them from him, than they to make any difficulty to restore them to him in the same case they were before. But, he said, as he was himself content with, so, he took God to witness, his greatest desire was, to observe always and maintain the law of the land ; and expected the same from his subjects ; and believed the mutual observance of that rule, and neither of them to fear what the law feared not, to be, on both parts, a better cure for that dangerous disease of fears and jealousies, and a better means to establish a happy and perpetual peace, than for him to divest himself of those trusts, which the law of the land had settled in the crown alone, to preserve the power and dignity of the prince, for the better protection of the subject, and of the law, and to avoid those dangerous distractions, which the interest of any sharers with him would have infalliby produced."

The committee neither offered to answer his majesty's reasons, nor to oppose other reasons to weigh against them ; but only said, " That they were commanded by their instructions, to insist upon the desires of both houses formerly expressed." To which the king made no other answer, " than that he conceived it all the justice in the world for him to insist, that what was by law his own, and had been contrary to law taken from him, should be fully restored to him, without conditioning to impose any new limitations upon him, or his ministers, which were not formerly required from them by the law ; and he thought it most unreasonable, to be pressed to diminish his own just rights himself, because others had violated and usurped them." This was the sum of what passed in the treaty upon that proposition.

To the first proposition of the two houses, " That his majesty would be pleased to disband his armies, as they likewise would be ready to disband all their forces, which they had raised, and that he would be pleased to return to his parliament ;" the king answered, " That he was as ready and willing that all armies should be disbanded, as any person whatsoever ; and conceived the best way to it, would be a happy and speedy conclusion of the present treaty ; which, if both houses would contribute as much as he would do to it, would be suddenly effected. And as he desired nothing more than to be with his two houses, so he would repair thither as soon as he could possibly do it with his honour and safety."

The committee asked him, " if by a happy and speedy conclusion of the present treaty, he intended a conclusion upon the two first propositions, or a conclusion of the treaty in all the propositions of both parts." The king, who well knew it would be very ungracious to deny the disbanding of the armies, till all the propositions were agreed, some whereof would require much time, answered, " That he intended such a conclusion of, or in the treaty, as there might be a clear evidence to himself, and his subjects, of a future peace, and no ground left for the continuance or growth of those bloody dissensions ; which, he doubted not, might be obtained, if both houses would consent that the treaty should proceed without further interruption, or limitation of days." They asked him, " What he intended should be a clear evidence to him, and his good subjects, of a future peace, and no ground left for the continuance and growth of . those bloody dissensions ?" His majesty told them, " If the conclusion of the present treaty upon his first proposition, and the first proposition of both houses, should be so full, and perfectly made, that the law of the land might have a full, free, and uninterrupted course, for the defence and preservation of the rights of his majesty, and of themselves, and the rest of his subjects, there would be thence a clear evidence to him, and all men, of a future peace ; and it would be such a conclusion as he intended, never meaning that both armies should remain undisbanded until the propositions on both sides were fully concluded." To the other clause of their own proposition concerning the king's return to the parliament, they said, " they had no instructions to treat upon it ;" which the king much wondered at ; and finding that they had no other authority to treat, or debate what was necessary to be done in order to disbanding, but only to press him to appoint a day for the actual disbanding ; and that the forces in the north, where he had a great army, and they had none, might be first disbanded, he endeavoured to draw them to some propositions upon his return to the parliament ; from whence expedients would naturally result, if they pursued that heartily, which would conclude a general peace. And it seemed

very strange, that, after so many discourses of the king's
absence from the houses, from whence they had taught the
people to believe that most of the present evils flowed and
proceeded, when a treaty was now entered upon, and that
was a part of their own first proposition, that their committee should have no instructions or authority to treat upon it.
In the end they received new instructions, " to declare to
his majesty the desire of both houses, for his coming to his
parliament ; which, they said, they had often expressed with
full offers of security to his royal person, agreeable to their
duty and allegiance, and they knew no cause why he might
not repair thither with honour and safety." When the king
found he could not engage them in that argument to make
any particular overture, or invitation to him ; and that the
committee, who expressed willingness enough, had not in
truth the least power to promote, or contribute to, an accommodation, lest they should make the people believe, that he
had a desire to continue the war, because he consented not
to their proposition of disbanding the armies, he sent this
message, by an express of his own, to the two houses, after
he had first communicated it to their committee.

Oxford, April 12th, 1643.

" To shew[1] to the whole world, how earnestly his majesty longs for peace, and that no success shall make him desire the continuance of his army to any other end, or for
any longer time, than that, and until, things may be so settled, as that the law may have a full, free, and uninterrupted course, for the defence and preservation of the rights of
his majesty, both houses, and his good subjects :

1. "As soon as his majesty is satisfied in his first proposition, concerning his own revenue, magazines, ships, and
forts, in which he desires nothing, but that the just, known,
legal rights of his majesty, (devolved to him from his progenitors,) and of the persons trusted by him, which have vio-

[1] *This message is in the handwriting of Lord Clarendon's amanuensis.*

85*

lently been taken from both, be restored unto him, and unto
them; unless any just and legal exception against any of the
persons trusted by him (which are yet unknown to his majesty) can be made appear to him:

2. "As soon as all the members of both houses shall be
restored to the same capacity of sitting and voting in parliament, as they had upon the first of January 1641 ; the same,
of right, belonging unto them by their birthrights, and the
free election of those that sent them ; and having been voted
from them for adhering to his majesty in these distractions ;
his majesty not intending that this should extend either to
the bishops, whose votes have been taken away by bill, or
to such, in whose places, upon new writs, new elections
have been made :

3. "As soon as his majesty, and both houses, may be secured from such tumultuous assemblies, as to the great
breach of the privileges, and the high dishonour of parliaments, have formerly assembled about both houses, and awed
the members of the same ; and occasioned two several complaints from the lords' house, and two several desires of
that house to the house of commons, to join in a declaration against them ; the complying with which desire might
have prevented all these miserable distractions, which have
ensued ; which security, his majesty conceives, can be only
settled by adjourning the parliament to some other place,
at the least twenty miles from London, the choice of which
his majesty leaves to both houses:

" His majesty will most cheerfully and readily consent,
that both armies be immediately disbanded, and give a present meeting to both his houses of parliament at the time
and place, at and to which the parliament shall be agreed to
be adjourned : his majesty being most confident, that the
law will then recover due credit and estimation ; and that
upon a free debate, in a full and peaceable convention of parliament, such provisions will be made against seditious
preaching, and printing against his majesty, and the established laws, which have been one of the chief causes of the
present distractions, and such care will be taken concerning
the legal and known rights of his majesty, and the property

and liberty of his subjects, that whatsoever hath been published, or done, in or by colour of any illegal declaration, ordinance, or order of one or both houses, or any committee of either of them, and particularly the power to raise arms without his majesty's consent, will be in such manner recalled, disclaimed, and provided against, that no seed will remain for the like to spring out of for the future, to disturb the peace of the kingdom, and to endanger the very being of it. And in such a convention his majesty is resolved, by his readiness to consent to whatsoever shall be proposed to him, by bill, for the real good of his subjects, (and particularly for the better discovery and speedier conviction of recusants; for the education of the children of papists by protestants in the protestant religion;[1] for the prevention of practices of papists against the state; and the due execution of the laws, and true levying of the penalties against them,) to make known to all the world, how causeless those fears and jealousies have been, which have been raised against him; and by that so distracted this miserable kingdom. And if this offer of his majesty be not consented to, (in which he asks nothing for which there is not apparent justice on his side, and in which he defers many things highly concerning both himself and people, till a full and peaceable convention of parliament, which in justice he might now require,) his majesty is confident, that it will then appear to all the world, not only who is most desirous of peace, and whose fault it is that both armies are not now disbanded; but who have been the true and first cause, that this peace was ever interrupted, or those armies raised; and the beginning or continuance of the war, and the destruction and desolation of this poor kingdom (which is too likely to ensue) will not, by the most interested, passionate, or prejudicate person, be imputed to his majesty."

To this message the two houses returned no answer to the king,[2] but required the committee to return to West-

---

[1] His majesty was much more careful that his own rights should not be violated, than that the rights of nature should be observed.—W.

[2] It was no wonder. This was the most unguarded step the king ever made throughout the course of the war.—W.

minster (having been in Oxford with his majesty just twenty days) with such positive circumstances, that the house of
commons enjoined their members to begin their journey the
same day; which they obeyed; though it was so late, that
they were forced to very inconvenient accommodations; and
at their return, some of them were looked upon with great
jealousy, as persons engaged by the king, and disinclined to
the parliament; and this jealousy prevailed so far, that Mr.
Martin opened a letter from the earl of Northumberland to
his wife, presuming he should therein have discovered some
combination; and this insolence was not disliked.

Many were of opinion, that the king was too severe in
this treaty,[1] and insisted too much upon what is his own by
right and law; and that if he would have distributed offices
and places liberally to particular men, which had been a condescension in policy to be submitted to, he might have been
repossessed of his own power. And I have heard this
alleged by many, who at that time were extremely violent
against all such artifices. The committee themselves (who
at that time perfectly abhorred the proceedings of the parliament, or rather the power and superiority of the earl of Essex) seemed exceedingly desirous of such an accommodation, as all good men desired; and to believe, that if the
king would have condescended so far, as to nominate the
earl of Northumberland to be lord high admiral, that it would
have made so great a division in the houses, that the treaty
would have been continued, and his majesty been satisfied
in all the other propositions. And the earl of Northumberland, to private friends, did make as full professions of future
service to his majesty, and as ample recognitions of past errors and mistakes, as could reasonably be expected from a
wary nature, before he could be sure what reception such

---

[1] Well they might. In an equal treaty, when made by the parties
sword in hand, were not concessions to be made on both sides, if a
peace was desired by either? But this unhappily was not the case.
While the hopes of each party were equal, the talk of treaties and of
peace was only to cajole the people who languished after it; and
each was to affect to labour after it, to throw the public odium on their
adversaries.—W.

professions and vows would find.   But the king thought the
power and interest of that committee would be able to do
little, if it could not prevail for the enlarging the time of the
treaty, in which they seemed heartily to engage themselves.
And he was resolved at least to have a probable assurance
of the conclusion, before he would offer such concessions, as
taking no effect might prove prejudicial to him : as the nominating the earl of Northumberland to be admiral (though he
would willingly have done it, as the price and pledge of an
honourable peace) would have discontented all who had,
how unreasonably soever, promised themselves that preferment ; and many would have imputed it to an unseasonable
easiness, (from which imputation it concerned the king, at
that time, as much to purge himself, as of unmercifulness
and revenge,) upon promises and hopes, to have readmitted
a man to a charge and trust, he had so fatally betrayed and
broken, against more solemn promises and obligations, than
he could now enter into ; and therefore it concerned the
king to be sure of some advantage, in lieu of this visible
hazard.

I am one of those, who do believe that this obligation, at
this time, laid upon the earl of Northumberland, with such
other circumstances of kindness as would have been fit to
accompany it, would have met real gratitude and faithful-
ness in him, (for as, originally, he had, I am persuaded, no
evil purposes against the king ; so he had now sufficient disdain and indignation against those who got him to tread their
ways, when he had not their ends,) and that it would have
made some rent and division in the two houses, (which could
not but have produced some benefit to the king,) and that it
might probably have procured some few days' addition for
the continuance of the treaty ; the avowed ground of denying
it being, because the king had not, in the least degree, consented to any one thing proposed by them : but, I confess, I
cannot entertain any imagination, that it would have produced a peace, or given the king any advantage, or benefit in
the war : what inconvenience it might have produced hath
been touched before.[1]   For, besides that the stirring and

---

[1] This advantage it would certainly have given him : it would have

active party, who carried on the war, were neither gracious
to the earl of Northumberland, nor he to them, their favourite
at sea being then the earl of Warwick, who had the possession of the fleet, and whom alone they believed fit to be
trusted with the navy; whoever calls to mind what was done
in the houses, during the time of the treaty, and by their directions; that by their own authority they directed all the
lands of bishops, deans, and chapters, to be sequestered, and
inhibited their tenants to pay any rent to them; that, under
pretence of searching for arms, and taking away superstitious
pictures, they caused the queen's chapel at Somerset-house
(where she was to exercise her devotion, if they ever meant
she should return again to London) to be most licentiously
rifled; in which license with impunity, her lodgings were
plundered, and all her furniture and goods of value taken away
and embezzled; that there was an order made in the house
of commons, when they sent their messengers every day to
Oxford without any formality or control, " that whatsoever
person should come from Oxford, or any part of the king's
army, to London, or the parts adjacent, without the warrant
of both houses of parliament, or of the lord general the earl
of Essex, he should be apprehended as a spy and intelligen-
cer, and be proceeded against according to the rules and
grounds of war:" by virtue of which order of the house of
commons only, and without any communication that notice
might be taken of it, a servant of the king's, for discharging
the duty of his place, was executed; which shall be remembered in its place; all which, except the execution of that
man, was transacted during the time of the treaty at Oxford.

Whosoever remembers the other proposition upon which
the treaty was founded, and the bills then presented to the
king for his royal assent; that there was no unreasonable
thing demanded in the nineteen propositions, which was not
comprehended in these fourteen, and many additions made,

shewn the people that he was ready to sacrifice his own interest for
their sake, by procuring them what they so much wanted, *a peace.*
The *inconvenience* it would have produced, was the displeasing per-
haps some of the most powerful of his self-interested and factious fol-
lowers.—W.

that were not in the former ; that they demanded the total abolition and extirpation of archbishops, bishops, deans, and chapters, and the whole frame of the government of the church ; and another bill for the calling an assembly of divines, nominated by themselves, (which was a presumption, as contrary to the policy and government of the kingdom, as the most extravagant act they had done,) and consisting of persons the most deeply engaged in the most unwarrantable acts that had been done ; and yet his majesty was required to promise to pass such other bills for settling church-government, as, upon consultation with that assembly of divines, should be resolved on by both houses of parliament: that all the other bills then presented to the king for his royal assent, and insisted on by their fourth proposition, though they had specious and popular titles, contained many clauses in them contrary to common equity, and the right of the subject, and introduced proceedings very different from the known justice of the kingdom; and therefore, besides the time and circumstances of the passing those acts, (when the nation was in blood,) not like to meet with his majesty's approbation ; I say, whosoever remembers and considers all this, (to say nothing of the limitations by which their committee were bound, without any power of debating, or other capacity than to deliver the resolutions of the two houses, and to receive the king's answer, which might as effectually have been done by any one single ordinary messenger,) cannot, I conceive, believe, that the king's consenting to make any one person among them high admiral of England, would have been a means to have restored the kingdom to a present peace, and the king to his just authority and rights.[1] And if all these considerations be not sufficient to render that supposition improbable, that, which follows next in order of story, will abundantly confute it.

On Saturday the 15th of April, which was the very day on which the treaty expired at Oxford, being the last of the

[1] Certainly not. But because the king could not get all by this treaty, was he to neglect the getting any thing? And he certainly would have got a great deal, by shewing the people that he was ready to sacrifice a great deal for them.—W.

twenty days which were first assigned, and to which no importunity of the king's could procure an addition, the earl of Essex marched with his whole army from Windsor, and sat down before Reading; which preparation would not have been so exactly made, and the resolution so punctually taken, if they had meant any reasonable concessions[1] from the king should have frustrated that vast charge, and determined all further contentions. The earl had never before been in the head of so gallant an army, which consisted of about sixteen thousand foot, and above three thousand horse, in as good an equipage, and supplied with all things necessary for a siege, as could be expected from an enemy which knew no wants, and had the command of the Tower of London, and all other stores of the kingdom. In the town were above three thousand foot, and a regiment of horse consisting of near three hundred; the fortifications were very mean to endure a formed siege, being made only to secure a winter quarter, and never intended for a standing garrison. And it is very true, that it was resolved at a council of war at Oxford, " that before the end of April," (before which time it was conceived the enemy would not adventure to take the field,) " sir Arthur Aston should slight those works, and draw off his garrison to the king;" and that which made it less able to bear a siege, than the weakness of their works, was their want of ammunition; for they had not forty barrels of powder; which would not have held a brisk and daring enemy four hours. And as this defect proceeded not from want of foresight, so it was not capable of being supplied, at least in that proportion as was worthy the name of a supply. For the king had no port to friend, by which he could bring ammunition to Oxford; neither had he been yet able to set up any manufacture for any considerable supply. So that what he brought up with him after the battle of Edge-hill, which was the remainder of the four hundred barrels brought by the ship called the Providence, before the setting up of his standard, had served for all his expeditions,

[1] Reasonable concessions? Why the king had made none; and that I suppose they foresaw.—W.

being distributed into the several garrisons ; and was still to furnish all his growing occasions ; and that magazine now at Reading (which was no greater than is before mentioned) was yet double to what was in any other place, Oxford only excepted ; wherein, at this time, there was not above one hundred barrels of powder, and in no one place match proportionable to that little powder : and this defect is wholly to be imputed to the lowness and straitness of the king's condition ; for there was no want of industry, but all imaginable care and pains taken to prevent and supply it.

Notwithstanding all these difficulties, the town looked upon the enemy with courage and contempt enough ; and, to say the truth, both officers and soldiers were as good, as in the infancy of a war could be expected ; and they had no apprehension of want of victual, with which they were abundantly stored. The soldiers without were, for the most part, newly levied, and few of their officers acquainted with the way and order of assaulting towns ;[1] and this was the first siege that happened in England. Upon the first sitting down before it, after they had taken a full view of the ground, their general advised with his council of war, in what manner he should proceed, whether by assault or approach ; in which there was great diversity of opinions. " The works were weak ; the number of the assailants sufficient ; all materials in readiness ; the soldiers in the town full of apprehensions, and a very considerable party of the inhabitants disaffected to the garrison, who in the time of a storm would be able to beget a great distraction. That they might be able to storm it in so many places at once, that the number of the soldiers within would not be able to defend all ; and if they prevailed in any one, their whole body of horse might enter, and be immediately masters of the town : if they prevailed this way, their army would have that reputation, and carry that terror with it, that no power of the

---

[1] And in this ignorance they continued throughout the whole war. For marshal Turenne, in his Memoires, tells us, that the six thousand brave English foot which Cromwell sent the French, to assist at the siege of Dunkirk, were mere savages in the knowledge of such a service.---W.

king's would hereafter be able to abide it ; but they might march over the kingdom, and subdue every part of it : whereas if they delayed their work, and proceeded by way of approach, those in the town would recover heart, and, after they had digested the present fears and apprehensions, contemn their danger ; and their own soldiers, who were yet fresh and vigorous, would every day abate in courage, and their numbers in a few weeks lessen as much by sickness and duty, as they should probably do by an assault." On the other hand it was objected, " that the army consisted most of new levies," (and in truth there were not, of all that gallant army that was at Edge-hill, among the foot, three thousand men,) " who would be hardly brought to begin upon so desperate service; that it was the only army the parliament had, upon which all their hopes and welfare depended ; and if in the spring it should receive an eminent foil, they would not recover their courage again all the sum-mer.   That they were not only to look upon the taking of Reading, but, pursuing that in a reasonable way, to keep themselves in a posture and condition to end the war by a battle with all the king's forces ; which would no doubt ap-ply themselves to their relief ; and no place under heaven could be so commodious for them to try their fortune in, as that.   Whereas if they should hastily engage themselves upon an onslatt, and receive a repulse, and should be after-wards forced to rise to fight with the king, they should never make their men stand ; and then their cause was lost."   For the danger of sickness among the soldiers, who were not ac-quainted with hardness, it was urged, " that though it were earlier in the year than the armies usually marched into the field, yet they had much better accommodation and provision than armies use to have ; their horse (to whom that time of the year is commonly most formidable, through the want of forage) being plentifully provided for with hay and oats by the benefit of the river, and all supplies being sent for the foot out of London."

And in truth it is hardly credible what vast quantities (besides the provisions made in a very regular way by the commissioners) of excellent victual ready dressed were every

day sent in wagons and carts from London to the army,
upon the voluntary contributions from private families, according to their affections to the good work in hand ; the
common people being persuaded, that the taking of Reading
would destroy all the king's hopes of an army, and that it
would be taken in very few days. Upon these arguments
and debates, (in which all these reasons were considered on
both sides,) the major part of the council inclined, and with
that the general complied, to pursue the business by approach. It was reported, that the officers of horse in the
council were all for a storm, and the foot officers for approaching.[1] The chief care and oversight of the approaches
was committed to Philip Skippon, a man often mentioned in
the first part of this history, who had been an old officer,
and of good experience in the Low Countries, and was now
made sergeant-major-general of the army, by the absolute
power of the two houses, and without the cheerful concurrence of the earl of Essex ; though sir John Merrick, who
had executed that place by his lordship's choice from the
beginning, was preferred to be general of the ordnance.

The approaches advanced very fast, the ground being in
all places as fit for that work as could be, and the town lying
so low, that they had many batteries, from whence they shot
their cannon into the town and upon their line at a near distance, but without any considerable execution ; there being
fewer lost by that service than will be believed,[2] and but
one man of note, lieutenant colonel D'Ews, a young man of
notable courage and vivacity, who had his leg shot off by a
cannon bullet, of which he speedily and very cheerfully died.
From the town there were frequent sallies with good success ; and very many soldiers, and some officers, of the enemy
were killed ; more, hurt ; who were sent to hospitals near
London ; and those that were sent to London, as many cart-
loads were, were brought in the night, and disposed with

---

[1] This is slyly said in reproach of Essex's army. For in a storm
the foot were to make way for the horse. So the former were exposed
to all the slaughter, and the latter shared in all the honour of the success.---W.

[2] This shews their total ignorance in the service.---W.

great secrecy, that the citizens might take no notice of it :
the stratagems of this kind are too ridiculous to be particularly set down, though pursued then with great industry,
insomuch as some were punished for reporting that there
were very many soldiers killed and hurt before Reading ;
and it was a mark of malignity to believe those reports ; so
unfit the people were to be trusted with all truths.

Within a week after the beginning of the siege, sir Arthur
Aston the governor being in a court of guard near the line
which was nearest to the enemy's approaches, a cannon shot
accidentally lighted upon the top of it, which was covered
with brick-tile, a piece whereof, the shot going through, hit
the governor in the head, and made that impression upon
him, that his senses shortly failed him, so that he was not
only disabled afterwards from executing in his own person,
but incompetent for counsel or direction ; so that the chief
command was devolved to colonel Richard Fielding, who was
the eldest colonel of the garrison.   This accident was then
thought of great misfortune to the king, for there was not in
his army an officer of greater reputation, and of whom the
enemy had a greater dread.   The next night after this accident, but before it was known at Oxford, a party from thence
under the command of Mr. Wilmot, the lieutenant general
of the horse, without any signal opposition, put in a supply
of powder, and a regiment of five hundred foot into the town,
but received advertisement from thence of the governor's
hurt, and that they must expect to be relieved within a week,
beyond which time they should not be able to hold out.
How ill the king was provided for such an expedition, will
best appear by remembering how his forces were then scattered, and the present posture he was then in at Oxford.

The nimble and the successful marches of sir William
Waller, whom we left triumphing in Wales, after his strange
surprise of the lord Herbert's forces near Gloucester, caused
the king to send prince Maurice with a strong party of horse
and dragoons to attend him, who moved from place to place
with as great success as speed, after his success at Hynam ;
and to make the shame of those officers the less, with the
spirit of victory doubled upon him, he came before Hereford,

a town very well affected, and reasonably well fortified, having a strong stone wall about it, and some cannon, and there being in it some soldiers of good reputation, and many gentlemen of honour and quality ; and three or four hundred soldiers, besides the inhabitants well armed ; yet, without the loss of one man on either side, to the admiration of all who then heard it, or have ever since heard of it, he persuaded them fairly to give up the town, and yield themselves prisoners upon quarter ; which they did, and were presently by him sent for their better security to Bristol.

From thence he marched to Worcester, where his conquests met some stop ; for though the town was not so strong, nor the garrison so great, (I mean of soldiers ; for the inhabitants were more,) as Hereford, nor one officer in it of more experience than he had gotten this unhappy war, the inhabitants had the courage to resolve not to admit any summons or messenger from him ; and when his drum, against all signs made to him from the walls not to approach, did notwithstanding refuse to return without delivering his message, they shot at him, and killed him ; and when sir William Waller himself, to revenge that affront, marched with his whole body towards them, (there being only an old gate, without bridge or work, before it, to hinder his entrance into the town, they entertained him so roughly, that he was forced to retire with the loss of some officers, and about twenty common men ; after which, his men having not been accustomed to such usage, he got over the Severn again, and, with quick night marches, so avoided prince Maurice, (who took no less pains to meet with him,) that with some few light skirmishes, in which he received small loss, he carried his party safe, and full of reputation, through Gloucester to the earl of Essex's army before Reading ; himself being sent for to London, upon a design that must be hereafter mentioned.

The great want at Oxford (if any one particular might deserve that style, where all necessary things were wanted) was ammunition ; and the only hope of supply was from the north ; yet the passage from thence so dangerous, that a party little inferior in strength to an army was necessary to convey it ; for though the earl of Newcastle, at that time, was master of the field in Yorkshire, yet the enemy was much superior in all the counties between that county and Oxford ; and had planted many garrisons so near all the roads, that the most private messengers travelled with great hazard, three being intercepted for one that escaped. To clear these obstructions, and not without the design of guarding and waiting on the queen to Oxford, if her majesty were ready for that journey, at least to secure a necessary supply of powder, prince Rupert resolved in person to march towards the north, and about the beginning of April (the treaty being then at Oxford, and hopes that it would have produced a good effect, at least that the earl of Essex would not have taken the field till May) his highness, with a party of twelve hundred horse and dragoons, and six or seven hundred foot, marched towards Litchfield ; which if he could reduce, and settle there a garrison for the king, lay most convenient for that northern communication ; and would with it dissolve other little adjacent holds of the enemy's, which contributed much to their interruption. In his way thither, he was to march through Bromicham, a town in Warwickshire before mentioned, and of as great fame for hearty, wilful, affected disloyalty[1] to the king, as any place in England. It is before remembered, that the king in his march from Shrewsbury, notwithstanding the eminent malignity of that people, had shewed as eminent compassion to them ; not giving way that they should suffer by the undistinguishing license of the soldier, or by the severity of his own justice ; which clemency of his found so unequal a return, that, the next day after his remove thence, the inhabitants of that place seized on his carriages, wherein were his own plate and furniture, and conveyed them to Warwick castle; and had from that time, with unusual industry and vigilance, apprehended all messengers who were employed, or suspected to be so, in the king's service; and though it was never made a garrison by direction of the parliament, being built in such a form, as was indeed hardly capable of being fortified, yet they had so

[1] Meaning affectionate.---W.

great a desire to distinguish themselves from the king's good subjects, that they cast up little slight works at both ends of the town, and barricadoed the rest, and voluntarily engaged themselves not to admit any intercourse with the king's forces.

In this posture prince Rupert now found them, having in the town with them at that time a troop of horse, belonging to the garrison of Litchfield, which was grown to that strength, that it infested those parts exceedingly; and would in a short time have extended itself to a powerful jurisdiction. His highness hardly believing it possible, that, when they should discover his power, they would offer to make resistance, and being unwilling to receive interruption in his more important design, sent his quartermasters thither to take up his lodging; and to assure them, " that if they behaved themselves peaceably, they should not suffer for what was past :" but they had not consciences good enough to believe him, and absolutely refused to let him quarter in the town; and from their little works, with mettle equal to their malice, they discharged their shot upon him; but they were quickly overpowered, and some parts of the town being fired, they were not able to contend with both enemies; and, distracted between both, suffered the assailant to enter without much loss; who took not that vengeance upon them they deserved, but made them expiate their transgressions with paying a less mulct than might have been expected from their wealth, if their wickedness had been less.

In the entrance of this town, and in the too eager pursuit of that loose troop of horse that was in it, the earl of Denbigh (who from the beginning of the war, with unwearied pains, and exact submission to discipline and order, had been a volunteer in prince Rupert's troop, and been engaged with singular courage in all enterprises of danger) was unfortunately wounded with many hurts on the head and body with swords and poll-axes; of which, within two or three days, he died. And but for which accident, (and to remember the dismal inequality of this contention, in which always some earl, or person of great honour or fortune, fell, when, after the most signal victory over the other side, there was sel-

dom a man of any known family, or of other reputation, than
of passion for the cause in which he fell,) I should not have
wasted so much paper in mentioning an action of so little
moment, as was this of Bromicham : which I shall yet enlarge with the remembrance of a clergyman, who was here
killed at the entering of the town, after he had not only refused quarter, but provoked the soldier by the most odious
revilings and reproaches of the person and honour of the
king, that can be imagined, and renouncing all allegiance to
him ; in whose pockets were found several papers of memorials of his own obscene and scurrilous behaviour with several women, in such loose expressions, as modest ears cannot
endure.   And this man was the principal governor and in-
cendiary of the rude people of that place against their sovereign.   So full a qualification was a heightened measure of
malice and disloyalty for this service, that it weighed down
the infamy of any other lewd and vicious behaviour.

From Bromicham, the prince, without longer stay than to
remove two or three slight garrisons in the way, which made
very little resistance, marched to Litchfield, and easily possessed himself of the town, which lay open to all comers ;
but the close (which contained the cathedral church and all
the clergymen's houses) was strongly fortified, and resolved
against him.   The wall, about which there was a broad
and deep moat, was so thick and strong, that no battery
the prince could raise would make any impression ; the governor, one colonel Rouswell, very resolute ; and the garrison of such men as were most transported with superstition
to the cause in which they were engaged, and in numbers
equal to the ground they were to keep, their provisions ample for a longer time than it was fit the prince should stay
before it.   So that it was believed, when his highness had
in vain endeavoured to procure it by treaty, he would not
have engaged before it ; for his strength consisted, upon the
matter, wholly in horse ; his foot and dragoons being an inconsiderable force for such an attempt.   But whether the
difficulties were not thoroughly discerned and weighed at
first, or whether the importance of the place was thought so
great, that it was worth an equal hazard and adventure, he

resolved not to move till he had tried the uttermost ; and, to that purpose, drew what addition of force he could out of the country, to strengthen his handful of foot ; and persuaded many officers and volunteers of the horse to alight, and bear their parts in the duty ; with which they cheerfully and gallantly complied ; and in less than ten days he had drawn the moat dry, and prepared two bridges for the graff.   The besieged omitted nothing that could be performed by vigilant and bold men ; and killed and wounded many of the besiegers ; and disappointed and spoiled one mine they had prepared.   In the end, early in the morning, the prince having prepared all things in readiness for the assault, he sprung another mine ; which succeeded according to wish, and made a breach of twenty foot in the wall, in a place least suspected by those within ; yet they defended it with all possible courage and resolution, and killed and hurt very many ; some, officers of prime quality ; whereof the lord Digby,[1] colonel Gerrard, colonel Wagstaffe, and major Leg, were the chief of the wounded ; and when they had entered the breach, they continued the dispute so fiercely within, (the narrowness of the breach, and the ascent, not suffering many to enter together, and no horse being able to get over,) that after they had killed colonel Usher, and some other good officers, and taken others prisoners, (for both colonel Wagstaffe and William Leg were in their hands,) they compelled the prince to consent to very honourable conditions ; which he readily yielded to, as thinking himself a gainer by the bargain.   And so the garrison marched out with fair respect, and a princely testimony of having made a courageous defence ; his highness being very glad of his conquest, though the purchase had shrewdly shaken his troops, and robbed him of many officers and soldiers he much valued.   At this time, either the day before or the day after this action, prince Rupert received a positive order from the king, " to make all possible haste, with all the strength he had, and all he could draw together from those parts, to the relief of Reading ;"

[1] Lord Digby's purpose in being of this party was to pay his court to the queen.—W.

which was in the danger we but now left it.   Upon which
his highness, committing the government of Litchfield to
colonel Baggot, a son of a good and powerful family in that
county, and appointing his troops to make what haste was
possible after him, himself with a few servants came to Oxford to attend the king, whom he found gone towards Reading.

The importunity from that garrison for relief was so peremptory, and the concernment so great in their preservation, that the king found it would not bear the necessary delay of prince Rupert's returning with his forces; and therefore his majesty in person, with those horse and foot which
he could speedily draw together, leaving very few behind
him in Oxford, or in any other garrison, advanced towards
Reading ; hoping, and that was the utmost of his hope, that
he might, with the assistance of the garrison, be able to force
one quarter, and so draw out his men ; and by the advantage of those rivers which divided the enemy, and by the
passes, be able to retire to Oxford ; for being joined, he
could not have equalled one half of the enemy's army.   When
he drew near the town, the day being passed whereon they
had been promised, or had promised themselves, relief, he
was encountered by a party of the enemy, which defended
their post, and being quickly seconded by supplies of horse
and foot from all their quarters, after a very sharp conflict,
in which many fell on both sides, the king's party, commanded by the earl of Forth himself, (the general,) consisting of
near one thousand musketeers, was forced to retire to their
body; which they did the sooner, because those of the town
made no semblance of endeavouring to join with them;
which was what they principally relied upon.   The reason
of that was, the garrison, not seeing their relief coming, sent
for a parley to the enemy, which was agreed to, with a
truce for so many hours, upon which hostages were delivered; and a treaty begun, when the king came to relieve it.
Upon the view of the enemy's strength and intrenchment,
all were of opinion that the small forces of the king would
not be able to raise the siege, or to join with those in the
town ; and in this melancholic conclusion his majesty retired

for the present, resolving to make any other reasonable attempt the next day.   In the mean time, some soldiers found means to escape out of the town, and colonel Fielding himself in the night came to the king, and told him the state they were in ; and "that they were in treaty, and he believed might have very good conditions, and liberty to march away with all their arms and baggage ;" which was so welcome news, that the king bid him, prince Rupert being then present, " that, if he could procure such conditions, he should accept them :" for indeed the men and the arms were all that the king desired, and the loss of either of which was like to prove fatal to him.   The king continued still at Nettlebedd, a village seven or eight miles distant from Reading, to attend the success of the treaty ; resolving, if it succeeded not, to try the utmost again for their redemption : but all men praying heartily for liberty to march off upon the treaty, the next day these articles were agreed on.

1. " That the governor, commanders, and soldiers, both horse and foot, might march out with flying colours, arms, and four pieces of ordnance, ammunition, bag and baggage, light match, bullet in mouth, drums beating, and trumpets sounding.

2. " That they might have free passage to his majesty's city of Oxford, without interruption of any of the forces under the command of his excellency the earl of Essex ; provided the said governor, commanders, and soldiers, use no hostility until they come to Oxford.

3. " That what persons were accidentally come to the town, and shut up by the siege, might have liberty to pass without interruption ; such persons only excepted, as had run away from the army under the command of the earl of Essex.

4. " That they should have fifty carriages for baggage, sick, and hurt men.

5. " That the inhabitants of the town of Reading should not be prejudiced in their estates, or persons, either by plundering or imprisonment ; and that they who would leave the town, might have free leave, and passage, safely to go to what place they would, with their goods, within the space of six weeks after the surrender of the town.

6. "That the garrison should quit the town by twelve of the clock the next morning; and that the earl of Essex should provide a guard for the security of the garrison soldiers, when they began to march."

Upon these articles, signed by the earl of Essex, the town was delivered on the 27th day of April, (being within a fortnight after the siege began,) and the garrison marched to the king, who stayed for them, and with him to Oxford. But at their coming out of the town, and passing through the enemy's guards, the soldiers were not only reviled, and reproachfully used, but many of them disarmed, and most of the waggons plundered, in the presence of the earl of Essex himself, and the chief officers; who seemed to be offended at it, and not to be able to prevent it; the unruliness of the common men being so great. And as this breach of the articles was very notorious and inexcusable, so it was made the rise, foundation, and excuse for barbarous injustice of the same kind throughout the greatest part of the war; insomuch as the king's soldiers afterward, when it was their part to be precise in the observation of agreements, mutinously remembered the violation at Reading, and thereupon exercised the same licence; from thence, either side having somewhat to object to the other, the requisite honesty and justice of observing conditions was mutually, as it were by agreement, for a long time after violated.

There had been, in the secret committee for the carrying on the war, forming those designs, and administering to the expenses thereof, a long debate with great difference of opinion, whether they should not march directly with their army to besiege Oxford, where the king and the court was, rather than Reading; and if they had taken that resolution, as Mr. Hambden, and all they who desired still to strike at the root, very earnestly insisted upon, without doubt they had put the king's affairs into great confusion. For, besides that the town was not tolerably fortified, nor the garrison well provided for, the court, and multitude of nobility, and ladies, and gentry, with which it was inhabited, bore any kind of alarum very ill. But others, who did not yet think their army well enough composed to resist all temptations, nor enough subdued in their inclinations to loyalty, and reverence towards the person of the king, had no mind it should besiege the very place where the king himself was; and the earl of Essex himself, who was yet the soul of the army, had no mind to that enterprise: and so the army marched, as hath been said, directly to Reading, with the success that is mentioned.

Though, at the instant, the parliament was highly pleased with the getting the town, and the king as well contented, when he saw his entire garrison safely joined to the rest of his army, (for it cannot be denied the joy was universal through the king's quarters, upon the assurance, that they had recovered full four thousand good men, whom they had given for lost,) yet, according to the vicissitudes in war, when the accounts are cast up, either party grew quickly dissatisfied with its success. The king was no sooner returned to Oxford, but, upon conference between the officers and soldiers, there grew a whisper, "that there had not been fair carriage, and that Reading had been betrayed," and from thence made a noise through Oxford; and the very next day, and at the same time, colonel Fielding, upon whom the discourses reflected, came to the king to desire, "that an account might be taken of the whole business at a council of war for his vindication;" and the common soldiers, in a disorderly manner, "to require justice against him for betraying and delivering up the town to the rebels;" which they avowed with so much confidence, with the mention of some particulars, "as having frequent intercourse with the earl of Essex, and hindering and forbidding the soldiers to issue out of the town to join with the king, when he came to relieve them, albeit their officers had drawn them up to that purpose, and were ready to lead them;" and the like; with some rash and passionate words disrespectful to his majesty; so that he gave present order for his commitment, and trial at a court of war; the king himself being marvellously incensed against him, for that clause in the third article, which gave liberty to all who were accidentally come to the town, and shut up by the siege, to pass without interruption, wherein there was an exception of such persons

who had run away from the earl of Essex's army, and by
virtue of that exception some soldiers of that kind were
taken after the rendering of the town, and were executed.
And though the colonel excused himself, "as being no more
concerned to answer for the articles, than every member of
the council of war, by which they were agreed;" yet it
was alleged, "that the council of war had been induced to
consent to those articles, upon the colonel's averment, that
the king had seen them, and approved of them." Whereas
his majesty had never seen any articles in writing, but only
consented, that they should march away with their arms and
baggage, if the enemy agreed to those conditions. I have
not known the king more afflicted than he was with that
clause, which he called no less "than giving up those poor
men, who, out of conscience of their rebellion,' had betaken
themselves to his protection, to be massacred and murdered
by the rebels, whom they had deserted;" and, for the vindication of himself therein, he immediately published a proclamation, in which he took notice of that clause; and declared to all the world,

"That he was not privy to, or, in the least degree, consenting to that exception, but held the same most prejudicial
to his service, and derogatory from his honour; and that he
would always choose to run any hazard or danger, the violence or treason of his enemies could threaten, or bring upon
him, rather than he would withdraw or deny his protection
to any, who, being convinced in their conscience of their disloyalty, should return to their duty, and betake themselves to
his service. And as he had referred to a court of war the
full examination of all the particular proceedings, in the delivery of that town, that so justice might be done accordingly; so he did declare, that he would always proceed with all
severity against such, as should, by the like dishonourable
conditions, expose his subjects, and bereave them of his protection that had returned to their obedience to him."

At the trial, it was objected against the colonel, "that the

' I make no doubt but these deserters from both armies were the
greatest scoundrels in them, and the least swayed by conscience.—W.

town might have been longer defended, there being want of no necessary provision, and as much powder, at the giving it up, as there was when the enemy came first before it; for, besides the first supply, sixteen barrels were put in during the skirmish, when the king came to relieve it : that several colonels pressed very earnestly to sally, when the king's forces were engaged, and that they were expressly hindered and forbidden by him : that he frequently gave his pass to a woman to go out of the town, who went into the earl of Essex's army, and returned again : that he persuaded the council of war to consent to the articles, by protesting that the king had well approved them, and reproached those officers who were of another opinion;" with some other particulars of licence and passion, which reflected more upon his discretion, than his honesty, or conduct.

He justified himself " to have done nothing towards the delivery of the place, but upon full consideration, advice, and approbation of the council of war : that he was in his own conscience and judgment satisfied, that the substance of the articles were advantageous for his majesty's service ; and though it was true, by that last supply of ammunition, their store was near as much as when the siege begun ; yet it was in all but thirty-two barrels, which would have lasted but few hours, if the enemy, who had approached within little more than pistol-shot of some parts of their works, should attack them in that manner as they had reason to expect ; and if they had held out longer, when it had appeared that the king was not strong enough to relieve them, they should not have been admitted to such conditions : and therefore, that he believed a hazard of so great a concernment was not to be run, when he well knew his majesty's former resolution of slighting the garrison ; and that it would not be now done above a fortnight sooner than was intended : that he had no knowledge of his majesty's approach, till the forces were engaged, when a truce was concluded, and their hostages in the enemy's hands ; and therefore, that he conceived it against the law of arms to make any attempt from the town ; and before they could sufficiently deliberate it in council, his majesty's forces retired : that the woman, to whom he gave a pass, was one he often employed as a spy, with very good effect; and he did believe, the advantage he received by it was greater than she could carry to the enemy by any information she could give : that he did persuade the council of war to consent to the conditions, because he believed them very profitable to his majesty, and he had averred only his majesty's approbation of the general substance of the articles, never applied it to the clause of the third article, which he much desired to have altered, but could not obtain the consent of the enemy. If he had been intemperate, or passionate to any, who were of another opinion, or had used any passionate expressions in the debate, it proceeded only from his zeal to the service, and his apprehension of the loss of so many good men, upon whom he well knew the king much depended : that he might have committed many indiscretions, for which he desired pardon, but had not failed in point of fidelity : that, by the unfortunate hurt of the governor, the command was devolved upon him by his right of seniority, not any ambitious design of his own : that he had, from time to time, acquainted sir Arthur Aston with the state and condition they were in; and though his indisposition of health was such, that he would not give positive orders, he seemed to approve of all that was done ; and though, for the former reason, he refused to sign the articles, yet they were read to him, and he expressed no dislike of them." The truth of it is, sir Arthur Aston was believed by many, not to be in so incompetent a condition to command as he pretended ; and that albeit his head was so much swoln, that he might not in person venture upon any execution, yet that his understanding, or senses, were not much distempered, or discomposed ; and that he only positively waved meddling, out of dislike of the condition they were in. And it is true, that, when he came to Oxford, he could speak as reasonably of any matter, as ever I knew him before, or after.

Notwithstanding all the defence the colonel could make for himself, and that there was not indeed any colour of proof, that he had acted any thing treacherously, he was, upon an article " of not obeying orders," (for in this agitation he had received some such, which he had not precisely

observed,) " sentenced to lose his head ;" which judgment,
after long and great intercession, was, in the end, remitted
by the king ; but his regiment disposed to another ; and he
never restored to that command.   And though he had been
always before of an unblemished reputation for honesty and
courage, and had heartily been engaged from the beginning
of the troubles, and been hurt in the service, and he appeared afterwards as a volunteer, with the same courage, in the
most perilous actions, and obtained a principal command in
another of the king's armies, he never recovered the misfortune and blemish of this imputation.   And yet I must profess for my part, being no stranger to what was then alleged
and proved on either party, I do believe him to have been
free from any base compliance with the enemy,[1] or any cow-
ardly declension of what was reasonably to be attempted.
So fatal are all misfortunes, and so difficult a thing it is to
play an after-game of reputation, in that nice and jealous
profession.

The inconveniences and mischiefs, that resulted to the
king from this accident, were greater than were at that time
taken notice of ; for from this, the factions in court, army,
and city (which afterwards grew very troublesome to the
king) were dated, and took their original ; great animosities
grew between the officers of the army ; some being thought
to have been too passionate and solicitous in the prosecution
of the colonel, and too much to have countenanced the rage
and fury of common soldiers in demanding justice on their
officer ; for from such a kind of clamour it began.   Others
again were as much condemned for a palpable avowed protection of him, thereby to shew their power, that a person
they favoured should not suffer ; and of both these, some
were more violent than they should have been ; which several inclinations equally possessed the court, some believing
that he was really guilty of treachery, though not so clearly
proved ; and therefore that, being within the mercy of the

[1] In other words, *I believe him to be unjustly condemned ;* and so will
every one who admits this representation of the case to be a true one.
--W.

law, upon another article, no mercy ought to be shewed to
him ; others as really supposing him innocent, and therefore
thinking it great pity, severely to take the forfeiture, upon
such a point, as few officers of the army did not know themselves guilty in : these supposing the former too full of rigour
and uncharitableness ; and they again accusing the other of
too much lenity and indulgence; whilst many gentlemen of
honour and quality, whose fortunes were embarked with the
king, grew extremely jealous, that the parliament had corrupted some of the king's officers with rewards, and that
others had power to protect them from punishment and discovery ; and the soldiers again as much incensed, that their
lives must be sacrificed, upon casual and accidental trespasses,
to the animosity and jealousy of those who run not the same
dangers with them.

But these indispositions and distempers were the effects
of the exigents of that time, (I wish the humours had been
impaired when the times mended,) and very many, who saw
the king's condition very low in an instant, and believed the
rebels to be most flourishing, would look no further for a
reason, than the loss of Reading ; though they had all still,
but the town ; which was never intended to be kept.   It is
most certain, that the king himself was so far from believing
the condition he was in to be tolerable, that, upon the news
of the earl of Essex's advance towards Oxford, within four
or five days after the loss of Reading, he once resolved, and
that by the advice of the chief officers of his army, to march
away towards the north, to join with the earl of Newcastle.
And if the earl of Essex had, at that time, but made any
show of moving with his whole body that way, I do verily
persuade myself, Oxford itself, and all the other garrisons of
those parts, had been quitted to them ; but those fears were
quickly composed, by an assurance of the earl's stay at Reading ; and that he was not in a posture for a present march,
and that his numbers had been shrewdly lessened by the
siege : whereupon the king resolved to abide him, and give
him battle about Oxford, if he advanced ; and, in the mean
time, encamped his foot upon the down, about a mile from
Abingdon ; which was the head quarter for his horse.   The

earl of Essex had as little joy of his conquests : the city murmured, and thought they were betrayed : they expected the reducing of Reading, by taking or destroying the garrison that was in it, which they were assured comprised above one half of the king's army; so that being defeated, the war would be at an end : whereas by giving them leave to march to the king with their arms, they had enabled him to fight a battle with them, which he could no otherwise have done : all that vast expense of money about the siege had been to no purpose, and had only recovered a town, which would have been left to them within one fortnight without any loss of men or money. They were now very angry that he had not marched to Oxford, when he first sat down before Reading, which if he had taken, (as with the same expense he might have done,) Reading must have yielded without a blow : and indeed there had been consultation at Windsor, before the expedition began, whether they should besiege Oxford or Reading first ; and the earl himself inclined to Oxford, but was advised to the other, for the conveniency of being supplied with provisions from London, and out of an apprehension that if the whole army should go before Oxford, and leave so strong a garrison at Reading behind them, they might not only be much infested from thence in their siege, but more frequent alarums would come from that place to the houses and the city than they would well bear : which without doubt was as great an oversight as any they committed ; for if they had at that time, with that full army they were then masters of, marched to Oxford, prince Rupert being, as is before remembered, at Litchfield, they had found the place every way worse provided for a siege than Reading, the fortifications being very slight and unfinished, and no public magazines of victual in store ; so that, though it may be, the king himself might with his horse have escaped, before they could have environed the town, the place, having a very thin garrison of soldiers, and a great company of lords and ladies, and persons of quality, not easy to be governed and commanded, could not probably have long held out, and then Reading must have been at their devotion ; and in the mean time, they had horse enough belonging to the city, and their gar-

rison at Windsor, to secure them from those excursions. But
that which troubled the earl of Essex more than these discourses, was the ill condition his army was in; they had
contracted in this short siege so great a sickness, and such an
indisposition to action, and so many were killed and run
away, that he was in no posture to pursue his advantage.

When the season of the year grew ripe for taking the
field, the earl of Essex found that his too early march had
nothing advanced his affairs; the soldiers having performed
so strict duty, and lodging upon the ground, in frost and rain,
before Reading, had produced great sickness and diseases in
his army, which had wasted abundance of his men; so that
he wanted rather another winter quarter to recover and recruit his men, than an opportunity to engage them in action;
which he found would be too often administered. He sent
daily importunities to the parliament for supplies of all kinds,
which they were not enough furnished with to satisfy him;
new divisions and animosities arose there, to perplex their
counsels. Their triumph upon the taking of Reading, which
they had celebrated with loud festivity, and made the city
believe, that all those benefits would attend it, which they
knew would be most grateful to them, appeared now without
any fruit; the king had all his forces and army entire, and
had only lost a town that he never meant to keep, and which
they knew not what to do with; and was now ready to
come into the field, when theirs was destitute of health, and
all those accommodations, which must enable them to march:
and their general every day reiterated his complaints, and
reproached them with the unskilful orders they had sent him,
by which, against all the advice and arguments he had given
them, he was reduced to that extremity.

The absurd and uncivil breaking off of the treaty with the
king was urged by their commissioners; who thought themselves disobliged by it, and published the king's gracious disposition, and the temper of the council in Oxford, to be different from what the parliament desired it should be believed.
They complained of jealousies which had been entertained
of their integrity; and the earl of Northumberland, having
discovered, that Harry Martin had opened a letter, which he

had writ from Oxford to his wife, to know what was included in it, took him aside, after a conference in the painted
chamber between the two houses, and questioned him upon
it ; and the other giving him some rude answers in justification of it, the earl cudgelled him in that presence ; upon
which many swords were drawn, to the great reproach and
scandal of the parliament.

These and the like instances of distraction and confusion
brought the reputation of that party low ; and made it looked upon, as like to destroy itself without an enemy ; whilst
the king's party, at that distance, seemed to be more united,
and to have recovered their spirits, of which they received
frequent evidence by the news of some of their quarters
being beat up, and many of their men being lost by the unexpected incursions of the king's horse ; whereof some parties, by night marches, and unusual lanes, went often near
London, and took many prisoners, who thought themselves
secure, in their houses, and in journeys they made ; and who
were put to ransom themselves with good sums of money :
so that, after all those mountains of promises, and undertakings, the wants were greater, and the city more importuned
for money, and the parliament visibly more necessitated for
want of it, than they had been before ; and instead of dispersing the king's army, and bringing the king back to his parliament, a sudden direction was given, and a vigorous execution of that direction was begun, to draw a line about the
city of London and Westminster, and to fortify it ; lest the
king's forces might break in upon them ; which made the
people suspect the state of their affairs to be worse than in
truth it was ; and so far were they from any thoughts of
peace and accommodation, that the house of commons raged
more furiously than ever ;[1] and every day engaged themselves in conclusions more monstrous than they had yet entered upon.   For the supply of the charge of the war, they

[1] This was consequential. The leaders in the house of commons
wanted some extraordinary security against the king's vindictive temper on his return to power ; and the last treaty had shewn that he
would not give it to them ; so they grew resolved that the sword
should decide all.--W.

proposed settling and imposing an excise upon such commodities as might best bear it; which was a burden the people of England had hitherto reproached other nations with, as a mark of slavery, and as never feared by themselves; and for the exercise of the sovereign power, they resolved it fit to make a new great seal, to be always resident with the houses. But the lords were not yet arrived at that presumption, but plainly refused to concur with them in either.

Whilst both armies lay quiet, the one about Reading, the other about Abingdon, or Oxford, without attempting one upon the other, or any action, save some small enterprises by parties, (in which the king got advantage; as the young earl of Northampton fortunately encountered a party of horse and foot from Northampton, which thought themselves strong enough to attempt upon Banbury: and having routed their horse, killed above two hundred of their foot, and took as many more prisoners, most whereof were shrewdly hurt, the young earl that day sacrificing to the memory of his father,) the king received from the earl of Newcastle, by a strong party of horse, a good and ample supply of ammunition; the want whereof all men looked upon with great horror. As soon as this was arrived, and the king heard that his armies, both in the north and west, began to flourish, and thought himself well provided to encounter the earl of Essex, if he desired it; his majesty resolved once more to try, whether the two houses would incline to a reasonable peace; and to that purpose sent a message to them by an express servant of his own, in these words:

"Since[1] his majesty's message of the 12th of April (in which he conceived he had made such an overture[2] for the immediate disbanding of all armies, and composure of those

---

[1] *This message is in the handwriting of lord Clarendon's amanuensis.*

[2] A mere farce to cajole the people. He could never imagine that, when he had granted nothing, the calling that nothing an *overture for composing the public distractions* could give the parliament any inclination to comply with what he wanted: but, as appears by page 1387. there was another purpose in it, the better by this means to carry on the correspondence between the king and his friends in the parliament and the city.—W.

miserable and present distractions, by a full and free convention of parliament, that a perfect and settled peace would have ensued) hath in all this time, above a full month, procured no answer from both houses, his majesty might well believe himself absolved, both before God and man, from the least possible charge of not having used his utmost endeavours for peace : yet, when he considers, that the scene of all this calamity is in the bowels of his own kingdom; that all the blood, which is spilt, is of his own subjects ; and that what victory soever it shall please God to give him, must be over those who ought not to have lifted up their hands against him ; when he considers, that these desperate civil dissensions may encourage and invite a foreign enemy, to make a prey of the whole nation ; that Ireland is in present danger to be totally lost ; that the heavy judgments of God, plague, pestilence, and famine, will be the inevitable attendance of this unnatural contention ; and that in a short time there will be so general a habit of uncharitableness and cruelty contracted through the whole kingdom, that even peace itself will not restore his people to their old temper and security ; his majesty cannot but again call for an answer to that his gracious message, which gives so fair a rise to end these unnatural distractions. And his majesty doth this with the more earnestness, because he doubts not the condition of his armies in several parts ; the strength of horse, foot, artillery, his plenty of ammunition, (when some men lately might conceive he wanted,) is so well known and understood, that it must be confessed, nothing but the tenderness and love to his people, and those Christian impressions, which always live, and he hopes alway shall dwell, in his heart, could move him once more to hazard a refusal. And he requires them, as they will answer to God, to himself, and all the world, that they will no longer suffer their fellow-subjects to welter in each other's blood ; that they would remember by whose authority, and to what end, they met in that council, and send such an answer to his majesty, as may open a door to let in a firm peace, and security to the whole kingdom. If his majesty shall again be disappointed of his intentions therein, the blood, rapine, and destruction, which may follow in England and Ireland, will be cast upon the account of those who are deaf to the motive of peace and accommodation."

This message was received by the house of peers (to whom it was directed) with all demonstration of respect and duty, and the messenger very civilly entreated by them : but when they communicated it with the house of commons, and desired their concurrence in preparing an address to the king suitable to his gracious invitation, that house was so far from concurring with them,[1] that they gave immediate order (which was executed accordingly) for the apprehension and commitment of the gentleman who brought the message ; and declared, " that they would proceed against him at a council of war," upon the order formerly mentioned, made by them when the treaty was at Oxford, " that any person coming from Oxford without their general's pass, or one from the houses, should be punished as a spy ;" to which order as the peers never consented, so the king had never, till this commitment, notice of it ; and themselves, after the making it, had sent several messengers to the king, without any formality of pass or trumpet.

The lords did what they could, publicly and privately, to dissuade this course ; but they could not prevail : the house of commons finding that the very imagination that a peace might be concluded, infinitely retarded their carrying on the war, and made not only those, who were yet free, not easy to be drawn in ; but many, who were engaged, remiss, and willing to retire ; and therefore they resolved to proceed with that vigour and resolution, that no reasonable man should believe it possible for the king to gain a peace but by subduing them, which seemed at least equally impossible.   To this purpose, instead of returning any answer to the king's message, within three days after the receiving it they impeached the queen of high treason, " for assisting the king her husband with arms, and ammunition, in the prosecution of the war against them ;" an attempt as unheard of among all the acts of their predecessors, and as unimagined as any thing they had yet ventured upon : their clergy sounded their trumpets louder

---

[1] It was no wonder they were a little out of humour for being thus bantered.—W.

to war than ever, if it was possible ; and they resolved, that
assembly of divines, to which they had at the treaty urged
the king's consent, should now meet by an ordinance of their
own, with an addition of some members of either house to
that number.

There had been, some months before, a design of prince
Rupert upon the city of Bristol, by correspondence with
some of the chief inhabitants of the city, who were weary of
the tyranny of the parliament ; but it had been so unskilfully or unhappily carried, that, when the prince was near the
town, with such a party of horse and foot, as he made choice
of, it was discovered, and many principal citizens apprehended by Nathaniel Fiennes, son to the lord Say, and then
governor of that city for the parliament ; at this time, special direction and order was sent thither, " that he should,
with all severity, and expedition, proceed against those conspirators," (as they called them ;) and thereupon, by a sentence and judgment of a council of war, alderman Yeomans,
who had been high sheriff of the city, and of great reputation in it, and George Bouchier, another citizen of principal
account, were (against all interposition his majesty could
make) both hanged ; and all other imaginary acts done, to
let all the world see that there was no way to peace but by
the sword.

There fell out now an accident at London, which gave
great advantage to them in the fierce prosecution of the war,
a discovery of a plot, which produced a public thanksgiving
to God for their deliverance, a wonderful animosity against
the king, and a covenant, and union among themselves, and
throughout the city a prejudice to all moderate men, who
promoted an accommodation, and a brand upon all overtures
of accommodation and peace as stratagems upon the city and
the parliament.   Of this plot, there being never such a formed relation made by those who made great use of it, that
men can collect what the design was, or that it was laid
with any probable circumstances, by which a success might
be expected, I shall briefly and faithfully set down all that I
know, have heard, or can reasonably conjecture to be in it ;
and it was thought by many, and averred by others who I

87*

believe did not think so, " that I knew as much of it as most men."

There was of the house of commons, one Mr. Waller, a gentleman of a very good fortune and estate, and of admirable parts, and faculties of wit and eloquence, and of an intimate conversation and familiarity with those who had that reputation. He had, from the beginning of the parliament, been looked upon by all men, as a person of very entire affections to the king's service, and to the established government of church and state ; and, by having no manner of relation to the court, had the more credit and interest to promote the rights of it. When the ruptures grew so great between the king and the two houses, that very many of the members withdrew from those councils, he, among the rest, with equal dislike absented himself; but at the time the standard was set up, having intimacy and friendship with some persons now of nearness about the king, with the king's approbation, he returned again to London ; where he spake, upon all occasions, with great sharpness and freedom ; which (now there were so few there that used it, and there was no danger of being overvoted) was not restrained ; and therefore used as an argument against those, who were gone upon pretence " that they were not suffered to declare their opinion freely in the house; which could not be believed, when all men knew, what liberty Mr. Waller took, and spake every day with impunity, against the sense and proceedings of the house." This won him a great reputation with all people who wished well to the king ; and he was looked upon as the boldest champion the crown had in both houses ; so that such lords, and commons, who really desired to prevent the ruin of the kingdom, willingly complied in a great familiarity with him, as a man resolute in their ends, and best able to promote them. And it may be they believed his reputation at court so good, that he would be no ill evidence there, of other men's zeal and affection ; and so all men spake their minds freely to him, both of the general distemper, and of the passions and ambition of particular persons: all men knowing him to be of too good a fortune, and too wary a nature, to engage himself in designs of danger or hazard.

Mr. Waller had a brother in law, one Mr. Tomkins, who had married his sister, and was clerk of the queen's council, of very good fame for honesty and ability. This gentleman had good interest and reputation in the city, and conversed much with those who disliked the proceedings of the parliament, and wished to live under the same government they were born ; and from those citizens received information of the temper of the people, upon accidents, in the public affairs. And Mr. Waller and he, with that confidence that uses to be between brethren of the same good affections, frequently imparted their observations and opinions to each other ; the one relating, how many in both houses inclined to peace ; and the other making the same judgment upon the correspondence he had, and intelligence he received from the most substantial men of London ; and both of them again communicated what one received from the other, to the company he used to converse with ; Mr. Waller imparting the wishes and power of the well affected party in the city, to the lords and gentlemen whom he knew to be of the same mind ; and Mr. Tomkins acquainting those he durst trust of the city, that such and such lords and gentlemen, who were of special note, were weary of the distractions, and would heartily and confidently contribute to such an honourable and honest peace, as all men knew would be most acceptable to the king. And from hence they came reasonably to a conclusion, that if some means were found out to raise a confidence in those who wished well, that they should not be oppressed by the extravagant power of the desperate party ; but that if they would so far assist one another, as to declare their opinions to be the same, they should be able to prevent or suppress those tumults, which seemed to countenance the distractions ; and the houses would be induced to terms of moderation.

In this time the lord Conway, being returned from Ireland, incensed against the Scots, and discontented with the parliament here, finding Mr. Waller in good esteem with the earl of Northumberland, and of great friendship with the earl of Portland, he entered into the same familiarity ; and, being more of a soldier, in the discourses administered questions, and considerations, necessary to be understood by men that either meant to use force, or to resist it ;[1] and wished "that they who had interest and acquaintance in the city would endeavour by a mutual correspondence to inform themselves of the distinct affections of their neighbours, that, upon any exigent, men might foresee whom they might trust;" and these discourses being again derived by Mr. Waller to Mr. Tomkins, he, upon occasion, and conference with his companions, insisted on the same arguments ; and they again conversing with their friends and acquaintance, (for of all this business, there were not above three who ever spoke together,) agreed, "that some well affected persons, in every parish and ward about London, should make a list of all the inhabitants; and thereupon to make a reasonable guess of their several affections," (which at that time was no hard thing for observing men to do,) and thence a computation of the strength and power of that party, which was notoriously violent against any accommodation.

I am persuaded the utmost project in this design was (I speak not what particular men might intend, or wish upon their own fancies) to beget such a combination among the party well affected, that they would refuse to conform to those ordinances of the twentieth part, and other taxes for the support of the war; and thereby, or by joint petitioning for peace, and discountenancing the other who petitioned against it, to prevail with the parliament to incline to a determination of the war. And it may be, some men might think of making advantage of any casual commotion, or preventing any mischief by it ;[2] and thereupon that inquiry where the magazines lay, and discourse of wearing some distinguishing tokens, had been rather mentioned, than pro-

---

[1] From these words it appears, that this was as much a plot against the parliament at Westminster, in which force was to be employed, as any plot could be. It is therefore surprising that the noble historian could say, so few lines after, that the whole design was only to oppose the petitioners against peace, by petitioning the parliament for it.—W.

[2] This is a miserable way of evading the evidence, that the plotters intended force.—W.

posed. For it is certain, very many who were conscious to
themselves of loyal purposes to the king, and of hearty dislike of the parliament's proceedings, and observed the violent, revengeful, and ruinating prosecution of all men, by
those of the engaged party, were not without sad apprehensions that, upon some jealousy, and quarrel picked, even a
general massacre might be attempted of all the king's friends;
and thereupon, in several discourses, might touch upon such
expedients, as might in those seasons be most beneficial to
their safety. But that there was ever any formed design,
either of letting in the king's army into London, which was
most impossible to be contrived, or of raising an army there,
and surprising the parliament, or any one person of it, or of
using any violence in or upon the city, I could never yet
see cause to believe ; and if there had, they would have
published such a relation of it,' after Mr. Waller had confessed to them all he knew, had heard, or fancied to himself, as might have constituted some reasonable understanding of it ; and not contented themselves with making conclusions from questions that had been asked, and answers
made, by persons unknown, and forcing expressions used by
one, to relate to actions of another, between whom there
had been never the least acquaintance or correspondence;
and joining what was said at London to somewhat done at
Oxford, at another time, and to another purpose: for, before I finish this discourse, it will be necessary to speak of
another action, which, how distinct soever from this that is
related, was woven together to make one plot.

From the king's coming to Oxford, many citizens of good
quality, who were prosecuted, or jealously looked upon in
London, had resorted to the king, and hoping, if the winter
produced not a peace, that the summer would carry the king
before that city with an army, they had entertained some
discourse " of raising, upon their own stocks of money and
credit, some regiments of foot and horse, and joining with

' If the parliament had only *published* the circumstances, which the
noble historian here delivers as fact, it would have been sufficient to
have convinced all impartial men that the plotters intended force.—W.

some gentlemen of Kent, who were likewise inclined to such
an undertaking." Among these was sir Nicholas Crisp, a
citizen of good wealth, great trade, and an active spirited
man, who had been lately prosecuted with great severity by
the house of commons; and had thereupon fled from London, for appearing too great a stickler in a petition for peace
in the city. This gentleman industriously preserved a correspondence still there, by which he gave the king often
very useful intelligence, and assured him " of a very considerable party, which would appear there for him, whenever his own power should be so near, as to give them any
countenance." In the end, whether invited by his corres-
pondents there, or trusting his own sprightly inclinations and
resolutions too much, and concluding that all, who were
equally honest, would be equally bold, he desired his majesty, " to grant a commission to such persons, whom he
would nominate, of the city of London, under the great seal
of England, in the nature of a commission of array, by virtue
whereof, when the season should come, his party there
would appear in discipline and order; and that this was desired by those, who best knew what countenance and authority was requisite; and being trusted to them would not
be executed at all, or else at such a time as his majesty
should receive ample fruit by it; provided it were done with
secrecy, equal to the hazard they should run who were employed in it."

The king had no exception to it but " the improbability
that it could do good, and that was the less because the failing could do no hurt but to the undertakers." The promo-
ter was a very popular man in the city, where he had been
a commander of the trained bands, till the ordinance of the
militia removed him; which rather improved, than lessened,
his credit; and he was very confident, it would produce a
notable advantage to the king : however, they desired it who
were there, and would not appear without it; and therefore
the king consented to it; referring the nomination of all persons to be named in the commission to him; who, he verily
believed, had proceeded by the instruction and advice of
those who were nearest the concernment; and for the se-

crecy of it, the king referred the preparing and despatch of
the commission to sir Nicholas Crisp himself, who should
acquaint no more with it than he found requisite; so, without the privity or advice of any counsellor, or minister of
state, he procured such a commission as he desired (being
no other than the commission of array in English) to be
signed by the king, and sealed with the great seal.

This being done, and remaining still in his custody, the
lady Aubigney, by a pass, and with the consent of the houses,
came to Oxford to transact the affairs of her own fortune
with the king upon the death of her husband, who was killed
at Edge-hill; and she having in few days despatched her
business there, and being ready to return, sir Nicholas Crisp
came to the king, and besought him, " to desire that lady"
(who had a pass, and so could promise herself safety in her
journey) " to carry a small box" (in which that commission
should be) " with her, and to keep it in her own custody,
until a gentleman should call to her ladyship for it, by such
a token : that token," he said, " he could send to one of the
persons trusted, who should keep it by him till the opportunity came, in which it might be executed."   The king accordingly wished the lady Aubigney to carry it with great
care and secrecy; telling her, " it much concerned his majesty's service;" and to deliver it in such manner, and upon
such assurance, as is before mentioned : which she did, and,
within few days after her return to London, delivered it to
a person who was appointed to call for it.   How this commission was discovered, I could never learn ;[1] for though
Mr. Waller had the honour to be admitted often to that lady,
and was believed by her to be a gentleman of most entire
affections to the king's service, and consequently might be
fitly trusted with what she knew, yet her ladyship herself,
not knowing what it was she carried, could not inform any
body else.

[1] What more easy? Would not Mr. Tomkins's well disposed citizens naturally confer with sir Nicholas Crisp's? And would this commission remain an uncommunicable secret between them? But the
historian goes upon what he would have his reader believe, that Tomkins and Crisp knew nothing of one another's plot.---W.

But about this time, a servant of Mr. Tomkins, who had often cursorily overheard his master and Mr. Waller discourse of the argument we are now upon, placed himself behind a hanging, at a time they were together ; and there, whilst either of them discoursed the language and opinion of the company they kept, overheard enough to make him believe his information, and discovery, would make him welcome to those whom he thought concerned ; and so went to Mr. Pym, and acquainted him with all he had heard, or probably imagined. The time when Mr. Pym was made acquainted with it is not known ; but the circumstances of the publishing it were such, as filled all men with apprehensions. It was on Wednesday the thirty-first of May, their solemn fast-day, when, being all at their sermon, in St. Margaret's church in Westminster, according to their custom, a letter or message is brought privately to Mr. Pym ; who, thereupon, with some of the most active members, rise from their seats ; and, after a little whispering together, remove out of the church : this could not but exceedingly affect those who stayed behind ; immediately they sent guards to all the prisons, as Lambeth-house, Ely-house, and such places, where their malignants were in custody, with directions " to search the prisoners ;" and some other places which they thought fit should be suspected. After the sermons were ended, the houses met ; and were only told, " that letters were intercepted going to the king and the court at Oxford, that expressed some notable conspiracy in hand, to deliver up the parliament and the city into the hands of the cavaliers ; and that the time for the execution of it drew very near." Hereupon a committee was appointed " to examine all persons they thought fit ; and to apprehend some nominated at that time." And the same night, this committee apprehended Mr. Waller and Mr. Tomkins ; and, the next day, such others as they thought fit.

Mr. Waller was so confounded with fear and apprehension, that he confessed whatever he had said, heard, thought, or seen ; all that he knew of himself, and all that he suspected of others ; without concealing any person of what degree or quality soever, or any discourse that he had ever, upon any occasion, entertained with them : what such and such ladies of great honour, to whom, upon the credit of his great parts, and very good reputation, he had been admitted, had spoke to him in their chambers of the proceedings of the houses ; and how they had encouraged him to oppose them ; what correspondence and intercourse they had with some ministers of state at Oxford ; and how they derived all intelligence thither.   He informed them, " that the earl of Portland and the lord Conway had been particular in all the agitations which had been with the citizens ; and had given frequent advice and directions how they should demean themselves ; and that the earl of Northumberland had expressed very good wishes to any attempt, that might give a stop to the violent actions and proceedings of the houses, and produce a good understanding with the king."

When the committee were thus furnished, they took the examinations of Mr. Tomkins, and such other as they thought necessary, and having at the same time, by some other means, discovered (or concealed it till this time) that commission which is before discoursed of, and gotten the very original into their hands, they kneaded both into one plot and conspiracy ;' and, acquainting the houses with so much as they thought yet seasonable to publish, they declared, (without naming any lords, or other persons, to be interested in the design, save those only who were imprisoned ; among whom the lady Aubigney was one : and without communicating any of the examinations, which, they pretended, were not to be common till the conspirators were brought to trial,) " that the original of this conspiracy was from the late London petition for peace," which was spoken of about Christmas last in the book precedent ; " and that, under pretence of peace and moderation, a party was to be formed, which should be able to suppress all opponents, and to awe

¹ One would wonder the noble historian should be so solicitous to discredit this plot ; since this was fair war, and only counterplotting the plotters. But the king's reputation with the public was so bad, that plotting against a parliament in arms against him, was understood to be an indication that he wanted to resume his exercise of arbitrary power.---W.

the parliament : that, to this purpose, some of those who were the principal movers and fomenters of that petition, did continue, in the nature of a committee, still to carry on the design : that they held intelligence in both armies, court, and parliament ; took a general survey of the numbers and affections of the several inhabitants throughout the wards and parishes of the city, and places adjacent ; and distinguished all under the titles of men affected, or averse to the king ; or indifferent, and neutral persons, carried only by the success and power of the prevailers : that they were well instructed in the number and inclinations of the trained bands of London ; the places where the magazines were kept ; where the commanders for the parliament dwelt ; had thought of places for rendezvous, and retreat, upon any occasion, and of colours, and marks of distinction between the different parties.

" That Mr. Waller and Mr. Tomkins were the principal persons employed, and trusted to give advertisement to, and correspond with, the king's ministers at Oxford ; and receive advertisements and commands from thence, for the completing the work ; that they two held constant intelligence and intercourse with the lord Falkland, then principal secretary to the king ; and that from him they received the signification of the king's pleasure ; and that those directions, counsels, and encouragements had been principally sent by those messengers which had been employed by his majesty to the parliament, under the pretence of peace ; and especially by Mr. Hambden ; who came with the last message, and was a cousin-german to Mr. Waller. That the lady Aubigney, who had been lately at Oxford, had brought thence a commission to them from the king, by force of arms to destroy, kill, and slay the forces, raised by the parliament and their adherents, as traitors and rebels ; and that they had lately sent a message to Oxford by one Hassel, a servant of the king's, to acquaint the lord Falkland, that the design was come to good perfection ; unto which, answer was returned, that they should hasten it with all speed :

" That the particulars of the design appeared to be : 1. To seize into their custody the king's children. 2. To seize several members of both houses, the lord mayor, and committee of the militia, under pretence of bringing them to a legal trial.   3. To seize upon the outworks, forts, Tower of London, magazines, gates, and other places of importance in the city.   4. To let in the king's forces to surprise the city, and to destroy all those who should oppose them by authority of the parliament.   5. By force of arms to resist all payments imposed by authority of parliament, raised for the support of the armies employed for their just defence, &c. to suspend, if not alter, the whole government of the city, and, with assistance of the king's force, to awe and master the parliament."[1]

When both houses were awakened, and startled with this report, the first thing agreed on was, " a day of thanksgiving to God for this wonderful delivery ;" which shut out any future doubts, and disquisitions, whether there had been any such delivery; and, consequently, whether their plot was in truth, or had been so framed.   Then it was said, " that as the design was the most desperate, so the carriage was the most subtle, and among persons of reputation, and not suspected; and that there was reason to suspect, many members of both houses were privy to it; and therefore there ought to be all possible care taken to make the discovery perfect, and to unite themselves for the public defence : that if any part were left undiscovered, it might prove fatal to the commonwealth."   This finding a full consent, it was propounded, " that a protestation might be drawn up, by which every member of the two houses might purge himself from any guilt of, or privity in, that conspiracy; and likewise oblige himself to resist and oppose any such combination."   They who were under the character of moderate men, and usually advanced all motions of peace and accommodation, durst not oppose the expedient, lest they should be concluded guilty; most of them having had familiarity with Mr. Waller, and, no doubt, upon sundry occasions,

---

[1] It was a thing surely to be wished by all who loved the established constitution, that this faction of a parliament should be destroyed; but then they would wish it to be done by a lover of public liberty, which few at that time thought the king was.—W.

spoken with that freedom to him, as might very well incur a severe interpretation, if, upon this occasion, what they had said should be scanned. And so, before the rising, there was framed by the house of commons, a vow and covenant to be taken by the members of both houses, and afterwards by the city, and their army; for their jealousy was now spread over all their own quarters; which covenant, for the rareness of it both in title and style, I think necessary here to insert in the very terms; which were these:

A sacred vow[1] and covenant, taken by the lords and commons assembled in parliament, upon the discovery of the late horrid and treacherous design, for the destruction of this parliament and the kingdom:

"Whereas there hath been, and now is, in this kingdom, a popish and traitorous plot for the subversion of the true protestant reformed religion,[2] and the liberty of the subject; and, in pursuance thereof, a popish army hath been raised, and is now on foot in divers parts of this kingdom; and whereas there hath been a treacherous and horrid design, lately discovered by the great blessing and especial providence of God, of divers persons, to join themselves with the armies raised by the king, and to destroy the forces raised by the lords and commons in parliament, to surprise the cities of London and Westminster, with the suburbs; by arms to force the parliament; and finding by constant experience, that many ways of force, and treachery, are continually attempted, to bring to utter ruin and destruction the parliament and kingdom; and that which is dearest, the true protestant religion: and that, for the preventing and withstanding the same, it is fit, that all, who are true hearted, and lovers of their country, should bind themselves each to other in a sacred vow and covenant:

"I *A. B.* in humility, and reverence of the Divine Majesty, declare my sorrow for my own sins, and the sins of

[1] *In the handwriting of Lord Clarendon's amanuensis.*

[2] Just such another farce as the king's last message for peace.—W.

this nation, which have deserved the calamities and judgments that now lie upon it ; and my true intention is, by God's grace, to endeavour the amendment of my own ways : and I do further, in the presence of Almighty God, declare, vow, and covenant, that, in order to the security and preservation of the true reformed protestant religion, and liberty of the subject, I will not consent to the laying down of arms, so long as the papists, now in open war against the parliament, shall by force of arms be protected from the justice thereof : and that I do abhor and detest the said wicked and treacherous design, lately discovered : and that I never gave, nor will give, my assent to the execution thereof, but will, according to my power, and vocation, oppose and resist the same, and all other of the like nature. And in case any other like design shall hereafter come to my knowledge, I will make such timely discovery, as I shall conceive may best conduce to the preventing thereof. And whereas I do in my conscience believe, that the forces, raised by the two houses of parliament, are raised and continued for their just defence, and for the defence of the true protestant religion, and liberty of the subject, against the forces raised by the king; that I will, according to my power, and vocation, assist the forces raised and continued, by both houses of parliament, against the forces raised by the king without their consent : and will likewise assist all other persons that shall take this oath, in what they shall do in pursuance thereof; and will not directly, or indirectly, adhere unto, nor shall willingly assist the forces raised by the king, without the consent of both houses. And this vow, and covenant, I make in the presence of Almighty God, the Searcher of all hearts, with a true intention to perform the same, as I shall answer at the great day, when the secrets of all hearts shall be disclosed."

Though many were much startled at this covenant, and took time to consider of it, there being in the preamble, and positive part, much which very few believed, and in the promissory part a more direct denouncing war against the king, than had been in plain terms before avowed by them, and an absolute protestation against peace, till the king were at their mercy; yet the fear of being concluded guilty of the plot, made them swallow all the rest; and the example of one prevailing with many, there was not a member of either house that took it not : and being thus fettered and entangled themselves, they sent their committee into the city, to acquaint them with their " happy discovery, and how miraculously God had preserved them, and to engage them in the same sacred vow, and covenant;" which was readily submitted to ; and, by the industry of their clergy,' sooner than can be imagined, taken throughout that people. Then it was, with equal diligence and solemnity, transmitted to the army, that their fears of inconvenience from thence might be likewise purged; and thence it grew the mark of distinction, to know their friends and enemies by ; and whosoever refused to take that covenant, needed no other charge to be concluded, and prosecuted, as the highest malignant.

Being this way secure from any future clamours for peace, they proceeded to try Mr. Tomkins ; Mr. Chaloner, a citizen of good wealth and credit, and most intimate with Tomkins ; Mr. Hambden, who brought the last message from the king; one Hassel, a messenger of the king's, who passed often between London and Oxford, and sometimes carried letters and messages to the lord Falkland ; and some citizens, whose names were in the commission sent from Oxford ; by a council of war ; by whom Mr. Tomkins and Mr. Chaloner were condemned to be hanged ; and were both, with all circumstances of severity and cruelty, executed : the one on a gibbet, by his own house in Holborn ; where he had long lived with singular estimation ; and the other, by his house in Cornhill, near the Old Exchange. Hassel the messenger saved them further trouble, and died in prison the night before his trial : and there being no evidence against Mr. Hambden, but what Mr. Waller himself gave, they gave no judgment against him, but kept him long after in prison, till he died : neither proceeded

---

' There was without doubt many a lay rogue amongst these patrons of liberty. But none of them came near their clergy in malignity, corruption, hypocrisy, and impiety.--W.

they capitally against those citizens whose names were in the commission, it not appearing that their names were used with their consent and privity ; though the brand of being malignants served the turn for their undoing ; for all their estates were seized, as theirs were who had been executed.

And there is nothing clearer than that the commission sent from Oxford by the lady Aubigney, had not any relation to the discourses passed between Mr. Waller, Tomkins, and those citizens ; or that they, who knew of one, had not any privity with the other : which if they had had, and intended such an insurrection, as was alleged, Mr. Waller, and Mr. Tomkins, or some one of those lords who were supposed to combine with them, would have been in the commission. Or if the king's ministers had been engaged in the consultation, and hoped to have raised a party which should suddenly seize upon the city and the parliament, they would never have thought a commission granted to some gentlemen at Oxford, (for the major part of the commissioners were there,) and a few unknown private citizens, would have served for that work. I am very confident, and I have very much reason for that confidence, that there was no more known, or thought of at Oxford, concerning the matter of the commission, than I have before set forth ; nor of the other, than that Mr. Tomkins sometimes writ to the lord Falkland, (for Mr. Waller, out of the cautiousness of his own nature, never writ word,) and by messengers signified to him, " that the number of those who desired peace, and abhorred the proceedings of the houses, was very considerable ; and that they resolved, by refusing to contribute to the war, and to submit to their ordinances, to declare and manifest themselves in that manner, that the violent party in the city should not have credit enough to hinder any accommodation." And the lord Falkland always returned answer, " that they should expedite those expedients, as soon as might be, for that delays made the war more difficult to be restrained." And if I could find evidence, or reason, to induce me to believe, that there was any further design in the thing itself, or that the king gave further countenance to it, I should not at all conceal it. No man imagining, that if the king could have entertained any probable hope of reducing London,[1] which was the fomenter, supporter, and indeed the life of the war ; or could have found any expedient, from whence he could reasonably propose to dissolve, scatter, and disperse those who, under the name of a parliament, had kindled a war against him, but he would have given his utmost assistance and countenance thereunto, either by public force, or private contrivance.

There were very great endeavours used, to have proceeded with equal severity against the earl of Portland, and the lord Conway, (for the accusation of the earl of Northumberland, it was proceeded tenderly in ; for though the violent party was heartily incensed against him, as a man weary of them, yet his reputation was still very great,) who were both close prisoners ; and, to that purpose, their lordships and Mr. Waller were confronted before the committee ; where they as peremptorily denying, as he charging them, and there being no other witness but he against them, the prosecution was rather let alone than declined, till after a long restraint they procured enlargement upon bail.   Mr. Waller himself, (though confessedly the most guilty ; and by his unhappy demeanour, in this time of his affliction, he had raised as many enemies as he had formerly friends, and almost the same,) after he had, with incredible dissimulation, acted such a remorse of conscience, as his trial was put off out of Christian compassion, till he might recover his understanding, (and that was not, till the heat and fury of the prosecutors was reasonably abated with the sacrifices they had made,) and, by drawing visitants to himself, of the most powerful ministers of all factions, had, by his liberality, and penitence, his *preces*, and his *lacrymæ*, his receiving vulgar and vile sayings from them with humility and reverence, as clearer convictions and informations than in his life he had

---

[1] This is said with a great deal of good sense. Tampering with the army in the north, when the parliament was beginning their redress of grievances, was to be condemned ; but now the king and parliament were formed into two parties, and both agreed to appeal to the sword, the king's attempt to disperse the parliament in this manner was justifiable policy.---W.

ever had ; and distributing great sums to them for their
prayers and ghostly counsel ; so satisfied them, that they
satisfied others ; was brought, at his suit, to the house of
commons' bar ; where (being a man in truth very powerful
in language; and who, by what he spoke, and in the manner
of speaking it, exceedingly captivated the good-will and be-
nevolence of his hearers ; which is the highest part of an
orator) with such flattery, as was most exactly calculated to
that meridian, with such a submission, as their vulgar pride
took delight in, and such dejection of mind, and spirit, as was
like to cozen the major part, and be thought serious ; he laid
before them " their own danger and concernment, if they
should suffer one of their own body, how unworthy and
monstrous soever, to be tried by the soldiers, who might
thereby grow to that power hereafter, that they would both
try those they would not be willing should be tried, and for
things, which they would account no crimes ; the inconvenience and insupportable mischief whereof all wise common-
wealths had foreseen, and prevented, by exempting their
own members from all judgments but their own :" he prevailed, not to be tried by a council of war ; and thereby
preserved his dear-bought life ; so that, in truth, he does as
much owe the keeping his head to that oration, as Cataline
did the loss of his to those of Tully : and by having done ill
very well, he, by degrees, drew that respect to his parts,
which always carries some compassion to the person, that he
got them to compound for his transgression, and to accept of
ten thousand pounds (which their affairs wanted) for his
liberty ; and so he had leave to recollect himself in another
country (for his liberty was to be in banishment) how
miserable he had made himself, to have leave to live out of
his own. And there cannot be a greater evidence of the inestimable value of his parts, than that he lived, after this, in
the good affection and esteem of many, the pity of most, and
the reproach and scorn of none.

These high proceedings at London, and in the houses,
were not seconded with any notable success abroad ; but it
appeared plainly, by the slow coming in of monies, and more
slow coming in of men, that the hearts of the people were

88*

generally more devoted to peace, than to the continuance of
those distractions ; and the earl of Essex found that he paid
dear for the time he had gotten in the spring, that little lying
in the field during the siege at Reading having so much
weakened his army, and his soldiers having contracted by it
so many diseases and such a general sickness, that very many
of them died ; and with all the supplies of money and recruits of men he could get, he was not, in near six weeks,
able to remove from Reading ; by which many men concluded,[1] which could not be reasonably foreseen, that if Reading had held out many days longer, he would have been
compelled to raise his siege; and that was the reason the
earl gave for granting so good conditions : for if he could
have stayed longer before it, he well knew, they must have
yielded on worse terms ; neither feared he the king would be
able to relieve it.   In the end, there being no other way to
quiet the city of London, he marched towards Oxford ; but,
in truth, rather to secure Buckinghamshire, which was now
infested by the king's horse, than to disquiet that place.
And, to that purpose, he fixed his head quarter at Thame,
ten miles from Oxford, and upon the very edge of the other
county.   At the same time when the earl of Essex began
his march from Reading, colonel Urry, a Scotchman, who
had served in that army from the beginning with great reputation, (as he was an excellent commander of horse,) till the
difference that is before spoken of between the English and
Scotch officers ; after which he laid down his commission ;
though, out of respect to the earl of Essex, he stayed some
time after with him as a volunteer ; and now came to the
king to Oxford, having before given notice to the earl of
Brainford that he meant to do so.   He came no sooner thither, than, to give proof that he brought his whole heart with
him, he proposed to prince Rupert to wait on him, to visit
the enemy's quarters, and being well acquainted with their
manner of lying and keeping their guards, undertook to be
his guide to a quarter where they were least expected : and

---

[1] The recording of these superstitions of the times, except where
they had an influence on the public affairs, is unworthy so great an
historian.---W.

the prince willingly consenting to the proposition, drew out a strong party of one thousand horse and dragoons, which he commanded himself, and marched with colonel Urry to a town four or five miles beyond the head quarter, where were a regiment of horse and a regiment of dragoons, and about daybreak fell upon them; and with little resistance, and no loss of his own men, he killed and took the whole party, except some few, who hid themselves in holes, or escaped by dark and untrodden paths. From thence, on his way back, according to purpose, he fell upon another village, where some horse and a regiment of foot were quartered; where he had the same success, and killed and took and dispersed them all. So he having fortunately performed all he hoped, his highness hastened his retreat as fast as he could to Oxford; having appointed a regiment of foot to attend him at a pass in the way for his security. But the alarum had passed through all the enemy's quarters; so that before the prince could reach the pass where his foot expected him, he found the enemy's whole army was drawn out, and a strong party of their horse, almost equal to his own in number, so hard pressed him, that, being then to enter a lane, they would disorder his rear before he could join with his foot, which were a mile before. He had very little time to deliberate, being even at the entrance into the lane. If he could have hoped to have retired in safety, he had no reason to venture to fight with a fresh party, excellently armed and in number equal, his own being harassed and tired with near twenty miles' march, and laden with spoil and prisoners, scarce a soldier without a led horse: but the necessity obliged him to stay; and after a short consideration of the manner of doing it, directing as small a convoy as was possible to guard the prisoners, and to hasten with all the unnecessary baggage and led horses, he resolved to keep the ground he had in the plain field, and after as short a pause, to charge the party that advanced, lest the body might come up to them. And they came on amain, leaving it only in his election, by meeting them, to have the reputation of charging them, or, by standing still, to be charged by them. Hereupon they were quickly engaged in a sharp encounter,

the best, fiercest, and longest maintained that hath been by
the horse during the war : for the party of the parliament
consisted not of the bare regiments and troops which usually
marched together, but of prime gentlemen and officers of all
their regiments, horse and foot, who, being met at the head
quarter upon the alarum, and conceiving it easy to get between prince Rupert and Oxford, and not having their own
charges ready to move, joined themselves as volunteers to
those who were ready, till their own regiments should come
up; and so the first ranks of horse consisting of such men,
the conflict was maintained some time with equal confidence.
In the end, many falling and being hurt on both sides, the
prince prevailed, the rebels being totally routed, and pursued,
till the gross of the army was discovered, and then his highness, with the new prisoners he had taken, retired orderly
to the pass where his foot and former purchase expected
him ; and thence sending colonel Urry to acquaint the king
with the success, who knighted the messenger for his good
service, returned, with near two hundred prisoners, and
seven cornets of horse, and four ensigns of foot, to Oxford.
On the king's part in this action were lost, besides few common men, no officers of note, but some hurt : on the enemy's side, many of the best officers, more than in any battle
they fought, and amongst them (which made the news of the
rest less inquired after by the one, and less lamented by the
other) colonel Hambden, who was shot into the shoulder
with a brace of pistol bullets, of which wound, with very
sharp pain, he died within ten days, to as great a consternation of all that party, as if the whole army had been defeated and cut off.

In the beginning of the war, the army in Scotland having
been lately disbanded, many officers of that nation, who had
served in Germany and in France, betook themselves to the
service of the parliament ; whereof many were men of good
conduct and courage ; though there were more as bad as the
cause in which they engaged. Of the former sort colonel
Urry was a man of name and reputation, and an excellent
officer of horse, and had commanded those horse at Edge-hill
under Balfour, which had preserved their army there ; and

finding himself afterwards not so well regarded, as, he thought, he had deserved, as it was no easy thing to value that people at the rate they did set upon themselves; and being without any other affection for their service, than their pay inclined him to, he resolved to quit them, and to go to the king; in order to which, he had kept some correspondence with the earl of Brainford, the king's general; under whose command he had formerly served in Germany. Whilst the earl of Essex remained at Thame, and his army quartered thereabout, Urry came to Oxford, in the equipage that became a colonel of horse who had received good pay; and the very next day after he came, having been very graciously received by the king, to give proof that he brought his whole heart with him, he went to prince Rupert, acquainted him where the parliament horse lay, and how loose they were in their quarters; and, to give a testimony of his fidelity to the king, he desired to march a volunteer with a good party, to make an attempt upon the enemy; and the prince assigning a strong party for the service, he accompanied, and conducted them out of the common road, till they came to a town; where a regiment of the parliament's horse was quartered; which they beat up, and killed or took most of the officers and soldiers; and then fell upon those other quarters, by which they had passed before, with the like success; so he returned to Oxford with many prisoners, and with notable damage to the enemy.

And as soon as he returned, he made another proposition to the prince for the attacking the quarters near Thame; through which he had passed, when he came to Oxford, and so was well acquainted with the posture in which they were; and assured the prince, " that, if he went about it time enough, before there should be any alteration in their quarters, which he believed the general would quickly make, the enterprise would be worthy of it." And the prince was so well satisfied with what he had already done, that he resolved to conduct the next adventure himself, which he did very fortunately. They went out of the ports of Oxford in the evening upon a Saturday, and marched beyond all the quarters as far as Wickham, and fell in there at the further end of the town towards London, from whence they expected no enemy, and so kept no guards there. A regiment of horse, and of foot, were lodged there ; which were cut off, or taken prisoners; and all the horses and a good booty brought away. And from thence they marched backward to another quarter, within less than two miles of the general's own quarters; where his men lodged with the same security they had done at Wickham, not expecting any enemy that way ; and so met with the same fate the others had done; and were all killed, or made prisoners. And having performed at least as much as they had proposed to do, and being laden with prisoners and booty, and the sun being now rising, the prince thought it time to retire to Oxford, and so gave orders to march accordingly with all convenient speed, till they came to a bridge which was yet two miles from them, where he had appointed a guard to attend, to favour their retreat.

But the alarm had been brought to the earl of Essex from all the quarters, who quickly gathered those troops together, which were nearest ; and directed those to follow the prince, and to entertain him in skirmishes, till himself should come up with the foot, and some other troops ; which he made all possible haste to do. So that when the prince had almost passed a fair plain, or field, called Chalgrave field, from whence he was to enter a lane, which continued to the bridge ; the enemy's horse were discovered marching after them with speed ; and as they might easily overtake them in the lane, so they must as easily have put them into great disorder. Therefore the prince resolved to expect, and stand them upon the open field, though his horse were all tired, and the sun was grown very hot, it being about eight of the clock in the morning in May. And so he directed, " that the guard of the prisoners should make what haste they could to the bridge, but that all the rest should return;" for some were entered the lane : and so he placed himself and his troops, as he thought fit, in that field to receive the enemy ; which made more haste, and with less order than they should have done ; and being more in number than the prince, and consisting of many of the principal officers, who, having been present with the earl of Essex when the alarm came, stayed not for their own troops, but joined with those who were ready in the pursuit, as they thought, of a flying enemy, or such as would easily be arrested in their hasty retreat; and, having now overtaken them, meant to take revenge themselves for the damage they had received that night, and morning, before the general could come up to have a share in the victory, though his troops were even in view. But the prince entertained them so roughly, that though their fronts charged very bravely and obstinately, consisting of many of their best officers, of which many of the chiefest falling, the rest shewed less vigour, and in a short time they broke, and fled, and were pursued till they came near the earl of Essex's body; which being at near a mile's distance, and making a stand to receive their flying troops, and to be informed of their disaster, the prince with his troops hastened his retreat, and passed the lane, and came safe to the bridge before any of the earl's forces came up; who found it then to no purpose to go further, there being a good guard of foot, which had likewise lined both sides of the hedges a good way in the lane. And so the prince, about noon, or shortly after, entered Oxford, with near two hundred prisoners, seven cornets of horse, and four ensigns of foot, with most of the men he carried from thence; some few excepted, who had been killed in the action, whereof some were of name.

And the prince presented colonel Urry to the king with a great testimony of the courage he had shewed in the action, as well as of his counsel and conduct in the whole; which was indeed very dexterous, and could have been performed by no man, who had not been very conversant with the nature and humour of those he destroyed. Upon which, the king honored him with knighthood, and a regiment of horse as soon as it could be raised; and every body magnified and extolled him, as they usually do a man who hath good luck, and the more, because he was a Scotchman, and professed a repentance for having been in rebellion against the king. And he deserves this testimony, and vindication to be given him, against the calumnies which were raised against him, " as if he had broken his trust, and deserted

the service of the parliament, and betrayed them to the king,"
which is not true.   He had owned and published his discontents long before, and demanded redress and justice in some
particulars from the parliament, in which the earl of Essex
thought he had reason ; and wished he might receive satisfaction.   But the man was in his nature proud and imperious ; and had raised many enemies; and was besides of licence, and committed many disorders of that kind.   And had
little other virtue than being a very good officer in the field ;
regular and vigilant in marching, and in his quarters ; which
the parliament thought other men would attain to, who had
fewer vices ; and therefore granted nothing that he had desired ; upon which he declared, " he would serve them no
longer ;" and delivered up his commission to the earl of Essex; and being then pressed to promise, that he would not
serve the king, he positively refused to give any such engagement ; and after he had stayed in London about a month,
and had received encouragement from some friends in Oxford, he came thither in the manner set down before.

The prince's success in this last march was very seasonable, and raised the spirits at Oxford very much, and for some
time allayed the jealousies and animosities, which too often
broke out in several factions to the disquiet of the king.   It
was visibly great in the number of the prisoners ; whereof
many were of condition, and the names of many officers were
known, who were left dead upon the field, as colonel Gun-
ter, who was looked upon as the best officer of horse they
had, and a man of known malice to the government of the
church ; which had drawn some severe censure upon him
before the troubles, and for which he had still meditated revenge.   And one of the prisoners who had been taken in
the action said, " that he was confident Mr. Hambden was
hurt, for he saw him ride off the field before the action was
done, which he never used to do, and with his head hanging down, and resting his hands upon the neck of his horse ;"
by which he concluded he was hurt.   But the news the
next day made the victory much more important than it was
thought to have been.   There was full information brought
of the great loss the enemy had sustained in their quarters,

by which three or four regiments were utterly broken and lost : the names of many officers, of the best account, were known, who were either killed upon the place, or so hurt as there remained little hope of their recovery. Of which Mr. Hambden was one ; who would not stay that morning till his own regiment came up, but put himself a volunteer in the head of those troops who were upon their march, and was the principal cause of their precipitation, contrary to his natural temper, which, though full of courage, was usually very wary ; but now, carried on by his fate, he would by no means expect the general's coming up ; and he was of that universal authority, that no officer paused in obeying him. And so in the first charge he received a pistol shot in his shoulder, which broke the bone, and put him to great torture: and after he had endured it about three weeks, or less time, he died, to the most universal grief of the parliament that they could have received from any accident: and it equally increased the joy for the success at Oxford ; and very reasonably ; for the loss of a man, which would have been thought a full recompence for a considerable defeat, could not but be looked upon as a glorious crown of a victory.

Mr. Hambden hath been mentioned before as a very extraordinary person, and being now brought to his grave, before he had finished any part of the great model he had framed, and there [not] being hereafter an occasion to enlarge upon him, it is pity to leave him here without some testimony. He was, as hath been said, of an ancient family and a fair estate in the county of Buckingham, where he was esteemed very much, which his carriage and behaviour towards all men deserved very well. But there was scarce a gentleman in England, of so good a fortune, (for he was owner of above 1500 pounds in land yearly,) less known out of the county in which he lived than he was, until he appeared in the exchequer chamber to support the right of the people in the case of ship-money ; and, to avoid the payment of twenty shillings, which was required of him, engaged himself in a very great charge to make the illegality of it appear against the king, and the current of the court at that time, when it seldom met with a barefaced opposition in any council they [thought] fit to undertake and pursue. Yet the king, who had reason to believe his title to be good, from the counsel that advised it, who was his attorney-general Noy, a man of the most famed knowledge in the law, gave the direction to have his right defended, without the least discountenance or reproach to the person who contended with him. This contradiction of the king's power made him presently the most generally known, and the most universally esteemed, throughout the whole nation, that any private man at that time could be. In the beginning of the parliament he was not without ambition to be of power in the court, and not finding that satisfaction quickly, he changed it into another ambition of reigning over the court, and was deepest in all the designs to destroy it; yet dissembled that design so well, that he had too much credit with men most moderate and sober in all their purposes. *Erat illi consilium ad facinus aptum ; consilio autem neque lingua neque manus deerat.* No man seemed to have more modesty and more humility, and more to resign himself to those he conferred with, but always led them into his resolutions. In a word, he had a head to contrive, and a tongue to persuade, and a hand to execute any mischief; and his death appeared to be a great deliverance to the nation.

Among the prisoners, there were taken colonel Sheffield, a younger son of the earl of Mulgrave, and one colonel Beckly a Scotchman; who, being both visibly wounded, acted their hurts so well, and pretended to be so ready to expire, that, upon their paroles neither to endeavour nor endure a rescue, they were suffered to rest at a private house in the way, within a mile of the field, till their wounds should be dressed, and they recover so much strength as to be able to render themselves prisoners at Oxford. But the king's forces were no sooner gone, than they found means to send to their comrades, and were the next day strong enough, to suffer themselves to be removed to Thame, by a strong party sent from the earl of Essex; and, between denying that they had promised, and saying, that they would perform it, they never submitted themselves to be prisoners, as much

against the law of arms, as their taking arms was against
their allegiance.   But that which would have been looked
upon as a considerable recompense for a defeat, could not
but be thought a glorious crown of a victory, which was the
death of Mr. Hambden; who, being shot into the shoulder
with a brace of bullets, which brake the bone, within three
weeks after died with extraordinary pain ; to as great a consternation of all that party, as if their whole army had been
defeated, or cut off.

Many men observed (as upon signal turns of great affairs,
as this was, such observations are frequently made) that the
field in which the late skirmish was, and upon which Mr.
Hambden received his death's wound, Chalgrave field, was
the same place in which he had first executed the ordinance
of the militia, and engaged that county, in which his reputation was very great, in this rebellion : and it was confessed
by the prisoners that were taken that day, and acknowledged
by all, that upon the alarum that morning, after their quarters were beaten up, he was exceedingly solicitous to draw
forces together to pursue the enemy ; and, being himself a
colonel of foot, put himself among those horse as a volunteer, who were first ready ; and that when the prince made
a stand, all the officers were of opinion to stay till their body
came up, and he alone (being second to none but the general himself in the observance and application of all men) persuaded, and prevailed with them to advance ; so violently
did his fate carry him, to pay the mulct in the place where
he had committed the transgression, about a year before.

He was a gentleman of a good family in Buckinghamshire,
and born to a fair fortune, and of a most civil and affable deportment.   In his entrance into the world, he indulged to
himself all the licence in sports and exercises, and company,
which was used by men of the most jolly conversation.
Afterwards, he retired to a more reserved and melancholy
society, yet preserving his own natural cheerfulness and vivacity, and above all, a flowing courtesy to all men ; though
they who conversed nearly with him, found him growing into a dislike of the ecclesiastical government of the church,
yet most believed it rather a dislike of some churchmen, and

of some introducements of theirs, which he apprehended
might disquiet the public peace.   He was rather of reputation in his own country, than of public discourse, or fame in
the kingdom, before the business of ship-money: but then
he grew the argument of all tongues, every man inquiring
who and what he was, that durst, at his own charge, support the liberty and property of the kingdom, and rescue his
country, as he thought, from being made a prey to the court.
His carriage, throughout this agitation, was with that rare
temper and modesty, that they who watched him narrowly
to find some advantage against his person, to make him less
resolute in his cause, were compelled to give him a just testimony.   And the judgment that was given against him infinitely more advanced him,' than the service for which it
was given.   When this parliament begun, (being returned
knight of the shire for the county where he lived,) the eyes
of all men were fixed on him, as their *patriæ pater*, and the
pilot that must steer the vessel through the tempests and
rocks which threatened it.   And I am persuaded, his power
and interest, at that time, was greater to do good or hurt,
than any man's in the kingdom, or than any man of his rank
hath had in any time: for his reputation of honesty was universal, and his affections seemed so publicly guided, that no
corrupt or private ends could bias them.

He was of that rare affability and temper in debate, and
of that seeming humility and submission of judgment, as if
he brought no opinion with him, but a desire of information
and instruction ; yet he had so subtle a way of interrogating,
and, under the notion of doubts, insinuating his objections,
that he left his opinions with those from whom he pretended
to learn and receive them.   And even with them who were
able to preserve themselves from his infusions, and discerned
those opinions to be fixed in him, with which they could not
comply, he always left the character of an ingenious and con-
scientious person.   He was indeed a very wise man, and of
great parts, and possessed with the most absolute spirit of
popularity, that is, the most absolute faculties to govern the

---

¹ For *him*, the historian should have said *his cause.*--W.

people, of any man I ever knew.   For the first year of the
parliament, he seemed rather to moderate and soften the violent and distempered humours, than to inflame them.   But
wise and dispassioned men plainly discerned, that that moderation proceeded from prudence, and observation that the
season was not ripe, rather than that he approved of the
moderation ; and that he begat many opinions and motions,
the education whereof he committed to other men ; so far
disguising his own designs, that he seemed seldom to wish
more than was concluded ; and in many gross conclusions,
which would hereafter contribute to designs not yet set on
foot, when he found them sufficiently backed by majority
of voices, he would withdraw himself before the question,
that he might seem not to consent to so much visible unreasonableness ; which produced as great a doubt in some, as it
did approbation in others, of his integrity.   What combination soever had been originally with the Scots for the invasion of England, and what further was entered into afterwards in favour of them, and to advance any alteration in
parliament, no man doubts was at least with the privity of
this gentleman.

After he was among those members accused by the king
of high treason, he was much altered ; his nature and carriage seeming much fiercer than it did before.   And without
question, when he first drew his sword, he threw away the
scabbard ; for he passionately opposed the overture made by
the king for a treaty from Nottingham, and as eminently,
any expedients that might have produced any accommodations in this that was at Oxford ; and was principally relied
on, to prevent any infusions which might be made into the
earl of Essex towards peace, or to render them ineffectual, if
they were made ; and was indeed much more relied on by
that party, than the general himself.   In the first entrance into
the troubles, he undertook the command of a regiment of
foot, and performed the duty of a colonel, on all occasions,
most punctually.   He was very temperate in diet, and a
supreme governor over all his passions and affections, and
had thereby a great power over other men's.   He was of
an industry and vigilance not to be tired out, or wearied by
the most laborious ; and of parts not to be imposed upon by

the most subtle or sharp; and of a personal courage equal to
his best parts; so that he was an enemy not to be wished where-
ever he might have been made a friend; and as much to be
apprehended where he was so, as any man could deserve to
be.   And therefore his death was no less congratulated on
the one party, than it was condoled in the other.   In a word,
what was said of Cinna might well be applied to him ; " he
had a head to contrive, and a tongue to persuade, and a
hand to execute, any mischief."[1]   His death therefore seemed to be a great deliverance to the nation.

The earl of Essex's army[2] was so weakened by these defeats, and more by the sickness that had wasted it, that it
was not thought safe to remain longer so near his unquiet
and restless enemies.   The factions and animosities at London required his presence there ; and he thought the army
would be sooner recruited there, than at so great a distance;
so that he marched directly from Thame to London, where
he found jealousy and contention enough; leaving his army
quartered about St. Alban's.   Whilst the affairs of the parliament were in this distraction, the king's recovered great
reputation ; and the season of the year being fit for action,
all discontents and factious murmurings were adjourned to
the next winter.

[1] By *mischief*, the historian means no more than *reducing the king's
arbitrary by force*, [so MS.] ; which, on the historian's principles, was
a matter altogether unlawful.   This sense of the word *mischief* makes
all the parts of this fine drawn *character* consistent.   For every line
shews that the historian believed him to be a man of honour and virtue, acting on wrong principles.   As to the historian's account, that
he grew more *fierce* after his *accusation*, this may be easily accounted
for, without ascribing it to personal resentment.   Mr. Hambden saw
how obstinately the king struggled against all reform of his arbitrary
measures ; of which, the accusing the five members was one of many
flagrant instances of this truth.   He was led to think there was a necessity to use force for the securing what they had got.   This was
surely a mistake ; but such a mistake as an honest man might commit.
—W.

[2] *The ensuing lines of the History are taken from MS. B.; with which is
interwoven a short statement of the plot mentioned in page 1379, &c. and
also a brief account of the marquis of Hertford's proceedings in Cornwall :
all which is given in Appendix E.*

The end of the treaty, in which we left the chief commanders of the Cornish forces, with commissioners of the
other western counties, was like that in other places; for
notwithstanding those extraordinary obligations of oaths, and
receiving the sacrament, circumstances in no other treaty,
the parliament no sooner sent their votes and declarations to
them, (the same which are before mentioned upon the treaties in Yorkshire and Cheshire,) and some members of their
own to overlook and perplex them, but all peaceable inclinations were laid aside; so that (having in the mean time industriously levied money, throughout Somerset and Devon,
upon friends and enemies; and a good body of men) the
night before the expiration of the treaty and cessation, James
Chudleigh, the major general of the rebels, brought a strong
party of horse and foot within two miles of Launceston, the
head quarter of the Cornish, and the very next morning, the
cessation not being determined till after twelve of the clock
in the night, marched upon the town, where they were not
sufficiently provided for them.   For though the commanders
of the Cornish had employed their time, as usefully as they
could, during the cessation, in preparing the gentry of that
country, and all the inhabitants, to submit to a weekly tax
for the support of that power, which defended them; over
and above which, the gentlemen, and persons of quality,
freely brought in all their plate to be disposed of to the public; and though they foresaw, after the committee of parliament came into the country, that the treaty would conclude
without fruit, and therefore sir Ralph Hopton and sir Bevil
Greenvil repaired to Launceston the day before the expiration of the treaty, to meet any attempt should be made upon
them : yet, being to feed and pay their small forces out of
one small county, they had been compelled to quarter their
men at a great distance, that no one part might be more oppressed than was necessary: so that all that was done the
first day was, by the advantage of passes, and lining of
hedges, to keep the enemy in action, till the other forces
came up; which they seasonably did towards the evening;
and then the enemy, who received good loss in that day's
action, grew so heartless, that in the night they retired to

Okington, fifteen miles from the place of their skirmish.   After which many small skirmishes ensued, for many days,
with various success ; sometimes the Cornish advancing in
Devon, and then retiring again ; for it appeared now, that a
formed army was marching against them, so far superior in
number, that there was no reasonable hope of resistance.

Towards the middle of May, the earl of Stamford marched into Cornwall, by the north part, with a body of fourteen
hundred horse and dragoons, and five thousand four hundred
foot by the poll, with a train of thirteen brass ordnance, and
a mortar-piece, and a very plentiful magazine of victual and
ammunition, and every way in as good an equipage, as could
be provided by men who wanted no money ; whilst the king's
small forces, being not half the number, and unsupplied with
every useful thing, were at Launceston ; of whom the enemy
had so full a contempt, though they knew they were marching to them, within six or seven miles, that they considered
only how to take them after they were dispersed, and to
prevent their running into Pendennis castle, to give them
further trouble.   To which purpose having encamped themselves upon the flat top of a very high hill, to which the as-
cents were very steep every way, near Stratton, being the
only part of Cornwall eminently disaffected to the king's service, they sent a party of twelve hundred horse and dragoons,
under the command of sir George Chudleigh, father to their
major general, to Bodmin, to surprise the high sheriff and
principal gentlemen of the country ; and thereby, not only
to prevent the coming up of any more strength to the king's
party, but, under the awe of such a power of horse, to make
the whole country rise for them.   This design, which was
not in itself unreasonable, proved fortunate to the king. For
his forces which marched from Launceston, with a resolution
to fight with the enemy, upon any disadvantage of place or
number, (which, how hazardous soever, carried less danger
with it, than retiring into the county, or any thing else that
was in their power,) easily now resolved to assault the camp
in the absence of their horse ; and, with this resolution, they
marched on Monday, the fifteenth of May, within a mile of
the enemy ; being so destitute of all provisions, that the best

officer had but a biscuit a man a day, for two days, the enemy looking upon them as their own.

On Tuesday the sixteenth of May, about five of the clock
in the morning, they disposed themselves to their work;
having stood in their arms all the night.   The number of
foot was about two thousand four hundred, which they divided into four parts, and agreed on their several provinces.
The first was commanded by the lord Mohun and sir Ralph
Hopton ; who undertook to assault the camp on the south
side.   Next them, on the left hand,' sir John Berkley and
sir Bevil Greenvil were to force their way.   Sir Nicholas
Slanning and Colonel Trevannion were to assault the north
side ; and, on the left hand, colonel Thomas Basset, who
was major general of their foot, and colonel William Godolphin were to advance with their party ; each party having
two pieces of cannon to dispose as they found necessary :
colonel John Digby commanding the horse and dragoons,
being about five hundred, stood upon a sandy common which
had a way to the camp, to take any advantage he could on
the enemy, if they charged ;[2] otherwise to be firm as a reserve.

In this manner the fight began ; the king's forces pressing,
with their utmost vigour, those four ways up the hill, and
the enemy's as obstinately defending their ground.   The
fight continued with very doubtful success, till towards three
of the clock in the afternoon ; when word was brought to
the chief officers of the Cornish, that their ammunition was
spent to less than four barrels of powder ; which (concealing the defect from the soldiers) they resolved could be only
supplied with courage : and therefore, by messengers to one
another, they agreed to advance with their full bodies, without making any more shot, till they reached the top of the

[1] *Their ;* i. e. on the left hand of Slanning and Trevannion ; for the
left hand of the south was the west, and the left hand of the north was
the east ; so the hill would be assaulted by these four divisions on the
four quarters.—W.

[2] That this was the historian's meaning appears from the next page,
where he says, their few horse might have done great service.—W.

89*

hill, and so might be upon even ground with the enemy; wherein the officer's courage, and resolution, was so well seconded by the soldier, that they began to get ground in all places; and the enemy, in wonder of the men, who outfaced their shot with their swords, to quit their post. Major general Chudleigh, who ordered the battle, failed in no part of a soldier; and when he saw his men recoil from less numbers, and the enemy in all places gaining the hill upon him, himself advanced, with a good stand of pikes, upon that party which was led by sir John Berkley and sir Bevil Greenvil; and charged them so smartly, that he put them into disorder; sir Bevil Greenvil, in the shock, being borne to the ground, but quickly relieved by his companion; they so reinforced the charge, that having killed most of the assailants, and dispersed the rest, they took the major general prisoner, after he had behaved himself with as much courage, as a man could do. Then the enemy gave ground apace, insomuch as the four parties, growing nearer and nearer as they ascended the hill, between three and four of the clock they all met together upon one ground near the top of the hill; where they embraced with unspeakable joy, each congratulating the other's success, and all acknowledging the wonderful blessing of God; and being there possessed of some of the enemy's cannon, they turned them upon the camp, and advanced together to perfect the victory. But the enemy no sooner understood the loss of their major general, but their hearts failed them; and being so resolutely pressed, and their ground lost, upon the security and advantage whereof they wholly depended, some of them threw down their arms, and others fled; dispersing themselves, and every man shifting for himself: their general, the earl of Stamford, giving the example, who, (having stood at a safe distance all the time of the battle, environed with all the horse, which in small parties, though it is true their whole number was not above six or seven score, might have done great mischief to the several parties of foot, who with so much difficulty scaled the steep hill,) as soon as he saw the day lost, and some said sooner, made all imaginable haste to Exeter, to prepare them for the condition they were shortly to expect.

The conquerors, as soon as they had gained the camp, and dispersed the enemy, and after public prayers upon the place, and a solemn thanksgiving to Almighty God for their deliverance and victory, sent a small party of horse to pursue the enemy for a mile or two ; not thinking fit to pursue further, or with their whole body of horse, lest sir George should return from Bodmin with his strong body of horse and dragoons, and find them in disorder ; but contenting themselves with the victory they had obtained upon the place, which, in substance as well as circumstance, was as signal a one as hath happened to either party since the unhappy distraction ; for on the king's party were not lost in all above fourscore men ; whereof few were officers, and none above the degree of a captain ; and though many more were hurt, not above ten men died afterwards of their wounds. On the parliament side, notwithstanding their advantage of ground, and that the other were the assailants, above three hundred were slain on the place, and seventeen hundred taken prisoners, with their major general, and above thirty other officers. They took likewise all their baggage and tents, all their cannon, being, as was said before, thirteen pieces of brass ordnance, and a brass mortar-piece ; all their ammunition, being seventy barrels of powder, and all other sorts of ammunition proportionable, and a very great magazine of biscuit, and other excellent provisions of victuals ; which was as seasonable a blessing as the victory, to those who, for three or four days before, had suffered great want of food as well as sleep, and were equally tired with duty and hunger. The army rested that night and the next day at Stratton ; all care being taken by express messengers, to disperse the news of their success to all parts of that country, and to guard the passes upon the river Tamar, whereby to hinder the return of the enemy's horse and dragoons. But sir George Chudleigh had no sooner, with great triumph, dispersed the high sheriff, and gentlemen, who intended to have called the *posse comitatus*, according to their good custom, for the assistance of the king's party, and with little resistance entered Bodmin, but he received the fatal news of the loss of their camp and army at Stratton. Upon which, with as much haste and disorder, as so great a consternation could produce among a people not acquainted with the accidents of war, leaving many of his men and horses a prey to the country people, himself, with as many as he could get, and keep together, got into Plymouth; and thence, without interruption or hazard, into Exeter.

The earl of Stamford, to make his own conduct and misfortune the less censured, industriously spread abroad in all places, and confidently sent the same information to the parliament, " that he had been betrayed by James Chudleigh; and that, in the heat of the battle, when the hope of the day stood fair, he had voluntarily, with a party, run over to the enemy, and immediately charged the parliament forces; which begot in all men a general apprehension of treachery, the soldiers fearing their officers, and the officers their soldiers revolt; and thereupon the rout ensued." Whereas the truth is, as he was a young man of excellent parts and courage, he performed the part of a right good commander, both in his orders and his person; and was taken prisoner in the body of his enemy, whither he had charged with undaunted courage, when there was no other expedient in reason left. But this scandal so without colour cast on him, and entertained with more credit than his services had merited, (for, from the time of his engagement to the parliament, he had served not only with full ability, but with notable success, and was the only man that had given any interruption to the prosperity of the Cornish army, and in a night-skirmish, at Bradock Down near Okington, struck a great terror into them, and disordered them more than they were at any other time,) wrought so far upon the young man, together with the kind usage and reception he found as a prisoner among the chief officers, who loved him as a gallant enemy, and one like to do the king good service if he were recovered to his loyalty, that after he had been prisoner about ten days, he freely declared, " that he was convinced in his conscience and judgment of the errors he had committed;" and, upon promise made to him of the king's pardon, frankly offered to join with him in his service; and so gave some countenance to the reproach that was first most injuriously cast on him.

The truth is, he was of too good an understanding, and too much generosity in his nature, to be affected to the cause which he served, or to comply with those arts, which he saw practised to carry it on ; and having a command in Ireland when the war first broke out, he came thence into England, with a purpose to serve the king ; and to that purpose, shortly after his majesty's coming to Oxford, he came thither to tender his service : but he found the eyes of most men fixed on him with prejudice and jealousy there, both for his family's sake, which was notoriously disaffected to the king, and for some errors of his own, in that plot, that was so much spoken of, to bring up the northern army to awe the parliament ; in which business, being then a very young man, and of a stirring spirit, and desirous of a name, he had expressed much zeal to the king's service, and been busy in inclining the army to engage in such petitions and undertakings, as were not gracious to the parliament.   But when that discovery was made by Mr. Goring, as is before remembered, and a committee appointed to examine the combination, this gentleman, wrought upon by hopes, or fears, in his examination, said much that was disadvantageous to the court,[1] and therefore, bringing no other testimony with him to Oxford, but of his own conscience, he received nothing like countenance there ; whereupon he returned to London, sufficiently incensed that he was neglected ; and was quickly entertained for their western employment, where his nearest friends were thoroughly engaged.   But after this defeat, his former passion being allayed, and his observation and experience convincing him, that the designs of the parliament were not such as were pretended, he resigned himself to those who first conquered him with force, and then with reason and civility ; and, no doubt, was much wrought upon by the discipline and integrity of the forces, by whom he had been

---

[1] By the character the historian here gives of young Chudleigh, we must conclude he confessed nothing but the truth ; and if this was very disadvantageous to the court, we must conclude that plot was not so harmless a one as the historian, in the former part of his history, has represented it.---W.

subdued; and with the piety, temper, and sobriety of the chief commanders, which indeed was most exemplary, and worthy the cause for which they were engaged; the reputation and confession whereof had alone carried them through the difficulties and straits, with which they were to contend.

The army, willing to relieve their friends of Cornwall, from the burden which they sustained so patiently, hastened their march into Devonshire, not thoroughly resolved whether to attack Plymouth, or Exeter, or both; when advertisement came to them, by an express from Oxford, " that the king had sent prince Maurice, and the marquis of Hertford, with a very good body of horse, to join with them; and that they were advanced towards them as far as Somersetshire; and that sir William Waller was designed by the parliament, to visit the west, with a new army, which would receive a good recruit from those who escaped from the battle of Stratton:" so that it was necessary for all the king's forces in those parts to be united in a body, as soon as might be : hereupon it was quickly resolved to leave such a party at Saltash and Milbrook, as might defend faithful Cornwall from any incursions of Plymouth, and with their army to march eastward; their number increasing daily upon the reputation of their new wonderful victory; many volunteers coming to them out of Devonshire, and very many of their prisoners professing, they had been seduced, and freely offering to serve the king against those who had wronged both; who, being entertained under some of their own converted officers, behaved themselves afterwards with great honesty and courage. And so making no longer stay by the way, than was necessary for the refreshing of their troops, the Cornish army, for that was the style it now carried, marched by Exeter, where the earl of Stamford, with a sufficient garrison, then was; and staying only two or three days to fix small garrisons, whereby that town, full of fear and apprehension, might be kept from having too great an influence upon so populous a county, advanced to Tiverton, where a regiment of foot of the parliament, under colonel Ware, a gentleman of that country, had fixed themselves; hoping sir William Waller would be as soon with them for their relief, as the Cornish would be to force them ; which being easily dispersed, they stayed there to expect new orders from the marquis of Hertford.

When the loss of Reading was well digested, and the king understood the declining condition of the earl of Essex's army, and that he would either not be able to advance, or not in such a manner, as would give him much trouble at Oxford ; and hearing in what prosperous state his hopeful party in Cornwall stood, whither the parliament was making all haste to send sir William Waller, to check their good success ; his majesty resolved to send the marquis of Hertford into those parts, the rather because there were many of the prime gentlemen of Wiltshire, Dorsetshire, and Somersetshire, who confidently undertook, if the marquis went through those counties, with such a strength as they supposed the king would spare to him, they would in a very short time raise so considerable a power, as to oppose any force the parliament should be able to send.   When the marquis was ready for his journey, news arrived of the great victory at Stratton ; so that there was no danger of the marquis's being able to join with that little Cornish army ; and then there appeared indeed a visible body worthy the name of an army.   This put some persons upon desiring, that prince Maurice[1] (who was yet in no other quality of command, than of a private colonel of horse, but had always behaved himself with great courage and vigilance) might be likewise disposed into a command of that army.   Hereupon the king assigned him, and his highness willingly accepted to be lieutenant general under the marquis ; who for many reasons, besides that he was actually possessed of it, was thought only fit to have the superior power over those western counties, where his fortune lay, and the estimation and reverence of the people to him was notorious.   So the prince and the marquis, with prince Maurice's, and the earl of Carnarvon's, and colonel Thomas Howard's regiments of horse (the earl being general of the cavalry) advanced into the west; and staying only some few

---

[1] Another strong misconduct of the king, in his fondness for this unhappy family.---W.

days at Salisbury, and after in Dorsetshire, whilst some new
regiments of horse and foot, which were levying by the gentlemen in those parts, came up to them, made all convenient
haste into Somersetshire, being desirous to join with the
Cornish as soon as might be ; presuming they should be
then best able to protect their new levies, when they were
out of apprehension of being disturbed by a more powerful
force.   For sir William Waller was already marched out of
London, and used not to stay longer by the way than was
unavoidably necessary.

In the marquis's first entrance into the west, he had an
unspeakable loss, and the king's service a far greater, by the
death of Mr. Rogers, a gentleman of a rare temper, and excellent understanding ; who, besides that he had a great interest in the marquis, being his cousin-german, and so, out of
that private relation, as well as zeal to the public, passionately inclined to advance the service, had a wonderful great
influence upon the county of Dorset, for which he served as
one of the knights in parliament ; and had so well designed
all things there, that Poole and Lyme, (two port towns in
that county, which gave the king afterwards much trouble,)
if he had lived, had been undoubtedly reduced.   But by his
death all those hopes were cancelled, the surviving gentry
of that shire being, how well affected soever, so unactive,
that the progress, that was that year made there to the
king's advantage, owed little to their assistance.

About the middle of June, prince Maurice, and the marquis, with sixteen or seventeen hundred horse, and about
one thousand new levied foot, and seven or eight field-
pieces, came to Chard, a fair town in Somersetshire, nearest
the edge of Devonshire ; where, according to order, they
were met by the Cornish army ; which consisted of above
three thousand excellent foot, five hundred horse, and three
hundred dragoons, with four or five field-pieces ; so that, officers and all, being joined, they might well pass for an army
of seven thousand men ; with an excellent train of artillery,
and a very fair proportion of ammunition of all sorts, and so
good a reputation, that they might well promise themselves
a quick increase of their numbers.   Yet if the extraordinary

temper and virtue of the chief officers of the Cornish had not been much superior to that of their common soldiers,[1] who valued themselves high, as the men whose courage had alone vindicated the king's cause in the west, there might have been greater disorder at their first joining, than could easily have been composed. For how small soever the marquis's party was in numbers, it was supplied with all the general officers of a royal army, a general, lieutenant general, general of the horse, general of the ordnance, a major general of horse, and another of foot, without keeping suitable commands for those who had done all that was past, and were to be principally relied on for what was to come. So that the chief officers of the Cornish army, by joining with a much less party than themselves, were at best in the condition of private colonels. Yet the same public thoughts still so absolutely prevailed with them, that they quieted all murmurings and emulations among inferior officers, and common soldiers; and were, with equal candour and estimation, valued by the prince and marquis, who bethought themselves of all expedients, which might prevent any misunderstanding.

Taunton was the first place they resolved to visit, being the fairest, largest, and richest town in Somersetshire; but withal as eminently affected to the parliament, where they had now a garrison; but they had not yet the same courage they recovered afterwards: for the army was no sooner drawn near the town, the head quarters being at Orchard, a house of the Portmans, two miles from the town, but the town sent two of their substantial inhabitants to treat; which, though nothing was concluded, struck that terror into the garrison, (the prisoners in the castle, whereof many were men of good fortunes, imprisoned there as malignants, at the same time raising some commotion there,) that the garrison fled out of the town to Bridgewater, being a less town, but of a much stronger situation; and, with the same panic fear, the next day, from thence; so that the marquis was possessed, in three days, of Taunton, Bridgewater, and Dunstar

---

[1] Great injustice to the Cornish.---W.

castle, so much stronger than both the other, that it could not have been forced; yet by the dexterity of Francis Windham, who wrought upon the fears of the owner and master of it, Mr. Lutterel, was, with as little bloodshed as the other, delivered up to the king; into which the marquis put in him, that took it, as governor; as he well deserved.

The government of Taunton he committed to sir John Stawell, a gentleman of a very great estate in those parts; and who, from the beginning, had heartily and personally engaged himself and his children for the king; and was in the first form of those who had made themselves obnoxious to the parliament. The other government, of Bridgewater, was conferred upon Edmund Windham, high sheriff of the county, being a gentleman of a fortune near the place, and of good personal courage, and unquestionable affection to the cause. The army stayed about Taunton seven or eight days, for the settling those garrisons, and to receive advertisements of the motion or station of the enemy; in which time they lost much of the credit and reputation they had with the country. For whereas the chief commanders of the Cornish army had restrained their soldiers from all manner of licence, obliging them to solemn and frequent actions of devotion, insomuch as the fame of their religion and discipline was no less than of their courage, and thereupon sir Ralph Hopton (who was generally considered as the general of that army, though it was governed by such a commission as is before remembered) was greedily expected in his own country, where his reputation was second to no man's; the horse, that came now with the marquis, having lived under a looser discipline, and coming now into plentiful quarters, unvisited by an army, and yielding some excuse to this by the eminency of their disaffection, were disorderly enough to give the enemy credit in laying more to their charge than they deserved; and by their licence hindered those orderly levies, which should have brought in a supply of money, for the regular payment of the army. And this extravagancy produced another mischief, some jealousy, or shadow of it, between the lord marquis and prince Maurice; the first, as being better versed in the policy of peace, than in the mysteries of war, desiring to regulate the soldier, and to restrain him from using any licence upon the country; and the prince being thought so wholly to incline to the soldier, that he neglected any consideration of the country, and not without some design of drawing the sole dependence of the soldier upon himself. But here were the seeds rather sown of dislike, than any visible disinclination produced; for after they had settled the garrisons before mentioned, they advanced, with unity and alacrity, eastward, to find out the enemy, which was gathered together in a considerable body, within less than twenty miles of them.

Whilst so much time was spent at Oxford, to prepare the supplies for the west, and in settling the manner of sending them; which might have been done much sooner, and with less noise; the parliament foresaw, that if all the west were recovered from them, their quarters would by degrees be so straitened, that their other friends would quickly grow weary of them. They had still all the western ports at their devotion, those in Cornwall only excepted; and their fleets had always great benefit by it. And though most of the gentry were engaged against them, as they were in truth throughout the kingdom, yet the common people, especially in the clothing parts of Somersetshire, were generally too much inclined to them. So that they could not want men, if they sent a body of horse, and some arms, to countenance them; with the last of which they had stored the sea-towns which were in their hands sufficiently. And therefore they resolved, that, though they could not easily recruit their army, they would send some troops of horse, and dragoons, into the west, to keep up the spirits of their friends there. And for the conduct of this service, they made choice of sir William Waller, a member of the house of commons, and a gentleman of a family in Kent.

Sir William Waller had been well bred; having spent some years abroad, and some time in the armies there, returned with a good reputation home; and shortly after, having married a young lady, who was to inherit a good fortune in the west, he had a quarrel with a gentleman of the same family, who had the honour to be a menial servant to the king in a place near his person ; which, in that time, was attended with privilege and respect from all men. These two gentlemen discoursing with some warmth together, sir William Waller received such provocation from the other, that he struck him a blow over the face, so near the gate of Westminster-hall, that he got witnesses to swear, " that it was in the hall itself," the courts being then sitting ; which, according to the rigour of law, makes it very penal; and the credit the other had in the court made the prosecution to be very severe ; insomuch as he was at last compelled to redeem himself at a dear ransom ;[1] the benefit whereof was conferred on his adversary, which made the sense of it the more grievous: and this produced in him so eager a spirit against the court, that he was very open to any temptation, that might engage him against it ; and so concurring in the house of commons with all those counsels which were most violent, he was employed in their first military action, for the reducing of Portsmouth ; which he effected with great ease, as is remembered before : and when the earl of Essex had put the army into winter quarters, he had with some troops made a cavalcade or two into the west, so fortunately, that he had not only beat up some loose quarters, but had surprised a fixed and fortified quarter, made by the lord Herbert of Ragland near Gloucester ; in which he took above twelve hundred prisoners, with all the officers; being a number very little inferior to his own party; which is likewise particularly remembered before. So that he got great reputation with the parliament and the city ; and was called William the Conqueror. And it is very true, that they who looked upon the earl of Essex as a man that would not keep them company to the end of their journey, had their eyes

[1] Every now and then a story comes out which shews the court to have been exceedingly tyrannical, and abates all our wonder at the rage and malice of those who had been oppressed by it. It is a moot point which did the king most mischief, his court servants, whom he unreasonably indulged, or his country subjects, whom he as unreasonably oppressed. Gratitude had not the same influence on the affections of his servants, which thirst of revenge had on those who had been oppressed by their master.—W.

upon sir William Waller, as a man more for their turn ; and were desirous to extol him the more, that he might eclipse the other. And therefore they prepared all things for his march with so great expedition and secrecy, that the marquis of Hertford was no sooner joined to the Cornish troops, (in which time Bridgewater, and Dunstar, and some other places, were reduced from the parliament,) before he was informed that sir William Waller was within two days' march of him, and was more like to draw supplies to him from Bristol, and the parts adjacent, which were all under the parliament, than the marquis could from the open country ; and therefore it was held most counsellable to advance, and engage him, whilst he was not yet too strong ; and by this means they should continue still their march towards Oxford ; which they were now inclined to do.[1]

Though sir William Waller himself continued still at Bath, yet the remainder of those horse and dragoons that escaped out of Cornwall, after the battle of Stratton, and such other as were sent out of Exeter for their ease, when they apprehended a siege, and those soldiers who fled out of Taunton and Bridgewater, and other regiments of the country, were by Alexander Popham, Strode, and the other deputy lieutenants of the militia for Somerset, rallied ; and with the trained bands, and volunteer regiments of the country, drawn together, with that confidence, that when the marquis had taken up his head quarters at Somerton, the enemy, before break of day, fell upon a regiment of dragoons, quartered a mile eastward from the town ; and gave so brisk an alarm to the king's army, that it was immediately drawn out, and advanced upon the enemy, (being the first they had seen make any stand before them, since the battle of Stratton,) who making stands upon the places of advantage, and maintaining little skirmishes in the rear, retired in no ill order to Wells; and the king's forces still pursuing, they chose to quit that city likewise ; and drew their whole body, appearing in num-

---

[1] *The ensuing relation of the battles of Lansdown and Roundwaydown are taken from MS. C. An abridged description of each, which in MS. B. follows this character, &c. of sir W. Waller, will be found in Appendix F.*

ber as considerable as their pursuers, to the top of a hill,
called Mendip Hill, overlooking the city of Wells, which
they had left.   The day being far spent, and the march having been long, the marquis, with all the foot, and train, stayed at Wells; but prince Maurice, and the earl of Carnarvon,
with sir Ralph Hopton, and sir John Berkley, and two regiments of horse, resolved to look upon the enemy on the
top of the hill; who suffered them, without interruption, to
gain the top of the hill level with them, and then, in a very
orderly manner, facing with a large front of their horse, to
give their foot and baggage leisure and security, retired together as the prince advanced.   This, and the natural contempt the king's horse yet had of the enemy, which in all skirmishes and charges had been hitherto beaten by them, made
the prince judge this to be but a more graceful running away;
and therefore followed them over those large hills further
than before, till the enemy, who were anon to pass through
a lane, and a village called Chewton, were compelled, before their entrance into the lane, to leave their reserve;
which faced about much thinner than it was over the hill:
which opportunity and advantage was no sooner discerned,
as it had been foreseen, but the earl of Carnarvon (who always charged home) with incomparable gallantry charged
the enemy, and pressed them so hard, that he entered the
lane with them, and routed the whole body of their horse,
and followed the execution of them above two miles.

But this was like to have been a dear success; for sir
William Waller, who lay with his new army at Bath, and
had drawn to him a good supply out of the garrison at Bristol, had directed this body which was in Somerset, to retire
before the king's forces till they should join with him, who
had sent a fresh, strong party of horse and dragoons, to assist their retreat; which, by the advantage of a fog, had
marched without being discovered: so that the earl of Carnarvon, being a stranger in the country and the ways, pursued the flying enemy into sir William Waller's quarters,
and till himself was pressed by a fresh body of horse and
dragoons; when he was necessitated to retire in as good order as he could; and sent the prince, who followed him,

word of the danger which attended them. His highness hereupon, with what haste he could, drew back through the village ; choosing rather, with very good reason, to attend the enemy in the plain heath, than to be engaged in a narrow passage : thither the earl of Carnarvon with his regiment came to him, broken and chased by the enemy ; who immediately drew up a large front of horse and dragoons, much stronger than the prince's party, who had only his own, and the earl of Carnarvon's regiments, with some gentlemen volunteers. The strait, and necessity he was in, was very great ; for as he might seem much too weak to charge them, so the danger might probably be much greater to retire over these fair hills, being pursued with a fresh party much superior in number. Therefore he took a gallant resolution, to give the enemy a brisk charge with his own regiment upon their advance, whilst the earl rallied his, and prepared to second him, as there should be occasion. This was as soon and fortunately executed as resolved ; the prince in the head of his regiment charging so vigorously, that he utterly broke and routed that part of the front that received the impression. But almost half the enemy's horse, that, being extended larger than his front, were not charged, wheeled about, and charged the prince in the rear ; and at the same time the earl of Carnarvon, with his rallied regiment, charged their rear ; and all this so thoroughly performed, that they were mingled pallmall one among the other, and the good sword to decide the controversy, their pistols being spent in the close. The prince himself received two shrewd hurts in his head, and was beaten off his horse ; but he was presently relieved, and carried off ; and the enemy totally routed, and pursued again by the earl of Carnarvon ; who had a fair execution upon them, as long as the light countenanced his chase, and then he returned to the head quarters at Wells ; there having been in these skirmishes threescore or fourscore men lost on the prince's party, and three times that number by the enemy ; the action being too quick to take many prisoners.

At Wells the army rested many days, as well to recover the prince's wounds, being only cuts with swords, as to con-

sult what was next to be done ; for they were now within
distance of an enemy that they knew would fight with them.
For sir William Waller was at Bath with his whole army,
much increased by those who were chased out of the west ;
and resolved not to advance, having all advantages of provisions, and passes, till a new supply, he every day expected
from London, were arrived with him.   On the other side,
the marquis was not only to provide to meet with so vigilant
an enemy, but to secure himself at his rear, that the disaffection of the people behind him, who were only subdued,
not converted, upon the advance of sir William Waller,
might not take fresh courage.   Though Cornwall was reasonably secured, to keep off any impression upon itself from
Plymouth, yet Devonshire was left in a very unsafe posture :
there being only a small party at Columb-John, a house of sir
John Ackland's, three miles off Exeter, to control the power of
that city, where the earl of Stamford was ; and to dispute
not only with any commotion that might happen in the country, but with any power that might arrive by sea.   Upon
these considerations, and the intelligence, that the parliament
had sent directions to the earl of Warwick their admiral, "to
attend the Devonshire coast with his fleet, and take any advantage he could," the marquis, by the advice of the council
of war, sent sir John Berkley back into Devonshire, with
colonel Howard's regiment of horse, to command the forces
which were then there, and to raise what numbers more he
could possibly, for the blocking up that city, and reducing
the county ; and upon his arrival there, to send up to the
army sir James Hamilton's regiment of horse and dragoons ;
which had been left in Devonshire ; and, by the licence they
took, weakened the king's party ; so that, by sending this
relief thither, he did not lessen at all his own numbers, yet
gave great strength to the reducing those parts, as appeared
afterwards by the success.

    After this disposition, and eight or ten days' rest at Wells,
the army generally expressing a handsome impatience to
meet with the enemy, of which, at that time, they had a
greater contempt, than in reason they should have ; the
prince and marquis advanced to Frome, and thence to Brad-

ford, within four miles of Bath. And now no day passed
without action, and very sharp skirmishes ; sir William Waller having received from London a fresh regiment of five
hundred horse, under the command of sir Arthur Haslerig :
which were so prodigiously armed, that they were called by
the other side the regiment of lobsters, because of their
bright iron shells, with which they were covered, being perfect cuirassiers ; and were the first seen so armed on either
side, and the first that made any impression upon the king's
horse ; who, being unarmed, were not able to bear a shock
with them ; besides that they were secure from hurts of the
sword, which were almost the only weapons the other were
furnished with.

The contention was hitherto with parties ; in which the
successes were various, and almost with equal losses : for as
sir William Waller, upon the first advance from Wells, beat
up a regiment of horse and dragoons of sir James Hamilton's,
and dispersed them ;[1] so, within two days, the king's forces
beat a party of his from a pass near Bath, where the enemy
lost two field-pieces, and near an hundred men. But sir
William Waller had the advantage in his ground, having a
good city, well furnished with provisions, to quarter his army
together in ; and so in his choice not to fight, but upon extraordinary advantage. Whereas the king's forces must either
disperse themselves, and so give the enemy advantage upon
their quarters, or, keeping near together, lodge in the field,
and endure great distress of provision ; the country being so
disaffected, that only force could bring in any supply or relief. Hereupon, after several attempts to engage the enemy
to a battle upon equal terms, which, having the advantage, he
wisely avoided ; the marquis and prince Maurice advanced
with their whole body to Marsfield, five miles beyond Bath
towards Oxford ; presuming, that, by this means, they should
draw the enemy from their place of advantage, their chief
business being to hinder them from joining with the king.

[1] This was the disorderly regiment which was sent for out of Devonshire, on account of the hurt they did there to the king's cause ;
and this was a fate very likely to attend their irregularities.—W.

And if they had been able to preserve that temper, and had neglected the enemy, till they had quitted their advantages, it is probable they might have fought upon as good terms as they desired. But the unreasonable contempt they had of the enemy, and confidence they should prevail in any ground, with the straits they endured for want of provisions, and their want of ammunition, which was spent as much in the daily hedge-skirmishes, and upon their guards, being so near as could have been in battle, would not admit that patience ; for sir William Waller, who was not to suffer that body to join with the king, no sooner drew out his whole army to Lansdown, which looked towards Marsfield, but they suffered themselves to be engaged upon great disadvantage.

It was upon the fifth of July when sir William Waller, as soon as it was light, possessed himself of that hill ; and after he had, upon the brow of the hill over the high way, raised breast-works with fagots and earth, and planted cannon there, he sent a strong party of horse towards Marsfield, which quickly alarmed the other army, and was shortly driven back to their body. As great a mind as the king's forces had to cope with the enemy, when they had drawn into battalia, and found the enemy fixed on the top of the hill, they resolved not to attack them upon so great disadvantage; and so retired again towards their old quarters : which sir William Waller perceiving, sent his whole body of horse and dragoons down the hill, to charge the rear and flank of the king's forces ; which they did thoroughly, the regiment of cuirassiers so amazing the horse they charged, that they totally routed them ; and, standing firm and unshaken themselves, gave so great terror to the king's horse, who had never before turned from an enemy, that no example of their officers, who did their parts with invincible courage, could make them charge with the same confidence, and in the same manner they had usually done. However, in the end, after sir Nicholas Slanning, with three hundred musketeers, had fallen upon and beaten their reserve of dragooners, prince Maurice and the earl of Carnarvon, rallying their horse, and winging them with the Cornish musketeers, charged the enemy's horse again, and totally routed them ; and in the same manner received two bodies more, and routed and chased them to the hill; where they stood in a place almost inaccessible. On the brow of the hill there were breast-works, on which were pretty bodies of small shot, and some cannon; on either flank grew a pretty thick wood towards the declining of the hill, in which strong parties of musketeers were placed; at the rear was a very fair plain, where the reserves of horse and foot stood ranged; yet the Cornish foot were so far from being appalled at this disadvantage, that they desired to fall on, and cried out, " that they might have leave to fetch off those cannon." In the end, order was given to attempt the hill with horse and foot. Two strong parties of musketeers were sent into the woods, which flanked the enemy; and the horse and musketeers up the road way, which were charged by the enemy's horse, and routed; then sir Bevil Greenvil advanced with a party of horse, on his right hand, that ground being best for them; and his musketeers on the left; himself leading up his pikes in the middle; and in the face of their cannon, and small-shot from the breast-works, gained the brow of the hill, having sustained two full charges of the enemy's horse; but in the third charge his horse failing, and giving ground, he received, after other wounds, a blow on the head with a pole-axe, with which he fell, and many of his officers about him; yet the musketeers fired so fast upon the horse, that they quitted their ground, and the two wings, who were sent to clear the woods, having done their work, and gained those parts of the hill, at the same time they beat off their foot, and became possessed of the breast-works; and so made way for their whole body of horse, foot, and cannon, to ascend the hill; which they quickly did, and planted themselves on the ground they had won; the enemy retiring about demi-culverin shot behind a stone wall upon the same level, and standing in reasonable good order.

Either party was sufficiently tired, and battered, to be contented to stand still. The king's horse was so shaken, that of two thousand which were upon the field in the morning, there were not above six hundred on the top of the hill. The enemy was exceedingly scattered too, and had no mind

to venture on plain ground with those who had beaten them
from the hill ; so that, exchanging only some shot from their
ordnance, they looked one upon another till the night interposed. About twelve of the clock, it being very dark, the
enemy made a show of moving towards the ground they had
lost ; but giving a smart volley of small-shot, and finding
themselves answered with the like, they made no more noise :
which the prince observing, he sent a common soldier to
hearken as near the place, where they were, as he could ;
who brought word, " that the enemy had left lighted matches
in the wall behind which they had lain, and were drawn off
the field ;" which was true ; so that, as soon as it was day,
the king's army found themselves possessed entirely of the
field, and the dead, and all other ensigns of victory : sir
William Waller being marched to Bath, in so much disorder
and apprehension, that he left great store of arms, and ten
barrels of powder, behind him ; which was a very seasonable supply to the other side, who had spent in that day's
service no less than fourscore barrels, and had not a safe
proportion left.

In this battle, on the king's part, there were more officers
and gentlemen of quality slain, than common men ; and more
hurt than slain. That which would have clouded any victory, and made the loss of others less spoken of, was the
death of sir Bevil Greenvil ; who was indeed an excellent
person, whose activity, interest, and reputation, was the
foundation of what had been done in Cornwall ; and his
temper and affections so public, that no accident which happened could make any impressions in him ; and his example
kept others from taking any thing ill, or at least seeming to
do so.[1] In a word, a brighter courage, and a gentler disposition, were never married together to make the most cheerful and innocent conversation.

[1] It appears from what the historian all along observes, that these
Cornish troops, to whom the king owed so much, (and, had they been
well used, would have owed a great deal more,) had great reason to
complain of the ill return their services met with from the court and
court favourites.---W.

Very many officers and persons of quality were hurt ; as the lord Arundel of Wardour, shot in the thigh with a brace of pistol bullets ; sir Ralph Hopton, shot through the arm with a musket ; sir George Vaughan, and many others, hurt in the head of their troops with swords and pole-axes ; of which none of name died.　But the morning added much to the melancholy of their victory, when the field was entirely their own.　For sir Ralph Hopton riding up and down the field to visit the hurt men, and to put the soldiers in order, and readiness for motion, sitting on his horse, with other officers and soldiers about him, near a wagon of ammunition, in which were eight barrels of powder ; whether by trea-chery, or mere accident, is uncertain, the powder was blown up ; and many, who stood nearest, killed ; and many more maimed ; among which sir Ralph Hopton and sergeant major Sheldon were miserably hurt ; of which, major Shel-don, who was thought to be in less danger than the other, died the next day, to the general grief of the army, where he was wonderfully beloved, as a man of an undaunted cou-rage, and as great gentleness of nature.　Sir Ralph Hopton, having hardly so much life, as not to be numbered with the dead, was put into a litter, and then the army marched to their old quarters to Marsfield ; exceedingly cast down with their morning's misfortune, (sir Ralph Hopton being indeed the soldiers' darling,) where they reposed themselves the next day, principally in care of sir Ralph Hopton, who, though there were hope of his recovery, was not fit to tra-vel.　In this time many of the horse, which had been routed in the morning, before the hill was won, found the way to Oxford ; and, according to the custom of those who run away, reported all to be lost, with many particular accidents, which they fancied very like to happen when they left the field ; but the next day brought a punctual advertisement from the marquis, but, withal, a desire of a regiment or two of fresh horse, and a supply of ammunition ; whereupon the earl of Crawford with his regiment of horse, consisting of near five hundred, was directed to advance that way, with such a proportion of ammunition as was desired.

After a day's rest at Marsfield, it being understood that

sir William Waller was still at Bath, (his army having been rather surprised and discomforted with the incredible boldness of the Cornish foot, than much weakened by the number slain, which was not greater than on the king's part,) and that he had sent for fresh supply from Bristol ; it was concluded, rather to march to Oxford, and so to join with the king's army, than to stay and attend the enemy, who was so near his supplies : and so they marched towards Chippenham. But when sir William Waller had intelligence of the blowing up of the powder, of which he well knew there was scarcely enough before, and of the hurt it had done, he infused new spirit into his men ; and verily believed that they had no ammunition, and that the loss of sir Ralph Hopton (whom the people took to be the soul of that army, the other names being not so much spoken of, or so well known, and at this time believed to be dead) would be found in the spirits of the soldiers ; and having gotten some fresh men from Bristol, and more from the inclinations of the three counties of Wilts, Gloucester, and Somerset, which joined about Bath, in the most absolute disaffected parts of all three,[1] he followed the marquis towards Chippenham ; to which he was as near from Bath, as the other from Marsfield.

The next day, early in the morning, upon notice that the enemy was in distance, the prince and the marquis drew back the army through Chippenham, and presented themselves in battalia to the enemy ; being very well contented to fight in such a place, where the success was to depend more on their foot, who were unquestionably excellent, than on their horse, which were at best weary,[2] though their officers were, to envy, forward and resolute. But sir William Waller, who was a right good chooser of advantages, liked not that ground; relying as much upon his horse, who had gotten credit and courage, and as little upon his foot, who

[1] Pryn, the *utter barrister of Swanswick*, had done much to spread this disaffection.---W.

[2] Their licence, and Haslerig's cuirassiers, had lessened both their discipline and their courage.—W.

were only well armed, and well bodied, very vulgarly spirited, and officered : so that having stood all night in battalia,
and the enemy not coming on, the prince and marquis, the
next day, advanced towards the Devizes ; sir Nicholas Slanning, with great spirit and prudence, securing the rear with
strong parties of musketeers ; with which he gave the enemy, who pressed upon them very smartly, so much interruption, that sir William Waller, despairing of overtaking, sent
a trumpet to the marquis, with a letter, offering a pitched
field at a place of his own choosing, out of the way.   The
which being easily understood to be only a stratagem to beget a delay in the march, the marquis carried the trumpet
three or four miles with him, and then sent him back with
such an answer as was fit.   There were, all this day, perpetual and sharp skirmishes in the rear ; the enemy pressing very hard, and being always with loss repulsed, till the
army safely reached the Devizes.

Then the case was altered for their retreat to Oxford, the
enemy being upon them with improvement of courage, and
improvement of numbers ; sir William Waller having dispersed his warrants over the country, signifying " that he had beat-
en the marquis," and requiring the people " to rise in all places
for the apprehension of his scattered and dispersed troops ;"
which confidence, men conceived, could not proceed from
less than a manifest victory ; and so they flocked to him as
the master of the field.   The foot were no more now to
make the retreat, the situation of the place they were now
in, being such as they could move no way towards Oxford,
but over a campaign of many miles, where the stronger in
horse must needs prevail.

Hereupon, it was unanimously advised, and consented to,
that the lord marquis and prince Maurice should that night
break through, with all the horse, to Oxford; and that sir
Ralph Hopton (who, by this, was supposed past danger of
death, and could hear and speak well enough, though he
could not see or stir) with the earl of Marlborough, who
was general of the artillery, the lord Mohun, and other good
officers of foot, should stay there with their foot and cannon,
where it was hoped they might defend themselves, for a few

days, till the general might return with relief from Oxford ; which was not above thirty miles off. This resolution was pursued ; and, the same night, all the horse got safe away into the king's quarters, and the prince and marquis, in the morning, came to Oxford ; by which time sir William Waller had drawn all his forces about the Devizes. The town was open, without the least fortification or defence, but small ditches and hedges; upon which the foot were placed, and some pieces of cannon conveniently planted. The avenues, which were many, were quickly barricadoed to hinder the entrance of the horse, which were principally apprehended. Sir William Waller had soon notice of the remove of the horse ; and therefore, intending that pursuit no further, he brought his whole force close to the town, and beleaguered it round ; and having raised a battery upon a hill near the town, he poured in his shot upon it without intermission, and attempted to enter in several other places with horse, foot, and cannon ; but was in all places more resolutely re- sisted, and repulsed. At the same time, having intelligence (as his intelligence was always most exact in whatsoever concerned him) of the earl of Crawford's marching with a supply of powder, according to order, after the first notice of the battle of Lansdown, he sent a strong party of horse and dragoons to intercept him ; who, before he knew of the alterations which had happened, and of the remove of the horse towards Oxford, was so far engaged, that he hardly escaped with the loss of his ammunition, and a troop or two of his horse. .

Upon this improvement of his success, sir William Waller reckoned his victory out of question ; and thereupon sent a trumpet into the town to summon the besieged, to let them know, " that he had cut off their relief, and that their state was now desperate; and therefore advised them to submit them- selves to the parliament, with whom he would mediate on their behalf." They in the town were not sorry for the overture ; not that they apprehended it would produce any conditions they should accept, but that they might gain some time of rest by it : for the straits they were in were too great for any minds not prepared to preserve their honour

at any rates.   When the enemy came first before the town,
and the guards were supplied with ammunition for their duty, there was but one hundred and fifty weight of match left
in the store ; whereupon diligent officers were directed to
search every house in the town, and to take all the bed-
cords they could find, and to cause them to be speedily beat-
en, and boiled.   By this sudden expedient, there was, by
the next morning, provided fifteen hundred weight of such
serviceable match, as very well endured that sharp service.
Then the compass of the ground they were to keep was so
large, and the enemy pressed so hard upon all places, that
their whole body were upon perpetual duty together, neither officer or soldier having any time for rest ; and the activity of the chief officers was most necessary to keep up
the courage of the common men, who well enough understood the danger they were in, and therefore they were very
glad of this message ; and returned, " that they would send
an officer to treat, if a cessation were agreed to during the
time of the treaty ;" which was consented to, if it were suddenly expedited.

On the party of the besieged were proposed such terms,
as might take up most time in the debate, and might imply
courage and resolution to hold out.   Sir William Waller, on
the other hand, offered only quarter, and civil usage to the
officers, and leave to the common soldiers to return to their
houses without their arms, except they would voluntarily
choose to serve the parliament.   These being terms many
of the officers would not have submitted to in the latest extreme, the treaty ended ; after those in the town had gained
what they only looked for, seven or eight hours' sleep, and
so long time sparing of ammunition.   The truth is, sir William Waller was so confident that they were at his mercy,
that he had written to the parliament, " that their work was
done, and that, by the next post, he would send the number
and quality of his prisoners ;" neither did he imagine it possible that any relief could have been sent from Oxford ; the
earl of Essex, to whom he had signified his success, and the
posture he was in, lying with his whole army at Thame,
within ten miles of it.   But the importance was too well

understood by the king to omit any thing, that might, with
the utmost hazard, be attempted for the redeeming those
men, who had wrought such wonders for him. And therefore, as soon as the marquis and prince arrived at Oxford,
with the sad and unexpected news, and relation of the
distress of their friends, though the queen was then on her
march towards Oxford, and the king had appointed to meet
her two days' journey for her security, his majesty resolved
to take only his own guards of horse, and prince Rupert's
regiment, for that expedition; and sent the lord Wilmot with
all the rest of the horse, to march that very day, in which
the advertisement came to him, towards the Devizes; so
that the marquis and the prince coming to Oxford on the
Monday morning, the lord Wilmot, that night, moved towards the work; and prince Maurice returning with him as
a volunteer, but the lord Wilmot commanding in chief, appeared, on the Wednesday about noon, upon the plain within two miles of the town.

The lord Wilmot had with him fifteen hundred horse, and
no more, and two small field-pieces, which he shot off, to
give the town notice of his coming; having it in his hopes,
that, it being a fair campaign about the town, when the enemy should rise from before it, that he should be able, in
spite of them to join with the foot, and so to have a fair
field for it; which would be still disadvantageous enough,
the enemy being superior by much in horse, very few of
those who had broken away from the Devizes (except the
prince himself, the earl of Carnarvon, and some other officers) being come up with them, partly because they were
tired and dispersed; and partly because it was not desired
to have many of those who might have their old terror still
upon them. The enemy, careful to prevent the joining of
this party of horse with the foot, and fully advertised of
their coming, drew off, on all parts, from the town; and put
themselves in battalia upon the top of a fair hill, called
Roundway-down; over which the king's forces were necessarily to march, being full two miles off the town: they
within conceived it hardly possible, that the relief, they expected from Oxford, could so soon arrive; all the messen-

gers, who were sent to give notice of it, having miscarried
by the closeness of the siege; and therefore suspected that
the warning pieces from the plain, and the drawing off the
town by the enemy, to be a stratagem to cozen the foot from
those posts they defended, into the open field; and so, very
reasonably, being in readiness to march, waited a surer evidence, that their friends were at hand; which shortly arrived; and assured them, "that the prince was by, and expected them."

It will be easily conceived, with what alacrity they advanced; but sir William Waller had purposely chose that
ground to hinder that conjunction, and advanced so fast on
the lord Wilmot, that without such shifts and traverses, as
might give his men some apprehension, he could not expect
the foot from the town; and therefore he put his troops in order upon that ground to expect the enemy's charge, who were
somewhat more than musket-shot off in order of battle.

Here sir William Waller, out of pure gaiety, departed
from an advantage he could not again recover; for being in
excellent order of battle, with strong wings of horse to his
foot, and a good reserve placed, and his cannon usefully
planted, apprehending still the conjunction between the horse
and the foot in the town, and gratifying his enemy with the
same contempt, which had so often brought inconveniences
upon them, and discerning their number inferior to that he
had before (as he thought) mastered, he marched, with his
whole body of horse, from his foot, to charge the enemy; appointing sir Arthur Haslerig with his cuirassiers apart, to
make the first impression; who was encountered by sir John
Byron, in whose regiment the earl of Carnarvon charged as
a volunteer; and after a sharp conflict, in which sir Arthur
Haslerig received many wounds, that impenetrable regiment
was routed, and, in a full career, chased upon their other
horse. And at the same time, the lord Wilmot charging
them from division to division, as they were ranged, in half
an hour, so sudden alterations the accidents of war introduce,
the whole entire body of the triumphant horse were so totally routed and dispersed, that there was not one of them
to be seen upon that large spacious down; every man shift-

ing for himself with greater danger by the precipices of that
hill, than he could have undergone by opposing his pursuer.
But as it was an unhappy ground to fly, so it was as ill for
the pursuer; and after the rout, more perished by falls and
bruises from their horses, down the precipices, than by the
sword.   The foot stood still firm, making shew of a gallant
resistance; but the lord Wilmot quickly seized their cannon,
and turned them upon them, at the same time that the
Cornish foot, who were by this come from the town, were
ready likewise to charge them; upon which their hearts
failed; and so they were charged on all sides, and either
killed, or taken prisoners, very few escaping; the Cornish
retaining too fresh a memory of their late distresses, and re-
venging themselves of those who had contributed the least
thereunto.   Sir William Waller himself, with a small train,
fled into Bristol, which had sacrificed a great part of their
garrison in his defeat; and so were even ready to expire at
his entry into the town, himself bringing the first news of
his disaster.

This glorious day, for it was a day of triumph, redeemed
the king's whole affairs, so that all clouds that shadowed
them seemed to be dispelled, and a bright light of success
to shine over the whole kingdom.   There were in this battle slain, on the enemy's part, above six hundred on the
place; nine hundred prisoners taken, besides two or three
hundred retaken and redeemed, whom they had gathered up
in the skirmishes and pursuit; with all their cannon, being
eight pieces of brass ordnance; all their arms, ammunition,
wagons, baggage, and victual; eight and twenty foot ensigns,
and nine cornets; and all this by a party of fifteen hundred
horse, with two small field-pieces, (for the victory was perfect, upon the matter, before the Cornish came up; though
the foot were suffered to stand in a body uncharged, out of
ceremony, till they came; that they might be refreshed with
a share in the conquest,) against a body of full two thousand
horse, five hundred dragoons, and near three thousand foot,
with an excellent train of artillery.   So that the Cornish
had great reason to think their deliverance, and victory at
Roundway, more signal and wonderful than the other at

Stratton, save that the first might be thought the parent of the latter, and the loss on the king's party was less ; for in this there were slain very few ; and, of name, none but Dudley Smith, an honest and valiant young gentleman ; who was always a volunteer with the lord Wilmot, and among the first upon any action of danger.

Besides the present fruit of this victory, the king received an advantage from the jealousy, that, from thence, grew among the officers of the parliament armies.   For sir William Waller believed himself to be absolutely betrayed, and sacrificed by the earl of Essex, out of envy at the great things he had done, which seemed to eclipse his glories; and complained, " that he, lying with his whole army within ten miles of Oxford, should suffer the whole strength of that place to march thirty miles to destroy him, without so much as sending out a party to follow them, or to alarm Oxford, by which they would have been probably recalled."   On the other hand, the earl, disdaining to be thought his rival, reproached the other with " unsoldierly neglects, and want of courage, to be beaten by a handful of men, and to have deserted his foot and cannon, without engaging his own person in one charge against the enemy."   Wherever the fault was, it was never forgiven ; but, from the enmity that proceeded from thence, the king often afterwards reaped very notable and seasonable advantages ; which will be remembered in their places.   This thirteenth of July was a day of perfect joy to the king; for at the same time, and in the very hour, that the lord Wilmot vanquished that army at Roundway-down, the king met and received his royal consort the queen, to his unspeakable satisfaction, in that ground under Edge-hill upon which the year before he had fought his first battle : her majesty having left the earl of Newcastle in a great likelihood of being entirely master of the north ; whose actions there were so prosperous, and so full of notable accidents, that they deserve a history apart ; and therefore I shall only insert such of them in this place as were most signal, and which had the greatest influence upon the series of the greatest affairs.

Upon the queen's arrival, (which is before set forth at

large,) and the conversion of sir Hugh Cholmondley which
ensued thereupon, the king's affairs in the north, which
were in good growth and improvement before, flourished
with notable vigour ; and yet it must be confessed, the enemy in those parts, with whom the earl of Newcastle was to
contend, in courage, vigilance, and insuperable industry, was
not inferior to any who disquieted his majesty in any part of
his dominions, and who pursued any advantage he got further, and recovered any loss he underwent sooner, than any
other in the kingdom : so that there were more sharp skirmishes and more notable battles in that one county of York,
than in all the kingdom besides, and less alteration upon
them, than could be expected ; the lord Fairfax and his son
with incredible activity reducing towns when they had an
army, and when they were defeated in the field, out of small
towns recovering new armies.

This blessed defeat happened to be upon the same day,
and upon the same time of the day, when the king met the
queen upon the field near Keinton, under Edge-hill,[1] where
the battle had been fought in October before ; and before
their majesties came to Oxford, they received the happy
news of it.   It is easy to imagine the joy with which it was
received, all men raising their fallen spirits to a height too
proportionable, as though they should now go through all the
work without further opposition ; and this transportation to
either extremes was too natural upon all the vicissitudes of
the war ;[2] and it was some allay to the welcome news of the
victory to some men, that it had been obtained under the
command and conduct of Wilmot; who was very much in
prince Rupert's disesteem, and not in any notable degree of
favour with the king, but much beloved in all the good fel-
lowship of the army ; which was too great a body.   It was
now time for the king's army, victorious in so many encounters, to take the field ; upon what enterprise, was the ques-

[1] This observation was more becoming a small paltry courtier, than
this great historian.—W.

[2] Too natural for courts, where the mind is always found, or made
unbalanced.   Meaning, without doubt, prince Rupert himself.—W.

tion. This overthrow of Waller had infinitely surprised, and increased the distractions at London. They had seen the copy of his warrants, which his vanity had caused to be dispersed, after the action at Lansdown; in which he declared, " that he had routed the marquis's army, and was in pursuit of them ; and therefore commanded the justices of peace, and constables, to give order for the apprehension of them, as they fled dispersed ;" and expected every day, that the marquis would be sent up prisoner : and now to hear that his whole invincible army was defeated, and himself fled, upon the matter, alone, (for ill news is for the most part made worse, as the best is reported to be better than it is,) brought them to their wits end ; that they could little advance the recruiting the earl of Essex's army ; who in his person likewise grew more sullen towards them, and resented their little regard of him, and grew every day more conversant with the earls of Northumberland and Holland, and others who were most weary of the war, and would be glad of peace upon easy terms.[1]

The king's army received a fair addition, by the conjuncture[2] with those forces which attended the queen ; for her majesty brought with her above two thousand foot, well armed, and one thousand horse, with six pieces of cannon, and two mortars, and about one hundred wagons. So that as soon as their majesties came to Oxford, the earl of Essex, who had spent his time about Thame and Aylesbury, without any action after that skirmish in which Mr. Hambden was slain, save by small parties, of which there was none of name or note, but one handsome smart conflict between a party of five hundred horse and dragoons, commanded by colonel Middleton, a Scotchman, on the parliament par-

---

[1] In MS. B., from whence the last page is taken, there follows an account of the siege and capture of Bristol, and of the beginning of the jealousy between the princes Rupert and Maurice, and the marquis of Hertford ; which (as a fuller and more circumstantial account of both is inserted in this History from the other MS.) will be found in Appendix G.

[2] Conjunction.—W.

ty, and a regiment of horse, commanded by sir Charles
Lucas, on the king's; where, after a very soldierly contest, and more blood drawn than was usual upon such actions, the king's party prevailed, returning with some prisoners of name, and the slaughter of one hundred of their enemy, not without some loss of their own : retired with his
army broken, and disheartened, to Uxbridge, giving over
any thought of fighting with the king, till he should be recruited with horse, men, and money ; and suffering no less
in the talk of the people, (who began to assume a great freedom in discourse,) for not interposing to hinder the queen's
march to Oxford, and joining with the king, than for sitting
still so near Oxford, whilst the lord Wilmot went from thence
to the ruin of sir William Waller.

After which defeat, the lord Wilmot retired to Oxford to
attend his majesty ; and the Cornish army (for that name it
deservedly kept still, though it received so good an increase
by the marquis and prince's joining with them) drew back,
and possessed themselves of Bath, which was quitted, upon
the overthrow of Waller ; that garrison being withdrawn to
reinforce Bristol. At Bath they rested, and refreshed themselves, till they might receive new orders from the king ;
who, upon full advice, and consideration of the state he was
in, and the broken condition of the enemy, resolved to make
an attempt upon the city of Bristol; to which prince Rupert
was most inclined, for being disappointed in a former design ;
and where there were many well affected to the king's service from the beginning, and more since the execution of
those two eminent citizens. And the disesteem generally
of the courage of Nathaniel Fiennes, the governor, made the
design to be thought the more reasonable ; and so the marquis and prince Maurice returned to Bath,' upon agreement
to appear, on such a day, with their whole strength, before
Bristol, on the Somersetshire side, when prince Rupert with
the Oxford forces would appear before it, on the Gloucestershire side.

' i. e. from Oxford, whither they had gone to attend the council of
war.---W.

On the four and twentieth of July, both armies sat down
before it ; quartering their horse in that manner, that none
could go out or in to the city, without great hazard of being
taken ; and the same day, with the assistance of some seamen, who were prepared before, they seized all the ships
that were in King-road ; which were not only laden with
things of great value, as plate, money, and the best sort of all
commodities, which those who suspected the worst had sent
aboard, but with many persons of quality ; who, being unwilling to run the hazard of a siege, thought that way to
have secured themselves, and to have escaped to London ;
and so were all taken prisoners.   The next day, prince Rupert came to his brother, and the marquis, and a general
council of all the principal officers of both armies being assembled, it was debated, " in what manner they should proceed, by assault or approach."

There were in the town five and twenty hundred foot,
and a regiment of horse and dragoons ; the line about the
town was finished ; yet in some places the graff was wider
and deeper than in others.   The castle within the town was
very well prepared, and supplied with great store of provisions to endure a siege.   The opinions were several : the
officers of the Cornish were of opinion, " that it was best to
proceed by way of approach ; because, the ground being very
good, it would in a very short time be done ; and since there
was no army of the enemy in a possibility to relieve it, the se-
curest way would be the best ; whereas the works were so good,
that they must expect to lose very many men ; and, if they
were beaten off, all their summer hopes would be destroyed ;
it not being easy, again to make up the spirit of the army for
a new action.   Besides, they alleged, the well affected party
in the city, which was believed to be very great, would, after they had been closely besieged three or four days, have
a greater influence upon the soldier, and be able to do more
towards the surrender, than they could upon a storm ; when
they would be equally sensible of the disorder of the soldier,
and their own damage by plunder, as the other ; and the
too late example of the executed citizens would keep men
from offering at any insurrection in the city."

On the other hand, prince Rupert, and all the officers of his army, very earnestly desired to assault it; alleged " the work to be easy, and the soldiers fitter for any brisk attempt, than a dull patient design; and that the army would be more weakened by the latter than the former : that the city, not having yet recovered the consternation of sir William Waller's defeat, was so full of horror, that it would make a very weak defence : that there was no soldier of experience in the town, and the governor himself not like to endure the terror of a storm : whereas, if they gave them time to consider, and to look long upon them with a wall between, they would grow confirmed and resolute, and courage would supply the place of skill; and having plenty of all kinds of provisions within the town, they would grow strong and peremptory, whilst the besiegers grew less vigorous, and disheartened." These reasons, and the prince's importunity, with some insinuations of knowing more than was fit to be spoken, as if somewhat would be done within the town, that must not be mentioned, and a glorious contempt of danger, prevailed so far, that it was consented to, on all parts, to assault the town the next morning at three places on the Somersetshire side, and at three places on the Gloucestershire side, at the break of day. The truth is, both opinions, without any circumstances, were in themselves reasonable. For the Gloucestershire side, where prince Rupert was, might be stormed, the graff being shallow, and the wall, in some places, low and weak; which could not be easily approached, by reason the ground was rocky, and the redoubts high and very strong, which overlooked the ground; on the other side the ground was very easy to approach, and as inconvenient and dangerous to storm, by reason of a plain level before the line, and a broad and deep graff, and the line throughout better flankered than the other.

The next morning, with no other provisions fit for such a work, but the courage of the assailants, both armies fell on. On the west side, where the Cornish were, they assaulted the line in three places; one division led by sir Nicholas Slanning, assisted with colonel John Trevannion, lieutenant colonel Slingsby, and three more field officers; too great a

number of such officers to conduct so small a party as five hundred men, if there had not been an immoderate disdain of
danger, and appetite of glory : another division, on the right
hand, was led by colonel Buck, assisted by colonel Wagstaffe,
colonel Bernard Ashley, who commanded the regiment of
the lord marquis Hertford, with other officers of the field :
and the third division, on the left hand, led by sir Thomas
Basset, who was major general of the Cornish.   These three
divisions fell on together with that courage and resolution,
as nothing but death could control ; and though the middle
division got into the graff, and so near filled it, that some
mounted the wall, yet by the prodigious disadvantage of the
ground, and the full defence the besieged made within, they
were driven back with a great slaughter ; the common soldiers, after their chief officers were killed, or desperately
wounded, finding it a bootless attempt.

On prince Rupert's side, it was assaulted with equal courage, and almost equal loss, but with better success ; for
though that division, led on by the lord Grandison, colonel
general of the foot, was beaten off, the lord Grandison himself being hurt ; and the other, led by Colonel Bellasis, likewise had no better fortune ; yet colonel Washington, with a
less party, finding a place in the curtain (between the places
assaulted by the other two) weaker than the rest, entered,
and quickly made room for the horse to follow.   The enemy, as soon they saw the line entered in one place, either
out of fear, or by command of their officers, quit their posts ;
so that the prince entered with his foot and horse into the
suburbs ; sending for one thousand of the Cornish foot, which
were presently sent to second him ; and marched up to
Fromegate, losing many men, and some very good officers,
by shot from the walls and windows ; insomuch as all men
were much cast down to see so little gotten with so great a
loss ; for they had a more difficult entrance into the town than
they had yet passed, and where their horse could be of no
use to them ; when, to the exceeding comfort of generals and
soldiers, the city beat a parley ; which the prince willingly
embracing, and getting their hostages into his hands, sent
colonel Gerrard and another officer to the governor to treat.

The treaty began about two of the clock in the afternoon, and, before ten at night, these articles were agreed on, and signed by all parties.

1. " That the governor,¹ Nathaniel Fiennes, together with all the officers both of horse and foot, now within and about the city of Bristol, castle, and forts, may march out to-morrow morning by nine of the clock, with their full arms, bag and baggage, provided it be their own goods: and that the common foot soldiers march out without arms, and the troopers with their horses and swords, leaving their other arms behind them, with a safe convoy to Warminster; and after, not to be molested in their march, by any of the king's forces, for the space of three days.

2. " That there may be carriages allowed and provided to carry away their bag and baggage, and sick and hurt soldiers.

3. " That the king's forces march not into the town, till the parliament forces are marched out; which is to be at nine of the clock.

4. " That all prisoners in the city be delivered up ; and that captain Eyres and captain Cookein, who were taken at the Devizes, be released.

5. " That sir John Horner, sir John Seymour, Mr. Edward Stevens, and all other knights, gentlemen, citizens, and other persons, that are now in the city, may, if they please, with their goods, wives, and families, bag and baggage, have free liberty to return to their own homes, or elsewhere, and there to rest in safety, or ride, and travel with the governor and forces: and such of them, and their families, as shall be left behind, by reason of sickness or other cause, may have liberty, so soon as they can conveniently, to depart this town with safety ; provided that all gentlemen, and other persons, shall have three days' liberty to reside here, or depart with their goods, which they please.

6. " That all the inhabitants of the city shall be secured in their persons, families, and estates, free from plundering, and all other violence, or wrong whatsoever.

---

¹ *These articles are in the handwriting of lord Clarendon's amanuensis.*

7. " That the charters and liberties of this city may be preserved; and that the ancient government thereof, and present governors and officers, may remain and continue in their former condition, according to his majesty's charters and pleasure.

8. " That, for avoiding inconveniences and distractions, the quartering of soldiers be referred or left to the mayor, and governor of the same city for the time being.

9. " That all such as have carried any goods into the castle may have free liberty to carry the same forth.

10. " That the forces, that are to march out, are to leave behind them all cannon, and ammunition, with their colours, and such arms as is before expressed."

The next morning, if not before, (for the truth is, from the time that the treaty was first offered, they in the town kept no guards, nor observed any order; but their soldiers run away to the prince, and many of his soldiers went into the town,) his highness was possessed of Bristol, the enemy then marching away. Here the ill example at Reading, in the breach of the articles, was remembered, and unhappily followed; for all that garrison was now here. So that they, with some colour of right, or retaliation, and the rest, by their example, used great licence to the soldiers, who should have been safely conducted; which reflected much upon the prince, though he used his utmost power to suppress it; and charged colonel Fiennes to be accessary to his own wrong, by marching out of the town an hour before his appointment; and thereby his convoy was not ready; and at another gate than was appointed and agreed on. And as the articles were thus unhappily violated to those who went away, so they were not enough observed to those who stayed, and to the city itself: for many of colonel Fiennes' soldiers taking conditions, and entering with the king's army, instructed their new friends, who were most disaffected; so that one whole street upon the bridge, the inhabitants whereof lay under some brand of malignity, though, no doubt, there were many honest men among them, was almost totally plundered; which, because there was but little justice done upon the transgressors, was believed to be done

by connivance from the officers, and more discredited the
king's forces, and his cause, than was then taken notice of,
or discovered.　　It was a noble attribute given to the brave
Fabricius, *qui aliquid esse crederet et in hostem nefas.*　I
wish I could excuse those swervings from justice and right,
which were too frequently practised against contracts, under
the notion, that they, with whom they were made, were
rebels, and could not be too ill used ; when, as the cause
deserved, so it needed all the ingenuity and integrity, in the
propugners of it, to keep despair from the guilty, who were
by much too numerous for the innocent.

This reduction of Bristol was a full tide of prosperity to
the king, and made him master of the second city of his
kingdom, and gave him the undisturbed possession of one of
the richest counties of the kingdom, (for the rebels had now
no standing garrison, or the least visible influence upon any
part of Somersetshire,) and rendered Wales (which was before well affected, except some towns in Pembrokeshire)
more useful to him ; being freed of the fear of Bristol, and
consequently of the charge that always attends those fears ;
and restored to the trade with Bristol; which was the greatest support of those parts.　Yet the king might very well
have said, what king Pyrrhus heretofore did, after his second
battle, by the city of Asculum, with the Romans, where he
won the victory ; " If we win another at this price, we are
utterly undone."　And truly his majesty's loss before this
town was inestimable, and very hard to be repaired.　I am
persuaded there were slain, upon the several assaults, of
common men, but such as were tried and incomparable foot,
about five hundred ; and abundance of excellent officers,
whereof many were of prime command and quality.

On the Cornish side fell, besides major Kendall, and many
other inferior officers, excellent in their degree, colonel Buck,
a modest and a stout commander, and of good experience in
war : who having got over the graff, and even to the top of
the wall, was knocked down with a halbert, and perished in
the graff ; sir Nicholas Slanning, and colonel John Trevannion, the life and soul of the Cornish regiments, whose memories can never be enough celebrated ; who being led by
no impulsion, but of conscience, and their own observation

of the ill practices and designs of the great conductors, (for they both were of the house of commons,) engaged themselves with the first in the opposition; and as soon as sir Ralph Hopton, and those other gentlemen came into Cornwall, joined with them; and being both of singular reputation, and good fortunes there, the one in possession, the other in reversion after his father, they engaged their persons and estates in the service; rather doing great things, than affecting that it should be taken notice of to be done by them; applying themselves to all infirmities, and descending to all capacities, for removing all obstructions, which accidentally arose among those, who could only prosper by being of one mind. Sir Nicholas Slanning was governor of Pendennis castle, upon the credit and security whereof, the king's party in that country first depended, and, by the command it had of the harbour of Falmouth, was, or might be, supplied with all that was necessary. He was indeed a young man of admirable parts, a sharp and discerning wit, a staid and solid judgment, a gentle and most obliging behaviour, and a courage so clear and keen, as, even without the other ornaments, would have rendered him very considerable: they were both very young, neither of them above eight and twenty, of entire friendship to one another, and to sir Bevil Greenvil, whose body was not yet buried; they were both hurt almost in the same minute, and in the same place; both shot in the thigh with a musket bullet; their bones broken, the one dying presently, the other some few days after; and both had the royal sacrifice of their sovereign's very particular sorrow, and the concurrence of all good men's; and, that which is a greater solemnity to their memories, as it fares with most great and virtuous men, whose loss is better understood long afterwards, they were as often lamented, as the accidents in the public affairs made the courage and fidelity of the Cornish of greatest signification to the cause.

On the north side, of prince Rupert's army, fell very many good officers, the chief of whom was colonel Harry Lunsford, an officer of extraordinary sobriety, industry, and courage; by whom, his excellent lieutenant colonel Moyle was likewise hurt, and died within few days, both shot out of a window after they had entered the suburbs. There were hurt, the lord viscount Grandison, nephew to the great duke of Buckingham, who was colonel general of the king's foot ; colonel John Bellasis, since lord Bellasis ; colonel Bernard Ashley ; colonel sir John Owen ; and many other officers of name, of whom none of quality died of their wounds but the lord Grandison ; whose loss can never be enough lamented. He was a young man of so virtuous a habit of mind, that no temptation or provocation could corrupt him ; so great a lover of justice and integrity, that no example, necessity, or even the barbarity of this war, could make him swerve from the most precise rules of it ; and of that rare piety and devotion, that the court, or camp, could not shew a more faultless person, or to whose example young men might more reasonably conform themselves. His personal valour, and courage of all kinds, (for he had sometimes indulged so much to the corrupt opinion of honour, as to venture himself in duels,) was very eminent, insomuch as he was accused of being too prodigal of his person ; his affection, and zeal, and obedience to the king, was such as became a branch of that family. And he was wont to say, " that if he had not understanding enough to know the uprightness of the cause, nor loyalty enough to inform him of the duty of a subject, that the very obligations of gratitude to the king, on the behalf of his house, were such, as his life was but a due sacrifice :" and therefore, he no sooner saw the war unavoidable, than he engaged all his brethren, as well as himself, in the service ; and there were then three more of them in command in the army, when he was so unfortunately cut off.

As soon as the news of the taking of Bristol came to the king at Oxford, after a solemn thanksgiving to God for the success, which was immediately and publickly performed, his majesty assembled his privy-council, to consider how this great blessing in war might be applied to the procuring a happy peace ; and that this might be the last town he should purchase at the price of blood. It was evident, that, as this last victory added great lustre and beauty to the whole face of his affairs, so it would produce an equal paleness, and be an ominous presage to the parliament ; where the jealousies and apprehensions between themselves still grew higher, and new remedies still proposed, which were generally thought worse than the disease.

Upon the news of the lord Fairfax's being defeated in the north, they resolved presently to send a committee of the two houses into Scotland, " to desire their brethren of that kingdom presently to advance with an army for their relief;" which was thought so desperate a cure, that the lords naming the earl of Rutland, and lord Grey of Warke, for that embassy, the earl upon indisposition of health procured a release; and the other, who had never declined any employment they would confer on him, so peremptorily refused to meddle in it, that he was committed to the Tower; and, in the end, they were compelled to depute only commoners to that service: and so sir William Armyne, young sir Henry Vane, and two more, assisted with Mr. Marshall and Mr. Nye, two of their powerful clergy, were embarked in that negociation; upon which, they who sent them were so far from being confident, and so little satisfied, that they should be driven to bring in foreign forces, with the purpose whereof they had so long traduced the king, that there was, some few desperate persons only excepted, even a universal desire of peace; and the earl of Essex himself, writing to the speaker of the house of commons, of the defects in his army, and of his wants of horse, men, and money, advised, " that they would think of sending some reasonable propositions to the king, for the procuring a safe peace;" which being the first intimation he had ever given to that purpose, together with his familiarity and correspondence with those lords, who were known passionately to desire an accommodation, gave them sad apprehensions; which were increased by some severe messages they received from him, for his vindication from the foul aspersions and calumnies, which were generally and publicly laid on him, for his unactivity after the winning Reading, whilst the queen marched securely to Oxford, and sir William Waller was destroyed; as if " he would think of some way of righting himself, if they were not sensible on his behalf."

How to work upon these discomposed humours, and to

reduce them to such temper, that they might consent to the
kingdom's peace, was the argument of the king's consultations: but by what expedient to promote this, was the difficulty. After the breach of the last treaty, and when the
king had in vain laboured to revive it, and could not procure any answer from them to his last messages; but instead thereof his messenger imprisoned, tried before a council of war for his life, and still in custody, and a declaration,
"that whosoever should be employed by his majesty, on
any message to them, without their leave, should be proceeded against as a spy," (so that though they pretended to
be his great council, they upon the matter now protested
against any relation to his majesty,) he advised with his
council, "what might be fit for him to do, to lessen the reverence and reputation of them with the people:" for the superstition towards the name of a parliament was so general,
that the king had wisely forborne to charge the two houses
with the treason and rebellion that was raised, but imputed
it to particular persons, who were most visibly and actually
engaged in it. Some were of opinion, " that all the members who stayed there, and sat in either house, being guilty
of so many treasonable acts, thereby the parliament was actually dissolved, by the same reason as a corporation, by
great misdemeanour and crime, might forfeit their charter;
and therefore that the king should, by his proclamation, declare the dissolution of it, and then consider whether it were
fit to call another." But this opinion was generally disliked,
both " because it was conceived not to be just; for the
treason of those who were present could not forfeit the right
of those who were away ; neither was it evident, that all
present consented to the ill that was done ; and the king's
declaring a parliament to be dissolved, contrary to an act of
parliament, was believed, would prove an act so ungracious
to the people, for the consequences of it, that the king would
be an exceeding loser by such an attempt; and that many,
in such a case, would return thither, who out of conscience
had withdrawn from that assembly."

In conclusion, the advice was unanimous, " that his majesty should declare the orders and proceedings of one or both

houses to be void, by reason the members did not enjoy the
freedom and liberty of parliament ; and therefore require
his good subjects, no longer to be misled by them :" and,
to that purpose, the king had issued his proclamation six
weeks before this happy turn in his affairs, so that he could
not now send a message to them, as to two houses of parliament, lest he might seem to retract his former judgment
of them, which was concluded to be both regular and just.
Upon the whole matter, lest his majesty might be understood to be so much elated with his good successes, and the
increase of his strength, that he aimed at no less than a perfect victory, and the ruin of those who had incensed him,
(by which insinuations they, who could not forgive themselves, endeavoured to make all others desperate,) he was
resolved to publish such a declaration to the whole kingdom,
that both houses, and their army, could not but take notice
of, and might, if they were inclined to it, thence take a rise
to make any overtures to him towards an atonement.   And
to that purpose, the next day after he received the assurance of the taking of Bristol, his majesty published this ensuing declaration ; which being short I shall enter in his own
words.

*His majesty's[1] declaration to all his loving subjects, after
his victories over the lord Fairfax in the north, sir William Waller in the west, and the taking of Bristol by his
majesty's forces.*

" As the grievances and losses of no particular persons,
since these miserable bloody distempers have disquieted this
poor kingdom, can be compared to the loss and damage we
ourself have sustained, there having been no victory obtained but in the blood of our own subjects, nor no rapine or
violence committed, but to the impoverishment and ruin of
our own people ; so, a blessed and happy peace cannot be
so acceptable and welcome to any man, as to us.   Almighty
God, to whom all the secrets of our heart are open, who
hath so often and so miraculously preserved us, and to whose

---

[1] *In the handwriting of Lord Clarendon's amanuensis.*

power alone we must attribute the goodness of our present condition, (how unhappy soever it is with reference to the public calamities,) knows, with what unwillingness, with what anguish of soul, we submitted ourself to the necessity of taking up defensive arms. And the world knows with what justice and bounty we have repaired our subjects, for all the pressures and inconveniences they had borne,[1] by such excellent laws, as would for ever have prevented the like ; and with what earnestness and importunity we desired to add any thing, for the establishment of the religion, laws, and liberty of the kingdom. How all these have been disturbed, invaded, and almost destroyed, by faction, sedition, and treason, by those, who have neither reverence to God, nor affection to men, but have sacrificed both to their own ends and ambition, is now so evident, that we hope, as God hath wonderfully manifested his care of us, and his defence of his and our most just cause ; so he hath so far touched the hearts of our people, that their eyes are at last opened to see how miserably they have been seduced, and to abhor those persons, whose malice and subtlety had seduced them to dishonour him, to rebel against us, and to bring much misery and calamity upon their native country.

" We well remember the protestation voluntarily made by us, in the head of that small army we were master of in September last, to defend and maintain the true reformed protestant religion : and if it should please God, by his blessing upon that army, to preserve us from this rebellion, that we would maintain the just privileges and freedom of parliament, and govern by the known laws of the land ; for whose defence, in truth, that army was only raised, and hath been since kept. And there cannot be a more seasonable time to renew that protestation than now, when God hath vouchsafed us so many victories and successes, and hath rendered the power of those, who seek to destroy us, less

---

[1] The robberies of arbitrary power. These were indeed solidly *repaired* by the *excellent laws* he speaks of. But the doing all this with a very bad grace, and the ill opinion that was entertained of his sincerity, gave the enemies of the constitution credit for their very worst designs.—W.

formidable than it hath been, (so that we shall probably not fall under the scandalous imputation, which hath usually attended our messages of peace, that they proceed from the weakness of our power, not love of our people,) and when there is more freedom in many counties, for our good subjects to receive true information of their own and our condition; the knowledge whereof hath been, with equal industry and injustice, kept from them, as other acts of cruelty have been imposed on them.

" We do therefore declare to all the world, in the presence of Almighty God, to whom we must give a strict account of all our professions and protestations, that we are so far from intending any alteration of the religion established, (as hath been often falsely, scandalously, and against the conscience of the contrivers themselves of that rumour, suggested to our people,) or from the least thought of invading the liberty and property of the subject, or violating the just privileges of parliament, that we call that God to witness, *who hath covered our head in the day of battle,* that we desire from our soul, and shall always use our utmost endeavour, to preserve and advance the true reformed protestant religion, established in the church of England; in which we were born, have faithfully lived, and, by the grace of God, shall resolutely die : that the preservation of the liberty and property of the subject, in the due observation of the known laws of the land, shall be equally our care, as the maintenance of our own rights; we desiring to govern only by those good laws, which, till they were oppressed by this odious rebellion, preserved this nation happy. And we do acknowledge the just privileges of parliament to be an essential part of those laws, and shall therefore most solemnly defend and observe them. So that, in truth, if either religion, law, or liberty, be precious to our people, they will, by their submission to us, join with us in the defence of them; and thereby establish that peace, by which only they can flourish, and be enjoyed.

" Whether these men, that be professed enemies to the established ecclesiastical government, who reproach and persecute the learned orthodox ministers of the church, and into their places put ignorant, seditious, and schismatical preachers, who vilify the Book of Common Prayer, and impiously profane God's worship with their scurrilous and seditious demeanour, are like to advance that religion ; whether those men, who boldly, and without the least shadow or colour of law, impose insupportable taxes and odious excises upon their fellow subjects, imprison, torment, and murder them, are like to preserve the liberty and property of the subject: and whether those men, who seize and possess themselves of our own unquestionable revenue, and our just rights, have denied us our negative voice, have, by force and violence, awed and terrified the members of both houses, and lastly have, as far as in them lies, dissolved the present parliament, by driving away and imprisoning the members, and resolving the whole power thereof, and more, into a committee of a few men, contrary to all law, custom, or precedent, are like to vindicate and uphold the privileges of parliament, all the world may judge.

" We do therefore once more conjure our good subjects, by their memory of that excellent peace and firm happiness,[1] with which it pleased God to reward their duty and loyalty in time past ; by their oaths of allegiance and supremacy, which no vow or covenant, contrived and administered to and by themselves, can cancel or evade ; by whatsoever is dear and precious to them in this life, or hoped or prayed for in the life to come, that they will remember their duty, and consider their interest, and no longer suffer themselves to be misled, their prince dishonoured, and their country wasted and undone by the malice and cunning of those state impostors ; who, under pretence of reformation, would introduce whatsoever is monstrous and unnatural both to religion and policy : but that they rather choose quietly to enjoy their religion, property, and liberty, founded and provided for by the wisdom and industry of former times, and secured and enlarged by the blessings upon the present age, than to spend their

[1] How is this consistent with the *pressures* and *inconveniences* which, in this very declaration, he owns the subject had felt during his reign, before the calling of this last parliament ?—W.

lives and fortunes to purchase confusion, and to make themselves liable to the most intolerable kind of slavery, that is, to be slaves to their fellow subjects; who, by their prodigious, unheard of acts of oppression and tyranny, have given them sufficient evidence what they are to expect at their hands.

" And let not our good people, who have been misled, or, through want of understanding, or want of courage, submitted themselves to unwarrantable and disloyal actions, be taught, by these seducers, that their safety now consists in despair; and that they can only secure themselves for the ills they have done, by a resolute and peremptory disobedience. Revenge and blood-thirstiness have never been imputed to us,[1] by those, who have left neither our government, or nature, unexamined, with the greatest boldness and malice. And all those who, since those bloody distractions, out of conscience have returned from their evil ways to us, have found, that it was not so easy for them to repent, as for us to forgive. And whosoever have been misled by those whose hearts from the beginning have designed all this mischief, and shall redeem their past crimes by their present service and loyalty, in the apprehending or opposing such who shall continue to bear arms against us, and shall use their utmost endeavours to reduce those men to their due obedience, and to restore this kingdom to its wonted peace, shall have cause to magnify our mercy, and to repent the trespasses committed against so just and gracious a sovereign. Lastly, we desire all our good subjects who have really assisted, or really wished us well, now God hath done such wonderful things for us, vigorously to endeavour to put an end to all these miseries, by bringing in men, money, plate, horses, or arms, to our aid; that so we being not wanting to ourselves, may with confidence expect the continuance of God's favour, to restore us all to that blessed harmony of affections, which may establish a firm peace; without the speedy obtaining of which, this

---

[1] The *revenge* his enemies charged him with at one time, and the *forgiveness* he boasts of at another, were very consistent.—W.

poor kingdom will be utterly undone, though not absolutely lost."

What effect this proclamation produced, at least what accident fell out shortly after the publishing it, we shall have occasion anon to remember, when we have first remembered some unfortunate passages, which accompanied this prosperity on the king's part; for the sunshine of his conquest was somewhat clouded, not only by the number and quality of the slain, but by the jealousies and misunderstandings of those who were alive.   There was not, from the beginning, that conformity of humour and inclinations between the princes and the marquis of Hertford, as had been to be wished between all persons of honour, who were engaged in a quarrel that could never prosper but by the union of the undertakers.   Prince Maurice, and, on his behalf, (or rather the other by his impulsion,) prince Rupert, taking to heart, that a nephew of the king's should be lieutenant general to the marquis,[1] who had neither been exercised in the profession of a soldier, nor even now punctually studied the office of a general : on the other hand, the marquis, who was of the most gentle nature to the gentle, and as rough and resolute to the imperious, it may be liked not the prince's assuming to himself more than became a lieutenant general, and sometimes crossing acts of his with relation to the governing and disposing the affairs of the country, in which he knew himself better versed than the prince ; and when Bristol was taken, where the marquis took himself to command in chief, being a town particularly within his commission, and of which he was besides lord lieutenant, he thought himself not regardfully enough used, that prince Rupert had not

[1] He took to heart what doubtless had been infused into it by the uncle himself.   A ray of royalty in the court notions of that time diffused itself through all the branches of the sacred stem : otherwise, how could it possibly be thought, that a mere soldier of fortune, a foreigner, scarce of age, was hardly dealt with, or degraded, in being appointed lieutenant general to an English nobleman of the first quality and credit, who was made general of an army that was to be raised and kept together by his own interest in the country, and much at the expense of his own noble fortune ?—W.

only entered into the treaty without his advice, but concluded the articles without so much as naming him, or taking notice that he was there.   And therefore with as little ceremony to his highness, or so much as communicating it to either of the princes, the marquis declared that he would give the government of that city to sir Ralph Hopton.   Prince Rupert on the other hand conceived the town won by him, being entered on that side in which he commanded absolutely, and the Cornish on the other part absolutely repulsed ; and therefore that the disposition of the command and government of it wholly belonged to him.   But when he heard the resolution of the marquis concerning sir Ralph Hopton, who was not to be put into the scale of any private man, he gave over the design of conferring it upon any of the pretenders ; and by the same messenger, by whom he advertised his majesty of the good success, he desired, " that he would bestow the government of that city, reduced by him, upon himself ;" the which the king readily consented to, not suspecting any dispute to be about it.   And shortly after an express arrived likewise from the marquis, with an account of all particulars, and that his lordship had designed sir Ralph Hopton to be governor of the new-got city.

Then, and not before, the king understood what strait he was in ; and was exceedingly perplexed to find an expedient to compose the difference that he saw would arise.   He had passed his word to his nephew, of whom he was very tender,[1] and did in truth believe that his title to dispose the government was very just : so he had a very just esteem of the marquis, who had served him with all fidelity, and who clearly declared himself for him, when the doing otherwise would have been most prejudicial to his majesty : and, it could not be denied, no subject's affection and loyalty gave a greater lustre to the king's cause, than that of the marquis ; and that which was a circumstance of infinite moment, was the nominating sir Ralph Hopton ; who as he was a per-

---

[1] Had the king been always as *tender* of his word, as he was of the follies of those nearest to him, he had never been reduced to these straits.—W.

son of high merit from the king, so he was the most gracious
and popular to that city, and the country adjacent; and after
so great service, and suffering in the service, to expose him
to a refusal, was both against the kindness and goodness of
the king's nature, and his politic foresight into his affairs.
And as a presage how various the interpretation would be
abroad, of whatsoever he should determine, he found the
minds and affections of his own court and council, with more
passion than ordinary, ready to deliver their opinions.   The
marquis was generally loved, and where he was not enough
known to be so, his interest and reputation in the kingdom
was thought of wonderful consideration in the king's business : and many were very much troubled to see prince
Rupert, whose activity and courage in the field they thought
very instrumental, incline to get the possession of the second
city of the kingdom into his hands, or to engage himself so
much in the civil government, as such a command soberly
executed must necessarily comprehend : and this as it were
in contempt of one of the prime noblemen of the kingdom,
to which order the prince had not expressed himself very
debonair.   And these thought[1] " the king was, by counsel
and precept, to reform and soften the prince's understanding
and humour ; and to persuade him, in compliance with his
service, to decline the contest, and suffer the marquis to
proceed in his disposition, which, on all parts, was acknowledged to be most fitly designed."

Others again were of opinion,[2] " that the right of disposing the command to whomsoever he thought fit, entirely belonged to prince Rupert ; and therefore (besides that the
king had, by the same messenger who brought the suit, returned his consent) that he could not be reasonably refused,
when he desired it for himself ; which would take away all
possible imagination of disrespect from sir Ralph Hopton,
who could not take it ill, that the prince himself had taken a
command, that was designed to him : that the eyes of the
army were upon his highness, whose name was grown a terror to the enemy, as his courage and conduct had been very

[1] His country friends.---W.   [2] His court friends.---W.

prosperous to the king ;¹ and if, after so happy and glorious an achievement, he should now receive a repulse in so reasonable a pretence, though it would not lessen his own duty or alacrity in the service, it might have an unhappy influence upon his reputation and interest in the army ; which could receive no diminution without apparent damage to his majesty : and therefore, that some means should be used to the marquis, to wave his title, and to consent that the prince should enjoy his desires:" so that they who were only fit to be employed to persuade and alter either, seemed, and indeed were, passionately engaged against the thing they were to persuade. So that the king discerned that all depended upon his own royal wisdom; and therefore resolved to take a journey in his own person to Bristol, and there to give such a rule as he should find most necessary, ; to which, he presumed, both persons would conform themselves, as well cordially, as obediently.

That which the king proposed to himself was, to gratify his nephew with the name, and the marquis, by making sir Ralph Hopton enjoy the thing ; upon obliging whom the king's care was very particular. For though he knew his nature, as in truth it was, most exactly free from interrupting the least public service by private ends or thoughts, other men would be apt to conceive and publish a disrespect to be done to him, which himself apprehended not ; and therefore that he was not only, in his own princely mind, to retain a very gracious sense of his service, but to give evidence to all men, that he did so. And so after he had made a joyful entrance into Bristol, which was performed with all decent solemnity, and used all kind and obliging expressions to the marquis, and in private desired to consent, that 'he might perform his promise to his nephew, which he had passed before he had any imagination that his lordship otherwise had determined of it ; without speaking at all of any other title he had to it, but by his majesty's promise. He established prince Rupert in the government of Bristol, who

---

¹ He had only fought one pitched battle, that of Edge-Hill, and that he lost by his eminent misconduct. The like misconduct afterwards lost him the battle of Marston Moor.---W.

immediately sent a commission to sir Ralph Hopton, (who was now so well recovered, that he walked into the air,) to be his lieutenant governor; signifying likewise to him, by a confidant who passed between them, "that though he was now engaged for some time, which should not be long, to keep the superior title himself, he would not at all meddle in the government, but that he should be as absolute in it, as if the original commission had been granted to him."

Sir Ralph Hopton, who was exceedingly sorry that his name was at all used, and exposed, as an argument of difference and misunderstanding between persons of such eminent influence upon the public, quickly discerned that this expedient, though it seemed plausibly to lessen the noise of the debate, did in truth object him to the full envy of one party. For the marquis (who by the king's persuasions was rather quieted than satisfied) might, and he foresaw would, be persuaded to expect that he would refuse the commission from prince Rupert, both, as he might be thought to comply in an injury done to the marquis, to whom his devotion had been ancient, fast, and unshaken, and as the command now given him was inferior to what the marquis, who had the power of disposal, had conferred on him; and so that he should vindicate the title, which the king himself was loath to give a judgment upon. And he was the more troubled, because he found that, by submitting to this charge, he should by some be thought to have deserted the marquis out of a kind of revenge for his having deserted the enterprise, when he chose, the last year, rather to go into Wales than Cornwall, and deserting him again now, when he brought all new officers to command the army over their heads who had raised it, and made the way for the new to come to them. Whereas the first, as is before remembered, was done by his own advice, as well as his full consent; and the latter, he well knew, was rather to be imputed to prince Maurice than to his lordship, whose kindness and esteem had been ever very real to him. On the other hand, he saw plainly, that if he refused to receive this commission, with what specious circumstances of duty and submission soever, it might produce (as without doubt unavoidably it would) notable disturbances and interruptions in the

king's affairs; and that the marquis, to common understandings, had, to obey the king, declined the contestation, and
therefore that the reviving it, and the mischief that attended
it, would be imputed to his particular account.   Besides
that, he had always borne an avowed and declared reverence to the queen of Bohemia and her children, whom he
had personally and actively served in their wars, whilst they
maintained any, and for whose honour and restitution he
had been a zealous and known champion.   And therefore he
had no inclination to disoblige a hopeful prince of that house,
upon whom our own hopes seemed so much to depend.   So
that he resolved, according to his rare temper throughout
this war, to let him whom he professed to serve, choose in
what kind he would be served by him; and cheerfully received the commission from prince Rupert; upon which, all
discourse, or debate of difference, was for the present determined, what whisperings or murmurings soever remained.

The king found it now high time to resolve, to what action next to dispose his armies, and that their lying still so
long there (for these agitations had kept the main work from
going forward ten or twelve days, a time in that season unfortunately lost) had more weakened, than refreshed them;
having not lost more men by storming the city, than afterwards by plundering it: those soldiers, who had warmed
themselves with the burden of pillage, never quietly again
submitting to the carriage of their arms.

The question was first, " whether both armies should be
united, and march in one upon the next design?" And then,
" what that design should be?" Against the first, there were
many allegations.

1. " The condition of the west : Dorsetshire and Devonshire were entirely possessed by the enemy; for though sir
John Berkley with a daring party kept Exeter, and colonel
John Digby the north part (which was notoriously disaffected)
from joining with Plymouth, which would else quickly have
grown into an army strong enough to infest Cornwall, yet
they had no place to retire to upon distress ; and all the
ports upon the western coasts were garrisoned by them,
which, upon the fame of the approach of the king's forces,

and the loss of Bristol, might probably be, without much resistance, reduced.

2. " The Cornish army was greater in reputation, than numbers ; having lost many at Lansdown, and the assault of Bristol, and, by the death of their chief officers, very many were run away since ; besides they pretended some promise made to their country (which they conceived not to be enough secured against Plymouth) of returning speedily for the reduction of that town ; so that if they were compelled to march eastwards, to which they were not inclined, it was to be doubted they would moulder away so fast, that there would be little addition of strength by it. Whereas if they marched westward, it would be no hard matter to gather up those who were returned, and to be strong enough in a very short time, by new levies, for any enterprise should be thought reasonable to be undertaken." To which was added, " that having lost those officers, whom they loved and feared, and whose reverence restrained their natural distempers, they were too much inclined to mutiny ; and had expressed a peremptory aversion to the joining, and marching with the king's army." And the truth is, their humours were not very gentle and agreeable, and apt to think that their prowess was not enough recompensed, or valued. For though the king affected to make all possible demonstrations to them, of an extraordinary high esteem he had of their wonderful fidelity and courage, yet he was able to procure very little money for them ; and they had then, by the discipline under which they had been trained, (which was most regular, and full of that sobriety which promised good fortune,) an honest pride in their own natures, a great disdain of plundering, or supplying themselves by those vile arts, which they grew afterwards less tender to avoid.

3. " The great number of the king's horse ; which was so glorious a body, that when that part of it which was joined to the Cornish was away, he should march with at least six thousand horse, which were as many as would be able to live on any country within a due distance of quartering.

4. " Lastly, some correspondence with the chief gentlemen of Dorsetshire, who were ready to join with any con-

siderable party for the king, and had some probable hopes, that the small garrisons upon the coast would not make a tedious resistance."

There was another reason, which was not given, that if both armies had been kneaded into one, prince Maurice could have been but a private colonel : but there were enough besides to satisfy the king to keep them divided ; and so he gave order to the earl of Carnarvon to advance towards Dorchester (the chief town in that county, and the most malignant in England, where the rebels had a garrison) with the horse and dragoons, and the next day to prince Maurice to march after with the foot and cannon ; his majesty keeping with him the marquis of Hertford to attend his own person ; for though he well saw, he should undergo some inconveniences by withdrawing the marquis from that employment, the opinion of the soundness of his religion, and integrity of his justice, rendering him by much the most popular man in those parts, and was exceedingly tender of giving the least umbrage and distaste to his lordship, upon whose honour and affection he relied entirely, and would as soon have trusted his crown upon his fidelity, as upon any man's in his three kingdoms, yet he discerned plainly that the prince and the marquis would never agree together ;[1] and that there were persons about them, who would foment their indispositions to each other, with any hazard to his service ; and concluded, that he should sooner reduce his people by the power of his army, than by the persuasions of his counsel ;[2] and that the roughness of the one's nature might prevail more than the lenity and condescension of the other : and therefore he sent the prince on that employment ; using all imaginable means to remove any trouble, or jealousy of his favour from the marquis's mind ; his majesty freely and clearly communicating to him all his counsels, and the true grounds of his resolution ; and declaring to him, " that he

[1] All may discern plainly that the king did it to humour prince Maurice, in his impotent passion for being a general.---W.

[2] This gives us a glimmering of what was to be expected, now success ran high, if the king's arms should prevail.---W.

would make him a gentleman of his bedchamber, and groom of his stole, and that he would always have his company and advice about him ;" with which the marquis was satisfied, rather because he resolved not to disobey him, than that he was well pleased with the price of the obligations.

* And truly many wise and honest men were sorry for the king's election ; and though the marquis's years, and a long indulgence to his ease, had superinduced a kind of laziness and inactivity upon his nature, that was neither agreeable to his primitive constitution, nor the great endowments of his mind, (for he was a good scholar, and had a good judgment,) and less to the temper of this time, and the office of a general, insomuch as he often resigned an excellent understanding to those who had a very indifferent one, and followed the advice, and concluded upon the information of those, who had narrower and more vulgar thoughts than suited with his honour, and were not worthy of such a trust ; yet they thought the prince's inexperience of the customs and manners of England, and an aversion from considering them,[1] must subject him to the information and advice of worse counsellors than the other, and which would not be so easily controlled : and I am of opinion, that if the prince had waited on his majesty in that army, and never interposed in any command, not purely martial, and the marquis been sent with those forces into the west with the lord Hopton, (who was now to be left at Bristol to intend his health, and to form that new garrison ; which was to be a magazine for men, arms, ammunition, and all that was wanted,) and some other steady persons, who might have been assigned to special provinces, a greater tide of good fortune had attended that expedition.[2]

The next resolution to be taken, was concerning the king's own motion with that army. There was not a man, who did not think the reducing of Gloucester, a city within little more than twenty miles of Bristol, of mighty importance to

[1] This we see in the last page was the very reason for the king's preferring the prince to the marquis.---W.

[2] This is honestly confessed.---W.

the king, if it might be done without a great expense of
time, and loss of men : " It was the only garrison the rebels
had between Bristol and Lancashire, on the north part of
England ; and if it could be recovered, his majesty would
have the river of Severn entirely within his command ;
whereby his garrisons of Worcester, and Shrewsbury, and all
those parts, might be supplied from Bristol ; and the trade
of that city thereby so advanced, that the customs and duties
might bring a notable revenue to the king, and the wealth
of the city increasing, it might bear the greater burden for
the war : a rich and populous county, which hitherto rather
yielded conveniences of quarter, than a settled contribution,
(that strong garrison holding not only the whole forest division, which is a fourth part of the county of Gloucester, absolutely in obedience, but so alarmed all other parts, that
none of the gentry, who for the most part were well affected,
durst stay at their own houses,) might be wholly the king's
quarters ; and by how much it had offended and disquieted
the king, more than other counties, by so much the more
money might be raised upon them." Besides the general
weekly contributions, the yeomanry, who had been most forward and seditious, being very wealthy, and able to redeem
their delinquency at a high price, (and these arguments
were fully pressed by the well affected gentry of the county,
who had carried themselves honestly, and suffered very much
by doing so, and undertook great levies of men, if this work
were first done,) there was another argument of no less, if
not greater, moment than all the rest : " if Gloucester were
reduced, there would need no forces to be left in Wales, and
all those soldiers might be then drawn to the marching army,
and the contributions and other taxes assigned to the payment of it." Indeed the king would have had a glorious
and entire part of his kingdom, to have contended with the
rest.

Yet all these motives were not thought worth the engaging
his army in a doubtful siege ; whilst the parliament might
both recover the fear that was upon them, and consequently
allay and compose the distempers, (which, if they did not
wholly proceed from, were very much strengthened by,

those fears,) and recruit their army; and therefore that it
was better to march into some of those counties which were
most oppressed by the enemy, and there wait such advantage, as the distraction in and about London would administer, except there could be some probable hope that Gloucester might be got without much delay.   And to that purpose
there had been secret agitation, the effect whereof was hour-
ly expected.   The governor of that garrison was one colonel Massy, a soldier of fortune, who had, in the late northern
expeditions prepared by the king against Scotland, been an
officer in the king's army, under the command of William
Leg; and, in the beginning of these troubles, had been at
York with inclination to serve the king; but finding himself
not enough known there, and that there would be little gotten, but the comfort of a good conscience, he went to London, where there was more money, and fewer officers; and
was easily made lieutenant colonel to the earl of Stamford;
and being quickly found to be a diligent and stout officer,
and of no ill parts of conversation to render himself acceptable among the common people, was by his lordship, when
he went into the west, left governor of that city, where he
had behaved himself actively and successfully.   There was
no reason to despair, that this man (not intoxicated with any
of those fumes which made men rave, and frantic in the
cause) might not be wrought upon.   And Will. Leg, who
had the good opinion of most men, and the particular kindness of prince Rupert, had sent a messenger, who was like
to pass without suspicion to Gloucester, with such a letter
of kindness and overture to Massy, as was proper in such a
case from one friend to another.   This messenger returned
when the king's and the army's motion was under debate,
and brought an answer from the governor, in a very high
style, and seeming to take it much unkindly, " that he should
endeavour to corrupt him in his honesty and fidelity, and to
persuade him to break a trust, which, to save his life, he
would never do;" with much discourse " of his honour and
reputation, which would be always dear to him."   But the
messenger said withal, " that, after the governor had given
him this letter, and some sharp reproaches before company,

he was brought again, a back way, to a place where he was by himself; and then he told him, that it was most necessary he should write such an answer as he had done; which was communicated to those, who else would have been jealous what such a messenger should come to him about; but that he should tell Will. Leg, that he was the same man he had ever been, his servant; and that he wished the king well; that he heard prince Rupert meant to bring the army before that town; if he did, he would defend it as well as he could; and his highness would find another work than he had at Bristol; but if the king himself came with his army, and summoned it, he would not hold it against him:[1] for it would not stand with his conscience to fight against the person of the king; besides that in such a case, he should be able to persuade those of the town; which otherwise he could not do."

This message turned the scale; for though it might be without purpose of being honest, yet there was no great objection against the king's marching that way with his army; since it would be still in his power to pursue any other counsel, without engaging before it. And it was to some a sign that he meant well, because he had not hanged, or at least imprisoned, the messenger who came to him on such an errand. Hereupon the king resolved for Gloucester, but not to be engaged in a siege; and so sent his army that way; and the next day (having first sent sir Ralph Hopton a warrant to create him baron Hopton of Stratton, in memory of the happy battle fought there) with the remainder of his forces marched towards it. On Wednesday the tenth of August, the king ranged his whole army upon a fair hill, in the clear view of the city, and within less than two miles of it; and then, being about two of the clock in the afternoon, he sent a trumpet with this summons to the town.

" Out of our tender compassion to our city of Gloucester, and that it may not receive prejudice by our army, which

---

[1] Massey evidently said this to draw the king's army before Gloucester, and to gain himself honour and advancement in the service by a brave defence.—-W.

we cannot prevent if we be compelled to assault it, we are personally come before it to require the same; and are graciously pleased to let all the inhabitants of, and all other persons within that city, as well soldiers as others, know, that if they shall immediately submit themselves, and deliver this our city to us, we are contented, freely and absolutely to pardon every one of them, without exception; and do assure them, in the word of a king, that they, nor any of them shall receive the least damage or prejudice by our army in their persons or estates; but that we will appoint such a governor, and a moderate garrison to reside there, as shall be both for the ease and security of that city, and that whole county.   But if they shall neglect this proffer of grace and favour, and compel us, by the power of our army, to reduce that place, (which, by the help of God, we doubt not, we shall be easily and shortly able to do,) they must thank themselves for all the calamities and miseries must befall them.   To this message we expect a clear and positive answer, within two hours after the publishing hereof; and by these presents do give leave to any persons, safely to repair to and return from us, whom that city shall desire to employ unto us in that business: and do require all the officers and soldiers of our army, quietly to suffer them to pass accordingly."

Within less than the time prescribed, together with the trumpeter returned two citizens from the town, with lean, pale, sharp, and bald visages, indeed faces so strange and unusual, and in such a garb and posture, that at once made the most severe countenances merry, and the most cheerful hearts sad; for it was impossible such ambassadors could bring less than a defiance.   The men, without any circumstances of duty, or good manners, in a pert, shrill, undismayed accent, said, " they had brought an answer from the godly city of Gloucester to the king;" and were so ready to give insolent and seditious answers to any question, as if their business were chiefly to provoke the king to violate his own safe conduct.   The answer they brought was in writing, in these very words.

August 10*th*, 1643.

" We the inhabitants, magistrates, officers, and soldiers, within this garrison of Gloucester, unto his majesty's gracious message return this humble answer : That we do keep this city, according to our oaths and allegiance, to and for the use of his majesty, and his royal posterity : and do accordingly conceive ourselves wholly bound to obey the commands of his majesty, signified by both houses of parliament : and are resolved, by God's help, to keep this city accordingly."

This paper was subscribed by Wise the mayor, and Massy the governor, with thirteen of the aldermen, and most substantial citizens, and eleven officers of the garrison ; and as soon as their messengers returned, who were quickly dismissed, without attending to see what the king resolved, all the suburbs of the city, in which were very large and fair buildings, well inhabited, were set on fire ; so that there was no doubt, the king was to expect nothing there but what could not be kept from him. Now was the time for new debates, and new resolutions ; to which men came not so unbiassed, or unswayed, as they had been at Bristol. This indignity and affront to the king prompted thoughts of revenge ; and some thought the king so far engaged, that in honour he could not do less than sit down before the town, and force it : and these inclinations gave countenance and credit to all those plausible informations, " of small provisions in the town, either of victual, or ammunition ; that, where the town was strongest, there was nothing but an old stone wall, which would fall upon an easy battery ; that there were many well affected people in the town, who, with those who were incensed by the burning of the suburbs, and the great losses they must sustain thereby, would make such a party, that as soon as they were distressed, the seditious party would be forced to yield." It was alleged, " that the enemy had no army ; nor, by all intelligence, was like to form any soon enough to be able to relieve it ; and if they had an army, that it was much better for his majesty to force them to that distance from London, and to fight there, where he could be supplied with whatsoever he wanted, could choose his own ground, where his brave body of horse would be able to defeat any army they could raise, than to seek them in their own quarters."

Above all, the confidence of the soldiers of the best experience moved his majesty ; who upon riding about the town, and taking a near view of it, were clear of opinion, that they should be able in less than ten days by approach, for all thoughts of storming were laid aside upon the loss at Bristol, to win it. This produced a resolution in his majesty, not one man in the council of war dissuading it. And so the king presently sent to Oxford for his general the earl of Brentford " to come to him, with all the foot that could be spared out of that garrison, and his pieces of battery, and to govern that action :" prince Rupert wisely declining that province, and retiring himself into the generalship of the horse, that he might not be thought accountable for any accidents which should attend that service. At the same instant, orders were despatched to sir William Vavasour, who commanded all the forces in South Wales, (the lord Herbert having been persuaded so far to comply with the indisposition of that people, as to decline that command, or at least for a time to dissemble it,) " to draw all his men to the forest side of the town ;" where the bridges being broken down, a small strength would keep them in, and any from going to them, which within two days was done. Thus the king was engaged before Gloucester ; and thereby gave respite to the distracted spirits at London, to breathe, and compose themselves; and, more methodically than they had hoped to have done, to prepare for their preservation, and accomplishing their own ends; which at that time seemed almost desperate and incurable.

The direful news of the surrender of Bristol, which was brought to the two houses on the 31st of July, struck them to the heart, and came upon them as a sentence of death, after a vast consumption of money, and confident promises of destroying all the king's forces by a day, every tax and imposition being declared to be the last ; and for finishing the work, the earl of Essex was at the same time returned to

Kingston, within eight miles of them, with his broken and dismayed troops, which himself would not endure should have the title of an army. So that the war seemed to be even at an end in a sense very contrary to what they had undertaken; their general talking more, and pressing for reparation, and vindication of his honour from imputations and aspersions, than for a recruit of forces, or providing an army to defend them. Every man reproached his neighbour with his disinclination to peace, when good conditions might be had, and magnified his own wisdom, for having feared " it would come to this." The king's last declaration had been read by all men, and was magnified " as a most gracious and undeniable instance of his clemency and justice, that he was so far from being elated with his good successes, and power almost to have what he would, that he renewed all those promises, and protestations for the religion, laws, and liberties of the kingdom, and privileges of parliament; which had been out of their perverseness discredited before, as proceeding from the low condition he was in; and whereas they had been frighted with their representation of their own guilt, and the implacableness of the king's nature, as if he meant an utter conquest of them, his majesty had now offered all that could be honestly desired, and had expressed himself a prince not delighted with blood and revenge, but an indulgent father to the most disobedient children." In this reformation of understanding, the lords in their house debated nothing but expedients for peace : there were not of that body above five, at the most, who had any inclination to continue the war ; and the earl of Essex had sufficiently declared, " that he was weary of it," and held closest and strictest correspondence with those who most passionately pressed an accommodation. So that, on the fifth of August, they desired a conference with the commons ; and declared to them, " that they were resolved to send propositions to the king, and they hoped, they would concur in them :" the particulars proposed by them were,

1. " That both armies might be presently disbanded, and his majesty be entreated to return to his parliament, upon such security as should give him satisfaction.

2. " That religion might be settled with the advice of a synod of divines, in such a manner as his majesty, with the consent of both houses of parliament, should appoint.

3. " That the militia, both by sea and land, might be settled by a bill; and the militia, forts, and ships of the kingdom, put into such hands as the king should appoint, with the approbation of both houses of parliament : and his majesty's revenue to be absolutely and wholly restored unto him; only deducting such part, as had been of necessity expended for the maintenance of his children, and not otherwise.

4. " That all the members of both houses who had been expelled only for absenting themselves, or mere compliance with his majesty, and no other matter of fact against them, might be restored to their places.

5. " That all delinquents, from before the tenth day of January 1641, should be delivered up to the justice of parliament, and a general pardon for all others on both sides.

6. And lastly, " That there might be an act of oblivion, for all by-gone deeds, and acts of hostility."

When this conference was reported in the house of commons, it begot a wonderful long and a hot debate, which lasted till ten of the clock that night, and continued a day or two more; the violent party (for there were yet many among them of more moderate constitutions, who did, and ever had heartily abhorred their proceedings, though out of fear, and indisposition of health, or not knowing else well what to do, they continued there) inveighed furiously against the design itself of sending to the king at all, and therefore would not have the particular propositions so much as considered : " They had received much prejudice by the last treaty at Oxford, and therefore must undergo much more now their condition was much lower : the king had since that, upon the matter, declared them to be no parliament; for if they were not free, they could not be a parliament; so that till that point were vindicated, they could not treat in any safe capacity, but would be looked upon under the notion of rebels, as his majesty had declared them. They had sent members into Scotland to require assistance, which that kingdom was preparing with all brotherly affection and forwardness; and after such a discovery,' to treat for peace, without their privity, was to betray them; and to forfeit all hopes hereafter of relief from thence, what necessities soever they might be reduced to. That the city of London had expressed all imaginable readiness to raise forces for sir William Waller; and the counties near London were ready to rise as one man, whereby the earl of Essex would be speedily enabled to march, with a better army than ever he had, to give the king battle, except this discourse of peace did extinguish the zeal that was then flaming in the hearts of the people."

But notwithstanding these reasons, and the passion in the delivery, the terror of the king's successes suggested answers enough. "They had been punished for breaking off the treaty of Oxford, when they might have had better terms than now they could expect; and if they omitted this opportunity, they should fare much worse; that they were not sure of aid from Scotland, neither was it almost possible it should come time enough to preserve them from the ruin at hand. And for the city of London, though the common and meaner sort of people, who might promise themselves advantage by it, desired the continuance of the distractions, yet it was evident the most substantial and rich men desired peace, by their refusal to supply money for the carrying on the war; and if they should judge of the common people by their forwardness to engage their own persons, they had reason to believe they had no mind to the war neither; for their general was forced to retire even under their own walls, for want of men to recruit his army. However, the sending reasonable propositions to the king would either procure a peace, and so they should have no more need of an army; or, being refused, would raise more men and money, than all their ordinances without it." These reasons and arguments prevailed; and after the debate had lasted till ten of the clock at night, it was resolved upon the question, and carried by nine and twenty voices, "That they

' Disposition.—W.

93*

should insist upon the propositions, and send to his majesty."

And without doubt, if they had then sent, (as, if the power had been in the two houses of parliament, they had done,)
a firm peace had immediately ensued : for besides that if a
treaty and cessation had been in that conjuncture entered
upon, no extravagant demand would have been pressed,
only a security for those who had been faulty, which the
king would gladly have granted, and most religiously observed ; the fourth proposition, and consent to restore all
members to their places in parliament, would have prevented the kindling any more fire in those houses.   But this
was too well known to be suffered to pass; and therefore
the next day, being Sunday, the seditious preachers filled all
the pulpits with alarms of " ruin and destruction to the city,'
if a peace were now offered to the king ;" and printed papers were scattered through the streets, and fixed upon
gates, posts, and the most public places in the city and
suburbs, requiring " all persons well affected to rise as one
man, and to come to the house of commons next morning;
for that twenty thousand Irish rebels were landed ;" which
information was likewise given that day in many pulpits by
their preachers; and in other papers likewise set up, it was
declared, " that the malignant party had overvoted the good,
and, if not prevented, there would be a peace."

When the minds of the people were thus prepared, Pennington, their own lord mayor, though on Sunday, (on which they
before complained the king used to sit in council,) called
a common council; where a petition was framed to the house
of commons, taking notice " of propositions passed by the
house of peers for peace, which if consented to, and allowed,
would be destructive to religion, laws, and liberties ; and
therefore desired that house to pass an ordinance, according
to the tenor of an act of their common council," (which they
appointed to be annexed to their petition,) " which was for
the vigorous prosecuting the war, and declining all thoughts

' Thus the presbyterian clergy became the instruments of the overthrow of the constitution.—W.

of accommodation." With this petition, and such an attendance as those preparatives were like to bring, the lord mayor
himself, who, from the time of his mayoralty, had forborne
sitting in the house as a member, came to the house of commons, and delivered it, with such further insinuations of the
temper of the city, as were fit for the purpose ; the people
at the door behaving themselves as imperiously, and telling
the members of both houses, as they passed by them, " that
if they had not a good answer, they would be there the next
day with double the number." The lords complained of the
tumults, and sent to the commons to join with them in their
suppression ; instead whereof the commons (many of their
body withdrawing for fear, and others by fear converted, or
it may be by hope of prevailing) gave the city thanks " for
their petition, advice, and courage ;" and rejected the propositions for peace.

This raised a new contest in the city, which was not willing to lie under the perpetual brand of resisting and opposing peace, as they did of first raising the war. And therefore
the wise and sober part of it would gladly have discovered
how averse they were from the late act of the common council. But the late execution of Tomkins and Chaloner, and
the advantage which was presently taken against any man
who was moderately inclined, frighted all men from appearing in person to desire those things upon which their
hearts were most set. In the end, the women expressed
greater courage than the men ; and having a precedent of a
rabble of that sex, appearing in the beginning of these distractions with a petition to the house of commons, to foment
the divisions, with acceptance and approbation, a great multitude of the wives of substantial citizens came to the house
of commons with a petition for peace. Thereupon a troop
of horse, under the command of one Harvey, a decayed silk-
man, who from the beginning had been one most confided in,
were sent for ; who behaved themselves with such inhumanity, that they charged among the silly women, as an enemy
worthy of their courage, and killed and wounded many of
them, and easily dispersed the rest. When they were by
this means secured from further vexation of this kind, special

notice was taken of those members who seemed most importunate, and desirous of peace, that some advantage might be
taken against them.   Whereupon, they well discerning the
danger they were in, many both of the peers and the commons first absented themselves from the houses, and then
removed into those quarters where they might enjoy the
protection of the king ; and some of them came directly to
Oxiord.

Having diverted this torrent, which would have brought
peace upon them before they were aware, they considered
their strength, and applied themselves to the recovery of
the spirits of their general ; whose indisposition troubled
them more than any other distress they were in.   To this
cure they applied remedies of contrary natures, which would
yet work to the same end.   First they caressed sir William
Waller with wonderful kindness and esteem ; and as he was
met upon his return to London, after the most total defeat
that could almost be imagined, (for though few of his horse
were killed upon the place, they were so ruinously dispersed,
that of above two thousand, there were not three hundred
gotten together again for their service,) with all the trained
bands and militia of London, and received as if he had
brought the king prisoner with him ; so he was immediately
chosen governor and commander in chief of the forces and
militia of London, for the defence of the city ; and it was
now declared, " that they would forthwith supply him with
a good body of horse and foot, to take the field again, and
relieve their distressed friends in the west."   Then another
ordinance was passed to raise a vast army, under the command of the earl of Manchester, (who had been always
steady to his first principles, and never a friend to any overture of accommodation,) in order to opposing the earl of
Newcastle, and to take charge of all the associated counties ;
which were Essex, Hertford, Cambridge, Norfolk, Suffolk,
Huntington, and (by a new addition) Lincoln ; and for the
speedy raising men to join to those who would voluntarily
list themselves under these two beloved generals, there was
an ordinance passed both houses for the pressing of men ;
which seemed somewhat to discredit their cause, that, after

so much pretence to the hearts of the people, they should
be now compelled to fight, whether they would or no; and
was the more wondered at, because they had themselves
procured the king's consent to an act this parliament, that
declared it to be unlawful to press, or compel any of the freeborn subjects to march out of the county in which they lived,
if he were not willing so to do ; and direction was given by
other ordinances to press great numbers of men, to serve
both under the earl of Manchester and sir William Waller;
and having thus provided for the worst, and let the earl of
Essex discern, that they had another earl to trust to, and
more generals than one at their devotion, they sent a formal
committee of both houses to him, to use all imaginable art,
and application to him, to recover him to his former vigour,
and zeal in their cause.   They told him " the high value
the houses had of the service he had done, and the hazards,
dangers, and losses he had for their sakes undergone : that
he should receive as ample a vindication for the calumnies
and aspersions raised on him, as he could desire, from the
full testimony and confidence of the two houses; and if the
infamous authors of them could be found, their punishment
should be as notorious as their libels: that no other forces
should be recruited till his were made up ; and that all his
soldiers' arrears should be paid, and clothes presently sent
for his foot."

Whether these reasons, with the jealousy of the earl of
Manchester, upon whom he plainly saw the violent party
wholly depended, or the infusions poured into him by the
lord Say and Mr. Pym, of the desperateness of his own condition, with an opinion, by the conclusions upon the differences between the two princes and the marquis of Hertford,
that the marquis's services were not enough valued by the
king, (which many desired should be thought to have then
some influence upon the earl,)[1] or whether he had not courage enough to engage in so hazardous an enterprise, he
grew insensibly altered from his moderate inclinations, and

[1] i. e. many of the king's court, who were of the party or faction of
the marquis.---W.

desire of peace ; for it is most certain, that as the confidence
in him gave many lords the spirit to appear champions for
peace, who had been before as solicitous against it, so the
design was then the same, which hath been since prosecuted,
with effect, to a worse purpose,[1] for the members of both
houses who were of one mind, upon that signal riot, and
compelling the house of commons to renounce their former
resolution of propositions to the king, to have gone to the
earl of Essex, and there, under the security of their own
army, to have protested against the violence which was
offered, the breach of their privileges by the common council's taking notice of their counsels, and overruling their conclusions, and to have declared their want of freedom : by
means whereof, they made no doubt to have drawn the
houses to consent to such an agreement as the king would
well have approved of ; or to have entered upon such a
treaty themselves with the king, as all the moderate part of
the kingdom would have been glad to be comprehended
under.

But this staggering in their general frustrated that design,
and put them to other resolutions ; and so, having rendered
themselves very ungracious in the houses, and possibly suspecting the earl of Essex might discover some of their overtures, many of the lords left the town, and went either
directly to Oxford, or into the king's quarters ; the earl of
Portland, and the lord Lovelace, (of whose good affections
to his service the king had always assurance, and who had
only stayed there, as at a place where they might do him
more service, than any where else,) directly to Oxford ; and
the lord Conway shortly after them ; the earl of Clare into
Worcestershire, and from thence, by the king's free acceptation, to Oxford ; there being no other objection against his
lordship, than his staying so long amongst them ; but his
total differing with them in all their extravagances, he having no manner of relation to the court, rendered him to his
majesty's opinion under a very good character. The earls

---

[1] When the seceders of parliament went to the army under Fairfax
and Cromwell.---W.

of Bedford and Holland, not without some difficulty, their purpose being discovered or suspected, got into the king's garrison at Wallingford, from whence the governor gave advertisement of their arrival ; the earl of Northumberland, with the leave of the house, retired for his health to his house at Petworth in Sussex ; which though it was in a county entirely then at the parliament's devotion, yet it was near enough to be infested from some of the king's quarters, if he had not some assurance of being safe there.

The violent party carried now all before them, and were well contented with the absence of those who used to give them some trouble and vexation. For the better strengthening themselves with the people, they ordered the divines of the assembly to repair into the country to their cures, especially in the counties of the association under the earl of Manchester, to stir up the people, with all their eloquence, to rise as one man against their sovereign ; and omitted nothing within their power, which might contribute to the raising men or money ; being not a little joyed, when they understood the king had given them more time than they expected, to compose all disorders and divisions among themselves, by his staying with his army before Gloucester ;[1] which was the greater blessing, and preservation to them, because at the same time there were sudden insurrections in Kent against their ordinances and jurisdiction, in defence of the known laws, and especially of the Book of Common Prayer ; which, if the king's army had been at any distance to have countenanced, they would never have been able to suppress.

The fame of all these distractions and disorders at London exceedingly disposed men in all places to reproach his

[1] It is certain this was a false step. Had the disorders and divisions in London been between men who had the same *end*, and differed only in the *means*, the approach of a common enemy would have united them. But as their end as well as means was different, the king's approach would have quite broke them to p·eces, and reestablished his own power. The not seeing this difference in the king's council must give one a very indifferent idea either of their sense or sobriety.---W.

majesty's stay before Gloucester; his friends at London desiring that his majesty should march directly thither, to take the advantage of those distractions; and the lords of the council at Oxford, upon the intelligence and advice from thence, were very solicitous that the king would take that resolution, to which he was himself enough inclined. But his condition was believed to be, in both places, better than it was; and that he had now a victorious army, without an enemy to restrain his motion: whereas, in truth, it was a miserable army, lessened exceedingly by the losses it sustained before Bristol; and when that part of it that was marched with prince Maurice into the west, and which could not have marched any other way, the king had not much above six thousand foot to march with, though he left none at Bristol, but obliged the lord Hopton to garrison it as he could, which he shortly did; and that would have appeared a very small army to have marched towards London; though it is true the horse was a noble body, and superior in number to that of the foot. On the other side, the parliament had a garrison in Gloucester, the only place possessed by them on the Severn, (for the taking of Bristol had reduced Chepstow, and secured for the most part all South Wales;) and if that were recovered to the king's obedience, his majesty's quarters would extend from Bristol to Chester, and bring all the countries between into contribution and subjection, which was a noble quantity of ground; Wales would be entire at the king's devotion; and his army would receive a very great addition by a body of three thousand men, horse and foot, which were commanded by Vavasour, under lord Herbert on the Welsh side, to block up Gloucester from annoying that country, and would all march with the king, if that place were recovered; whereas they could not be drawn from thence whilst that garrison remained, and which, as soon as the king was marched from Bristol, would be a thorn in the sides of Gloucestershire and Wales, and would hinder all levies and contributions in those countries, and much hinder the settlement of Bristol itself. Gloucester was at that time under the government of colonel Massey, a soldier of fortune, and a very active and vigilant officer. He had been some-

times an officer under the command of Will. Leg, who was
then major to prince Rupert, and of near trust about him.
After the taking of Bristol, he had, with the king's privity,
written a letter to him, and received such an answer that
was interpreted to give encouragement to the king's army to
march thither, and as if the king's presence would have
opened the ports of the town ; though it appeared afterwards
that it was craftily and maliciously written to amuse the king.
However the town itself was no otherwise fortified than by
an old high stone wall and a dry ditch, there being likewise
a fair and well built suburbs without the town.   There did
not appear, when the king consulted it at Bristol, any difference of opinion against the king's marching thither with his
army ; and it was resolved that if he found, when he came
there,-that a summons would not put the town into his hands,
he might march on towards any other designs.

There was likewise another circumstance that favoured
this resolution, which was some good success the earl of
Newcastle had obtained in Yorkshire, which had broken all
the parliament forces, and driven them into Hull, and much
increased his own, with which he made little doubt in a
short time to be master of that important place.   Upon the
first news of the taking of Bristol, his majesty, before he left
Oxford, had sent an express to the earl of Newcastle, who
was then engaged before Hull, " that if he found the business of Hull to be more difficult than he expected, he should
leave it blocked up at a distance, which might restrain excursions into the country, and march with his army into the
associated counties;" which comprehended Norfolk, Suffolk,
Cambridgeshire, and Essex, which had associated themselves, by some agreement, to serve the parliament ; though
the better part of all those counties, especially of the two
greater, were most affected to the king, and wished for an
opportunity to express it; and if the earl would bring his
army through those counties towards London, his majesty
would then resolve, with his own, to march towards it on
the other side.   And in the very time that his majesty
came before Gloucester, and before he took the resolution to
sit down before it, that express returned from the earl of

Newcastle, who informed him, "that it was impossible for him to comply with his commands, in marching with his army into the associated counties, for that the gentlemen of the country, who had the best regiments, and were among the best officers, utterly refused to march, except Hull were first taken; and that he had not strength enough to march and to leave Hull securely blocked up :" which advertisement, with the consideration before mentioned, of the enlarging his quarters by the taking of Gloucester, and the concurrence of all the officers, that it would speedily be taken, produced that resolution of attempting it, notwithstanding that the queen herself writ so importunately against it,[1] that his majesty thought it necessary to make a journey himself to Oxford, to convince her majesty, and to compose some distempers which were risen among his council there, upon the news of the arrival of some of the lords mentioned before in those quarters.

The king was newly set down before Gloucester, when the governor of Wallingford sent notice to Oxford, of the arrival of those two earls; to whom the lords of the council returned direction, "that they should stay there, till the king's pleasure was understood ;" to whom the secretary had sent the information, and desired his majesty's will concerning their reception. The king well knew, any order he should give in it would be liable to many objections, and he had not so good an inclination to either of them, as to run any inconvenience for their sakes; the earl of Bedford having served in person against him, as the general of the rebels' horse ; and the earl of Holland, in the king's opinion, having done worse. And therefore his majesty commanded, "that his privy-council should debate the matter among themselves, and present their opinion and advice to him ; and he would then determine what kind of entertainment they should have." The opinions at the board were several; some thought, "that his majesty should receive them very graciously, and with all outward expressions of his ac-

---

[1] This was the first good counsel I find of her giving. But we see, by p. 1487, that it was out of no public motive.—W.

ceptance of their return to his service; and that the demeanour of all others to them should be such, as might make them think themselves very welcome, without the least taking notice of any thing formerly done amiss by them; which would be a great encouragement to others to come away too: so that the numbers and quality of those who stayed behind would probably in a short time be so small, that they would have no reputation in the kingdom to continue the war." Many differed diametrically from this; and were so far from thinking this advice agreeable to the dignity or security of the king, that they thought it not fit "to admit them presently to the king's or queen's presence, till, by their good carriage and demeanour, they should give some testimony of their affections: they had both taken the late covenant, of which one clause was, to assist the forces raised by the parliament, against the army raised by the king; with many reproaches, and known scandals upon that army. If they had felt a true remorse of conscience for the ill they had done, they would have left that party, when that convenant was to be imposed upon them; which since they did not, that they came now was to be imputed rather to the king's success, and the weakness of that power which they had hitherto served, than to any reformation of their understanding, or improvement of their allegiance: and that it was great reason, that they who had given such arguments of just jealousy and suspicion of themselves, should raise a confidence in their loyalty and affection by some act equal to the other; and therefore that none who had taken that covenant should be admitted to the presence of the king, queen, or prince, before he had taken some other oath or covenant, declaring an equal hatred and abhorring of the rebellious arms which were taken up against his majesty, and the counsels by which they were taken up."

It was said, " that the good or ill reception of these lords could have no influence upon the actions or deliberations at Westminster, or London, or any considerable persons there: that they were but single men, without any considerable dependence upon them. Whilst they had reputation and interest enough to do good or hurt, and the king's condition

needed their attendance, they chose to be engaged against
him; but now, when they were able to do him no more
harm, they came to receive benefit and advantage from him:
that it was a common argument men used to allege to themselves for their compliance with, and submission to, the commands of the parliament; that, if they did otherwise, their
severity and rigour was so great, that they and their families
were sure to be ruined; but, if the king prevailed, he was
gracious and merciful, and would remit their offences when-
soever they cast themselves at his feet; which presumption
if they should see confirmed in this example, it would make
the observation of conscience and loyalty of no price, and
encourage those who were risen against him, and exceedingly dishearten those who had been honest and faithful
from the beginning: that there could ensue no inconvenience from any reservedness and coldness towards them;
for they durst not return to London, having now made
themselves odious to that party, and had no hope but from
the acceptance of his majesty; which they should merit before they found." There was a third opinion between
these extremes, "that they should be neither courted nor
neglected, but be admitted to kiss the king's and queen's
hands, and to dispose themselves as they thought fit; and so
to leave the rest to their future demeanour:" and to resolve
which of these opinions to follow, was another motive for his
majesty's sudden journey to Oxford. The king followed
the last opinion; and so they came to Oxford, and were
admitted to kiss the queen's hands, and shortly after went
to the leaguer before Gloucester, and were in the same
manner received by the king: all which I have remembered
the more particularly, that it may appear whatsoever was
done in that point to have been deliberated; yet truly I
conceive it was one of the greatest, if not the only omission
on the king's part of any expedient, during the whole dis-
-tractions, which might reasonably have been depended on,
to promote or contribute towards a fair accommodation, upon
which we shall have occasion anon to say more.

The king found greater alterations in the minds and
spirits at Oxford, than he expected after so much great suc-

cess as had befallen him ; and that success was it, that had
made the alteration; it being the unlucky temper of that
place, and that company, to be the soonest and the most
desperately cast down upon any misfortune or loss, and to be
again, upon any victory, the most elated, and the most apt
to undervalue any difficulties which remained.　The taking
Bristol had so possessed them with joy, that they thought
the war even at an end, and that there was nothing left to
be done, but to take possession of London ; which they
were assured would be delivered to them upon demand.
Many members of both houses were come to Oxford, which
assured them, "the violent people there were even in despair; and after the news came of the surrender of Bristol,
that they had only kept up their spirits that the king would
engage his army in the siege of Gloucester, which some of
them had seemed to promise their friends would be the
case :" from whence they would infer, " that the king was
betrayed,[1] and that they who had persuaded him to undertake that design were corrupted by the parliament."　And
the envy and jealousy of all this fell upon sir John Colepepper, who was indeed of the opinion for the siege, but, without doubt, how much soever he suffered at that time, and
afterwards, under that reproach, he believed there was very
good reason for that engagement, and was most free from
any corrupt end, and of most sincere fidelity.

　　This discourse and imagination had made wonderful impression upon the queen ; who was inflamed with a jealousy
that there was a design to lessen her interest in the king,
and that prince Rupert was chief in that conspiracy, and
meant to bring it to pass by keeping the king still in the
army, and by hindering his coming to Oxford : and out of
this apprehension the queen had written so warmly and con-
cernedly to the king, who was the most incapable of any
such apprehensions,[2] and had her majesty in so perfect an

　　[1] No further than by the soldiery's desiring the continuance of the
war.—W.

　　[2] Which had brought him into this condition, and soon reduced him
to a worse.—W.

adoration,[1] that as soon as he received that letter, without
delay he came to Oxford, and quickly composed those mistakes; though the being engaged before Gloucester was
still very grievous, and reproaches were publicly cast upon
those who gave the advice.

But that which took up most of the time of that one day
that the king stayed at Oxford, was concerning the two
lords who were retained at Wallingford; which had been
agitated in the council with great passion before the king's
coming.   The king caused the council to meet the next
morning, and asked their advice, " whether the earls of
Bedford and of Holland should be admitted to come into
Oxford, or obliged to return from whence they came? or, if
admitted, how they should be received, or countenanced by
their majesties?"   And it cannot be enough wondered at,
that there should be any difference of opinion in that matter;
but it cannot be expressed, with how much earnestness and
unreasonableness the whole was debated, and how warmly
even they, who in all other debates still expressed all moderation and temper, did now oppose the receiving these
lords with any grace, with more passion, and other reasons,
than had been offered in their former conferences; so that
there was scarce known such an union in opinion at that
board, in any thing, where disunion was very inconvenient.

All exaggerated " the carriage and foul ingratitude of the
earl of Holland, from the beginning of the parliament; and
the earl of Bedford's being general of the horse in the earl
of Essex's army; and now when the parliament was low,
and they had lost their credit and interest there, they were
come to the king, whom they had so much offended; and
expected to be as much, it may be, more made of, than they
who had borne the heat of the day;[2] which would so much
reflect upon the king's honour, that men would be exceed-

---

[1] Were there no other proof, this very strange expression shews
how much the noble historian condemned the king's uxorious folly.—
W.

[2] They were afraid of having too many sharers in the king's good
fortune.—W.

ingly discouraged to serve him." Some moved, " that they
might be detained, and kept prisoners of war, since they
came into the king's quarters without any pass;" others as
plainly and more vehemently pressed, " that they might not
be suffered to come to Oxford, or where the king or queen
should be ; but permitted to live in some other place within
the king's quarters, until they should manifest their affections by some service." They who thought this too severe
and unpolitic, proposed " that they might be suffered to
come to Oxford, that thereby they might be kept from returning to the parliament," (which appeared to most to be
liable to many exceptions,) " but that being at Oxford, they
should not come to court; and that no privy-counsellor
should visit them."

In this whole debate, the chancellor of the exchequer,
who seldom spoke without some earnestness,[1] was the only
man (except another, who brought no credit to the opinion,
the lord Savile) who advised confidently, " that they might
be very graciously received by both their majesties, and
civilly be visited and treated by every body ; that other men
might, by the entertainment they received, be encouraged to
desert the parliament too." He said, " it would be too
great a disadvantage to the king, and to his cause, that whilst
the parliament used all the industry and artifices, to corrupt
the duty and affection of the subject, and had their arms
open to receive and embrace all, who would come to them,
his majesty should admit none to return to him, who had
been faulty, or not come so soon as they ought to have done ;
that if the king had a mind to gratify and oblige the parliament, he could not do it more to their hearts' desire, than
by rejecting the application of these lords, or suffering it to
pass unregarded." There was one argument against their
admission urged very loudly, " that it would disturb the
peace of the place ;" the earl of Bedford had commanded
that part of the army, which infested the marquis of Hertford, at his being at Sherborne, when the marquis had sent

---

[1] i. e. on some pressing occasion. For this is the sense of the words,
which have the face of a very different meaning.---W.

Harry Seymour, as is mentioned before, with a challenge to the earl to fight with him ; which the earl reasonably declined at that time ; and said, " he would be ready, when the business of the parliament should be over, to wait upon the marquis when he should require it " And some men, who were near enough to the marquis's counsels, undertook to know, that if the earl of Bedford should be in Oxford, the marquis, who was every day expected, would exact the performance of his promise ; which sure he was too wise to do.

The king, during the whole debate, did not express any thing of his own sense, save that he seemed well pleased with any sharpness that was expressed towards the earl of Holland. He said, " that he was bound to his good behaviour, by being under the common reproach of inclining too much to those who had used him worst ; of which he would not be guilty :" however, he did not think, at this time, that it would be good to make any persons desperate ; and therefore gave order, " that the governor of Wallingford should permit them to continue their journey to Oxford ; where all men might use what civilities they pleased to them ; and that himself and the queen would do that towards them, which, upon their application and address, they should think fit :" and though this determination was given, without the least discovery of grace towards the persons of those lords, and not without some reflections of prejudice towards them, it was not grateful to the table ; which was evident enough by their countenance. The next morning the king returned to the army.

There had been, as is said, very great divisions in the counsels at Westminster, from the time of the treaty, and the very abrupt breaking of it ; and the earl of Northumberland, resenting the affront done to him by Martin, had increased those divisions ; and the ill successes afterwards in the defeat of Waller, and the taking of Bristol, had given every man courage to say what he would. And then the proceeding upon Mr. Waller's discovery, and obliging all men to take a desperate engagement, which they durst not refuse, for fear of being declared guilty of the plot, as many

of them were, incensed very many: but above all, the prosperity of the king's affairs made every body wish to come
into his quarters.   A great number of the house of commons,
who were known always to wish well, came to Oxford: and
of the peers, the earl of Portland, who was always very
faithful to the king, and had stayed in the house of peers by
his majesty's leave, and had been accused by Mr. Waller to
be privy to that design, upon which he had endured a long
imprisonment, came at this time to Oxford, together with the
lord Conway, and the lord Lovelace; the former of which
had been likewise questioned, and imprisoned, and the latter
had been as knowing of the matter, and of constant duty
to the king; and all three had gotten liberty and opportunity to come away by swallowing that vow, and oath, which
could only set them free, and which they made haste to answer for to the king.   The return of the earl of Essex to London in ill humour, had given opportunity to the earl of Holland, and the rest, who were weary of the work in hand, to
inflame him to resentment of the neglects which had been
put upon him, and the jealousies which were entertained of
him.   The earl of Bedford had given up his commission of
general of the horse, and quitted the service, and never had
any affection to their ways in his judgment, which was not
great.   The earl of Clare had been with the king at York,
and had his leave to return to London, to intend his own
particular affairs; and, during his stay, had never concurred
in any malicious counsel against the king, but was looked
upon as a man, not only firm to the principles of monarchy,
but of duty to the person of the king.   He was a man of
honour, and of courage, and would have been an excellent
person, if his heart had not been set too much upon the
keeping and improving his estate;[1] he was weary of the
company he kept, and easily hearkened to the earl of Holland, in any consultation how to recover the king's authority,
and to put an end to the war.   The earl of Essex was, as

[1] The exact character of his son, the late duke of Newcastle, and
the first of the name of Holles.---W.

94*

is said before, enough provoked, and incensed, and willingly heard all the lords, and others, who inveighed against the violent proceedings of those who swayed the parliament, and differed not with them in his judgment of the men, and the matter : so that they believed that he would as readily be disposed to agree upon the remedy, as he did upon the disease.

Their end and design was, if they could draw him to a concurrence, that they, and all the rest of those who were accounted moderate men, that is who desired a peace, and to return to their duty to the king, (which was much the major part of both houses that remained at Westminster, after so many of both were gone to the king,) might all go to the army; and thereupon the general, and they, to write to the parliament together, and to send such propositions to them, as the parliament should transmit to the king, as the conditions of peace. If the king should refuse to consent to them, it would be an infallible way to unite all people to compel him to it : but if the parliament would refuse to transmit those propositions to the king, or to consent to a peace upon those conditions, they would then declare against them, for not adhering to the grounds upon which the war was first begun, and would join themselves to the king to force them to it. If this had been done in that conjuncture, when the authority and credit of the earl of Essex was not yet eclipsed, and before an independent army was raised, which was shortly after done, it could not probably have failed of the success desired. But the earl was too scrupulous and too punctual to that which he called a trust ; and this was too barefaced a separation for him to engage in : besides that he did believe, that he should be able to suppress that violent party by the parliament itself, and he thought that would bring all about which he desired ; and so he did not only reject what was proposed to him, but expressed such a dislike of the earl of Holland for proposing it, that he thought it high time to get himself out of his reach. The earl of Holland, who always considered himself in the first place, had, from the time of the queen's landing, privately made offer of his service to the queen, and renewed his old confidence and friendship with Mr. Jermyn; and knowing well to enhance the value of his own service, made great promises of notable service; and Mr. Jermyn easily persuaded her majesty, " that it was much better for her to restore an old servant, whom she knew so well, to her confidence, (though he had stepped out of the way,) than to rely upon the fidelity of any of those who were now about the king, and who were all upon the matter strangers to her, at least not enough known by her;" and then, "that, by laying hold upon this opportunity, she would, at her first coming to the king, carry his restoration with her, possess herself of the whole frame of his business, because all other designs would be laid aside; and so all the good, which would redound to the king and kingdom from this new negotiation, must, by the consent of all the world, be attributed to her majesty's wisdom and conduct." And this appearing hopeful to her majesty, and all that had any thing of hope was by the other always looked upon as certain, the correspondence was embraced; and the earl assured not only to be restored to his former station in all respects, but to a title to new interest. And upon this encouragement and obligation, when he found he could not prevail with the earl of Essex, that the king's affairs prospered, and that Bristol was now taken, and the queen come to Oxford, he resolved himself to go thither, and prevailed with the earls of Bedford and Clare to do the like; he assuring them, that they should be very well received. The earl of Clare made his journey by himself, out of the common road, and came without any interruption into Oxford, at the time appointed : the earls of Bedford and Holland came together to Wallingford, as is mentioned. The earl of Northumberland, who was naturally suspicious, went to his own house at Petworth in Sussex; by which he thought he shewed aversion enough to the counsels at Westminster, and would keep it in his own power to return, if he found that the reception of the other lords at Oxford was not answerable to their expectation; besides that he would expect the result of the lord Conway's negotiation, who was more trusted by him than any other.

The leave for the two earls to come from Wallingford to

Oxford, was declared but the night before the king returned
to the army; and was not sent thither till the next day.   So
that the lords came not to Oxford till two days after, much
mortified with the time they had been forced to spend at
Wallingford, and with the disputation they heard had been
held concerning them; of which they had received so particular information, that the earl of Holland writ a very civil
letter to the chancellor before he came to Oxford, taking
notice of "the affection he had shewed to him in his advice
to the king."   Both of them had friends enough there to
provide for their accommodation in convenient lodgings : so
that the one had a lodging at Magdalen college in Oxford, of
which house he had formerly been a member; the other lay
in Balliol college, where he had a daughter, who spared him
part of her lodgings.   But for any application to them by
the lords, or persons in authority there, they had no reason
to think themselves very welcome.   They went, in the first
place, to do their duties to the queen; who received them
coldly enough, not out of disinclination, or willingness
enough to shew them any countenance, but pure compliance
with the ill humour of the town,[1] which she detested : nor
did Mr. Jermyn, who still valued himself upon the impossible faculty to please all, and displease none, think fit to deal
clearly with them in that point, (having, no doubt, said more
in his letters of correspondence and advice, than he had authority to do; it being his custom to write and speak what
was most grateful to the persons ;) so that the earl of Holland, with whom alone the correspondence had been, began
to think himself betrayed, and invited to Oxford only to be
exposed to contempt.   He came one morning to visit the
chancellor of the exchequer, when there were the lord Cot-
tington, and two or three other privy-counsellors with him,
who all went presently away, without so much as saluting
him : which offended the chancellor as much as it did him,
and in truth obliged him to more ceremony and civility, than,
it may be, he would otherwise have exercised; and he did

[1] Nothing more shews the innate corruption of courtiers, than this
ill humour on this occasion.—W.

visit him again, and make all professions and offers of kindness and service to him ; which he did very heartily ; and
complied therein, not only with his own inclinations, but with
his judgment, as very important to the king's service ; and
did all he could to induce others to be of the same opinion ;
in which he had no great success.

The intelligence from London brought, every day, the resolution of the parliament, " to relieve Gloucester ;" and
that, if their levies did not supply them with men soon
enough, the trained bands of the city would march out with
the general for that service ; whereupon the three earls,
Bedford, Holland, and Clare, after some days stay in Oxford,
thought it necessary to offer their service to the king in the
army, and to bear their part in any danger that might happen
by an engagement between the armies ; and so went together to Gloucester ; where the king received them without
any disrespect, and spoke with them as they gave him occasion.

Whilst the king continued before Gloucester, his forces in
the west moved with a full gale and tide of success.   The
earl of Carnarvon marched with the horse and dragoons, being near two thousand, into Dorsetshire, two days before
prince Maurice moved with his foot and cannon from Bristol,
and had made a fair entrance upon the reduction of that
whole county, before his highness overtook him ; and it was
thought then, that, if the prince had marched more slowly,
he had perfected that work.   Upon the surrender of Bristol,
many of the gentlemen, and others of that county, who were
engaged in that city for the parliament, had visited their
houses and friends, in their journey to London, whither by
their safe conduct they went, and had made such prodigious
discourses of the fierceness and courage of the cavaliers, (as
most men who run away, or are beaten, extol the power of
the enemy which had been too hard for them,) that resisting
them begun to be thought a matter impossible.   One Mr.
Strode, a man much relied on in those parts, and of a good
fortune, after he had visited his house, took Dorchester in
his way to London, and being desired by the magistrates,
" to view their works and fortifications, and to give his judg-

ment of them ;" after he had walked about them, he told them, " that those works might keep out the cavaliers about half an hour ;" and then told them strange stories of the manner of assaulting Bristol ; " and that the king's soldiers made nothing of running up walls twenty foot high, and that no works could keep them out ;" which he said not out of any purpose to betray them, (for no man wished the king's army worse success,) but had really so much horror and consternation about him, and the dreadful image of the storm of Bristol imprinted in his mind, that he did truly believe, they had scaled all those forts and places which were delivered to them ; and he propagated this fear and trepidation so fruitfully where he came, that the earl of Carnarvon came no sooner near Dorchester with his horse and dragoons, (which, it may be, was understood to be the van of the victorious army which had taken Bristol,) but the town sent commissioners to him to treat ; and upon articles of indemnity, that they should not be plundered, and not suffer for the ill they had done, delivered up the town, (which was strongly situated, and might very well have been defended by the spirits of these people, if they had courage equal to their malice ; for a place more entirely disaffected to the king, England had not,) with all their arms, ammunition, and ordnance. The fame of the earl's coming had before frighted sir Walter Earl, who had for a long time besieged Corfe castle, (the house of the lord chief justice Banks, defended by his lady with her servants, and some few gentlemen, and tenants, who betook themselves thither for her assistance, and their own security,) from that siege; and he making more haste to convey himself to London, than generals use to do, who have the care and charge of others, his forces were presently dispersed. And now the surrender of Dorchester (the magazine from whence the other places were supplied with principles of rebellion) infused the same spirit into Weymouth, a very convenient harbour and haven : and that example again prevailed on the island and castle of Portland, (a place not enough understood, but of wonderful importance,) to all which the earl granted fair conditions, and received them into his majesty's protection.

Hither prince Maurice came now up with his foot and cannon, and neglecting to follow the train of the enemy's fears to Lyme and Poole, the only two garrisons then left in their possession, stayed with his army about Dorchester and Weymouth some days, under the notion of settling and disposing the government of those garrisons. Here the soldiers, taking advantage of the famous malignity of those places, used great licence; neither was there care taken to observe those articles which had been made upon the surrender of the towns; which the earl of Carnarvon, who was full of honour and justice upon all contracts, took so ill, that he quitted the command he had with those forces, and returned to the king before Gloucester; which published the injustice with the more scandal. Whether this licence, which was much spoken of, and, no doubt, given out to be greater than it was,[1] aliened the affections of those parts; or whether the absence of the marquis of Hertford from the army, which was not till then taken notice of, begot an apprehension that there would not be much lenity used towards those who had been high and pertinacious offenders; or whether this army, when it was together, seemed less formidable than it was before conceived to be, or that the terror, which had possessed and seized upon their spirits, was so violent that it could not continue, and so men grew less amazed, I know not: but those two small towns, whereof Lyme was believed inconsiderable, returned so peremptory a refusal to the prince's summons, that his highness resolved not to attack them; and so marched to Exeter, where he found all things in better order, and that city more distressed, than he had reason to expect, by the diligence and dexterity of sir John Berkley, who being sent from Wells by the marquis of Hertford, as is before remembered, to govern the affairs of Devonshire, with one regiment of horse, and another of new

---

[1] How could he say so, when he had but just before told us how lord Carnarvon resented it? But, as usual, he was tender of these foreign branches of the royal house. But that these injustices were chiefly to be laid at the door of the foreign officers, appears pretty plain by the familiar use of the German word *plunder*, then first introduced into the English tongue.---W.

levied and half-armed foot, had so increased his numbers by
the concurrence of the gentlemen of that county, that he
fixed strong quarters within less than a mile of the city, and
kept his guards even to the gates ; when the earl of Stamford was within, with a strength at least equal in number to
the besiegers.

The parliament commended the relief of this place, by
special instructions, to their admiral, the earl of Warwick ;
who after he had made show of landing men in several places
upon the coast, and thereby compelled sir John Berkley to
make quick and wearisome marches with horse and dragoons
from place to place, the wind coming fair, the fleet left those
who attended their landing about Totness, turned about, and
with a fresh gale made towards the river, that leads to the
walls of Exeter ; and having the command of both sides of
the river, upon a flat, by their cannon, the earl presumed
that way he should be able to send relief into the city : but
the admirable diligence and providence of sir John Berkley
had fortunately cast up some slight works upon the advantageous nooks of the river, in which his men might be in some
security from the cannon of the ships; and made great haste
with his horse to hinder their landing ; and so this attempt
was not only without success, but so unfortunate, that it discouraged the seamen from endeavouring the like again.
For after three or four hours pouring their great shot, from
their ships, upon the land forces, the tide falling, the earl of
Warwick fell off with his fleet, leaving three ships behind
him, of which one was burnt, and the other two taken from
the land, in view of his whole fleet ; which no more looked
after the relief of Exeter that way.

But whilst all the king's forces were employed in the
blocking up the town, and attending the coast, to wait upon
the earl of Warwick, the garrison of Plymouth increased
very fast, into which the fleet disburdened themselves of all
they could spare ; and the north parts of Devonshire gathered apace into a head for the parliament ; Barnstable and
Bediford being garrisoned by them ; which having an uninterrupted line of communication with Plymouth, resolved to
join their whole strength, and so to compel the enemy to draw

off from the walls of Exeter, which had been very easy to have been done, if they in the city had been as active for their own preservation. Sir John Berkley having notice of this preparation and resolution, sent colonel John Digby (who had, from their first entrance into Cornwall, commanded the horse) with his own regiment of horse, and some loose troops of dragoons, into the north of Devon, to hinder the joining of the rebels' forces. He chose Torrington for his quarter, and within few days drew to him a troop of new-raised horse, and a regiment of foot, raised by his old friends in Cornwall; so that he had with him above three hundred horse, and six or seven hundred foot. Those of Bediford and Barnstable, being superior in number, and apprehending that the king's successes eastward might increase his strength and power there, and weaken theirs, resolved to try their fortune; and joining themselves together, to the number of above twelve hundred foot, and three hundred horse, under the command of colonel Bennet, hoped to surprise colonel John Digby at Torrington; and he was upon the matter surprised: for albeit he had notice in the night from Barnstable, " that the forces drew out thence to Bediford in the night, and that they intended to fall on his quarters early in the morning;" and thereupon he put himself into a posture to receive them, and drew up all his forces together out of the town, upon such a piece of ground, as, in that enclosed county, could be most advantageous for his horse, having, through all the little enclosures, cut gaps, through which his horse might enter; yet, after he had attended their coming till noon, and heard no more of them, and his small parties, which were sent out to inquire, returned with assurance, that there was no appearance of an enemy, he believed they had given over their design; and so dismissed his horse to their several quarters, reserving only one hundred and fifty upon their guard, and returned himself into the town with the foot.

And, within less than an hour, he received the alarm, " that the enemy was within half a mile of the town." The confusion was very great, so that he resolved not to draw the foot out of the town; but having placed them in the best

manner he could, upon the avenues, himself went to the
horse out of the town, resolving to wait upon the rear of the
enemy ; who were drawn up on the same piece of ground,
on which he had expected them all the morning.   The
colonel, whose courage, and vivacity upon action, was very
eminent, and commonly very fortunate, intended rather to look
upon them, than to engage with them, before his other troops
came up ; but having divided his small party of horse, the
whole consisting but of one hundred and fifty, into several
parties, and distributed them into several little closes, out of
which there were gaps into the larger ground, upon which
the enemy stood, a forlorn hope of fifty musketeers advanced towards that ground where himself was ; and if they recovered the hedge, they would easily have driven him thence.
And therefore, as the only expedient left, himself, taking
four or five officers into the front with him, charged that forlorn hope ; which immediately threw down their arms, and
run upon their own body, and carried so infectious a fear
with them, that without making a stand, or their horse offering once to charge, the whole body routed themselves, and
fled ; colonel Digby following the execution with his horse,
till their swords were blunted with slaughter, and his numbers overburdened with prisoners; though the foot out of
the town hastened to the chase, as soon as they saw what
terror had possessed their enemies.

In this action (for it cannot be called a battle ; hardly a
skirmish ; where no resistance was made) there were near
two hundred killed, and above two hundred taken prisoners;
and those that fled contributed more to the victory, than the
prisoners, or the slain, for they were scattered and dispersed
over all the country, and scarce a man without a cut over
the face and head, or some other hurt ; that wrought more
upon the neighbours towards their conversion, than any sermon could be preached to them.   Some of the principal officers, and of their horse, got into Bediford and Barnstable ;
and not considering the inconvenience of acknowledging, that
God was extraordinary propitious to the cavaliers, told
strange stories of " the horror and fear that seized upon
them, and that nobody saw above six of the enemy, that

charged them;"[1] which proved a greater dismay to their friends, than their defeat.

At this time came prince Maurice to Exeter, the fame of whose arrival brought a new terror, so that the fort at Appledore, which commanded the river to Barnstable and Bediford, being delivered to colonel Digby, within two or three days after his victory, those two towns shortly after submitted to his majesty, upon promise of pardon, and such other articles as were of course; which colonel Digby saw precisely observed, as far as concerned the towns in point of plunder, or violence towards the inhabitants. And this success so wrought upon the spirits and temper of that people, that all the persons of eminent disaffection withdrawing themselves, according to their liberty by the articles; colonel Digby, within very few days, increased his small party to the number of three thousand foot, and eight hundred horse; with which he was by prince Maurice ordered to march to Plymouth, and to block up that place from making incursions into the country.

The loss of all their garrisons on the north coast, and despair of succour or relief from any other place, prevailed with the earl of Stamford, and that committee in Exeter, (to whom the earl was not superior,) to treat with the prince; and thereupon articles were agreed to; and that rich and pleasant city was delivered on the fourth of September, which was within fourteen or sixteen days after prince Maurice came thither, into the king's protection, after it had suffered no other distress, or impression from the besiegers, than the being kept from taking the air without their own walls, and from being supplied from the country markets.

There was an accident fell out a little before this time, that gave new argument of trouble to the king, upon a difference between prince Maurice and the marquis. The earl of Carnarvon, who was general of the horse of the western army, had marched from Bristol the day before the prince, and had taken Dorchester and Weymouth, before his high-

---

[1] These were the officers who charged with sir J. Digby in the front of the horse.

ness came up to the army, both considerable places, and the
seats of great malignity. The former was not thought necessary to be made a garrison; but the latter was the best
port town of that country, and to be kept with great care.
The marquis had made some promise of the government
thereof, when it should be taken, (of which they made no
doubt,) to sir Anthony Ashley Cooper, a young gentleman
of that country, of a fair and plentiful fortune, and one, who,
in the opinion of most men, was like to advance the place
by being governor of it, and to raise men for the defence of
it, without lessening the army; and had, in expectation of
it, made some provision of officers and soldiers, when it
should be time to call them together. Prince Maurice, on
the other side, had some other person in his view, upon
whom he intended to confer that charge, when it should
fall. In the moment that the town was taken, and before
the prince came thither, sir Anthony, hearing that the marquis came not with the army, but remained some time at
Bristol, made all the haste he could to him, and came thither
the same day the king left it; and applied himself to the
marquis, who remembered his promise, and thought himself
obliged to make it good, and that it was in his power so to
do, since it appeared, that the town was taken before the
king had declared to him, that he should not go to the army;
till when he ought to be looked upon as general of it. He
conferred with the chancellor upon it, as a matter in which
his honour was concerned, and on which his heart was set.
And sir Anthony came likewise to him, who was of his acquaintance, and desired his assistance, " that, after so much
charge he had been put to, in the expectation of it, and to
prepare for it, he might not be exposed to the mirth and
contempt of the country." It was evident, that if he returned with the commission from the marquis, (which he
was most inclined to give him,) both he and the commission
would be affronted, and the town would not be suffered to
submit to him. Therefore the chancellor was of opinion,
that there was no way but to appeal to the king, and desire
his favour, as well as his justice, in giving his commission to
the person designed by the marquis; which would remove

that part of the exception, which would most trouble the prince; and he offered to write himself very earnestly to the king.   And besides his desire to gratify the marquis, he did in truth believe it of great importance to his majesty's service, to engage a person of such a fortune and interest, so thoroughly in his quarrel, as he then believed such an obligation must needs do; the flexibility and instability of that gentleman's nature[1] not being then understood, or suspected.

He did write, with all the skill and importunity he could use, to the king; and wrote to the lord Falkland, " to take sir John Colepepper with him, if he found any aversion in the king, that they might together discourse, and prevail with him."   But his majesty positively and obstinately refused to grant it; and said, " he would not, to please the marquis in an unjust pretence, put a public disobligation and affront upon his nephew."[2]   So the express returned without effect, and the marquis was as sensibly touched as could be imagined; and said, " that he was fallen from any degree of credit with the king, and was made incapable of doing him further service; that his fidelity should never be lessened towards him," (as in truth he was incapable of a disloyal thought,) " but since he was become so totally useless to the king, and to his friends, he hoped his majesty would give him leave to retire to his own house; where, he doubted not, he should be suffered to live privately and quietly, to pray for the king."   The chancellor knew well the nature of the marquis, which would never give him leave to pursue any resolution which he found might prove inconvenient to his majesty, for whom he had all possible duty; yet he knew too, that the mischief was not small, from the observation that the marquis thought himself ill used, and that

---

[1] There was much both of intrigue and whim in the character of this first earl of Shaftsbury.—W.

[2] Had the king been as able in politics, as he was in the episcoparian squabbles, he would have sent this nephew back to Germany, after all the disorders he had countenanced, and the disaffection he had thereby created to the king's cause in the west.—W.

there were too many who would take the opportunity to foment those jealousies and discontents; and therefore resolved (having despatched all things which were incumbent on
him at Bristol, and used all freedom to the marquis, for the
dispelling all troublesome imaginations) to go himself to the
king, and to represent that affair to him, and the probable
consequences of it, with new instances. The king left
Bristol in the resolution and expectation formerly mentioned; and when he came near Gloucester, he sent a summons
to the governor, and drew up his army in the view of the
town from a reasonable ascent; and after he had expected
an answer some hours, one of the citizens of the town, of a
very ill aspect and rude behaviour, came to the king with
the answer from the mayor and aldermen, as well as from
the governor, and signed by them all, which the messenger
would read in a loud unmannerly voice. It did not only
contain a refusal to deliver the place, and a declaration that
they did and would keep it for the parliament; but had such
reproachful expressions in it, that together with the sauci-
ness of the messenger, as exceedingly incensed the king:
and the messenger was no sooner returned, but they gave
another evidence of their resolution, by setting all the
suburbs, in which there was a fair street and many good
houses, on a fire together. Though the king had resolved
before not to be engaged in the siege of this city, and he
received new instances from the queen, and intelligence
from London of the extraordinary distractions there, to confirm him in that resolution, and many members of both houses had left the parliament, whereof some came to Oxford,
(who shall be mentioned anon,) and all sent word, that if
the king now marched towards London, the city itself
would compel the parliament to make a peace; but these
unmannerly and insolent provocations from the town persuaded him that he was bound in honour speedily to chas-
tise it. Upon the drawing up his army, he found it much
weaker than he thought it to have been. The gentlemen
of Gloucestershire and of the Welsh side of the Severn came
to him, and made great professions how soon they would recruit his army, if he would remain some time there; that

the town would be taken in few days, and whilst he was taking it, his army should be increased every day; whereas if he marched presently away, besides the dishonour of it, he would not be able to carry away with him one man more than he had brought thither, which would appear a very small body to shew to the city of London for their encouragement to join with him. But that which made most impression was, that the express was now returned from the earl of Newcastle, who informed his majesty, that it was impossible for him to comply with his commands and expectation in marching with his army into the associated counties; for that the gentlemen of the country who had the best regiments, and were amongst the best officers, utterly refused to march, except Hull were first taken, and that he had not strength enough to march with any considerable body, and to leave Hull securely blocked up; which resolution made it, in the judgment of the king and of most of the officers, necessary for the king to engage in the siege of that town; and thereupon he sent for the general, who remained yet at Oxford, to attend him at Gloucester, with his greatest cannon, and such foot as could be spared out of Oxford; and thereupon he committed the care of one approach, which was resolved upon, to the general; and another, which was thought necessary, to another part of the town, to sir Jacob Ashley, the major general of the foot, who best understood that kind of service; and so disposed the whole army formally to the siege; his majesty himself quartering in a village about two miles distant from the city: and in this posture that affair stood, when the chancellor came to the king from Bristol. And at last, with very great difficulty, he did so far prevail with his majesty, that he gave a commission to sir Anthony Ashley Cooper, to be governor of Weymouth; which he was the more easily persuaded to, out of some prejudice he had to the person, who, he understood, was designed to that government. However, the marquis received it as a seasonable act of favour to himself, and, in a short time after, came from Bristol to Oxford, to attend upon his majesty according to his command. The king told the chancellor that it was necessary he should

make haste to Oxford, where he would find the lords in
great disorder for his having engaged the army before Gloucester, but more upon the news of the earl of Holland and
the earl of Bedford being coming to Oxford; that they were
already come to Wallingford, where the governor, col.
Blague, had civilly detained them, till he might understand
the king's pleasure, who seemed to be in some trouble and
irresolution in what manner to receive them. The chancellor stayed not above two hours with the king; but though
it was late, went to a gentleman's house five or six miles
from thence, and, after some hours sleep, made haste the
next morning to Oxford; where before night the king likewise arrived, of which he had no thought when the chancellor came away; but received that night some letter from
the queen, which made him believe that journey necessary,
bringing a small train with him; and after one day's stay he
returned to the siege, where his presence was in many respects very necessary.

At Gloucester the business proceeded very slowly: for
though the army increased wonderfully there, by the access
of forces from all quarters, yet the king had neither money
nor materials requisite for a siege,[1] and they in the town
behaved themselves with great courage and resolution, and
made many sharp and bold sallies upon the king's forces, and
did more hurt commonly than they received; and many officers of name, besides common soldiers, were slain in the
trenches and approaches; the governor leaving nothing unperformed that became a vigilant commander. Sometimes,
upon the sallies, the horse got between the town and them,
so that many prisoners were taken, who were always drunk;
and, after they were recovered, they confessed, " that the
governor always gave the party that made the sally, as much
wine and strong water as they desired to drink :" so that it
seems their mettle was not purely natural ; yet it it is very

---

[1] This shews the reason of *Chillingworth's* activity there in invent-
ing military machines for the service, and for which he was so much
abused by those miserable rascals, the presbyterian pulpit incendiaries.---W.

observable, that, in all the time the king lay there with a very glorious army, and after the taking of a city of much greater name, there was no one officer run from the town to him, nor above three common soldiers, which is a great argument, the discipline within was very good.   Besides the loss of men before the town, both from the walls, and by sickness, (which was not greater than was to be reasonably expected,) a very great licence broke into the army, both among officers and soldiers; the malignity of those parts being thought excuse for the exercise of any rapine, or severity among the inhabitants.   Insomuch as it is hardly to be credited, how many thousand sheep were in a few days destroyed, besides what were brought in by the commissaries for a regular provision; and many countrymen imprisoned by officers without warrant, or the least knowledge of the king's, till they had paid good sums of money, for their delinquency; all which brought great clamour upon the discipline of the army, and justice of the officers, and made them likewise less prepared for the service they were to expect.

In the mean time nothing was left at London unattempted, that might advance the preparation for the relief of Gloucester.   All overtures of peace were suppressed, and the city purely at the devotion of those who were most violent, who had put one compliment upon them at this time, that is not to be passed over.   It is remembered before, that, at the beginning of these distractions, before the king's going into the north, his majesty had, upon the reiterated importunity of the two houses, made sir John Coniers lieutenant of the Tower of London; who was a soldier of very good estimation, and had been the lieutenant general of his horse in that last preparation against the Scots, and governor of Berwick.   The parliament thought, by this obligation, to have made him their own creature, and desired to have engaged him in some active command in their armies, having the reputation of one of the best officers of horse of that time.   But he warily declined that engagement, and contained himself within the limits of that place, which, by the multitude of prisoners, sent to the Tower by the two houses, and the excessive fees they paid, yielded him a vast profit;

in the administration whereof he was so impartial, that those
prisoners who suffered most for his majesty, found no more
favour or indulgence from him than the rest.   About this
time, either discerning that they grew to confide less in him
than they had done, and that he must engage himself in their
service, or should shortly lose the benefit of their good opinion, or really abhorring to be so near those actions he saw
every day committed, and to lie under the scandal of keeping his majesty's only fort which he could not apply to his
service, he desired leave from the houses, " to go into Holland," where his education had been, and his fortune was,
without obliging himself to a time of return.   The proposition was not unwelcome to the houses ; and thereupon they
immediately committed that charge, the custody of the Tower of London, to the lord mayor Pennington ; that the city
might see they were trusted to hold their own reins, and
had a jurisdiction committed to them which had always
justled with their own.   And this compliment served to a
double purpose ; for thereby, as they made the city believe
they had put themselves under their protection, so they were
sure they had put the city under the power, or under the
apprehension of the power of him, who would never forsake
them out of an appetite to peace.

     The earl of Essex now declared, that he would himself un-
dertake the relief of Gloucester, whereas before sir William
Waller was designed to it, and, whencesoever it proceeded, was
returned to his old full alacrity against the king, and recovered
those officers and soldiers again to him, who had absented
by his connivance, or upon an opinion that he would march
no more ; yet his numbers increased not so fast as the occasion
required : for colonel Massy found means to send many messengers out of the town, to advertise the straits he was in,
and the time that he should be able to hold out.   Their
ordinance of pressing, though executed with unusual rigour,
insomuch as persons of good fortunes, who had retired to
London, that they might be less taken notice of, were seized
on, and detained in custody, till they paid so much money, or
procured an able man to go in their places, brought not in
such a supply as they expected ; and such as were brought

in, and delivered to the officers, declared such an averseness
to the work to which they were designed, and such a peremptory resolution not to fight, that they only increased
their numbers, not their strength, and run away upon the
first opportunity.   In the end, they had no other resort for
men, but to those who had so constantly supplied them with
money, and prevailed with their true friends, the city, which
they still alarmed with the king's irreconcilableness to them,
to send three or four of their trained-band regiments, or aux-
iliaries, to fight with the enemy at that distance, rather than
to expect him at their own walls, where they must be assured to see him as soon as Gloucester should be reduced;
and then they would be as much perplexed with the malignants within, as with the enemy without their city.

Upon such arguments, and the power of the earl of Essex,
so many regiments of horse and foot as he desired were assigned to march with him ; and so, towards the end of August, he marched out of London ; and having appointed a
rendezvous near Aylesbury, where he was met by the lord
Grey, and other forces of the associated counties, from thence
he marched by easy journeys towards Gloucester, with an
army of about eight thousand foot, and four thousand horse.
It would not at first be credited at the leaguer, that the earl
of Essex could be in a condition to attempt such a work ;
and therefore they were too negligent upon the intelligence,
and suspected rather that he would give some alarm to Oxford, where the queen was, and thereby hope to draw the
army from Gloucester, than that in truth he would venture
upon so tedious a march, where he must march over a cam-
pagnia) near thirty miles in length, where half the king's body
of horse would distress, if not destroy his whole army, and
through a country eaten bare, where he could find neither
provision for man nor horse ; and if he should, without interruption, be suffered to go into Gloucester, he could neither stay there, nor possibly retire to London, without being
destroyed in the rear by the king's army, which should
nevertheless not engage itself in the hazard of a battle.
Upon these conclusions they proceeded in their works before Gloucester, their galleries being near finished, and visi-

bly a great want of ammunition in the town; yet the lord Wilmot was appointed, with a good party of horse, to wait about Banbury, and to retire before the enemy, if he should advance towards Gloucester, and to give such impediments to their march, as in such a country might be easy to do; prince Rupert himself staying with the body of horse,[1] upon the hills above Gloucester, to join, if the earl of Essex should be so hardy as to venture.

The earl came to Brackley, and having there taken in from Leicester and Bedford the last recruits upon which he depended, he marched steadily over all that campaign, which they thought he feared, towards Gloucester; and though the king's horse were often within view, and entertained him with light skirmishes, he pursued his direct way; the king's horse still retiring before him, till the foot was compelled to raise the siege, in more disorder and distraction than might have been expected; and so with less loss, and easier skirmishes, than can be imagined, the earl, with his army and train, marched to Gloucester; where he found them reduced to one single barrel of powder; and all other provisions answerable. And it must be confessed, that governor gave a stop to the career of the king's good success, and from his pertinacious defence of that place, the parliament had time to recover their broken forces, and more broken spirits; and may acknowledge to this rise the greatness to which they afterwards aspired.

The earl of Essex stayed in that joyful town (where he was received with all possible demonstrations of honour) three days; and in that time, which was as wonderful as any part of the story, caused all necessary provisions to be brought in to them, out of those very quarters in which the king's army had been sustained, and which they conceived to be entirely spent: so solicitous were the people to conceal what they had, and to reserve it for them; which, without a connivance from the king's commissaries, could not have been done. All this time the king lay at Sudley cas-

[1] Here, where generalship was required, prince Rupert could do nothing worthy of his name.---W.

tle, the house of the lord Chandois, within eight miles of Gloucester, watching when that army would return ; which, they conceived, stayed rather out of despair than election, in those eaten quarters ; and, to open them a way for their retreat, his majesty removed to Esham, hoping the earl would choose to go back the same way he came ; which, for many reasons, was to be desired ; and thereupon the earl marched to Tewkesbury, as if he had no other purpose.　The king's horse, though bold, and vigorous upon action and execution, were always less patient of duty and ill accommodation than they should be ; and at this time, partly with weariness, and partly with the indisposition[1] that possessed the whole army upon this relief of the town, were less vigilant towards the motion of the enemy : so that the earl of Essex was marched with his whole army and train from Tewkesbury, four and twenty hours before the king heard which way he was gone : for he took the advantage of a dark night, and having sure guides, reached Cirencester before the breaking of the day ; where he found two regiments of the king's horse quartered securely ; all which, by the negligence of the officers, (a common and fatal crime throughout the war, on the king's part,) he surprised, to the number of above three hundred ; and, which was of much greater value, he found there a great quantity of provisions, prepared, by the king's commissaries, for the army before Gloucester, and which they neglected to remove after the siege was raised, and so most sottishly left it for the relief of the enemy, far more apprehensive of hunger than of the sword ; and indeed this wonderful supply strangely exalted their spirits, as sent by the special care and extraordinary hand of Providence, even when they were ready to faint.

From hence the earl, having no further apprehension of the king's horse, which he had no mind to encounter upon the open campaign, and being at the least twenty miles before him, by easy marches, that his sick and wearied soldiers

---

[1] Their indisposition should have been pointed against the earl of Essex, who raised the siege, and on whom a brave and vigilant enemy might have had its revenge.---W.

might overtake him, moved, through that deep and enclosed county of North Wiltshire, his direct way to London. As soon as the king had sure notice which way the enemy was gone, he endeavoured, by expedition and diligence, to recover the advantage, which the supine negligence of those he trusted had robbed him of; and himself, with matchless industry, taking care to lead up the foot, prince Rupert, with near five thousand horse, marched day and night over the hills, to get between London and the enemy before they should be able to get out of those enclosed deep countries, in which they were engaged between narrow lanes, and to entertain them with skirmishes till the whole army should come up. This design, pursued and executed with indefatigable pains, succeeded to his wish; for when the van of the enemy's army had almost marched over Awborne Chase, intending that night to have reached Newbury, prince Rupert, besides their fear or expectation, appeared with a strong body of horse, so near them, that before they could put themselves in order to receive him, he charged their rear, and routed them with good execution; and though the enemy performed the parts of good men, and applied themselves more dexterously to the relief of each other, than on so sudden and unlooked for an occasion was expected, yet with some difficulty, and the loss of many men, they were glad to shorten their journey, and the night coming on, took up their quarters at Hungerford.

In this conflict, which was very sharp for an hour or two, many fell of the enemy, and of the king's party none of name, but the marquis of Vieu Ville, a gallant gentleman of the French nation, who had attended the queen out of Holland, and put himself as a volunteer upon this action, into the lord Jermyn's regiment. There were hurt many officers, and among those the lord Jermyn received a shot in his arm with a pistol; owing the preservation of his life from other shots to the excellent temper of his arms; and the lord Digby a strange hurt in the face, a pistol being discharged at so near a distance upon him, that the powder fetched much blood from his face, and for the present blinded him, without further mischief; by which it was concluded, that the bullet had dropped out before the pistol was discharged : and may be reckoned among one of those escapes, of which that gallant person hath passed a greater number, in the course of his life, than any man I know.

By this expedition of prince Rupert, the enemy was forced to such delay, that the king came up with his foot and train, though his numbers, by his exceeding long and quick marches, and the licence which many officers and soldiers took whilst the king lay at Esham, were much lessened, being above two thousand fewer, than when he raised his siege from Gloucester. And when the earl, the next day, advanced from Hungerford, hoping to recover Newbury, which prince Rupert with his horse would not be able to hinder him from ; when he came within two miles of the town, he found the king possessed of it ; for his majesty, with his whole army, was come thither two hours before : this put him to a necessity of staying upon the field that night ; it being now the seventeenth day of September.

It was now thought by many, that the king had recovered whatsoever had been lost by former oversights, omissions, or neglects, and that by the destroying the army which had relieved Gloucester, he should be fully recompensed for being disappointed of that purchase. He seemed to be possessed of all advantages to be desired, a good town to refresh his men in, whilst the enemy lodged in the field, his own quarters to friend, and his garrison of Wallingford at hand, and Oxford itself within distance for supply of whatsoever should be wanting ; when the enemy was equally tired with long marches, and from the time that the prince had attacked them, the day before, had stood in their arms, in a country where they could not find victual. So that it was conceived, that it was in the king's power, whether he would fight or no, and therefore that he might compel them to notable disadvantages, who must make their way through, or starve ; and this was so fully understood, that it was resolved over night, not to engage in battle, but upon such grounds as should give an assurance of victory. But, contrary to this resolution, when the earl of Essex had, with excellent conduct, drawn out his army in battalia, upon a hill called Bigg's

Hill, within less than a mile of the town, and ordered his men in all places to the best advantage, by the precipitate courage of some young officers, who had good commands, and who unhappily always undervalued the courage of the enemy, strong parties became successively so far engaged, that the king was compelled to put the whole to the hazard of a battle, and to give the enemy at least an equal game to play.

It was disputed, on all parts, with great fierceness and courage; the enemy preserving good order, and standing rather to keep the ground they were upon, than to get more; by which they did not expose themselves to those disadvantages, which any motion would have offered to the assailants. The king's horse, with a kind of contempt of the enemy, charged with wonderful boldness, upon all grounds of inequality; and were so far too hard for the troops of the other side, that they routed them in most places, till they had left the greatest part of their foot without any guard at all of horse. But then the foot behaved themselves admirably on the enemy's part, and gave their scattered horse time to rally, and were ready to assist and secure them upon all occasions. The London trained bands, and auxiliary regiments, (of whose inexperience of danger, or any kind of service, beyond the easy practice of their postures in the Artillery Garden, men had till then too cheap an estimation,) behaved themselves to wonder; and were, in truth, the preservation of that army that day. For they stood as a bulwark and rampire to defend the rest; and when their wings of horse were scattered and dispersed, kept their ground so steadily, that, though prince Rupert himself led up the choice horse to charge them, and endured their storm of small shot, he could make no impression upon their stand of pikes, but was forced to wheel about: of so sovereign benefit and use is that readiness, order, and dexterity in the use of their arms,[1] which hath been so much neglected.

[1] A most judicious observation, which later times have abundantly supported. Skippon had disciplined these men in the Artillery Garden ever since the first beginning of the quarrel.—W.

It was fought all that day without any such notable turn, as that either party could think they had much the better. For though the king's horse made the enemy's often give ground, yet the foot were so immoveable, that little was gotten by the other; and the first entrance into the battle was so sudden, and without order, that, during the whole day, no use was made of the king's cannon, though that of the enemy was placed so unhappily, that it did very great execution upon the king's party, both horse and foot. The night parted them, when nothing else could; and each party had then time to revolve the oversights of the day. The enemy had fared at least as well as they hoped for; and therefore, in the morning early, they put themselves in order of marching, having an obligation in necessity to gain some place, in which they might eat and sleep. On the king's side there was not that caution which should have been the day before; and though the number of the slain was not so great, as, in so hot a day, might have been looked for, yet very many officers and gentlemen were hurt: so that they rather chose to take advantage of the enemy's motion, than to charge them again upon the old ground, from whence they had been, by order, called off the night before, when they had recovered a post, the keeping of which would much have prejudiced the adversary. The earl of Essex finding his way open, pursued his main design of returning to London, and took that way by Newbury, which led towards Reading; which prince Rupert observing, suffered him, without interruption or disturbance, to pass, till his whole army was entered into the narrow lanes; and then with a strong party of horse, and one thousand musketeers, followed his rear with so good effect, that he put them into great disorder, and killed many, and took many prisoners. However the earl, with the gross of his army, and all his cannon, got safe into Reading; and, after a night or two spent there to refresh and rest his men, he moved in a slow and orderly march to London, leaving Reading to the king's forces: which was presently possessed by sir Jacob Ashley, with three thousand foot and five hundred horse, and made again a garrison for the king: his majesty and prince Rupert, with the remainder of the army, retiring to Oxford, and leaving a garrison under the command of colonel Boys in Donnington castle (a house of John Packer's, but more famous for having been the seat of Geoffery Chaucer, within a mile of Newbury) to command the great road, through which the western trade was driven to London.

At this time sir William Waller was at Windsor, with above two thousand horse, and as many foot, as unconcerned for what might befall the earl of Essex, as he had formerly been on his behalf at Roundway hill : otherwise, if he had advanced upon the king to Newbury (which was not above twenty miles) when the earl was on the other side, the king had been in great danger of an utter defeat; and the apprehension of this was the reason, or was afterwards pretended to be, for the hasty engagement in battle.

The earl of Essex was received at London with all imaginable demonstrations of affection and reverence ; public and solemn thanksgiving was appointed for his victory, for such they made no scruple to declare it. Without doubt, the action was performed by him with incomparable conduct and courage ; in every part whereof very much was to be imputed to his own personal virtue ; and it may be well reckoned among the most soldierly actions of this unhappy war. For he did the business he undertook, and, after the relief of Gloucester, his next care was to retire with his army to London ; which, considering the length of the way, and the difficulties he was to contend with, he did with less loss than could be expected ; on the other hand, the king was not without some signs of a victory. He had followed, and compelled the enemy to fight, by overtaking him, when he desired to avoid it. He had the spoil of the field, and pursued the enemy the next day after the battle, and had a good execution upon them, without receiving any loss ; and, which seemed to crown the work, fixed a garrison again at Reading, and thereby straitened their quarters as much as it was in the beginning of the year ; his own being enlarged by the almost entire conquest of the west, and his army much stronger, in horse and foot, than when he first took the field. On which side soever the marks and public en-

signs of victory appeared most conspicuous, certain it is, that,
according to the unequal fate that attended all skirmishes
and conflicts with such an adversary, the loss on the king's
side was in weight much more considerable and penetrating;
for whilst some obscure, unheard of colonel or officer was
missing on the enemy's side, and some citizen's wife bewail-
ed the loss of her husband, there were, on the other, above
twenty officers of the field, and persons of honour, and public name, slain upon the place, and more of the same quality
hurt.

Here fell the earl of Sunderland, a lord of great fortune,
tender years, (being not above three and twenty years of
age,) and an early judgment; who, having no command in
the army, attended upon the king's person, under the obligation of honour;[1] and putting himself that day in the king's
troop a volunteer, before they came to charge, was taken
away by a cannon bullet.

This day also fell the earl of Carnarvon, who, after he
had charged, and routed a body of the enemy's horse, coming
carelessly back by some of the scattered troopers, was, by
one of them who knew him, run through the body with a
sword; of which he died within an hour.   He was a person,
with whose great parts and virtue the world was not enough
acquainted.   Before the war, though his education was
adorned by travel, and an exact observation of the manners
of more nations, than our common travellers use to visit,
(for he had, after the view of Spain, France, and most parts
of Italy, spent some time in Turkey, and those eastern countries,) he seemed to be wholly delighted with those looser

---

[1] These are lord Sunderland's own words to his wife, from the
king's camp, in 1642: "The king's condition is much improved of
late, which increaseth the insolency of the papists. Neither is there
wanting daily handsome occasion to retire, were it not for *grinning
honour.* For let occasion be never so handsome, unless a man were
resolved to fight on the parliament side, (which, for my part, I had
rather be hanged,) it will be said, without doubt, that a man is afraid
to fight. If there could be an expedient found to salve the *punctilio
of honour,* I would not continue here an hour." Sidney Papers, vol.
ii. p. 667.---W.

exercises of pleasure, hunting, hawking, and the like ; in which the nobility of that time too much delighted to excel. After the troubles begun, having the command of the first or second regiment of horse, that was raised for the king's service, he wholly gave himself up to the office and duty of a soldier ; no man more diligently obeying, or more dexterously commanding ; for he was not only of a very keen courage in the exposing his person, but an excellent discerner and pursuer of advantage upon his enemy. And had a mind and understanding very present in the article of danger, which is a rare benefit in that profession. Those infirmities, and that licence, which he had formerly indulged to himself, he put off with severity, when others thought them excusable under the notion of a soldier. He was a great lover of justice, and practised it then most deliberately, when he had power to do wrong : and so strict in the observation of his word and promise as a commander, that he could not be persuaded to stay in the west, when he found it not in his power to perform the agreement he had made with Dorchester and Weymouth. If he had lived, he would have proved a great ornament to that profession, and an excellent soldier, and by his death the king found a sensible weakness in his army.

But I must here take leave a little longer to discontinue this narration: and if the celebrating the memory of eminent and extraordinary persons, and transmitting their great virtues, for the imitation of posterity, be one of the principal ends and duties of history, it will not be thought impertinent, in this place, to remember a loss which no time will suffer to be forgotten, and no success or good fortune could repair. In this unhappy battle was slain the lord viscount Falkland ; a person of such prodigious parts of learning and knowledge,[1] of that inimitable sweetness and delight in conversation, of so flowing and obliging a humanity and goodness to man-

---

[1] So says this wise historian ; but an historian wiser than he, the honourable Mr. Horace Walpole, in his Lives of royal and noble authors, says, this noble lord was a weak man, and of very mean and ordinary parts.—W.

kind, and of that primitive simplicity and integrity of life, that if there were no other brand upon this odious and accursed civil war, than that single loss, it must be most infamous and execrable to all posterity.

Turpe mori, post te, solo non posse dolore.

Before this parliament, his condition of life was so happy that it was hardly capable of improvement. Before he came to twenty years of age, he was master of a noble fortune, which descended to him by the gift of a grandfather, without passing through his father or mother, who were then both alive, and not well enough contented to find themselves passed by in the descent. His education for some years had been in Ireland, where his father was lord deputy; so that, when he returned into England, to the possession of his fortune, he was unentangled with any acquaintance or friends, which usually grow up by the custom of conversation; and therefore was to make a pure election of his company; which he chose by other rules than were prescribed to the young nobility of that time. And it cannot be denied, though he admitted some few to his friendship for the agreeableness of their natures, and their undoubted affection to him, that his familiarity and friendship, for the most part, was with men of the most eminent and sublime parts, and of untouched reputation in point of integrity; and such men had a title to his bosom.

He was a great cherisher of wit, and fancy, and good parts in any man; and, if he found them clouded with poverty or want, a most liberal and bountiful patron towards them, even above his fortune; of which, in those administrations, he was such a dispenser, as, if he had been trusted with it to such uses, and if there had been the least of vice in his expense, he might have been thought too prodigal. He was constant and pertinacious in whatsoever he resolved to do, and not to be wearied by any pains that were necessary to that end. And therefore having once resolved not to see London, which he loved above all places, till he had perfectly learned the Greek tongue, he went to his own house in the country, and pursued it with that indefatigable industry, that it will not be believed in how short a time he was master of it, and accurately read all the Greek historians.

In this time, his house being within ten miles of Oxford, he contracted familiarity and friendship with the most polite and accurate men of that university ; who found such an immenseness of wit, and such a solidity of judgment in him, so infinite a fancy, bound in by a most logical ratiocination, such a vast knowledge, that he was not ignorant in any thing, yet such an excessive humility, as if he had known nothing, that they frequently resorted, and dwelt with him, as in a college situated in a purer air ; so that his house was a university in a less volume ; whither they came not so much for repose as study ; and to examine and refine those grosser propositions, which laziness and consent made current in vulgar conversation.

Many attempts were made upon him by the instigation of his mother (who was a lady of another persuasion in religion, and of a most masculine understanding, allayed with the passion and infirmities of her own sex) to pervert him in his piety to the church of England, and to reconcile him to that of Rome ; which they prosecuted with the more confidence, because he declined no opportunity or occasion of conference with those of that religion, whether priests or laics ; having diligently studied the controversies, and exactly read all, or the choicest of the Greek and Latin fathers, and having a memory so stupendous, that he remembered, on all occasions, whatsoever he read. And he was so great an enemy to that passion and uncharitableness, which he saw produced, by difference of opinion, in matters of religion, that in all those disputations with priests, and others of the Roman church, he affected to manifest all possible civility to their persons, and estimation of their parts ; which made them retain still some hope of his reduction, even when they had given over offering further reasons to him to that purpose. But this charity towards them was much lessened, and any correspondence with them quite declined, when, by sinister arts, they had corrupted his two younger brothers, being both children, and stolen them from his house, and transported them beyond seas, and perverted his sisters: upon which occasion he writ two large discourses against the principal positions of that religion, with that sharpness of style, and full weight of reason, that the church is deprived of great jewels in the concealment of them, and that they are not published to the world.

He was superior to all those passions and affections which attend vulgar minds, and was guilty of no other ambition than of knowledge, and to be reputed a lover of all good men; and that made him too much a contemner of those arts, which must be indulged in the transactions of human affairs. In the last short parliament, he was a burgess in the house of commons; and, from the debates which were then managed with all imaginable gravity and sobriety, he contracted such a reverence to parliaments, that he thought it really impossible they could ever produce mischief or inconvenience to the kingdom; or that the kingdom could be tolerably happy in the intermission of them. And from the unhappy and unseasonable dissolution of that convention, he harboured, it may be, some jealousy and prejudice to the court,[1] towards which he was not before[2] immoderately inclined; his father having wasted a full fortune there, in those offices and employments by which other men use to obtain a greater. He was chosen again this parliament to serve in the same place, and, in the beginning of it, declared himself very sharply and severely against those exorbitancies, which had been most grievous to the state; for he was so rigid an observer of established laws and rules, that he could not endure the least breach or deviation from them; and thought no mischief so intolerable as the presumption of ministers of state to break positive rules, for reasons of state; or judges to transgress known laws, upon the title of conveniency, or neces-

---

[1] Did he not, he could never be the man his historian here represents him.—W.

[2] i. e. *before the last short parliament.* But lord Falkland himself, in his printed speeches in the *last long* parliament, gives a better reason for his indisposition to the court, than his father's ill success there as a *courtier of fortune.*—W.

sity; which made him so severe against the earl of Strafford
and the lord Finch, contrary to his natural gentleness and
temper: insomuch as they who did not know his composition
to be as free from revenge, as it was from pride, thought
that the sharpness to the former might proceed from the
memory of some unkindnesses, not without a mixture of injustice, from him towards his father. But without doubt he
was free from those temptations, and was only misled by the
authority of those, who, he believed, understood the laws
perfectly; of which himself was utterly ignorant; and if the
assumption, which was scarce controverted, had been true,
" that an endeavour to overthrow the fundamental laws of
the kingdom had been treason,"[1] a strict understanding might
make reasonable conclusions to satisfy his own judgment,
from the exorbitant parts of their several charges.

The great opinion he had of the uprightness and integrity
of those persons who appeared most active, especially of
Mr. Hambden, kept him longer from suspecting any design
against the peace of the kingdom; and though he differed
from them commonly in conclusions, he believed long their
purposes were honest. When he grew better informed
what was law, and discerned in them a desire to control
that law by a vote of one or both houses, no man more opposed those attempts, and gave the adverse party more trouble by reason and argumentation; insomuch as he was, by
degrees, looked upon as an advocate for the court, to which
he contributed so little, that he declined those addresses,
and even those invitations which he was obliged almost by
civility to entertain. And he was so jealous of the least
imagination that he should incline to preferment, that he affected even a morosity to the court, and to the courtiers;
and left nothing undone which might prevent and divert the
king's or queen's favour towards him, but the deserving it.

[1] As much as to say, Strafford did indeed *endeavour to overthrow the*
fundamental laws of the kingdom. If this was true, his punishment
was certainly most just. An endeavour to overthrow a society, must
needs, from the very nature and end of society, be a capital crime.
It is not treason to this or that state, but to all community in general.—W.

For when the king sent for him once or twice to speak with
him, and to give him thanks for his excellent comportment
in those councils, which his majesty graciously termed
" doing him service," his answers were more negligent, and
less satisfactory,[1] than might be expected ; as if he cared
only that his actions should be just, not that they should be
acceptable, and that his majesty should think that they proceeded only from the impulsion of conscience, without any
sympathy in his affections ; which, from a stoical and sullen
nature, might not have been misinterpreted ; yet, from a
person of so perfect a habit of generous and obsequious
compliance with all good men, might very well have been
interpreted by the king as more than an ordinary averseness
to his service :[2] so that he took more pains, and more forced
his nature to actions unagreeable, and unpleasant to it, that
he might not be thought to incline to the court, than most
men have done to procure an office there.   And if any
thing but not doing his duty could have kept him from receiving a testimony of the king's grace and trust at that
time, he had not been called to his council ; not that he was
in truth averse to the court or from receiving public employment ; for he had a great devotion to the king's person,
and had before used some small endeavour to be recommended to him for a foreign negociation, and had once a desire to be sent ambassador into France ; but he abhorred an
imagination or doubt should sink into the thoughts of any
man, that, in the discharge of his trust and duty in parliament, he had any bias to the court, or that the king himself should apprehend that he looked for a reward for being
honest.

[1] Without doubt *little satisfactory* to a monarch unwilling even then
to part with illegal powers his parliament was wresting from him.—
W.

[2] Hitherto he plainly entertained violent suspicions of the court ;
nay, he seems to have done so to the last : and if his amiable friend,
the young lord Sunderland, was not mistaken in the picture he draws
of the court a few weeks before this battle, in which they both fell,
not without reason.—W.

For this reason, when he heard it first whispered, "that the king had a purpose to make him a counsellor," for which there was, in the beginning, no other ground, but because he was known sufficient, (*haud semper errat fama, aliquando et eligit*,) he resolved to decline it; and at last suffered himself only to be overruled, by the advice and persuasions of his friends, to submit to it. Afterwards, when he found that the king intended to make him secretary of state, he was positive to refuse it; declaring to his friends, "that he was most unfit for it, and that he must either do that which would be great disquiet to his own nature, or leave that undone which was most necessary to be done by one that was honoured with that place; for that the most just and honest men did, every day, that which he could not give himself leave to do." And indeed he was so exact and strict an observer of justice and truth *ad amussim*, that he believed those necessary condescensions and applications to the weakness of other men, and those arts and insinuations which are necessary for discoveries, and prevention of ill, would be in him a declension from his own rules of life : which he acknowledged fit, and absolutely necessary to be practised in those employments. And was so precise in the practic principles he prescribed to himself, (to all others he was as indulgent,) as if he had lived *in republica Platonis, non in fœce Romuli.*

Two reasons prevailed with him to receive the seals, and but for those he had resolutely avoided them. The first, the consideration that it might bring some blemish upon the king's affairs, and that men would have believed, that he had refused so great an honour and trust, because he must have been with it obliged to do somewhat else not justifiable. And this he made matter of conscience, since he knew the king made choice of him, before other men, especially because he thought him more honest than other men. The other was, lest he might be thought to avoid it out of fear to do an ungracious thing to the house of commons, who were sorely troubled at the displacing sir Harry Vane, whom they looked upon as removed for having done them those offices they stood in need of; and the disdain of so popular an incumbrance wrought upon him next to the other. For as he had a full appetite of fame by just and generous actions, so he had an equal contempt of it by any servile expedients : and he so much the more consented to and approved the justice upon sir Harry Vane, in his own private judgment, by how much he surpassed most men in the religious observation of a trust, the violation whereof he would not admit of any excuse for.

For these reasons, he submitted to the king's command, and became his secretary, with as humble and devout an acknowledgment of the greatness of the obligation, as could be expressed, and as true a sense of it in his heart. Yet two things he could never bring himself to, whilst he continued in that office, that was to his death ; for which he was contented to be reproached, as for omissions in a most necessary part of his place. The one, employing of spies, or giving any countenance or entertainment to them. I do not mean such emissaries, as with danger would venture to view the enemy's camp, and bring intelligence of their number, or quartering, or such generals as such an observation can comprehend ; but those, who by communication of guilt, or dissimulation of manners, wound themselves into such trusts and secrets, as enabled them to make discoveries for the benefit of the state. The other, the liberty of opening letters, upon a suspicion that they might contain matter of dangerous consequence. For the first, he would say, " such instruments must be void of all ingenuity, and common honesty, before they could be of use ; and afterwards they could never be fit to be credited : and that no single preservation could be worth so general a wound, and corruption of human society, as the cherishing such persons would carry with it." The last, he thought " such a violation of the law of nature, that no qualification by office could justify a single person in the trespass ;" and though he was convinced by the necessity, and iniquity of the time, that those advantages of information were not to be declined, and were necessarily to be practised, he found means to shift it from himself ; when he confessed he needed excuse and pardon for the omission : so unwilling he was to resign any thing in his nature[1] to an obligation in his office.

In all other particulars he filled his place plentifully, being sufficiently versed in languages, to understand any that are used in business, and to make himself again understood. To speak of his integrity, and his high disdain of any bait that might seem to look towards corruption, *in tanto viro, injuria virtutum fuerit.* Some sharp expressions he used against the archbishop of Canterbury, and his concurring in the first bill to take away the votes of bishops in the house of peers, gave occasion to some to believe, and opportunity to others to conclude, and publish, " that he was no friend to the church, and the established government of it ;" and troubled his very friends much, who were more confident of the contrary, than prepared to answer the allegations.

The truth is, he had unhappily contracted some prejudice to the archbishop ; and having only known him enough to observe his passion, when, it may be, multiplicity of business, or other indisposition, had possessed him, did wish him less entangled and engaged in the business of the court, or state : though, I speak it knowingly, he had a singular estimation and reverence of his great learning, and confessed integrity ; and really thought his letting himself to those expressions, which implied a disesteem of him, or at least an acknowledgment of his infirmities, would enable him to shelter him from part of the storm he saw raised for his destruction ; which he abominated with his soul.

The giving his consent to the first bill for the displacing the bishops, did proceed from two grounds : the first, his not understanding the original of their right and suffrage there : the other, an opinion, that the combination against the whole government of the church by bishops, was so violent and furious, that a less composition than the dispensing with their intermeddling in secular affairs, would not preserve the order. And he was persuaded to this by the profession of many persons of honour, who declared, " they did desire the one, and would not then press the other ;" which, in that

---

[1] i. e. virtuous disposition.---W.

particular, misled many men. But when his observation and experience made him discern more of their intentions, than he before suspected, with great frankness he opposed the second bill that was preferred for that purpose ; and had, without scruple, the order itself in perfect reverence ; and thought too great encouragement could not possibly be given to learning, nor too great rewards to learned men. And was never in the least degree swayed or moved by the objections which were made against that government, (holding them most ridiculous,) or affected to the other, which those men fancied to themselves.

He had a courage of the most clear and keen temper, and so far from fear, that he was not without appetite of danger ; and therefore, upon any occasion of action, he always engaged his person in those troops, which he thought, by the forwardness of the commanders, to be most like to be furthest engaged ; and in all such encounters he had about him a strange cheerfulness and companionableness, without at all affecting the execution that was then principally to be attended, in which he took no delight, but took pains to prevent it, where it was not, by resistance, necessary : insomuch that at Edge-hill, when the enemy was routed, he was like to have incurred great peril, by interposing to save those who had thrown away their arms, and against whom, it may be, others were more fierce for their having thrown them away : insomuch as a man might think, he came into the field only out of curiosity to see the face of danger, and charity to prevent the shedding of blood. Yet in his natural inclination he acknowledged he was addicted to the profession of a soldier ; and shortly after he came to his fortune, and before he came to age, he went into the Low Countries, with a resolution of procuring command, and to give himself up to it, from which he was converted by the complete inactivity of that summer : and so he returned into England, and shortly after entered upon that vehement course of study we mentioned before, till the first alarum from the north ; and then again he made ready for the field, and

though he received some repulse[1] in the command of a troop
of horse, of which he had a promise, he went a volunteer
with the earl of Essex.

From the entrance into this unnatural war, his natural
cheerfulness and vivacity grew clouded, and a kind of sadness and dejection of spirit stole upon him, which he had
never been used to ; yet being one of those who believed
that one battle would end all differences, and that there
would be so great a victory on one side, that the other
would be compelled to submit to any conditions from the vic-
tor, (which supposition and conclusion generally sunk into the
minds of most men, and prevented the looking after many
advantages, that might then have been laid hold of,) he resisted those indispositions, *et in luctu, bellum inter remedia
erat.*   But after the king's return from Brentford, and the
furious resolution of the two houses not to admit any treaty
for peace, those indispositions, which had before touched
him, grew into a perfect habit of uncheerfulness ; and he,
who had been so exactly unreserved and affable to all men,
that his face and countenance was always present, and vacant to his company, and held any cloudiness, and less plea-
santness of the visage, a kind of rudeness or incivility, became, on a sudden, less communicable ; and thence, very
sad, pale, and exceedingly affected with the spleen.   In his
clothes and habit, which he had intended before always
with more neatness, and industry, and expense, than is usual
to so great a mind, he was not now only incurious, but too
negligent ; and in his reception of suitors, and the necessary
or casual addresses to his place, so quick, and sharp, and
severe, that there wanted not some men, (who were strangers to his nature and disposition,) who believed him proud
and imperious, from which no mortal man was ever more
free.

The truth is, as he was of a most incomparable gentleness, application, and even a demissness, and submission
to good, and worthy, and entire men, so he was naturally

---

[1] I suppose on account of his declared indisposition to the court.—
W.

(which could not but be more evident in his place, which objected him to another conversation and intermixture, than his own election had done) *adversus malos injucundus;* and was so ill a dissembler of his dislike and disinclination to ill men, that it was not possible for such not to discern it. There was once, in the house of commons, such a declared acceptation of the good service an eminent member had done to them, and, as they said, to the whole kingdom, that it was moved, he being present, " that the speaker might, in the name of the whole house, give him thanks; and then, that every member might, as a testimony of his particular acknowledgment, stir or move his hat towards him;" the which (though not ordered) when very many did, the lord Falkland, (who believed the service itself not to be of that moment, and that an honourable and generous person could not have stooped to it for any recompense,) instead of moving his hat, stretched both his arms out, and clasped his hands together upon the crown of his hat, and held it close down to his head ; that all men might see, how odious that flattery was to him, and the very approbation of the person, though at that time most popular.

When there was any overture or hope of peace, he would be more erect and vigorous, and exceedingly solicitous to press any thing which he thought might promote it; and sitting among his friends, often, after a deep silence and frequent sighs, would, with a shrill and sad accent, ingeminate the word *Peace, Peace;* and would passionately profess, " that the very agony of the war, and the view of the calamities and desolation the kingdom did and must endure, took his sleep from him, and would shortly break his heart." This made some think, or pretend to think, " that he was so much enamoured on peace, that he would have been glad the king should have bought it at any price ;" which was a most unreasonable calumny. As if a man, that was himself the most punctual and precise in every circumstance that might reflect upon conscience or honour, could have wished the king to have committed a trespass against either. And yet this senseless scandal made some impression upon him, or at least he used it for an excuse of the daringness of his

spirit; for at the leaguer before Gloucester, when his
friends passionately reprehended him for exposing his person
unnecessarily to danger, (as he delighted to visit the trenches, and nearest approaches, and to discover what the enemy
did,) as being so much beside the duty of his place, that it
might be understood against it, he would say merrily, "that
his office could not take away the privileges of his age; and
that a secretary in war might be present at the greatest
secret of danger;" but withal alleged seriously, "that it
concerned him to be more active in enterprises of hazard,
than other men; that all might see, that his impatiency for
peace proceeded not from pusillanimity, or fear to adventure
his own person."

In the morning before the battle, as always upon action,
he was very cheerful, and put himself into the first rank of
the lord Byron's regiment, who was then advancing upon
the enemy, who had lined the hedges on both sides with
musketeers; from whence he was shot with a musket in the
lower part of the belly, and in the instant falling from his
horse, his body was not found till the next morning; till
when, there was some hope he might have been a prisoner;
though his nearest friends, who knew his temper, received
small comfort from that imagination. Thus fell that incomparable young man, in the four and thirtieth year of his age,
having so much despatched the business of life, that the
oldest rarely attain to that immense knowledge, and the
youngest enter not into the world with more innocence:
whosoever leads such a life, need not care upon how short
warning it be taken from him.

APPENDIX, A.

REFERRED TO IN PAGE 1069.

A<small>ND</small> they could not have used a more powerful argument to the king, to get his consent, than that it would not be accepted. However he was with wonderful difficulty brought to it, by the unanimous importunity of the whole board ; where, though there were some who in their judgments did not approve it, there was none durst speak against it ; and sir John Colepepper, who had most credit with him, was as earnest to persuade him to it as any man ; and the earl of Dorset was persuaded to concur in it, upon an assurance, that he should be one who should be sent with the message : and an opportunity to go to and return from London with safety was attended with many advantages, by their getting supplies of money to defray the great expenses they were at. In the end, being tired with the debate, the council sitting till it was very late, the king consented that there should be a message prepared against the next morning, and that the earls of Southampton and Dorset, with sir John Colepepper and sir William Udall, should carry the message, and deliver it to the houses whereof they were members ; the lord Falkland being left at York, to take care for the sending the arms and ammunition from thence, which was not yet come to Nottingham ; and then the earl of Southampton and sir John Colepepper were sent by the king to Mr. Hyde, to prepare the message against the next morning. The king was so exceedingly afflicted after he had given his consent, that he brake out into tears ; and the lord Southampton, who lay in the bedchamber that night, told Mr. Hyde the next morning, that the king had been in so great an agony that whole night, that he believed he had not slept two hours in the whole night, which was a discomposure his constitution was rarely liable to in the greatest misfortunes of his life. The message was made ready in the morning, in a softer and calmer style, than his majesty had been accustomed to for some months, and the persons began their journey towards London the same day.

The king continued very thoughtful and sad, and cared not to be entertained with any discourse, which he did not usually avoid, and fixing his eyes upon Mr. Hyde in the gallery, shortly after the lords were departed, he called him, and walked with him to the other end of the room, and observed that he looked sadder than he used to do, and said he had reason, for that he had been drawn to do that which must make all men sad, who had any love and kindness for him: and thereupon, with a countenance that had indeed much of sorrow in it, he related all that had passed in the two days before, and said, if he could have gotten any one of his council to have adhered to him in the refusal, he would never in this condition have been prevailed with to have made an address to those who had used him so reproachfully. He told him, he had once thought to have sent for him, to have advised with him upon the point, and that he might divert Colepepper from pursuing it so warmly, and prevent the earl of Dorset concurring in the advice, upon whom his majesty thought the other had some influence; but he said he forbore to do so, out of kindness to him, and that he might not expose him to the displeasure he might probably have incurred by opposing it. However he resolved he would send no message but what he prepared; and therefore he had sent Southampton to him, and that he confessed he was better pleased with the message itself, than the thought of sending to them; and that he had so far preserved his honour (for which he thanked him) that he had used no mean and base expressions of condescensions to them; and then enlarged with many passionate protestations, that if they should upon this message enter upon any treaty for an accommodation, he would never consent to any particular that might be to the prejudice of any of his friends who adhered, of which he required him to assure all men with whom he could converse. Mr. Hyde answered, that he had not apprehended any of that trouble in his own countenance, which his majesty had taken notice of; yet that he could not say he was without it, for he had that very morning received news of the death of a son of his, which did affect him, though it would not disturb him long; but he assured his majesty that his message or sending to the parliament did not in the least degree disorder him: for though there might have been many objections made against it, and some apprehension, that any condescension at this time might give some stop to his levies, and discourage those who had a purpose to resort to him or to declare for him, and that men might naturally believe, that if a treaty should be consented to by the parliament upon this application from his majesty, it would not be afterwards in his power to deny his concession to whatsoever should be required of him in that treaty; and that the interest of all particular persons must be subjected to that public convenience and peace, for which he protested he was himself very cheerfully prepared, and expected as sour a portion as would be assigned to any man in England: yet there were on the other side many appearances of benefit that might accrue to his majesty from their carriage and refusal: of which he conceived one might be, that they would be so amused with this message, and an opinion that an entire submission would shortly attend it, that they would sit still, and perform no act of hostility, till the effect of it was known ; which very sitting still would be of much advantage to him; (which his majesty said was a better argument than any that had been used to him :) and therefore, he said, he had nothing to do but to take all opportunities to persuade men, that it was very necessary for his majesty to send that message at that time ; and to that purpose he had always the message in his pocket, which he had read to many, who confessed that it was better than they imagined ; and that he gave copies of it to all who desired it, and which had already composed the minds of many. He concluded with an earnest desire to his majesty, that he would compose his own countenance, and abolish that infectious sadness in his own looks, which made the greatest impression upon men, and made them think that he found his condition to be more desperate than any body else believed it to be. The king was very well pleased with the discourse, and told him he was a very good comforter ; and that if he had as much credit with others as he had with him, as he doubted not he would have, the court would be shortly in a better humour.

The truth is, the consternation that at that time covered the countenance of most men cannot be imagined. The soldiers looked upon themselves as given up, and the war at an end. They who repaired to the king out of duty and conscience expected to be sacrificed to the pride and fury of the parliament, and the government both of church and state to be upon the point dissolved ; and there were many others, who thought the message would do no good, but that the king and they must be destroyed in so unequal a war.

APPENDIX, B.

REFERRED TO IN PAGE 1106.

WHILST this was preparing, the king made a journey to Chester, both to secure that place to his service, (which being the key of Ireland, was most necessary to be preserved in obedience to him,) and to countenance the lord Strange, who met with some opposition in those parts, to a degree he had not apprehended. When his majesty marched towards Shrewsbury, the earl of Essex, not knowing his purpose, went with his army towards Worcester, that he might keep himself between the king and London ; and prince Rupert chanced to be at the same time in Worcester, as is mentioned before, when he was informed that some of the parliament forces were even at the gates. Whereupon he drew out those few troops of horse which attended him, that he might take a view of the enemy; and they were no sooner in view, than they were engaged mutually in a brisk charge. The earl of Essex had sent Nathaniel Fiennes with a regiment of his best horse to take possession of Worcester, where he intended to be that night with the gross of his army. They were more in number, and much better provided than the prince's troops, but they were, by reason of the hedges, too near each other to part, before either thought to engage, many of the prince's troops being dismounted, as not looking for an enemy; when the first troops, where the prince was, charged the other so fiercely, that though they who were in the front behaved themselves well, the colonel himself and the greater part of his troops were routed very easily, and pursued as far as was fit. Wilmot, sir Lewis Dives, and some other officers, were hurt, but very few of the king's men killed, and none of name. Of the parliament side near a hundred were killed on the place; Sandys, and Wyndham, and Walton, and other officers of name, taken prisoners; whereof the first died of his wounds in few days after; and five or six cornets of horse taken. It was a brisk and a seasonable action, and made the prince's name and his troops terrible, and brake the spirits of the other as much; and did terribly break one of the best regiments of horse in that army. The prince understood by the prisoners how near the earl of Essex was, and therefore having come into the town that morning, and having nothing but horse there, and two or three companies of foot of new unarmed men, levied in the place, he drew all away from thence towards Bewly; but the earl of Essex meeting the marks and evidence of the defeat of his troops, and not knowing what reception he should find at Worcester, stopped his march, and did not enter that city in three days after this action. The king was at Chester when this fell out, whither the prince gave him notice of it, and sent the colours he had taken by his servant Crane, who was knighted for his news; and the king thought it necessary, in regard of the earl of Essex's being at Worcester, to return to Shrewsbury sooner than he intended, and before he had finished the business he went upon: and so the lord Strange suffered an affront at Manchester, and the town then shutting their gates against him, they continued in rebellion during the war: and at the same time the earl of Derby died, and the lord Strange succeeded him in that title.

APPENDIX, C.

REFERRED TO IN PAGE 1107.

As soon as the earl of Essex came to Worcester, he found himself obliged to send to the king. The parliament found very sensibly that they had lost much of the people's veneration, by having rejected the king's proposition for peace, and that very many, who had talked loud, and were for raising an army, whilst they thought it impossible for the king to raise any, when they now saw the king was like to be in the head of an army too, repented heartily what they had done, - and wished nothing more, than to prevent the two armies meeting in battle; which could be no otherwise done but by a treaty; and they who had, as they believed, proceeded too far to be capable of security by any other expedient than by victory, and by reducing the king into the same straits he was in before he had an army, which they had no reason to despair of, were yet too wise to profess that they desired the war; but seemed only to wish for such a peace, as might be security to the people against all such oppressions as they had formerly undergone; and therefore they now prepared a message to the king, which should be sent to the earl of Essex, and by him to his majesty; and made the people believe that they had now made such an address to the king, as would prevent the shedding of blood, and that a peace would be quickly concluded. The earl of Essex sent this message from Worcester, by a gentleman who was only a trooper in his guards, one Fleetwood, a son of sir Miles Fleetwood, the same man who had afterwards so great power in the army, and was so much spoken of. This person, with a trumpet, came to Worcester, with a letter from the earl of Essex to the earl of Dorset, in which the message was enclosed, the letter containing some civil expression of confidence, that he to whom it was directed did desire the peace of the kingdom, and to prevent a civil war; and therefore desired him to deliver that message to the king; which message renewed their old professions of duty, and how desirous they were to prevent a civil war, and to return to their obedience; and therefore desired him to withdraw from his evil counsellors, who had so much misled him, and to return to his parliament, who thought of nothing but to make him great and glorious. And in order to his safety, and to defend him from his enemies, they had appointed the earl of Essex to receive him who would perform all the offices of respect and duty to him which could be expected; and when he was returned to his parliament he should find that all the professions they had made to him were very sincere. Though the king had indignation enough for such an invitation, it was not thought worthy of any answer from him, and the earl of Dorset did not think himself obliged by the employment, or by any expressions of their good opinion; and so it was concluded that the messenger should return without any answer.

Within little more than twenty days from the time that the king came to Shrewsbury, he was in a posture convenient to find out the enemy. Wales had yielded him two or three good regiments of foot, and some troops of horse; and Cheshire and Lancashire as many. The lord Grandison and sir John Byron had brought in their regiments of horse well completed, and the lord Digby had drawn together some troops of his. The greatest defect was, that many of the horse and foot were so much without arms, that some regiments of foot had not above two or three companies which had any arms, and the rest only had cudgels; and few of the horse had any fire arms, and some without swords. However sitting still would bring no supply of that kind, and therefore the king resolved to march; and when he had got what he could from the train-bands, that the soldiers must do the rest upon the charge of the enemy, with whom every body desired to encounter. And as on the parliament side, the opinion that the king could never raise an army was the true cause, was the true reason why they did raise one; and so the cause of the war, together with the general opinion that the parliament would never raise a rebellion: so on the king's side, the confidence that one battle would end and determine the war, in a total subduing one party, and extinguishing all the fire that kindled it, and consequently all counsels being directed to that one end of fighting, was the principal cause of continuing the war: whereas if the king had only stood upon the defensive in all places where he had power, and declined all occasions of fighting as much as had been possible, and so ordered all contributions and supplies of money to the equal support of the army, it would probably have succeeded better; and those divisions would sooner have fallen out in the parliament party, which at last ruined themselves, after it had first destroyed the king and ruined the kingdom. But the making head against a rebellion and the supporting a civil war, was so much above the comprehension of any man, that very few guessed aright what they would do, or could judge what was fit to be done by the king. The truth is, so many contrary causes contributed to the production of the same effects, that the prophecy of Esdras seemed to be accomplished in that time: *And salt waters shall be found in the sweet, and all friends shall destroy one another; then shall wit hide itself, and understanding withdraw itself into his secret chamber.* 2 Esdras v. 9.

APPENDIX, D.

REFERRED TO IN PAGE 1117.

Upon Saturday the 22d of October, the king quartered at Edgeworth, the house of sir William Cherry; from whence the king resolved, having then no notice of the enemy, the next morning to march to a house of the lord Say, near Banbury, which was then garrisoned by the parliament forces, which lay in a very pleasant and open country. But about daybreak on Sunday the 23d of October, prince Rupert sent the king word, that the parliament army lay all quartered together about a village called Keinton, within three or four miles of Warwick; that there was a large field near the town, in which both armies might very well be drawn up; and therefore that he had appointed all the horse to rendezvous upon the top of the hill called Edge-hill, which overlooked the field and the enemy's quarters, where he would expect the king's pleasure; and if all the foot could meet there in any time, they might oblige the enemy to fight that day. The earl of Lindsey was quartered in a village, called Culworth, about a mile distant from the court, in which village likewise the earl of Dorset, the lord Falkland, sir John Colepepper, and Mr. Hyde were quartered, who quickly received advertisement from the general, of the posture things were in, and made all the haste they could to the king, who was gone from Edgeworth, leaving orders for all men to repair to Edge-hill. The army was quartered at so great a distance, that they could not quickly be drawn together, so that it was afternoon before they could be brought to the rendezvous, and were then to file down a very steep hill, where three horse could not go abreast together, till they came into the field, which was large enough. The earl of Essex had no better intelligence of the king's motions, and the first notice he had was by the appearance of the king's horse in a body from the top of the hill. Some of his artillery, and some of his regiments, both horse and foot, were a day's march behind; but he found many objections in retiring to join with them, and therefore resolved to put himself in order to expect the king's army in the same place; and so put his whole body in battalia, within less than half a mile of the village, at very near a mile's distance from the hill, without moving till the king's army came to charge them. He had the entire choice of the ground, and was in battalia before one company of the king's went down the hill; and if he had chosen his place

VoL. III.   97

near the hill, it would not have been possible for the king's army to have drawn down that steep narrow way without infinite prejudice : but the enemy standing at so great a distance, there was no other inconvenience than in the long time that was spent in their descent ; by reason whereof it was near three of the clock in the afternoon before the battle began. It was as fair a day as that season of the year could yield, the sun clear, no wind or cloud appearing. The relation of that battle is not proper of this place, in which there were many notable accidents, which if they had been pursued by either side, would have produced other effects. Prince Rupert charged the right wing of the enemy's horse so furiously, that they bore not the charge, but turned and fled in all the confusion imaginable, few of that body looking behind them till they came to St. Alban's, and many of them fled to London with news of the total defeat ; and the greater part of the king's horse which charged that wing pursued them so far, and they who did not, entertained themselves with the plunder of the carts and carriages, which were all in the village, that none of that wing could be ever rallied together that night, when there was need enough of their service. Wilmot had the command of the left wing, where were the lord Carnarvon, lord Grandison, and many other gallant gentlemen with their regiments and troops, who finding very little resistance from that party which they were to choose, many of them followed their friends of the right wing, to have a share of what might be gotten in the pursuit. And that which was worst of all, the reserve, which was intrusted to a very gallant gentleman, who had never been in action before, seeing no body of horse to charge, thought they might likewise follow the chase ; and so pursued it accordingly : nor did that gentleman, who upon all occasions gave as great testimony and evidence of courage as any man, ever acknowledge that he had orders, or understood himself to be left with a reserve ; so great a want there was of punctuality in that day's service. But if the horse of both wings had been contented with doing the business they were appointed to do, and had been less vehement in pursuing their enemy when they had quitted the field, that day had put a glorious end to the king's troubles and to the parliament's pretences ; and the earl of Essex thought the work so near an end, that he alighted from his horse, and put himself into the head of his regiment of foot, with a pike in his hand, resolving to die there, and to take no quarter, as he confessed to the countess of Carlisle at his return to London. But the behaviour of the king's horse lost all those advantages ; and the reserve of the parliament horse, commanded by sir William Balfour, a Scotchman, who is mentioned before, observing the field quitted by both their wings, kept themselves at a distance, moving up and down the field, and were taken to be the reserve of the king's horse, until they found an opportunity to do good service. The foot stood their ground with great courage; and though many of the king's soldiers were unarmed, and had only cudgels, they kept their ranks, and took up the arms which their slaughtered neighbours left to them; and the execution was great on both sides, but much greater on the earl of Essex's party; and the king's general, in the head of his regiment on foot, was come within little more than pistol shot of that body where the earl of Essex was, (which was the thing he most desired in the world,) when Balfour with his reserve of horse charged the flank of that body of foot, and so broke it; and, whether from the horse or the foot, the earl of Lindsey fell, his leg being broke short off, and the lord Willoughby his son, being in the head of the king's regiment of horse-guards, which he commanded, making haste to the relief of his father, they were both taken prisoners, and the whole body of the king's foot exceedingly shaken and broken, which changed exceedingly the fortune of the day: and if that wing of horse had sooner began, when there were no other horse upon the field but the few gentlemen who attended about the persons of the king and the prince, he might have taken them both prisoners. When the king discerned how doubtfully affairs stood, he commanded the prince of Wales and duke of York, who were both very young, to withdraw to the top of the hill, attended only by his company of pensioners, and commanded Mr. Hyde to wait upon them, and not depart from them; and as they went towards the hill, the evening now approaching, they saw a body of horse, which they made no doubt was the king's, and so moved towards them, when sir Richard Grime, an equery of the king's, rode very little before, to know them, which he quickly did, and was beaten off his horse, and so well counterfeited being killed that he was presently stripped: all which being in the prince's view gave him advertisement what they were, so that he diverted his course to the other hand, and that body moved as quickly from him, being evidently in great apprehension; which if they had not been, the number about the prince was so very small, that they could have made very little resistance, if Balfour had charged them: so that the preservation of those two young princes was a great blessing of that day: and they had not been long upon the hill, before the king sent order that they should go to Edgeworth, where his majesty had laid the night before,

Though the king's horse sustained no loss, and they who followed the enemy too far yet returned before it was night, either the officers would not or could not rally so many of them together as would charge that small reserve, which still went about the field without standing in any place to expect a charge. The lord Falkland, who in all such actions forgot that he was secretary of state, and desired to be where there would probably be most to do, had that day chosen to

97*

charge with Wilmot, who charged on the left wing, declining, upon the former expostulation, to be on the other wing with prince Rupert, used to protest that he saw no enemy that day of the horse that made any resistance, and observing that body under Balfour whole up and down, he spake to Wilmot that he might go and charge them, which the other seeming not to consider, he pressed him again ; to which the other made no other answer but, " My lord, we have got the day, and let us live to enjoy the fruit thereof;" and after it was found, too late, what mischief that small body had done, and continued to do, the officers could not rally their horse together, albeit they were all in the field. From the time that the battle began, it was not above an hour and an half before the evening stopped the heat of the fight, and all men were content to stand still without making any advance ; and the king continued upon his horse, with some of the lords and other principal officers about him, in no degree satisfied with the posture they were in. Though they were sure they could not have lost many of the horse in the action, they knew not what was become of them, and the foot appeared very thin, as long as they could be discerned by the light ; and therefore they concluded they would be much thinner, when the darkness should cover their withdrawing. So there wanted not those who proposed that the king would draw off the field, and with as many horse as he could rally hasten into the west, and leave both the foot and the cannon to the enemy. Which proposition received so much countenance from some great officers, that many thought it would have been resolved upon ; until sir John Colepepper, who had that day charged with prince Rupert with much gallantry, (as his courage was always unquestionable,) did oppose it with great warmth and passion, and told the king he was ruined if he hearkened to it, which his majesty was not inclined to do, and so silenced the debate, declaring that he would not stir from the place till the morning ; and so the night was passed, with inconvenience and trouble enough : for besides the expectation of a very melancholy prospect in the morning, the night itself was as cold as a very great frost and a sharp northerly wind could make it at that season of the year. Nor did the morning appear more auspicious ; the troops of horse and foot appeared very thin, yet many, both officers and soldiers, who had sought warmer lodgings in the cold night, returned in the morning to see what was become of their friends ; and so the numbers increased. The ordnance was all safe, and though the field was covered with the dead, yet nobody could tell to what party they belonged ; and that which composed the minds of the soldiers most was, that the enemy's troops appeared as thin, as broken, and as dispirited as they could wish ; so that they who could longest endure the station they were in, were likely to remain masters of the field. As soon as it was light, and the king had gotten a little sleep in his coach, whither he betook himself about daybreak, it was wished that the horse, which had yet endured no other shock than of the cold of the night, would make one brisk charge with that body of horse which remained of the enemy; but the officers, who without doubt had as much courage themselves as could be expected, had no mind to undertake for their men. They said, the bodies which were in view were rather an assembly of all the horse of the army, than regiments or troops under their officers, and so they knew not how to draw them out, or to depend upon them; that the horses were so weak that they would not be able to make a charge, and the men had not eaten or drank in more than four and twenty hours; in effect, that they had with much ado prevailed with them to keep the field, the king continuing there himself, but they much doubted, that as soon as it should be known that they were to renew the battle, many of them would directly run away. Upon the whole matter, it was thought most counsellable, that they should be in as good a posture to receive the enemy as was possible, if they advanced, otherwise that they should only keep the ground, and expect what the enemy would do: and it was believed by many, then and after, that which side soever had assumed the courage to have attacked the other would have proved victorious.

In this interval, those things occurred to memory which had been forgotten, or rather which could not be executed according to former resolutions before the battle. The proclamation, mentioned before, was now delivered to sir William Le Neve, Clarencieux king at arms, who in his robe of office carried it towards the earl of Essex's army, as it stood still in the field, intending to have proclaimed it at the head of the troops; but he was met by a guard before he came thither, and charged upon his life, with pistols at his breast, neither to read any thing or to speak a word, being likewise blinded, and so conducted to the general, before whom he expostulated in vain of the indignity and injury done to his office, contrary to the law of nations, which the standers by laughed at; and when he began to read the proclamation, it was violently snatched from him with new reproaches and threats, if he presumed to say any thing to that purpose, or to scatter or let fall any of those proclamations. The earl of Essex asked him, whether the king and the prince were in the field; and when the herald said they were, and had been exposed to the same danger with the rest, he seemed not to believe it, and said he knew the king was not there: and if he had not really thought so, he would never have asked the question in the hearing of so many, who thereby were informed of what they had not before known or believed: for care had been taken, that the soldiers should think that they fought against those malignants who kept the king from the parliament, and that his majesty himself was not present in the field. The herald was suffered to stay very little time, and blinded again, and conducted by a guard to the outmost limits of the army; and so returned with the news of the death of the earl of Lindsey, the king's general, and of many officers being prisoners, who were thought to be dead. The king remained in the field till the evening, and till the enemy quitted it and marched away; and then orders were sent to the foot and to the horse, to draw off to their former quarters, where they had been the night before the battle; and his majesty likewise repaired to Edgeworth, from whence he had gone on Sunday morning; not resolving till the next morning what counsel to pursue; and he rested likewise the next day, to be better informed of the enemy's motions, and that the soldiers might, by so much longer rest in their quarters, recover their spirits.

APPENDIX, E.

REFERRED TO IN PAGE 1408.

The earl of Essex's army was so weakened by these defeats, and more by the sickness that had wasted it, that it was not thought safe to remain longer so near unquiet and restless enemies; and the factions and animosities at London required his presence there; and he thought the army would be sooner recruited there than at so great a distance; so that about the beginning of May, or soon after, he marched from Thame to London, where he found jealousy and contention enough, leaving his army quartered about St. Alban's. There was newly discovered a design amongst some citizens of name, with the privity of members of both houses of the best rank, to compel the parliament by force to make peace with the king, the correspondence between the persons of honour and the citizens being managed by Mr. Waller, who, upon a light discovery made by a false servant who had overheard some discourses, very frankly confessed all he knew, named lords and ladies, and gentlemen and merchants, whereof some were condemned and executed, and others of all sorts imprisoned. The relation of that whole affair, and his miserable behaviour in it, deserved to be the part of a more formal discourse. It was not thought prudent to examine that business to the bottom, in which they found very considerable persons engaged or privy ; but having taken the lives of some with all the circumstances of terror, causing them to be executed in the streets before their own doors, in the sight of their neighbours ; whereof one was a gentleman of good reputation, who had married the sister of Mr. Waller, and had been very assistant to him in his education, whom he sacrificed now without the least reluctancy. They thought it best to take the words of all the members of both houses for their own indemnity, by their severally pronouncing a solemn protestation and vow, that they had no hand or privity in that design or plot ; and in which they promised always to adhere to the parliament, and to assist the forces raised by the parliament against the army raised by the king, which was an expression never before heard of; and so all jealousies were extinguished, no man refusing or pausing to take it, choosing rather to run the hazard of that, than to be made a spectacle as their other friends were ; though as soon as they had secured themselves by that sacred vow, they made what haste they could to the king for better security, and where they might procure God's pardon as well as the king's, without incurring any danger for asking it. Mr. Waller would have been glad to have got his own liberty at the same price, or of any other oath or vow; but he was kept in prison, and continually threatened with death, which he feared and abhorred, till at last he redeemed himself at a ransom of ten thousand pound, to supply the affairs of the parliament; and as much more spent upon divines and other intercessors, besides marrying a wife whose friends had contributed to his absolution ; and besides the disposing them to accept all this by a speech pronounced by him at the bar of the house of commons, of the greatest flattery and the greatest falsehood ; such a meanness and lowness of spirit, that life itself was no recompense for it.

Whilst the affairs of the parliament were in this distraction, the king recovered great reputation, and the season of the year being fit for action, all discontents and factious murmurings were adjourned to the next summer. Sir Ralph Hopton, and that handful of gentlemen which in the beginning of the troubles had been forced to seek refuge in Cornwall, had, with the countenance and assistance of some faithful persons there, so good success, that they had mastered all unquiet spirits in that county, and had sent to the king, that if his majesty would supply them with some troops of horse and ammunition, of which they stood in great need, they would march into Somersetshire, and there wait his majesty's further commands. The queen soon after her landing, and before she could be ready for her own march, sent a good supply of arms and ammunition to Oxford, where there was so great want of it, that if the earl had come before Oxford, there was not powder enough for the action of four hours, nor a hundred spare arms in the magazine. This seasonable supply being now come, the king thought it necessary to give such a countenance to his Cornish troops (for the whole body was raised in Cornwall) as might reduce all the western counties to his devotion, where though the parliament had in every country, Cornwall now excepted, some garrisons upon the sea-coast, yet they consisted only of the inhabitants and men drawn out of the adjacent villages, and they could not all together send out a party of horse and foot strong enough to give any trouble to the little Cornish army, or to interrupt their march.

The principal gentry of Somersetshire were now in Oxford, and were all joint suitors to the king to send the marquis of Hertford again into the west; and both the king and the marquis consented to it; and the king appointed them all to meet every day at the chancellor of the exchequer's lodging, whom he commanded to assist them, in adjusting all that was to be done in order to a present march; the king declaring what troops he would spare for that service, and what ammunition should be ready: the rest they were to advance by their own industry and with their own money; for it was in secret that the king had none. The marquis himself was content to come to the chancellor of the exchequer's lodging to confer with the gentlemen, and every man subscribed what he would provide before he went out of the town, and what he would undertake to have ready in several counties where his interest lay, and some brought in money towards carrying on the work; so that in few days a great advance seemed to be made. But now the fame of new successes in the west, and the general good inclinations of the several counties, and the visible distractions at London, raised new thoughts; and whereas before nothing was thought of, but how to convoy this body of Cornish foot, which had performed so many brave actions, after the petty garrisons in the country should be suppressed, which could not take very much time, to increase the body of the king's army, that it might march near London, if it should appear counsellable, it being hoped that those western gentlemen would be presently able to raise strength enough in their several counties to keep these in peace and quiet; it was now thought necessary, upon the stock and credit of those forces, and the good conjuncture to raise a new army, which should never join with the king's, but after subduing the lesser garrisons might take Portsmouth, and so visit Sussex and those parts even to Surrey and Kent, where there were likewise some undertakers to be ready to expect and assist them. And now, not only those officers who had undertaken to raise troops and regiments to bring into the king's army, for which they had received commissions, and found they could not perform, desired to be a part of the new army; but many others, who were weary of their superior officers in the army, or hoped to be superiors, were all contriving how to carry away the troops they had into this army, where they expected to find more benefit and preferment; and the marquis was willing to hearken to any of these propositions as the best way to increase his own strength, and so consented to the making general officers for a royal army, without thinking upon his old friends, who had raised that body in Cornwall, and were of quality and abilities for command superior to most of this new model, and could never submit to be commanded by them.

Prince Rupert, who had always looked upon the interest and credit of the marquis of Hertford as somewhat that eclipsed him, and seeing him like now to be in the head of a royal army, which was to be increased with troops drawn from his command, used all the means he could by himself, and those few others who were trusted by him, that the king might be persuaded that his brother prince Maurice (who had only a regiment in the army) would be fit to be made general of this army. The king always loved his family immoderately, and with notable partiality, and was willing to believe that their high quality could not be without all those qualities and qualifications which were equal to it, if they had an opportunity to manifest those endowments, easily entertained that overture, and believed the marquis himself would easily resign his pretences, and be contented to serve under a grandson of king James, and the king's nephew. He made choice of the chancellor of the exchequer to dispose the marquis to this condescension, but he did not only excuse himself from undertaking the office, but used all the means and endeavours he could to dissuade the king from his design, telling him, that he thought it easy to dissuade the marquis from undertaking the enterprise, which nothing but affection to his majesty's service could dispose him to, the marquis loving his ease, and abhorring any fatigue, and having no military quality but courage, in which he abounded: but if his majesty would have him engaged in the enterprise, he would not find that he would take any inferior command; which his majesty upon further endeavour found to be true; and judging that the presence of the marquis was absolutely necessary for the disposing and reconciling all those western counties to his service, his fortune, which was very great, lying in many of them, he appointed his nephew prince Maurice to be lieutenant general under the marquis, which nobody believed would produce any good effect, there being no two men of more contrary natures and dispositions. The prince never sacrificed to the Graces, nor conversed amongst men of quality, but had most used the company of ordinary and inferior men, with whom he loved to be very familiar. He was not qualified with parts of nature, and less with any acquired; and towards men of the best condition, with whom he might very well have justified a familiarity, he maintained at least the full state of his birth, and understood very little more of the war, than to fight very stoutly when there was occasion. The marquis was of a very civil and affable nature, and knew well what respect to pay to the other, if he were fairly encouraged to it; but he was withal very great hearted, and when more was expected, he would give less than was due: nor was there any third person of quality and discretion, who had interest enough in either of them to prevent misunderstandings, which there were too many industrious enough to foment: so that at their leaving Oxford, (which was about the middle of May,) it was not hard to divine that that subordination would not last long, nor produce any good effects.

APPENDIX, F.

REFERRED TO IN PAGE 1423.

FOR six or seven days there were continual skirmishes, Waller retiring with great order and little loss, and the marquis advancing with some little advantage, till they came near Bath; and then Waller, having drawn a regiment or two of foot from the garrison of Bristol, and others out of the country, by the credit and countenance of Hungerford and Popham, appeared near Lansdown, an open plain within two miles of Bath, where both sides drew up in good order, having room enough. The action was performed on both sides with courage and resolution, till the night parted them, when Waller drew to the lower ground, to the shelter of a hedge and wall. Many officers and gentlemen of quality fell on both sides, and if the Cornish foot had not stood very firm, when the horse was shaken, it would have proved a sad day; but sir Bevil Greenvil, in the head of his pikes, bore the shock of Waller's horse, and broke them, and forced them to retire, though himself lost his life in the service, to the universal grief of the army, and indeed of all who knew him. He was a gallant and a sprightly gentleman, of the greatest reputation and interest in Cornwall, and had much contributed to all the service that had been done there, and to the leading the army out of the country; and by the gentleness of his spirit, accompanied with courage and authority, had restrained much of the licence, and suppressed the murmur and mutiny, to which that people were too much inclined, especially after they were joined to the marquis's troops, and made subject to the command of new officers. All men exceedingly lamented his loss at the time he fell, and had cause to renew the lamentation very often afterwards. Though the day had proved sad and melancholy enough, the evening was by much the more tragical; for when the troops were content to breathe on both sides, some of the officers repairing to the artillery to see in what state it was, and to give order to send ammunition to those places where it was wanted, by what accident was never known, a wagon of powder was blown up, which blew up and killed all the persons about it, whereof some were of name. Col. Thomas Sheldon, who commanded prince Maurice's regiment of horse, was at some distance from it, yet his horse was killed under him, and himself so hurt from head to foot, that he died within two days, a gentleman of great courage and generally beloved; and (which made up the tragedy) sir Ralph Hopton, whose name had been much and deservedly magnified in all the western service, being yet further from the wagon, was by the blast of the powder thrown from his horse, which was killed, and so hurt, that he was looked upon as dead for many days, though, by the diligence of his servants, with God's blessing, he recovered afterwards to give signal marks of his fidelity to the king; but the marks of that ill accident were never worn out, and deprived him of that gracefulness and lustre in his person and countenance, which he formerly had.

In the morning after this battle, it appeared that Waller had drawn off all his men in the night, leaving lighted matches in the wall and hedge, to amuse the enemy; which raised their spirits very much, and was an evident sign that the victory remained on the marquis's part, and gave them cause to believe that the loss was very great on that side, and that they should be troubled no more with him; so that after a day's repose in the neighbour villages, which was in many respects necessary, the marquis continued his march towards Oxford by the way of Chippenham; but quickly found that Waller, with the same repose, and the fresh supplies he received every day from the country, attended upon his rear very near, so that both horse and foot were engaged every day, and they now found the loss of the wagon of powder which was blown up at Lansdown, for they had not enough left to make a stand, or to line the hedges to secure their rear, and keeping the enemy back; so that when they came to the Devizes, an open market town in Wiltshire, of receipt enough for the men, they found it necessary that all the foot, their cannon, and their sick and wounded men, which had necessarily made their march slow, should remain there, whilst the horse went away, as they easily might, to Oxford; from whence they doubted not to send fresh succour to the

APPENDIX, F.

rest before they should be overpressed or overpowered by Waller, who was not yet come out, and found difficulties enough in his pursuit. When they came into the Devizes, they found they had not match enough to keep their guards, so that both the marquis and prince Maurice in the night thought fit likewise to leave them, and so make haste to Oxford, where the old jealousies between the prince and the marquis were presently revived; the friends of either making all the disadvantageous reports they could of the other, whilst most men thought neither of them had done honourably in abandoning the army, and coming themselves to call for help. In the mean time the small army in the Devizes was upon the matter left without command; for the forces which had been brought or raised by the marquis, and were much less in number than the Cornish, would only obey the officers they had known, and the lord remained so ill, and so obliged not to come into the air, that he would not assume the command, whom all would obey; notwithstanding all which, and though Waller was now come before the town, and summoned them, the officers agreed so well, and took pains by beating all the bed-cords in the town into matches, and barricadoing the avenues, that Waller durst not assault them, so that they relied upon succour in time; and expected it accordingly, and without any other impatience than giving account to Oxford of the truth of their condition.

This sudden unexpected news, for the last account had brought the issue of the battle at Lansdown, where the victory was understood to be on the king's side, or at least the enemy to be dismayed, raised such a damp at Oxford, (as the ebb and flows of fortune made always great impressions there,) that all men were dispirited, and the arrival of the prince and the marquis in the break of the day, spread the rumour through the town that that army was totally lost. The queen was now come from York, and upon her march towards Oxford; and the king had sent to her, that he would not fail to meet her such a day at a place a good day's journey from Oxford; and that appointment must of necessity hold, and good troops attend the king, who was to march very near the garrison of Warwick, belonging to the parliament. However it was evident that if the Devizes was not instantly relieved, that gallant party must be lost. It was therefore quickly resolved, that Wilmot, lieutenant general of the horse, should march away with a good party of about 1200 horse and some dragoons, there being sent before a regiment of horse under the command of the earl of Crawford, with a supply of as much powder and match as could well be carried by the troopers on their horses, which was lost, and that regiment disordered by the enemy, which had blocked up all the passages to the town. Waller had not so soon notice of the approach of the king's horse, as his vigilance might have expected, and he received it first by the interception of a messenger, who was sent to inform those in the town of it, that they might be ready to draw out as soon as the enemy could be obliged to draw off; and upon this advertisement, and fearing to be enclosed between the horse which were coming, and the foot of the town, which he knew to be superior in courage to his, and having great confidence in his horse, he drew off his horse, foot, and cannon to an open plain piece of ground, upon the top of a steep hill from the town, and about a mile's distance from thence, called Round-way hill, where the enemy was to pass, and there he put his men in order, and expected them. Wilmot, finding them in this posture, with horse, foot, and cannon, much superior to him in number, and hearing nothing of the foot from the town, though he had made all signs to them from another part of the hill, according to what he had appointed them to expect by his messenger, that body of foot being the strength upon which he relied, knew not what to do; but calling his officers together, amongst whom there was the earl of Carnarvon, who was general of the horse under the marquis of Hertford in the west, and had been engaged in all the actions with Waller, and so knew his manner of fighting, who came now only as a volunteer in the regiment of sir John Byron, they all found it necessary to fight, since they could not expect the foot longer than the enemy would give them leave; and observing that Waller had placed all his horse in several small bodies at some distance each from other, and all be-tween them his foot and cannon, Carnarvon said that the regiment of cuirassiers, who were all covered with armour, and commanded by sir Arthur Haslerig, and which stood nearest to them, were the men upon whom Waller principally depended, and therefore desired Wil-mot that their whole body might charge them; and if they could rout them, it was probable it might have a good effect upon their whole army: which advice being followed, had the effect desired; for that body being charged by all the king's horse, though they stood well, and longer than was expected, could not bear that shock; and when they were broken, they fell upon their own next body of horse, and disordered them, and all their horse fell upon and into their body of foot, and routed them more than the enemy could have done; and thereupon Waller himself, Haslerig, sir Edward Hungerford, and such other officers as were best horsed, without making further resistance, fled the nearest way in all the confusion imaginable; many running their horses down the steep of the hill, and so falling, were either kill-ed with the fall, or so hurt that they became prisoners. By this time the body of the foot in the Devizes was come up, without having re-ceived any other advertisement, till after they came out of the town, than the seeing the enemy in some disorder drawing themselves together from their several quarters, which at first they believed to be upon design, but soon after, by their march towards the plain, they concluded that the relief was come from Oxford ; and so they quickly got their men together who were in health, (for sir Ralph Hopton and many other sick and wounded men were still left behind in the town ;) and when they were drawn out, they received another direction from Wilmot, which way they were to march ; and so they came to the top of the ground when the enemy was in that confusion, and lost no time in falling upon the foot, to revenge what they had suffered, and sacrificed too many to the memory of their beloved Greenvil. In this total general defeat many were slain, without the loss of any officer of name on the king's side, and about twelve hundred men taken prisoners, whereof many of their considerable officers, all their baggage and cannon, and a rich booty to the soldiers, who upon this good fortune had leisure to repose themselves in the quarters they were before weary of, and to expect new orders from the king.

APPENDIX, G.

REFERRED TO IN PAGE 1441.

There had been the winter before an unhappy design for the surprise of Bristol, upon intelligence with some citizens not maturely ripened ; which being discovered, an alderman, and another citizen of good account, had been tried before a council of war, and executed in the streets, and many others had fled out of the city, which, though it disappointed the design, had exceedingly enraged a great part of the city, which longed to be freed from the yoke of servitude they were under. And now the strength of that garrison had been drawn out, and lost under Waller at Roundway, very few of them returning to Bristol, so that it seemed very counsellable to the king to make his first enterprise upon Bristol, where the little reputation the governor

Nathaniel Fiennes had in war, and the general prejudice the city and country had against him, made the attempt appear the more hopeful; and it was therefore resolved accordingly. The marquis of Hertford, with prince Maurice, was to return to his western troops, who remained about the Devizes still, and with them to march to that side of Bristol which lay next to Somersetshire, and to quarter as near the city as they conveniently could, that nothing might go in or out. And prince Rupert was with the horse and foot of the king's army to march and quarter upon that side of the city that lies next Gloucestershire, to straiten it likewise as close as on the other side; and a day was agreed upon, that they might compute both armies might by that time be come to their several quarters, and then the generals on both parts might consult and conclude what was further to be done for the attacking the town; and they did all meet accordingly.

Upon a full conference, it was agreed that the next morning they would assault the city in several places at once; the marquis with his forces on that side on which he was quartered, and the prince on the other. The works on the Somersetshire side being much higher and stronger, and the graff deeper than they were on the Gloucestershire side, where prince Rupert lay; and the very place assigned for the marquis's assault was much harder than many other places upon that line, which might with less danger and as much benefit have been entered; which made the Cornish (who use to say what they think) murmur loudly, that they were carried thither to be paid for the service they had done. On the western side, after a continued assault of near three hours, they were beaten off, and upon the matter quite gave over the assault, with a very great loss of common men and inferior officers of very good reputation. There fell likewise sir Nicholas Slanning and colonel Trevannion, the heads of the Cornish, with sir Bevil Greenvil and sir Brutus Buck, colonel of the marquis's own regiment. Sir Nicholas Slanning was brought off the field, his thigh broken with a musket bullet, of which he died a fortnight after, when the king was in Bristol. He was a young gentleman of about 25 years of age, of a small stature, but very handsome, and of a lovely countenance, of excellent parts and invincible courage. He was master of a fair estate in land, and had the government of Pendennis castle, and was vice-admiral of the Castle; both which offices and commands in so dexterous and active a hand were of infinite benefit to the king's service; he being a man well loved and obeyed, and there being an entire friendship between him, Greenvil, and Trevannion, with a firm conjunction with John Arundel of Trerice, and his two sons John and Richard, both very active men, and in command. Cornwall was quickly disposed to serve the king, as soon as sir Ralph Hopton, and the other gentlemen named before, came into that county. He was of a very acceptable presence, great wit, and spake very well, and with notable vivacity, and was well believed by the people. He was in all the actions and in all parties where there was action, in signal command, and never received hurt or wound, till this last fatal assault. He told the chancellor of the exchequer, who visited him after the king came to Bristol, that he had always despised bullets, having been so used to them, and almost thought they could not hit him. He professed great joy and satisfaction in the losing his life in the king's service, to whom he had always dedicated it, and desired the chancellor (with whom he had always friendship) to recommend his wife and his son (who was born the very day upon which he received his wound at Pendennis castle) to the king's favour, and died the next day, to the great grief of all who knew him. Trevannion was about the same age of 24 or 25 years, the eldest, if not the only son of his father, sir Charles Trevannion, and newly married to the daughter of Arundel of Trerice. He was a steady young man, of a good understanding, great courage, but of few words; yet what he said was always to the purpose. Both he and Slanning were members of the house of commons, and the more abhorred the rebellion by having been present, and observed by what foul artifices it had been promoted; and as they always gave what opposition they could to those practices whilst they remained there, so they were amongst the first who drew their swords to suppress them. Brutus Buck was an old soldier, having been an officer of a very good esteem in the voyage to Rochelle, and in the action in the isle, and ever after lived in a command the king had given him in the Isle of Wight, with the reputation of a civil and a stout gentleman. He was killed in the head of his regiment with a musket bullet in the forehead, when he was getting upon the wall, and fell dead in the graff. He was a man generally beloved, and had no enemies.

On prince Rupert's side, where the line indeed was very weak and low, but there were two or three high castles of earth, upon which store of cannon was planted with many musketeers, all which infested those who assaulted the line, which was otherwise slenderly guarded; but there was within the line a great space of meadow ground, upon which two or three regiments of horse might be drawn up, who might quickly have broken such foot as should enter the line, the assault here was more prosperous and successful, though with the loss of many, and some very excellent persons. The line was entered in the weakest place, and where it was least guarded; and they who entered it easily made way for some horse to follow them, who quickly made the few horse which were placed within to give ground, and retire into the town, which raised confusion there; and some more of the horse and foot of the prince's likewise entered the line, and leaving those castles behind them, marched directly into the suburbs, where the streets being narrow, many soldiers and officers were killed from the windows and tops of houses, which stopped their advance;' and no doubt, if the governor had understood his business well, that party which was entered might very well have been driven back, before any other could have come to their assistance. But the confusion within the town was very great, and the apprehension that the army was already entered, and that they should all be made a prey to the soldiers, if there were no articles made and conditions obtained for them, made the people so clamorous, that the governor yielded to their importunities, and sent a trumpet to the prince to treat upon surrender; which overture was easily accepted, and upon hostages sent, colonel Gerrard, a haughty young man, of a very different temper from colonel Fiennes, was sent to treat with him. He talking loud to the people of firing the town, if they did not forbear shooting out of the windows, which they continued to do, hectored the governor himself to such a temper, that he forthwith gave orders to forbear all acts of hostility in all places, which they in the castles hardly obeyed, but still continued to shoot, and did much mischief; and then concluded upon the ordinary conditions, to march out of the town the next day with his troops, and to surrender the city to the king, which was done accordingly, to the no small joy of the commanders.

Of the prince's side there fell that day many good officers, amongst which were colonel Harry Lunsford, and his lieutenant colonel Nathaniel Moyle, both officers of the first rank in their reputation of courage and conduct, and were both killed out of a window, when they had entered the suburbs; the former dead on the place, the other lived near a month, and then died. Colonel John Bellasis had a hurt of a very strange nature, and worth the mentioning. Being a gallant gentleman, of much honour and courage, as he was marching in the head of his regiment of foot, with his sword drawn in his hand, upon which a musket bullet struck the flat of the blade with such force that it bowed like a bow, and remaining still in his hand, was driven upon his forehead that he fell to the ground, but rose presently of himself without help, and seeing no blood, he believed the hurt not considerable, and continued in his business; but he found it necessary within less than an hour to be carried off, his head with the contusion for many days swelling to that prodigious proportion, that when the king came to Bristol, and the chancellor of the exchequer went to see him, he knew not who he was, there being no appearance of eyes or nose, so that it was thought trepanning would be the only way to preserve him, and that not a certain one: but he having his senses very perfect, would not endure so rude a remedy ; and after the swelling was at the height, it declined and sunk as fast ; and when the army removed from Bristol, was well enough, and attended his charge in it, without any mark or blemish. The lord viscount Grandison was then likewise wounded with a musket-shot in the leg, of which, though he was carried to Oxford, and thought past danger, he died two months after. He was a very beautiful person, of great virtue and eminent courage, and of manners not to be corrupted. He was a very great loss, when the age stood in need of such examples, and was particularly lamented by the chancellor of the exchequer with very vehement passion, there being a most entire friendship between them for many years without any intermission.

The town being thus happily taken, (though the price that was paid for it was grievous,) the old embers of jealousy and discontent, which had been lightly raked up and covered between the two princes and the marquis of Hertford, broke out now into a flame. The town was within the marquis's commission, and so he concluded that the government was in his disposal, and designed it to sir Ralph Hopton, who by this time was past all danger, and in all respects was preferable to any man that could be named. On the other side, prince Rupert believed the right of conferring it to be in him, since it was taken by the forces under his command, when those under the marquis were beaten off ; and he had a purpose to confer it upon sir Arthur Aston, who had been governor of Reading, and lost much reputation there in respect of his nature and manners, not of his soldiery, which stood as it did before. But when the prince had thought better of his own power, and weighed the difference between sir Ralph Hopton and sir Arthur Aston in the eyes of the world, he changed his purpose, and both the prince and the marquis sending expresses to give the king notice of the success, the prince made it his humble suit to the king that his majesty would bestow the government of Bristol upon his highness ; and the marquis, after he had given an account of the taking the town, in which he gave all the attributes to the prince which were due to him, he told the king that he had conferred the government upon sir Ralph Hopton, which he knew his majesty would approve, since no man could be so fit for it, nor had deserved better from his majesty. *The remainder of this relation is inserted in the Life of lord Clarendon.*

END OF THE THIRD VOLUME.

LaVergne, TN USA
29 December 2009

168442LV00010B/102/A